Praise

"In a world where the very survival of business is dependent on the absorption, assimilation and effective utilization of digital technology, business and technology are fast becoming indistinguishable from one another. The practical wisdom of this book will help organizations and individuals excel in this new world."

– Amarendra Narayan, Former Secretary General, Asia Pacific Tele community (APT), Bangkok

"'Aligned To Win' is a book with a difference. It is a story of experiences skilfully woven to take you on a journey that would remind of several workplaces challenges you dealt with while managing business affairs. Technology is all around and defines our way of life today. Business has become e-business and society has become e-society. We now talk about 5-10G, IoT and Industry 4.0. These are terms beyond sense of integration. It refers to technology entrenched beyond any chance of visualising it as separate entity. With business outcomes being increasingly influenced by information technology (IT), the alignment between Business and IT has become a crucial success factor for an enterprise in this digital age. This book is an intuitive and practical guide to discovering the power of Business-IT alignment and channelling it for personal and organizational growth. The many examples, exercises, and assessment tools in the book make it not only an insightful reference, but also a practical handbook for managing real-world issues. It is an important read for practitioners and students alike."

– Dr MP Gupta, Head, Department of Management Studies, Indian Institute of Technology, Delhi.

ALIGNED TO WIN

Plugging-in IT to light up your Business Value

About the Author

Ashish Pachory is an Information and Communication Technology (ICT) consultant and leadership guide. Till 2016, he was the Chief Information Officer (CIO) of the telecom services venture of the Tata group in India.

Before joining Tata in 2011, Ashish worked on the other side of the IT/Telecom value chain, in business, operations and delivery management functions with globally renowned technology companies like Nokia, Amdocs, Lucent (Bell-Labs) and Wipro. Ashish's work on measuring the business value of IT was recognized among the top IT innovations in 2013 by the Dynamic CIO (Achievers series). He was conferred Telecom Icon 2015 by the Centre of Recognition and Excellence (CORE), and as one of India's most Influential Technology Leaders (ET). Also in 2015, he was recognized among the top 25 Global Business CIOs by iCMG.

As a thought leader on technology trends and its adoption for business, he has been active as a speaker and panelist at industry forums and has contributed several thought-provoking articles and interviews in various industry and general publications, including The Economic Times, Business Standard and The Hindu.

Ashish is a Telecommunications engineer and lives in Gurgaon with his wife, Seema. His interests include astronomy, reading, cryptic crosswords and cricket.

He invites you to connect on Linkedin or Twitter (@apachory) to share views and ideas.

ALIGNED TO WIN

Plugging-in IT to light up your Business Value

ASHISH PACHORY

ZORBA BOOKS

ZORBA BOOKS

Published in India by Zorba Books, 2018

Website: www.zorbabooks.com
Email: info@zorbabooks.com

ISBN Print Book - 978-93-87456-10-5
ISBN eBook - 978-93-87456-11-2

Zorba Books Pvt. Ltd.(opc)
Gurgaon, INDIA

Printed at Repro Knowledgecast Limited, India

Contents

Acknowledgements

If there is one thing I learned from writing this, my first book, it is that I could not have done it alone. I took a decision – which I consider among my boldest – to step down from corporate life into the uncharted world of writing, to fulfil an abiding passion. The support and encouragement I received from my family, most notably my mother, Mrs. Madhuri Pachory, and my wife, Seema, in this difficult transition is invaluable. It is what made this book possible. I, therefore, dedicate it to them, with gratitude and pride. The role played by my children, Arjun and Sanjana, in offering unfettered feedback, while never losing their trust in me, was a constant source of strength and confidence.

This book is interspersed with many examples and stories from my long experience in the industry. Each of these stories is related to real people who have remained unnamed here, but without whom the narrative would have been incomplete. I am sure those amongst them who are reading this book will have no difficulty in identifying their part. I am grateful to them for their immense contribution to this book. I also wish to gratefully acknowledge the role played by many of my colleagues and associates who gave valuable insights through interviews and survey responses, patiently bearing with my persistence. I wish I could name each one individually and express my deep gratitude.

This book is but a compilation of the ideas, thoughts, experiences, and stories of the many wonderful people with whom I was privileged to share my long work experience. The life-lessons, which make up the essence of this book, are drawn from these brilliant folks who will never cease to inspire, and to whom I shall be forever indebted.

A work of this nature, based as it is on diverse – sometimes conflicting – topics cutting across numerous segments arduously stitched together into a common theme, needs constant reinforcement. Without this, it is more likely than not to bite the dust midway. For their ready advice and continuous encouragement, I humbly acknowledge the immense contribution of my extended family members, friends, and well-wishers. And last but not the least, while mentioning the credits, how can I forget the brilliant people behind Wikipedia for assiduously, if unwittingly, helping in framing my thoughts, particularly with the concise definitions in the Glossary.

As I said, writing a book is not a road on which you travel alone. To all who have walked beside me on this exhilarating path, I can only say this: thank you for being the wind beneath my wings.

Introduction

Great things happen at intersections. Some of our finest creations are a product of intersecting ideas. Think about it. On its own spoken language was a great idea, but when intersected with the human aptitude for sketching, it gave us *writing,* and thus a way to chronicle information. The rest, of course, is history! The idea of the internal combustion engine when intersected with improved production processes gave us the automobile revolution. Electric power and vapor compression crossed paths to create refrigeration which, in turn, intersected with shipping to alter the eating habits of people around the world. More recently the intersection of telephony with radio has given us the mobile revolution. Mobile technology has intersected with computer software to place a smart device in our hands that has changed our socializing, banking and shopping ways forever. It has also replaced many older devices – like camera, video recorder, audio player, calculator, alarm-clock – by further intersecting with advances in micro-miniaturization. The possibilities are limitless, as you can verify by imagining any two diverse concepts and crossing them in your mind. Try it – it's fun, and you may well herald the next breakthrough!

The magic of intersection has worked on professions too. Through much of history though, occupations have existed in isolation – often under a religious authority or diktat – unable to realize their combined potential and forge new advancement. In my view, this was the root-cause for the Dark Ages (circa 500AD to 1500AD) – a period of human history almost entirely devoid of cultural or scientific advancement. *Cross-fertilize or perish* is the clear message reaching us from across the centuries.

Fortunately, we have learned some lessons from history. We do understand now the value of *collaboration* and *teamwork* in our day to day business. For many of us, our careers have been liberally interspersed with team-building workshops, soft skills training programs, cross-functional task forces, and personal effectiveness goals, all aimed at increasing collaborative interworking between the various functions in the organization. There is negligible emphasis on achieving *Alignment,* however, since this is assumed to be a derivative of

Teamwork. As we shall explore in this book, ALIGNMENT goes much *beyond* teamwork. Let us look at some quick points of difference between Teamwork and Alignment.

	Teamwork	**Alignment**
1	Bound by common *Goals and Objectives*	Bound by shared *Purpose* (strategic fit)
2	Impermanent: Accomplish goal and disband	Never Changing
3	Answers the question "***What are we going to do***?" [Examples: launch cloud-based Mobile banking solution in 8 months; Open four more branch offices in North India by EOY]	Answers the question "***Who do we intend to be***?" [Examples: Consistently ahead of competition in Service Quality; Market leaders in product category X]
4	Hierarchical structure, led by a team leader – where the buck stops. Dedicated formation	Does not conform to specific structure or hierarchy. Ownership driven.

Many years ago, I participated in my company's national customer service conference in Bangalore. This was attended by regional service heads from across the country, all of whom made energetic and impressive presentations to the top management on the accomplishments of their teams towards *exceeding* their service delivery targets consistently. There was applause and cheer all around, and the chatter around the dinner table later in the evening couldn't have been livelier. However, when the conference resumed with an address from the management the next morning, we were all in for a shock. We were told that as a company, we had *not* met our customers' service expectations and this had negatively impacted the sales performance. There was a stunned silence. How could this happen? A lot of straight talk followed, and the root-causes were debated. What emerged was that (a) customer service targets were set unilaterally on a one-size-fits-all assumption, (b) a lot of national accounts did not have clear ownership within a region, and (c) there was hardly any interaction between the sales and service functions. In fact, in many regions, they were operating out of different premises – and this was *before* the email and mobile era! Thinking back, I can now see this as an instance where each team performed, but there was no *alignment* to a common, larger purpose, leading to organizational failure.

Let us cut to the present. In the increasingly complex and dynamic business world of today, what is a company's biggest source of competitive advantage? That's an easy one – it's obviously the trust and confidence of its customers, you would say. And you'd be right! After all, what greater wealth than a solid base of happy and loyal customers? Hasn't it been proved time and again that the voice of a happy customer reaches far beyond the most creative marketing campaign? Sure. We all believe this and therefore strive hard to keep our customers happy and loyal, often through some nifty teamwork between the front-end client relationship (business) and the back-end service delivery (technology) organizations.

However, we don't always succeed. In my over three decades of experience with some great companies, I have found that good intentions abound, but a sustained *alignment* of Business and Technology to a common purpose is still at best a platitude. A lot of times IT teams have no idea of the competitive pressures and market dynamics that lead to stiff Time-to-Market demands from Business. Tight bondage to internal SLAs, a fixation about keeping the light bulbs on, and a take-it-or-leave-it kind of inflexibility regarding its policies and deliverables give the IT team a rather formidable hue. On their part, Business teams often do not engage with IT until the last moment, define their requirements somewhat vaguely and are not always realistic about commitments to the external world. As the wave of digitization sweeps the world, one must emerge from this stifling climate into a more positive ambiance where business-technology alignment is not a platitude but a driver of business success.

Let's pause here to get to common ground on the terms "Business" and "Technology" (or "IT"). These terms are used here to denote separate *functions* in the organization. In general, "Business" refers to the responsibilities of a business team or SBU – like pre-sales, sales, marketing, product management, account management, channel partnerships, customer relationships, business finance, SCM and Legal. "Technology" or "IT", on the other hand, refers to the responsibilities of the CTO, CIO, Engineering, R&D, Consulting, Customer Service, and Operations team. These include the evaluation, planning, design, development, deployment, service, support, operations, advisory, analysis, and measurement of technology products, services, and solutions, built either in-house or in collaboration with external technology partners.

I have introduced the term **BITA** in this book to refer to **Business-IT Alignment**, but as IT and Technology are interchangeable in all but the most high-tech industries (like Telecom), the term BITA equally applies to **B**usiness-**T**echnology **A**lignment. The essential principles of alignment with business are unchanged by whether IT and Technology refer to the same or separate entities.

BITA is a lot more than a pain-reliever. As we saw earlier, *intersection is a powerful multiplier of value*. Thus, when modern business intersects with current technology, new possibilities instantly emerge that go far beyond easing existing pain and open new avenues of growth, create and deliver greater value to customers, improve employee engagement, and reduce uncertainty.

Technology forms the backbone of business in today's world. Few would deny the role, indeed the power, of technology in imparting that vital edge when it comes to delivering the personalized services which every customer rightfully expects from a bank, retail chain, hotel, utility service provider or virtually any business. It amazes me no end that very few organizations have done enough to bring Business and Technology together as a strategic force-multiplier to drive their growth. Since I entered the workforce in 1982, a lot of things have changed on both the business and technology dimensions. However, the transactional nature of Business-IT interaction has largely remained the same, and thus a lot of the potential remains locked up.

To be fair, while appreciating the importance of BITA in today's world is quite natural, getting to a high level of BITA requires a great deal of conscious effort and cannot be left to chance. This book is about discovering the power of BITA and harnessing it for personal and organizational development. It is not just a discourse on the virtues of BITA, but a simple and practical guidebook outlining clear steps towards its attainment. The viewpoints and anecdotes here are an extract of insights and experiences gained over three decades of managing business and technology, many of them learned the hard way! It should, therefore, help not only organizations in unlocking their true potential by avoiding the usual bumps and roadblocks but also individual employees in getting the right orientation towards business and improve their chances of succeeding in the technology-dominated world.

The chapters that follow will take you on an excursion to BITA in two phases – first Discovery and then Conquest. Think of BITA as you would of good health. The general importance of good health is not lost on you, but your primary interest is in understanding the specific dose and mix, exercises, diet, etc. that would lead YOU personally to good health. The Discovery section dwells on the overall relevance of BITA, but more importantly on diagnosing YOUR specific condition relating to BITA. I have tried to present tips and tools that would help you gauge where you are on the BITA Index in Chapter6. You thus enter the Conquest phase with a fair understanding of your strengths and weaknesses and can accordingly vary the emphasis on the individual practices suggested. The Conquest phase is your handbook on using BITA to drive success in a digitally-powered enterprise.

There are seven defining dimensions of alignment presented in this work which I have found are essential for driving excellence through BITA. Your progress along these dimensions will not only help with building and sustaining BITA but will contribute to a culture of collaboration and improve the predictability and efficiency of technology-driven services to customers and internal functions.

Before we start our journey, let me reiterate a couple of familiar but essential points on BITA. First, an alignment between Business and Technology does not take away the importance of personal touch in your business interactions, particularly with your customers. Quite the contrary, in fact. As technology advances, human-to-human interactions are far fewer, and hence the value of each interaction is much greater. We must never forget this.

Second, and this is very important, individuals and organizations that have *customer orientation* in their DNA have a more natural path to BITA. In such organizations, Customer Service is not just one department. Instead, the entire organization sees itself as one large customer service department. Everyone – from the CEO to the Accounts clerk – recognizes their primary role as being a CUSTOMER SATISFIER. If this is true in your organization, you have already taken a crucial first step towards BITA. In this book though, instead of an idealistic approach, I have taken the view that most organizations may have to put in just that little *extra* effort initially during takeoff, but in due course will land safely in BITA territory.

Of course, healthy functional alignment between other parts of the organization – e.g., business and HR, or IT and SCM - is also relevant in the current business context and most of the principles in this book may apply to these as well. However, as this book is about achieving success in the digital economy for which BITA has been highlighted as a critical factor by most respondents that I approached (results in Chapter-5), the emphasis is on Business-IT alignment. All the same, greater alignment *across* the organization is an unbeatable strength and I trust this book will set you in the right direction towards attaining it.

The purpose of this book is to *awaken*, and not *teach*. We already have been taught a lot through learning and experience, of which we probably use 10% through our lives. Esoteric or academic concepts that may sound exalted but lack practical appeal are, therefore, passed over. Most ideas in this book will have a ring of familiarity, and that is by design. It is backed by my trust that you, the reader, will build upon the familiar notions put together in this book in your unique environment to make a difference. In any case, for mastering BITA, you need not be exceptional in Business or Technology. It is not an S-M-E thing! The aim of this book is thus to enable *everyone* to acquire the essential skills and mindset which will help them wade through the digital ocean where all of us are going to find ourselves soon, if not already immersed. This does not mean that BITA just happens and all one must do is to 'ride the wave.' Quite like customer-orientation, BITA is all about your attitude and drive for excellence, which this book will guide you to discover and develop.

Part-I:
DISCOVERY

1 *The Way Things Were...*

The universe, they say, started with a big bang and went through a phase of hyper-inflationary growth before things cooled down and the expansion rate stabilized. Once this happened, conditions evolved that produced stars, planets, life (at least here on Earth) and eventually, pockets of *intelligence.*

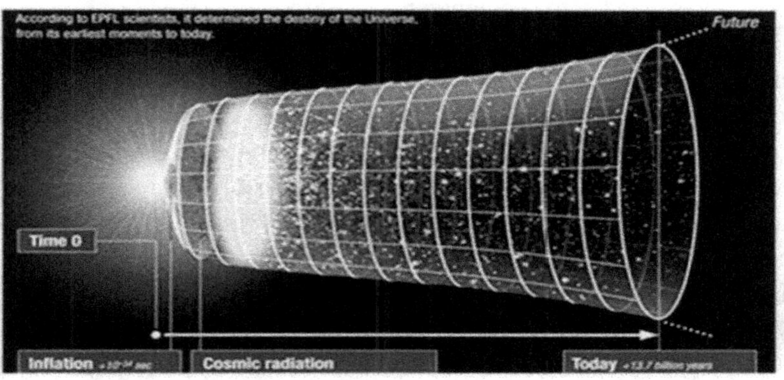

As it morphed into its present form, the Universe also created its own *dimensions*. There was no concept of space and time prior to the creation event. Don't get alarmed yet - this is not a book on the physics of the Big Bang! The reason I bring up the subject in the opening lines is that the Universe is the best model to explain the concept of hyper-inflationary growth along multiple dimensions. As we shall see in later chapters, the concept of dimensions has a special significance in this book.

Let's turn to Information Technology. Unlike the Universe, Information Technology did not have very spectacular origins. There was no Big Bang. Information processing systems arrived on the scene around the middle of the twentieth century in successive stages. It was, however, not until the 1980s that computing and networking technology scaled up sufficiently to make computers

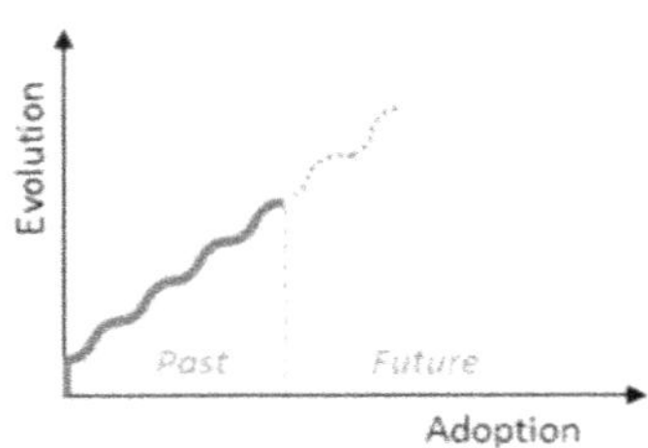

accessible (easy-to-use) and feasible (fit-to-use) in the business environment. This intersection of technology with business released a continuous wave of evolution and adoption, which drove not just the growth of IT, but created – ultimately – an entirely new paradigm in which IT became inseparable from Business.

We will return to this subject but for now, let us go back to the origins of IT and the way things *were* for the Business-IT ecosystem. While the first computer, called ENIAC, arrived in 1946, it would be inaccurate to say that it spawned an IT revolution. Gradual advancements led to computers finally emerging from highly specialized, dedicated, and often secret environments into the public domain on a time-share basis. IBM System 360 *mainframe computer* was a ground-breaking step in facilitating this movement as it heralded a shift from discrete transistors and relays to integrated circuits, marking the entry of *electronic computer systems*. This pioneered the concepts of scalability and compatibility – the importance of which has not diminished with time. CDC, DEC, HP, and others followed, and by about the early-to-mid seventies, several scientific institutions and business corporations were relying on mainframe computers for bulk data processing. The sturdy mainframe remained well entrenched in our business, educational, financial, and research institutions at least up to the mid-1980s. In those days, electronic display, storage, and information-sharing capabilities were somewhat limited, so *printing* was very central to computing.

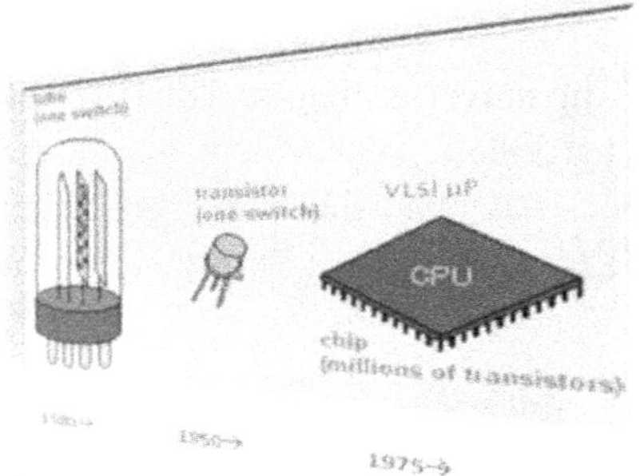

I recall visiting computer installations in 1983 where it was a routine matter to schedule print jobs for the 1403 IBM Line Printer from the IBM 1401 central processing system in the evening, and it would be found happily chugging away, spewing paper, when you came back to the office the next morning – or next Monday! The early computers were built for sturdiness and manual-work reduction more than for speed and versatility – at least in comparison to current trends.

The Way Things Were...

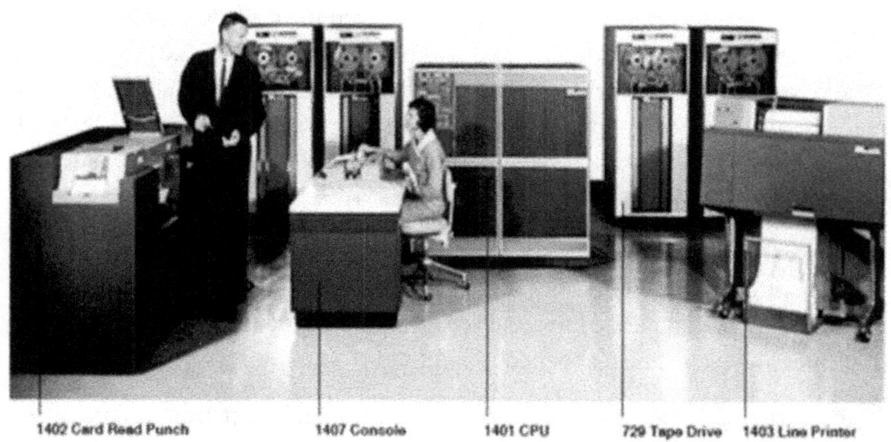

The IT story is marked by significant and frequent generational shifts, driven by new technology. With each generation, things have become simpler for the user, thus increasing the rate of *adoption*. Up to about 1980, there was a specialized group of people, notably computer engineers, scientists, and programmers, who alone could lay claim to knowledge of IT and its limited applications. Look where we are now with the adoption of IT! The story of the *evolution* of technology, helped by Moore's law, is similar. What took a room-full of hardware then, comfortably fits into your pocket now! This steady growth in technological evolution and rate of adoption thus takes the form of an ice-cream-cone when plotted on a time-scale.

Many of us – and I consider myself privileged to be one such – in our lifetimes have seen IT evolve from centralized Big Iron (Mainframes) to Networking

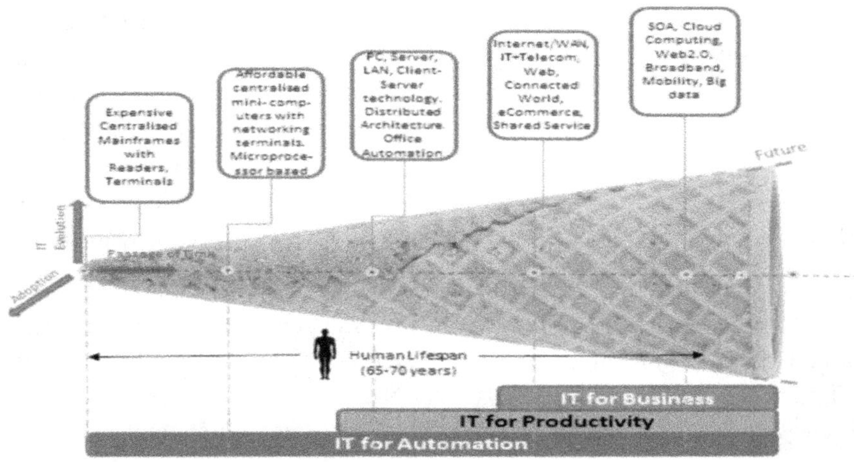

terminals (Minicomputers), to Client-Server architecture (PC, LAN, Servers) to Internet (Telecom/WAN) to Cloud Computing (SOA, Web 2.0). That is *five* generations of IT in *one* of ours! With the spawning of each new generation, the realization that IT can play a larger role than keeping the traditional light bulb on gradually dawned, but it took almost four generations to realize the potential of IT as a real *business enabler*.

IT's potential in the organization has enlarged over the generations from an instrument of *automation* to a tool for *productivity,* and finally an enabler of *business*. We are concerned in this book primarily with the emergence of *IT as a business enabler.* This happened around the 4th generation of IT.

In the earlier generations, the picture was starkly different from what we see today. Actually, there was no picture at all, as IT was completely invisible to all but itself. An IT (or EDP – short for Electronic Data Processing – as it was then called) 'department' was where data was keyed-in manually from vouchers on to diskettes which were fed into batch-processing minicomputers running COBOL programs, with programmers within shouting distance always, because you never knew! In the background used to be boisterous 'Line Printers', always printing away on reams of lined paper. To this day I wonder who consumed those reports and why! Then Y2K, the biggest damp squib in recorded history, happened and people woke up to the existence of IT, though no one was quite sure of its role in their lives.

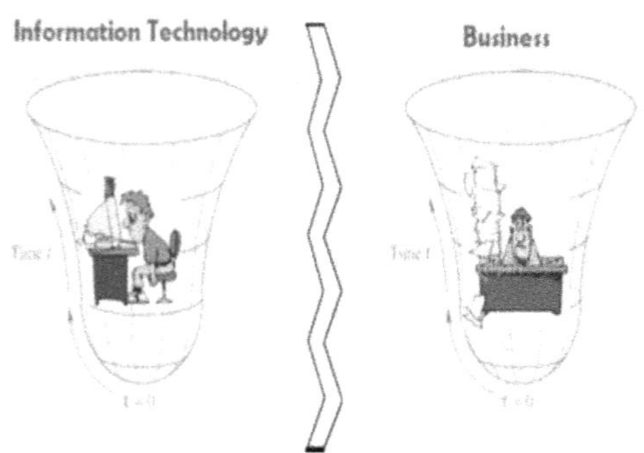

In the above scenario, Business and IT existed in completely different, non-intersecting universes. The advent of PCs and rudimentary LAN made a case for IT to be seen (though still not heard) around the office. Even as IT was gaining some acceptance as an enhancer of office productivity in the early 80s, it was still not in the realm of being a real *business enabler*. Business-IT Alignment was beyond even the remote reaches of imagination in those times.

Things started changing rather swiftly with the arrival of the public Internet around 1983. The operating word here is *public,* for the Internet had existed in a limited way since the late 1960s when the US Advanced Research Projects Agency (ARPA) interconnected some university computers and created the first ever 'network' of computers, called ARPANET. The ARPANET served the interests of scientific users only and had limited extent. However, it was the earliest demonstration of *packet-based* communication – which means sending information in small units over different paths and reconstructing the units at the destination. This formed the basis of the TCP/IP (which is an acronym for the rather grandiloquent *Transport Control Protocol over Internet Protocol*, but you can ignore this. Just call it 'packet transfer'), which allowed for an orderly expansion of the network to include more and more computers. TCP/IP became the lifeline of what we now know as the Internet and is still used as the dominant protocol for Internet communication.

Two other things happened in the early 1980s that brought the Internet into the public arena. One, the creation of the *world wide web* enabling sharing of documents over a TCP/IP network and two, the introduction of the *web browser*.

In 2013, the web completed 30 years of existence. A lot has changed since its arrival. In a snippet, I gave to *Information Week* magazine on this occasion (captioned), I spoke about the struggles and triumphs that we faced during the early days of the Internet.

ASHISH PACHORY, HEAD-IT, TATA TELESERVICES

"The Internet may be 30 today, bordering on middle age in our human terms, but in my experience it is still a budding teenager! I first encountered this phenomenon in 1994. I was in Switzerland for business, and was used to exchanging data on 1.2 MB floppy disks. True to this, my patrons provided me a floppy disk titled "World Wide Web" that could potentially access unlimited amounts of data (far more than 1.2 MB). Somewhat puzzled, I brought this disk to India, but found that we did not have the tools in my office to exploit it!

In the early nineties, the world was yet to wake up from the era of EDP. Communications meant DoT POTS network, which completely failed to anticipate anything other than voice and telex. The Internet was clearly ahead of its time.

Arrival of ISPs on the scene proliferated Internet use. The ISP offered dial-up access over phone lines, and a rudimentary browser. The first browser I recollect was Netscape with its constant meteor shower that gave you the assurance that something was going on, don't give up! E-mail and chat were the killer apps. No one talked of speed. Just connecting and doing anything at all was an achievement!

Considering that we did not have even the basic technologies and systems, like abundant disk and system memory, communication bandwidth, software and graphics, the Internet was indeed a phenomenon waiting to happen. And it did happen. It had its ups and downs — hindered by Y2K, then spurred by Dotcom — but it never stopped happening.

What an extraordinary transformation in 30 years! From being a mysterious, difficult to use, clunky and restricted system to something that has touched almost all of humanity in ways that no one could have imagined. And yet, this is just a beginning.

In retrospect, I consider myself more fortunate than my kids. I have seen both worlds, from birth to infancy to teenage of the Internet. How can a generation, which gets bewildered over a delay of a few seconds while online 30,000 feet above the Atlantic, grasp the meaning of Internet evolution? They missed out on the fun, the thrill, the excitement — and the frustration at times — of watching the biggest phenomenon of our times take shape."

Information Week Feb 2013

An understanding of the state of business-technology relationship in the *pre-internet era* is an integral part of appreciating the power of Business-IT Alignment (BITA). For far too long, IT systems operated invisibly in the back-end run by the dedicated staff of a (now mostly defunct) department called 'electronic-data-processing' (EDP). The other genre associated with IT was the computer scientist – the erudite product of a top technological institute whose work was mostly confined to research on how to build better computers and not on how to make better use of computers for business. Hence most of these scientists went to work for technology firms, usually manufacturers of computer equipment, and not to EDP departments.

In this scenario, most companies had no means to see beyond the usual invoice-printing, MIS and other routine batch-processing jobs performed by 'minicomputers' (as per today's standards they were mini in everything but size!) and there was very little attempt to exploit the power of computers for anything beyond *automation* of existing – mostly financial – processes. The following is an example from that era.

The year was 1984. I was a maintenance engineer for minicomputer systems in the Delhi area. On one Saturday morning, there was a person from office at my door with a message (since there was no phone in my apartment) which stated that I must call a number, which happened to be a customer (a large manufacturer of textile yarn) located about 80 km from Delhi. I called back from a nearby public booth and was told that a catastrophic event had occurred, and could I report immediately, please. I took a public (state transport) bus to reach the site by afternoon. Went straight to the EDP manager's glass cabin (they were always glass cabins, probably so that a sharp eye could be kept on IT equipment and staff). It turned out that on the previous day (Friday) an urgent meeting had taken place between the company's top management, the sales managers and the Finance team which ended with the decision to revamp the material coding system to reflect product categorization. It was further agreed that this would be the highpoint of the meeting with the managing director during his forthcoming visit next Tuesday (yes, 3 days later), where itemized sales would be presented for the first time.

There was no one from IT (EDP) present during that Friday meeting. However, it was cheerily stated by the Finance Head that 'we have a computer, so we can easily do it. After all, what are computers for?' Obviously, the material code was linked to several programs and data-sets like invoicing, and the change of code would need to be run on volumes of records which were kept on tapes, as disk capacity was limited to 34MB! The EDP manager was understandably flustered. He had quit smoking a year ago but restarted that day! The Finance Manager (his boss) wouldn't listen to him. There wasn't much he could do, and nor could I – except for giving some moral support! Of course, those of us familiar with modern ERP would wonder why this is even a problem. But this was way back in the days of batch processing. Anyhow, with all the smart scripting, retrievals, etc. that we tried, the job could not be done, and the EDP manager had the unpleasant task on Monday evening to ask for an additional 14 days from his superiors. I was told later that the meeting with the MD on Tuesday did not go well for the Finance Manager and commitments on some new product launches were slipped, which probably affected revenues and disconcerted the sales folks as well. It took days to recover from the effects of one wrong communication that could have been avoided had there been some sort of alignment with IT either prior to or during a crucial meeting. But such instances were commonplace as IT did not merit a say on crucial decisions that it was asked to implement.

As evident from the example above, IT was only a back-end tool for *automation*. Nothing more. It had no place in decision making. There was also no attempt to use IT for any optimization or improvement of processes to deliver any value other than saving time. Even the accuracy of calculations was doubted - I have seen folks sitting with computer-generated reports, verifying the totals on a calculator!

To be fair, the minicomputer had its limitations as an enabler of Business-IT interface. It was a batch processing system which relied on data fed through offline data-entry machines. There was no 'non-IT' interface envisaged in its construction. As seems quite inevitable in retrospect, it soon yielded to another interesting development in the early 80s – the arrival of the Personal Computer, or simply the PC. IBM, which was almost synonymous with computers up to the 70s, had somehow missed the minicomputer leg. But it rode the 'microcomputer' wave remarkably well – belying all expectations – and came up with the IBM-PC which soon became the de facto standard which others were required to emulate – and did. There were variants of the PC, in the form of PCXT, PCAT etc. which differed in hardware configuration, but were essentially similar. The personal computer filled a very crucial gap – it heralded the use of computers for rudimentary business purpose, *directly by the end user*. The computer had finally broken out of the lab and the EDP department!

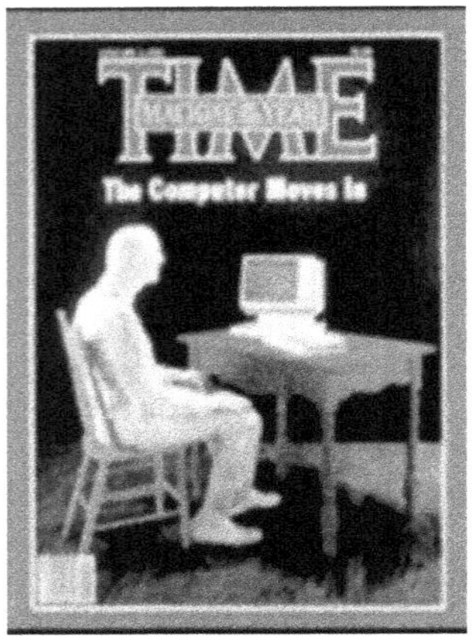

The early business use, of course, was mostly limited to word-processing and spreadsheets. While it was indeed a boost for individual *productivity*, computers and IT were still very far from being enablers of business in the real world and the concept of BITA was entirely alien. It was an era when the *device* defined the landscape of IT and trumped data and applications. Still, the computer age had now firmly arrived. I think it was uncannily prophetic of TIME magazine to break tradition and declare the PC, a machine, as its 'Person' of the year in 1983!

The PC helped usher another very significant development. For the first time, people could *transfer their data to another unconnected computer*, by *saving* it on the humble floppy disk with its limited (1.2MB) capacity, and thus allowed *data sharing*. (Strangely, the 'Save' icon on most applications (like Word) is still in the shape of a floppy disk. Ever wonder why?) Theoretically, the data transfer was possible with mainframes and minicomputers as well, but as there was no *universal operating system* that different computers could understand, it was restricted to very tight, allied groups. This sharing of data between disjoint computers (PCs) was largely possible with the arrival of Microsoft on the scene with its MS-DOS operating system, which was easy for everyone to learn, enabled sharing across computers and allowed portable applications for the first time, thus revolutionizing the way people used computers. So, did everyone now rush to hop on to the IT bandwagon? Not by a long shot, unfortunately.

IT was still considered an expensive indulgence by most institutions in the 80s, at least here in India. Protests against 'computerization' were common. There was very little understanding of the gain that the computer could bring, and most of the contemplation was around the perceived pain it entailed. Far from being an enabler of business success, the PC was seen as an avoidable extravagance and a threat to job security. I was in Lucknow in 1985 to meet with the head of a renowned scientific institution - a very learned man, well-grounded but with eyes to the sky. His problem was that despite having used his available grant to have high-end personal computers (PC-ATs) installed in his institute, he was unable to convince his team of scientists and research associates to use those computers, which would justify the investment. On probing further, it emerged that using the PCs for the work would result in some of the on-going programs finishing much ahead of schedule, which was not desirable since the stipend of the lab staff was linked to the duration of the project! Certainly, this was a problem that was not envisaged at the time of the business-case preparation! I was asked to join his staff meeting that day, to convince the team of the benefits of using computers, as an outside 'expert.' Incredible as it may seem, we could not succeed, and the project went ahead without using the computers though there was some agreement that future programs would factor in the use of computers after due training etc. was provided. However, I was happy that I could convince the team to use the computers for some required documentation at least, which could prove beneficial later by easing the storage, retrieval and editing process. This case highlights the state of affairs even in relatively very learned communities of those times. Attitudes and mindsets were not aligned with the ready adoption of technology.

Stances towards the adoption technology for business started becoming more favorable with the advent of the **client-server** model of computing. This book is not a discourse on the minutiae of computing technology. The client-server architecture, however, heralded a new era which would eventually spawn many of the services (like Email, Web) that contributed to BITA. A quick refresher on the high-level basics of client-server architecture would thus be in order. For more on this, you can always refer to Wikipedia or other web sources.

The client-server architecture pre-existed the microcomputer era. In the age of mainframes and minicomputers, a number of 'dumb' terminals were connected to a central and powerful *server* (the mainframe) which did all the hard work and delivered (or 'served') its output to the terminals, or *clients*. The clients just placed inquiries to the server and could receive and display the response in a readable format. Later, such 'dumb' terminals came to be known as 'thin' clients, as opposed to 'thick' clients which had some built-in business logic for processing and storing the data served up by their servers.

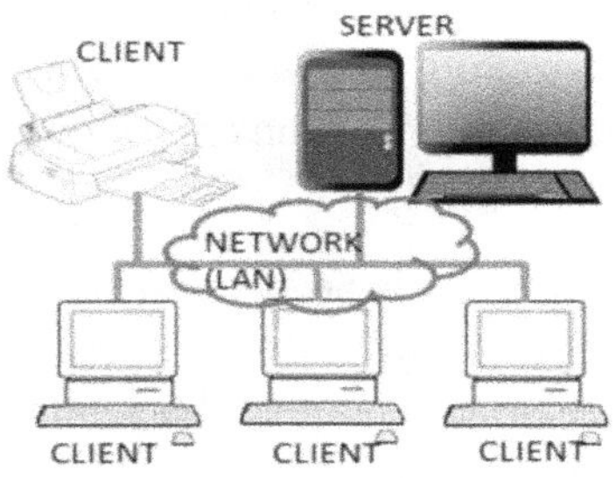

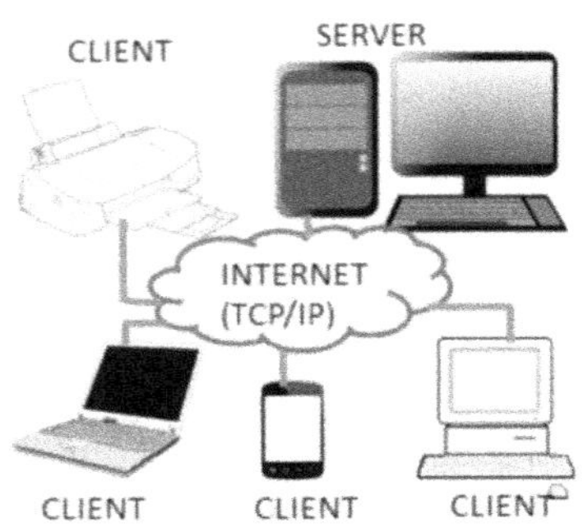

As *microcomputers* (PCs etc.) became more affordable and increasingly powerful, protocols evolved to interconnect them and share their combined computing power. This gave rise to the *Local Area Network* which is a system of interconnected computers (hosts) communicating through a well-defined protocol, permitting seamless expansion of the network. In this system of interconnected computers (computers are called *hosts* in network jargon) *any* individual computer or process could play the role of *either* a server *or* a client or *both*. A client or server could be an *application* (and not necessarily a computer), running on a *host* (which is necessarily a computer). In a typical computer network, there are centralized servers serving applications, data etc. to the networked clients. The email that you routinely use is an excellent example of a client as it enables you to send messages to an unseen mail server which processes the message to decide on further action – like forwarding it to its intended destination client.

In a nutshell, *clients* are applications that rely on servers for processing power. *Servers* are centralized processing systems that manage all the resources like files and data and execute all the process requests from the clients, while the *network* connects the servers and clients so that they can communicate and share information with each other.

The client-server architecture is an important milestone in the evolution of the Internet. The Internet is merely a vast network of interconnected hosts (running as clients *or* servers) communicating via a defined protocol (TCP/IP) for sharing information (web pages) using client-server architecture.

We have come a long way from the days of the IBM 360. Today we have a vibrant Internet which encompasses many diverse developments in computing architecture, communication networks, devices, and software which happened independently of each other. The internet is a living demonstration of the power of intersection.

We come across mind-boggling statistics on Internet adoption every day, and on its innovative use in social, business, scientific, educational and indeed almost every human endeavor. Now, in fact, the Internet has gone beyond human use and is making fast strides into another realm – the Internet of *Things*, opening the road to smart cities and beyond! As far as technology is concerned, the Internet may be just another example of what successive intersections of ideas

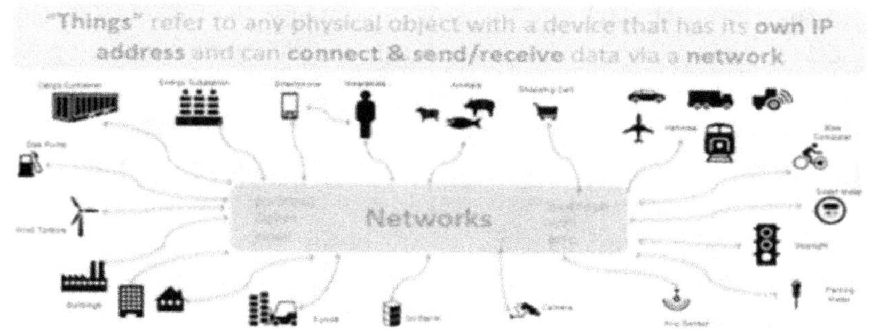

can achieve, but for business, it unveils completely new vistas that call for a quick rebooting of the very fundamentals of strategy, customer management, go-to-market, survival. In the Internet world, Business and IT *together* create business value. They do not just complement each other. They are inseparable.

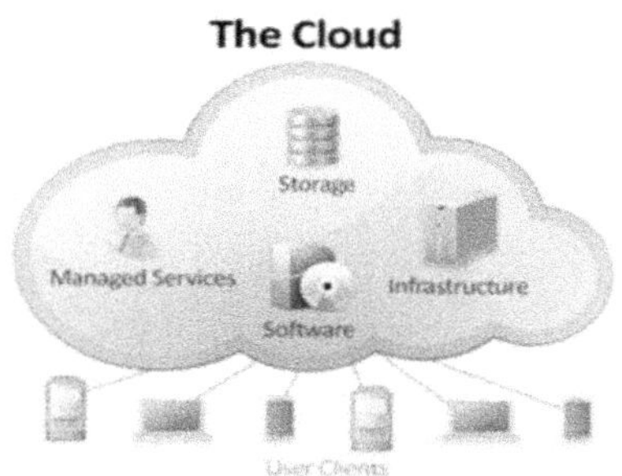

There's a lot more to the Internet story. You are no longer restricted in your access to your private or business data and applications by your location or device. That's because your content (data, applications) can now reside on a "cloud" instead of locally on your device, and this cloud can be accessed from anywhere. Connectivity has become ubiquitous and it no longer matters whether you are using your office laptop, your personal smartphone or your friend's borrowed tablet. Your internet experience is completely independent of your device or location. This is *Mobility* – another new trend spawned by the Internet, which along with the Cloud, has had a profound impact on the social and business landscape. The second generation of the World Wide Web is already on its way. Web2.0 will increase the scope for online collaboration and provide better structure and organization of content.

The Internet saga continues. To accommodate more users (which would now include 'things', or 'machines'), the current addressing system for identifying individual users is being revamped. Addressing refers to the capacity to identify unique devices on the Internet. As the Internet is based on a binary (i.e., base of 2) system, the current 32-bit addressing protocol, known as IPv4, can identify up to 2^{32}, or 4.3 billion users. The *new* addressing system (IPv6) would use *128*-bits! By the way, this is not just 4 times increase in capacity, but a staggering 2^{96} times (which is around 72 billion billion billion times)! Information Technology is certainly going the Universe way in the numbers game!

This chapter has been a rather breezy journey through the various stages of IT evolution and adoption. It is intended to help us gain an understanding of the way things were, as a precursor to defining the way things should be in the new Business-IT ecosystem. Business and IT have become inseparably intertwined by the web and its progeny. The opportunities for both Business and IT in this environment are limitless. However, making the most of these opportunities requires a conscious effort on the part of both business and IT participants. They must be aligned to a common purpose, and this is what we shall be discussing in the rest of this book.

2 Business-IT Alignment: Platitude Or Survival?

If you are still in an organization where alignment of IT with business is a mere platitude, let me offer this advice to you: get off the bus before it tumbles down the ravine. Business-IT alignment (BITA) is not another well-tossed transformation brew stirred up by hype rather than value. It is a ground-up reality brought upon us by compelling and irreversible changes in our environment – market, economic, social and of course, technological. It is survival.

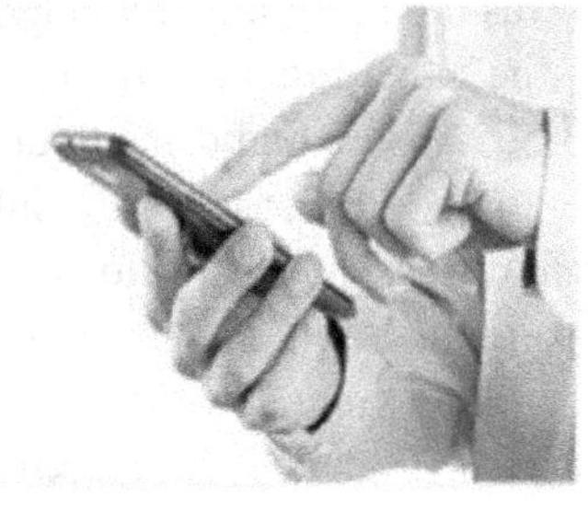

We saw in the previous chapter that for most of their history, business and IT existed in completely different, non-intersecting universes. Let us cut to the present. The amalgamation of IP (Internet Protocol)-centric technologies, an abundance of bandwidth, the explosion of data, the proliferation of smart mobile devices, and a growing hunger for actionable information anywhere and anytime, have resulted in the creation of the new-age digital ecosystem which has turned all traditional concepts on their heads. The foundation of the integrated Business-Technology edifice of the future has been laid. Alignment of IT with Business in this backdrop is not about platitudes or catchy slogans, or even mission statements. It is about Business and IT thinking, building and operating *together* for a shared goal, and that is to make the business successful. If this simple tenet is demonstrated in the day to day *behavior* of the entire IT workforce, you have already taken a significant first step towards alignment of IT with Business. For the new-age digital enterprise, this must become the new normal.

We will return to the new normal in a moment, but first, let us be clear about 'the demonstration of day to day *behavior*' since this is at the very root of

BITA. Quite like customer-orientation and quality-focus, BITA is part of the organization's *character*. It cannot be attained unless everyone in Business, IT and beyond is passionate about their individual responsibility towards the attainment of *organizational* (and not only departmental) success and feel connected to the larger mission of the company regardless of their level or role. BITA can never truly happen as a response to a directive or compliance with a policy. It must be a voice from *within* which makes you act it out instinctively and naturally.

The below example has nothing to do with IT and not much to do with Business either, but it's a great demonstration of intrinsic *behavior* which collectively builds organizational character. I have used this in many of my discourses to make a point about the individual's role in influencing company image.

It was a typically hot summer afternoon in Delhi. For the benefit of those who have not experienced it, summers are quite extreme in Delhi: 44°C (111°F) being quite common, with hot and dusty winds blowing which could give you a stroke if you are not protected. The era was mid-nineties – before mobile phones and ATMs were prolific. My wife was at home with my daughter who was then four months old. At about noon, there was a sudden need for money due to an urgent delivery, and as it happened, there wasn't enough cash in the house. I had driven our (only) car to work, so there was no transport. My wife could not leave the infant at home, nor venture out with her in the heat and dust, and walk to the bank for drawing the money. In earlier visits to our bank, which was about 1.5km away, we had come across a teller whom we had frequently dealt with and thus knew his name. From the landline, my wife called the bank and asked for this gent by name, and fortunately, he came on the line. She explained to him her predicament. He told her not to worry and that he will come to our house with the required cash, and my wife could then hand a cheque over to him. True to his word, he dropped in 15 minutes later with the cash, took the cheque, and left. Think about it –this is an experience with a public-sector (govt owned and run) bank, as a 'small' (read non-HNI) customer. The teller would have been well within his rights to ask his customer (my wife) to come to the bank for the money. Yet he chose to brave the heat on a two-wheeler scooter, to do a job which was not part of his charter but meant a lot to his customer. More than 20 years later, I still recall this incident because it was such an exceptional show of positive behavior. It made me think very highly of this bank, and to this day I not only stay loyal but also an advocate.

What individuals in a group consciously, consistently and collectively demonstrate in their thinking and behavior becomes its culture. It is true of all communities, including business corporations. That is why many companies have belief systems, which is an *unchanging* set of behaviors – for example, serving the customer well, conducting business ethically, setting high standards of quality, etc. – that every employee is expected to emulate in word and spirit. It's the belief system, shared by all the employees, that builds the *culture* of the organization. An organization has *character* when it does not compromise on its belief system irrespective of inducements, compulsions or consequences. I recall an incident that brings out the character of the organization very aptly.

This is an unfortunate example which depicts the corruption that has set in in some government institutions. It also exemplifies how a robust belief system becomes your guide in making right decisions in ambiguous situations. During the early days of computerization, my company was expecting a large order for microcomputers (PCs) from a government agency. The order was almost 'in the bag', and we had even begun the task of 'site-inspection', a mandatory requirement in those days as computers were very fussy about their installation environment. During the very last stages, a senior official called our area sales manager and asked him for a 'small favor'. He wanted my company to arrange (and pay for) transportation for personal guests of his to visit a nearby hill-station. For him, the government official, this was a very trivial and routine request which was not at all out of place! The request was indeed a small one compared to the size of the order and considering that these were days of very stiff competition in the hardware market. Yet this request was politely refused, as it was against our core belief of ethical business conduct. Many such examples abound, but unfortunately, there are also examples where inducements have subordinated beliefs. We did not get the order right then, but eventually, we did and in a completely clean and transparent way. However, we were all prepared to lose the deal rather than compromise on our values. There was not even a question raised about it. It was a great show of character by the company which left us all feeling very proud.

How do you inculcate a strong belief system across the length and breadth of the organization? As this is driven by a *shared passion* there is no standard formula here, but a few pointers could be useful:

- The leadership of the company reinforces the belief system by living it, commenting on it, measuring it and communicating it at every opportunity.

- The leadership always decides in favor of the belief system during organizational crises. Their reactions are guided by the belief system, and they act as role-models for the organization.
- It is made mandatory for every person in the organization to participate at least annually in coaching sessions *by the leadership itself* to reinforce the belief system.
- The company's rewards and recognition programs are modeled on the belief system
- Alignment to the belief system forms the most important and uncompromising criteria for recruitment, performance assessments and progression.

Outcome-based IT:

Let us return now to the new normal. From being isolated entities driven by functional objectives, Business and IT are now bound by a *common mission* that requires them to think, build, and operate *together* for a shared goal, which is to make the business successful (I said this before and am repeating it here given its centrality to our subject).

In other words, the new normal is about IT being an equal stakeholder in the achievement of business results, or *outcomes*. The true measure of IT's performance is the impact it has on the *outcome* of *business processes.* Internal measures like RoI, uptime of IT servers, adherence to response-time SLA etc. are fast fading away and becoming irrelevant in business-led IT organizations. Clearly, IT is no longer just an emergency-response team to cater to outages and 'issues.' Outcome-based IT is focused on the *purpose*, that is, on *what* was achieved, rather than on *how* it was achieved. Being bound by a common purpose is at the core of any alignment. The outcome-based model of IT is thus the essence of BITA.

The good news is that outcome-based IT has quickly come to a point where it is well entrenched in our everyday lives. Consider these examples.

Manufacturing: Traditionally IT has been tasked with automation of the process workflow in a manufacturing environment while the actual outcome of those processes is the shop-floor persons' responsibility. In the outcome-based model, the role of IT would be achieving JIT manufacturing and lean production to reduce cost (a *business* outcome).

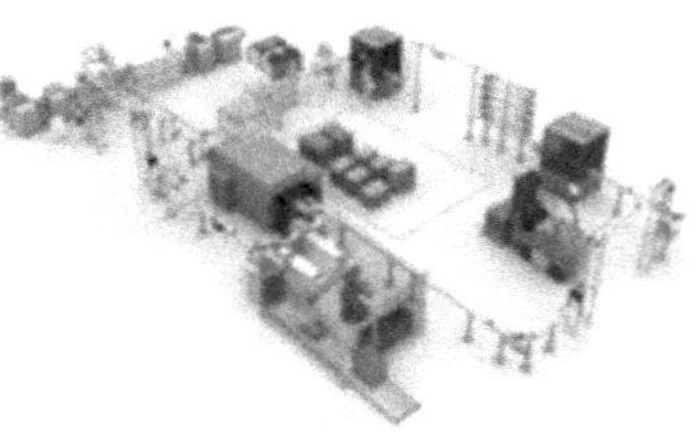

Banking: IT is no longer just the agency for 'computerization' of operations, but is a primary stakeholder in the growth of the banking business through the enablement of Internet and Mobile Banking and adapting quickly to changing customer preferences. For example, in the outcome-based model, IT would be responsible for ensuring that the customer's last transaction is reflected in his statement after, say, thirty minutes of the transaction. Providing secure online banking without causing irritation – like fast OTP delivery – is also a measure of IT success, as is the fulfillment of customer's expectation of publishing latest investment portfolio status each morning. These are clear *business* outcomes which are a measure of *IT* effectiveness, and go to show the extent to which IT and business are intertwined in the modern banking scenario.

Telecom: In high-tech sectors like Telecom, IT has an even higher influence on the business outcome, not only as an early *implementer* of new solutions (short TTM) required by the Business but also as a leading light to the Business in *proposing* innovative solutions in areas like monetization of data and business analytics. The primary business outcomes like rapid customer acquisition, quick recharge, timely port-in/port-out or accuracy of billing are measures of IT success in the outcome-based model. The outcome of many of the new telecom services like mobile wallet, m-health, m-education etc. is dependent on a healthy Business-IT association. This trend is likely to only increase, especially with the many over-the-top services now becoming an inseparable part of the telecom world.

Airlines: The speed and convenience with which you can book an airline ticket while on the move, or at home, is an example of Business-IT alignment at work in an outcome driven model. Not just that, but the ease and precision with which an airline can offer seat-selection, meal preferences, flight status, check-ins, discounts and loyalty programs to its customers are a measure of IT's contribution to the achievement of business outcomes – in this case getting you airborne comfortably, conveniently and cost-effectively. Conversely, is IT accountable for the dwindling loyalty of the airline's customer base? In the outcome-based model, it most certainly is.

In all the above scenarios, any discussion on the return on IT investment, workforce productivity, or the uptime of an IT server would be at best an academic one. Frankly, no one cares. In any case, how do you effectively measure RoI for systems whose benefits cannot be measured in money terms – like a mobile portal, customer relationship management system, ERP, etc.? This is another reason that the RoI model is losing sheen in favor of the outcome-based model. All that matters is how well IT has been able to contribute to the success of the business and its stakeholders. This trend is not likely to abate down the road.

On the flip side, there is this terrifying tale from a *high-tech* company – where the usual equation between IT and Business is a relatively good one. I was in Singapore in the mid-nineties to attend the APAC service conference of our principal, a global leader in high tech equipment. The theme of the workshop was "service strategy as a market differentiator" – a novel idea for those times! Presentations on service strategy were made by the service managers from twelve countries, including yours truly from India. We were all mildly surprised to see not one but *two* people stepping up for the presentation by one of the participant countries. It turned out that one was the service manager while the other was the sales manager. Why the *sales* manager? This was, after all, a service conference! It was not very common to see sales and service folks together, except when they were pointing fingers at each other! Our curiosity was soon satiated. It had so happened that a few months ago, there was a frantic call one afternoon to the company's salesperson from a hospital-cum-research facility that had purchased advanced medical equipment from this company. It was the operator of the MRI scanner machine. His worst nightmare had come true. There was an unconscious patient whose magnetic scan (or imaging) was being done for which he had been placed on the sliding table and pushed into the tubular scanner. The trouble was it wouldn't retract and open! The patient being unconscious could not operate the emergency button inside. The machine had a console from where the operator ran it, but he could not retract the patient from the scanner. The operator did not even have the service engineer's phone number and instead called the sales guy, as it was the only number he had. On hearing the story, the sales guy also tensed up and tried to reach the IT service engineer for help. The IT person left for the hospital in haste, but would he make it in time? Probably because of an in-built time-out mechanism, the machine opened on its own after a few extremely tense minutes, and the patient was saved! But it imparted

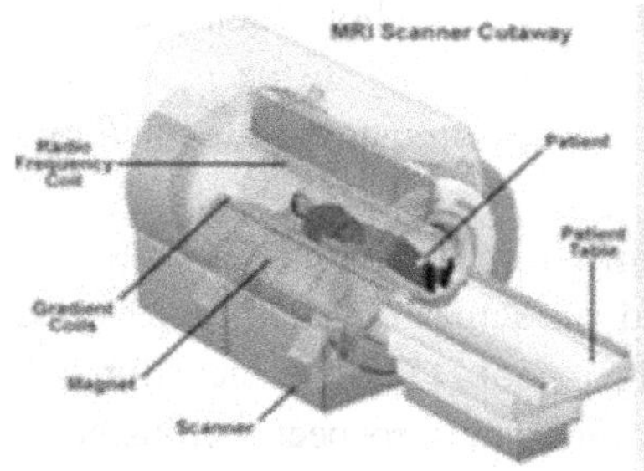

some crucial lessons. First, the service (IT) team was measuring itself on parameters like MTBF, MTTR, and FCRE – none of which would save a patient's life in a big crisis like above. The focus was clearly internal and not on the *outcome,* which in this case was ensuring the safety of the patient and providing accurate diagnostics. Secondly, there was no interaction between sales and service which would have helped plan an emergency response along with the sales, service, and hospital (customer) teams – like training the operator, remote control center manned by IT team, on-site IT availability etc. (all focused on the outcome). The good thing was that after this incident the company's management decided that sales and service teams would henceforth create their strategy and operations plans jointly and communicate them to the world *together*. That is, be equal stakeholders. Which is why the sales and service managers were together on the stage, presenting the service strategy. A big round of applause followed! A good lesson learned the hard way. Though I did not recognize it then, this was my earliest introduction to the importance of outcome-based IT.

For true and sustained alignment that goes well beyond platitudes and slogans, it is clear that there must be strong *interdependency* between Business and IT. After all, both Business and IT are bound by a common purpose and are targeting the same outcomes, so can they still afford to be in different universes? In the outcome-based model, the answer is a resounding NO.

So, what do companies (and individuals) that have strong BITA in their DNA and are therefore driven by the outcome-based model of IT do *differently*? This is one of the critical questions that this book attempts to answer, and is the subject of later sections, where we go into individual dimensions of BITA. For now, let us look at just a few examples of behaviors that I have found commonly displayed in almost all companies where BITA is a lot more than a platitude or a slogan.

1. In companies that are serious about Business-IT alignment, it is typical for the CIO and the IT team to be measured not only on benefits of IT to business, but the 'cost' at which these benefits are delivered as well. This is best indicated by *Business and IT regularly monitoring and reviewing the **Business Value of IT** (BVIT)* – a concept we shall be introducing later in this book. In these companies, no one cares about internal measures.

It is the *business* outcome that matters. For example, how accurately and quickly can customer information be made available to the call-center agent? What was the lost revenue due to delayed customer acquisition? Etc.

2. Business and IT have moved away from a formula based allocation of IT costs towards a costing model based on actual consumption by the Business. There is no common IT budget pool. IT is business-funded. Thus, the stakes for Business are much higher and prospects of business-aligned IT delivery much brighter. *This requires sound systems in place to measure IT consumption and to tie back the business benefits of a solution to the investment made in its roll-out.*
3. *Business and IT operate as two-in-a-box.* There is a robust governance framework in place, but it does not substitute constant and informal interaction between the teams. IT teams participate in discussions around business plans and Business teams join in discussions on IT strategy and product/ vendor selection
4. The IT organization is business-led. This means that there is an empowered business champion (call it business analyst, or business information officer) whose sole responsibility is to assure that *IT priorities are never out of sync with the business priorities* and that the entire IT team is focused on doing what is right for the *business*. There is at least one such Business-IT champion for each Line of Business.
5. IT team works as a *thought-leader to the business team*, rather than as an order-taker. As domain experts, the IT organization must be a trusted advisor to the business, providing thought-leading insights on trends and technologies that help the business succeed.
6. *The IT strategy and architecture are continually evaluated against the business roadmap.* The most common reason for misalignment is a divergence in strategies which lead to an IT architecture that is not supportive of future business requirements.
7. IT processes are simple and painless, designed to *serve the needs of the business*, and not the needs of IT. All processes are dynamic and adaptable to the changing business climate. *It is business that drives the IT processes and not the other way!*

Attainment of strong BITA calls for several concerted and well-thought-out actions on the part of both Business and IT. While this can be achieved through guidance and effort, it is important to emphasize that many of the factors involved are non-trivial and require a fair degree of maturity in Business, Finance, and IT processes. As a first step, we need to establish our current bearings, that is, find out where we stand presently and what the areas that require improvement are. This is the subject of Chapter-6. Having established *what* we need to do, we will go into Section-II and nail down *how* we are going to do it.

There's a lot of heavy stuff above, and this is a good time to take a story-break which will also help to grasp this more tightly.

We were executing a major business transformation project with a leading telecom service provider in the Asia Pacific recently. The project revolved around building the core revenue (billing) and credit control (receivables etc.) platform and was highly time-bound. The customer's ability to launch new services in the market hinged strongly on the availability of this system. There were many parties involved – customer's own IT team, billing product supplier, system integrator (my team) and few other smaller suppliers of adjunct products. Six months into the project, we were slipping milestones and anticipated a major derailment that would take us a year or more from the *original plan* – which incidentally was already communicated to the top management and the market. The primary reasons for slippage were a delay in agreeing on the scope, and frequent changes in the business requirements which in turn necessitated regressive development, redesign and cost escalations requiring pre-approval, etc. The project was led by a very astute CIO who fully understood that the situation called for some drastic steps as missing the business commitment was out of the question. I heard with dismay the presentation from the senior executive of the product company, whose pitch was on one aspect only – that projects of this magnitude are universally delayed, so there was nothing unique in this situation. And hence 'don't worry', was his guidance, 'your management will understand'! There was no word from him on how the project could be herded back on track. I don't think he got the customer on his side with his rather insensitive advice.

A couple of days later, the customer's CEO called all the stakeholders to a meeting. All participants in the consortium arrived with their senior folks as well as the project leaders. There was a great deal of censure and reprimand, but more disturbingly there was a visible disappointment on the CEO's face. He even reproached his CIO and the team. Finally, he said that what was clearly missing was an alignment between the various teams involved, particularly with the business, thereby eroding the sense of urgency around the project which he expected to see. It seemed that no one was accountable, and the CIO was being pulled in too many directions. To cut things short the meeting ended with an agreement amongst the stakeholder on a few decisive actions:

(1) Any delay in billing to end-customers will be the accountability of the IT team, who will if required do the billing *manually* or adopt a workaround, but the new cut-over date for the project will NOT be changed
(2) The business team will have two of their representatives permanently assigned to this project, with no other assignments until this was completed. There will be no more weekly 'hothouses.' Issues will be dealt with as and when they surfaced.
(3) The business team was also brought into an agreement on the *scope-freeze* date, beyond which all requirements will go into the subsequent phases. This caused some murmurs, but these were soon silenced.
(4) Importantly, business teams will fund all future change requirements from their *business* budget and not from the available project budget. Thus, stringent approval process would be followed before a change could be approved.
(5) Lastly, the CEO asked that a weekly progress update be given to him face-to-face, with very solid reasons given for any further slippage. He set aside 30 minutes each week for this review.

A new baseline was created and agreed with business, close to the earlier one. The sense-of-urgency was palpable. We ended up taking the project into production on the deadline. Confidence grew in the collaboration, and I know now that another key transformation project is underway with the same constitution of partners. Such is the power of BITA, even if it was an enforced one in this instance.

Many organizations follow the concept of Business being an 'internal customer' to IT. While this is fine for *the shared-services* model which is typically driven by an SLA (and not by business outcome), *the internal-customer concept does not work best for BITA.* An internal customer approach often causes confusion about who is the real customer being served and imparts – to the IT team – a feeling of being one layer removed from the end customer. The customer always means the *end*-customer, who pays for your services or products. Remember this: in a BITA driven organization, both IT and Business are *Customer Satisfiers* and that is the ONLY role they play. It does not matter what their business cards proclaim.

The outcome-driven model follows a cycle in which both Business and IT are participants. They are fully aligned in their view of the desired outcome early in the cycle. That is, both Business and IT have a clear and well-coordinated plan to achieve the outcome as a common mission, instead of IT teams just 'turning the wheel' without being aware of the purpose. I cannot over-emphasize this. *Unless Business and IT are aligned early in the game on the need and the desirability of an action, there will never be an alignment on the* ***outcome***.

Further, in an outcome-based model, the agreement between Business and IT goes beyond the traditional *requirements sign-off.* Here Business and IT *agree* and *own* the final deliverable, or outcome, and have an equal stake in its impact on the business. Hence it is important that they *both* answer **'Yes'** to all the questions in the cycle (see figure). In this case, we have considered the launch of a Mobile Self-Service portal, but the surrounding questions apply equally to other initiatives. Draft your own questions if you will. But always test your alignment *early in the game* through clear responses to such questions.

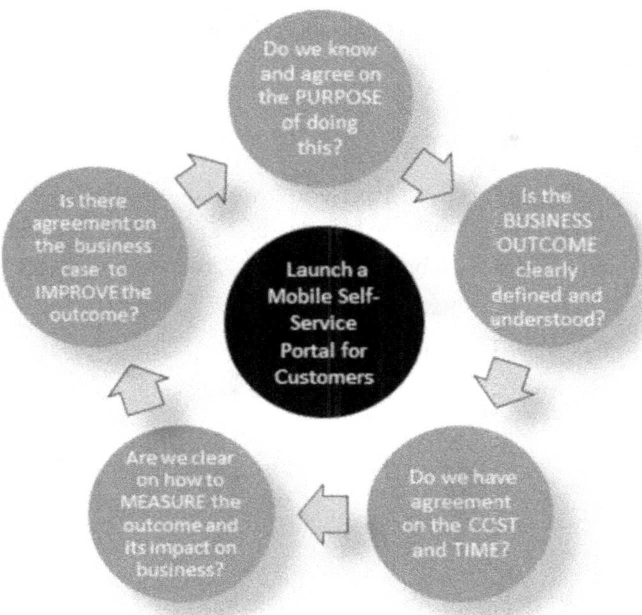

In summary, (1) defining the outcome must be the *starting point* of an engagement and not a corollary and (2) the outcome must be commonly understood and owned by both Business and IT.

There is no organized industry today where IT does not have a role in shaping the product that reaches the end customer. Can an airline today claim to offer the level of customer convenience that it does without packaging online reservations, seat selection, web check-in and a variety of other value-adds enabled by IT? Or a Bank, Hotel-chain, telecom service provider, even governments? While this may be less evident in case of manufactured goods, the role of IT is equal, if not higher, here as IT is behind many of the real-time processes, material and inventory tracking, control systems etc. that result in the final product being created and retailed. Even behind-the-scenes IT is at work alongside marketing teams in launching campaigns, benchmarking with competition, analyzing customer behavior and preferences, and enabling efficient customer service delivery.

In such a scenario, imagine for a moment that Business and IT are NOT aligned, and are still in the state of 80s and 90s described in the previous chapter. It is not just that chaos will ensue, which it inevitably will. More to the point, Business, which survived even Y2K, will come to a grinding halt. IT is at the very CORE of business today. In fact, it is indistinguishable from Business. For the new age enterprise, Business *IS* IT. And vice-versa.

The Cycle of Interdependence

The cycle of interdependence as depicted here is at the core of Business-IT alignment. In an organization where Business and IT are truly aligned, they are also interdependent. Let us look briefly at the various aspects of interdependence

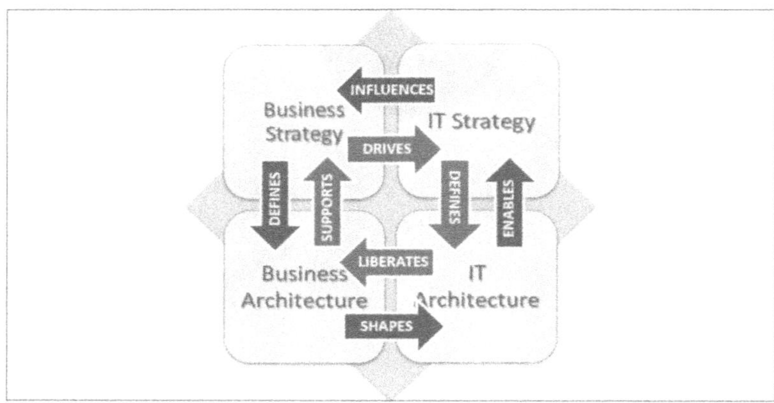

1. Business Strategy DRIVES IT Strategy

The Business Strategy lays the foundation for the IT strategy. One of the defining characteristics of BITA-led organizations is that their IT strategy flows down from a very clear and uncomplicated charter: *IT exists to make the business succeed.* Period. The IT strategy is to ensure that Business stays ahead in terms of speed-to-market and in capitalizing on key indicators to create differentiation. Hence the IT strategy ensures that two objectives are met. First, IT is aligned with the business roadmap, i.e., IT organization, systems and processes can effectively and efficiently support, enable and execute the company's *business* plan. Second, IT transformation is a continuous process, i.e., IT Service Delivery and Application Architecture are continuously *evolving* to keep up with the dynamic business environment.

2. IT Strategy DEFINES IT Architecture

This would seem rather obvious. However, a lot of organizations find themselves constrained by their IT architecture, which over the years has become clunky and patchy. They have no option but to allow the architecture to influence their strategy – a gross mistake. In the fast-changing technology scenario, your IT architecture may be the biggest constraint in delivering those Mobility-driven (cloud-enabled) services that your customer expects and your competitor is already providing. Or in searching through humungous data repositories (like call data records in telecom companies) to ascertain customer behavior patterns which would facilitate customized offerings. Even though your strategy envisages these benefits, your IT architecture is clearly not aligned with the vision. In a BITA-driven organization, the IT architecture is built-for-the-future. This is not as difficult as it sounds. There are standards available which provide for modularity and scalability so that the architecture can keep step-locked with the evolving strategy. For some companies, this may be a somewhat involved process requiring a one-time financial and time commitment, but it may be well worth it for achieving BITA and reaping its benefits.

3. IT Architecture LIBERATES Business Architecture

The Business Architecture is what enables organizations to visualize their business *as a whole*, rather than as small pieces that somehow fit together. It is a description of the structure and interaction between the business strategy, organization, functions, processes, and information needs. In short, business architecture is the *blueprint* for aligning the organization with its mission and forms the bridge between a company's business strategy and its successful execution ("how to?"). In organizations with strong Business-IT alignment, the IT architecture can truly liberate the business architecture by incrementally transforming and adapting itself to the changing needs of the business. For example, the ease and alacrity with which an organization can perform its business process re-engineering, considering that most process workflows are IT-enabled, would be a good indicator of the liberating (or constraining) effect of the IT architecture on the Business architecture.

4. **Business Architecture SUPPORTS Business Strategy**

As we said, Business Architecture is the bridge, or path, between the Business strategy and its execution. Hence, a supportive business architecture ensures better chances of the business strategy being successfully carried out. Since the Business architecture and strategy are tightly coupled with the IT architecture and strategy respectively, IT is at the very core of this successful execution.

The cycle of interdependence also works in the reverse direction:

5. **IT Strategy INFLUENCES Business strategy**

In the digital world where business outcomes are increasingly dependent on IT, a business strategy is also increasingly influenced by the IT strategy. A Business strategy cannot by itself drive business success in the current technology-driven environment. The business, therefore, must factor in the IT capabilities and roadmap to arrive at a winning strategy. Both Business and IT understand that to win in the market, differentiation is the key and this differentiation rides very heavily on Business and IT having a converged strategy. Here's an example –A hotel chain based its business model on seamless services to *corporate* customers across its different geographical locations. The hotel's business team leveraged the IT strategy (of moving all corporate data and applications on a private cloud) to instantly offer unused privileges (like left-over Wi-Fi hours, restaurant coupons, spa facilities etc.) at a discount to corporate guests the next time they checked in into *any* of their hotels. This gave business the much-needed differentiation that went a long way in building customer loyalty. I am informed that the said chain is now mulling IP-based room-to-room conferencing across hotels in different locations to aid corporates who have several guests staying at its many properties at the same time. Such examples are a direct outcome of an IT strategy and Business strategy that are joined at the hip to create innovative, differentiated services leading to positive business outcomes consistently. In the digital world, this is not something in the realms of idealism. It is survival.

6. Business Strategy DEFINES Business Architecture

The Business architecture is the blueprint that aligns the organization with the business strategy. While this is an important facet in the construction of a successful and contemporary business model, it is a subject for another book. However, this is a good time to recollect that the *IT strategy* being increasingly intertwined with business strategy, influences – and is influenced by –the organization, functions, processes, and information needs of the enterprise. In short, the business architecture.

7. Business Architecture SHAPES IT Architecture

The IT architecture in high BITA organizations is not a static body. It is *designed* to quickly and efficiently respond to changes in the business strategy. When the business strategy changes, the business architecture may also require to be changed since it is the blueprint for execution of the business strategy. Hence the business architecture is the trigger for reshaping the IT architecture. This flow must be built into the foundation of the IT architecture for BITA to succeed.

8. IT Architecture ENABLES IT Strategy

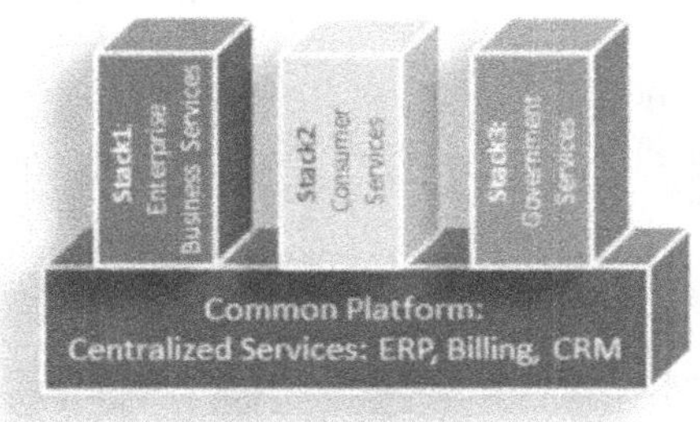

We mentioned above that a non-supportive IT architecture is a constraint to new business offerings. On the other hand, a modular and scalable architecture enables quick, efficient and seamless launch of new services which is part of any good IT strategy. To support a dynamic IT strategy a typical IT architecture would have a 'platform' that consists of all the common and reusable components (typically ERP, Revenue Control (Billing etc.), CRM, SRM, Analytics etc.) and has the capability to support independent 'stacks' on top of it, representing different services. These stacks can be added/removed/modified quickly without impacting the overall architecture. For example, if your company wants to launch Insurance based products, it only needs to build the relevant applications and data and interface them (through APIs) to the common platform. Each stack is a collection of applications and datasets unique to the service. (However, this is an over-simplistic view, as the 'real' architecture would need to factor in high-availability, virtualization etc. as well. Also, depicted here is only *one* possible form of architecture out of many, and should not be considered universally applicable.) The short of the story is that an elegant architecture is strongly conducive to launch of new and differentiated services quickly and effortlessly.

A lot of people have asked me: what's your IT strategy? My answer to this question is always the same: IT exists to make the business succeed. Period. The best strategy for IT is, therefore, to harmonize the IT people, processes and systems with the *business* goals so that IT's success is a function of business success. You cannot have an IT that is successful while the business is a failure.

A strategy is nothing but a plan to achieve the mission of the company. The mission is created for the company *as a whole*, defining the purpose of its existence and what it wants to become. Business and IT are constituents of a larger entity – the organization – guided by the same mission. Hence it is truly a no-brainer that the IT strategy and business strategy, if not overlapping, must be fully convergent. In my experience as a CIO, I have found this rule greatly to my advantage. I now do not have to spend weeks formulating a specific strategy for IT. The template, or the boiler-plate, is already available in the form of the business strategy and I just need to conform to this.

Structure follows strategy. Therefore, the convergence of Business strategy and IT strategy has obvious implications on the constitution of the organization structure. In this environment, business people are required to be tech-savvy and IT people are required to be business savvy. There must be a lot of common elements in the KRAs of Business and IT teams. Indeed, IT organizations are now emphasizing business-mindedness in hiring for technical roles. Lines are blurring. We may soon see more Business Managers becoming CIOs and CIOs becoming CEOs. In most business-aligned IT organizations, the core IT team is a group of 'influencers', serving as navigators and facilitators towards accomplishing the business mission. Typically, all routine operations are outsourced to like-minded partners. This trend helps in directing the organizations' energies to its core strategic (business) areas and is insulation against technological upheavals requiring trending skill-sets in large numbers.

Business-IT Alignment is certainly not a platitude in today's tech-dominated business world. It is a *requisite* for the business to succeed today. However, it is not a trivial task to accomplish and should not be under-estimated. Organizations must consciously and consistently strive to achieve it. We shall see how.

First, let us take a quick guided tour to explore the new world of IT, which is vastly different from the one we came across in the first chapter. Here, IT does not just influence the business, but *shapes* it, as we shall see in the next chapter.

3 *Redefining IT in the Times of BITA*

IT and business no longer exist in separate universes. As a direct stakeholder in the creation of business value, IT is now cast in a new mold. Let us look at some of the new elements that are redefining IT, like Cloud-computing, Big Data, Enterprise Mobility, Social Media, etc., which are essentially *business enablers* powered by Technology, or IT. The introduction of these enablers has made the Business-IT correlation more critical, even indispensable. Of course, traditional systems like ERP, CRM, in-house software, etc. continue to be part of the IT eco-system, but it is these new trends that have resulted in Business and IT becoming *integral* to each other, as I am sure the future will exemplify even more sharply. Quite clearly IT has broken free of the back-office, and it is time to redefine it using a new set of building blocks.

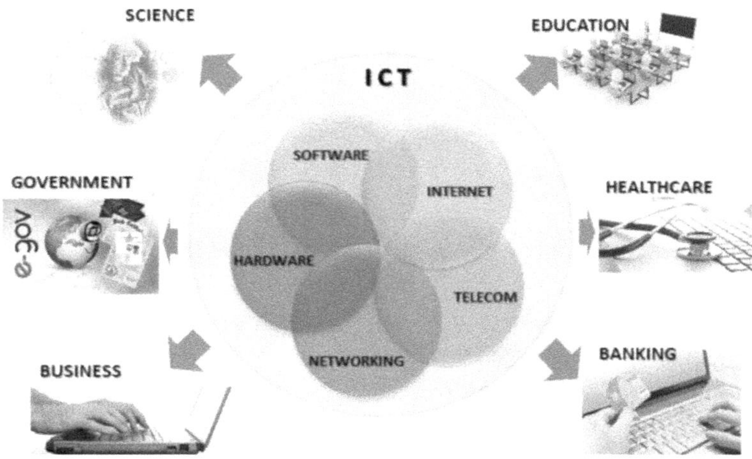

Much of the technological revolution that we see around us is a result of new technologies *converging* with the old. The smartphone, laptop computer, IP-TV, Voice-over-IP are some familiar examples of convergence from the IT and Telecom world.

Convergence is the merging of existing media (domains, technologies) to give rise to new or more enhanced media, spawning fresh products and applications. It is quite common to use the term **ICT** (Information and Communication Technology) to refer to *converged* IT, Telecommunication and Media streams. ICT covers any product or service that can store, retrieve, manipulate, transmit or receive information in digital form. While IT and Telecom are primary *enablers* of ICT, the reach of ICT extends to every industry, as depicted. Trends in ICT enable new developments – sometimes entirely new markets – in banking, healthcare, education, government and other industry verticals. Hence our discussion on new technology trends here is focused on *ICT* related developments. Of course, if the pace of technology trends, particularly in ICT, continues to be anything like it has been over the last two decades, chances are that by the time you read this, much of the cutting-edge stuff of today would be well into or even past the adoption curve. That is, no longer cutting edge, but mainstream.

Interestingly, there's an ICT development index, or IDI, which is published by the International Telecommunication Union (ITU – A United Nations body). IDI measures and compares ICT performance of various countries on certain defined parameters based on ICT infrastructure, usage/adoption, and skills available. It's one of the most valuable tools for benchmarking the important indicators of information society globally. Countries with high ICT development index are the most high-income countries where the quality of life is better than the average. ICT is thus an indicator of the economic development of nations. With the decline in global poverty index, there has been increased ICT adoption.

It would be beyond the scope of this book to go into all the social, political, economic and environmental implications of ICT. The World Economic Forum

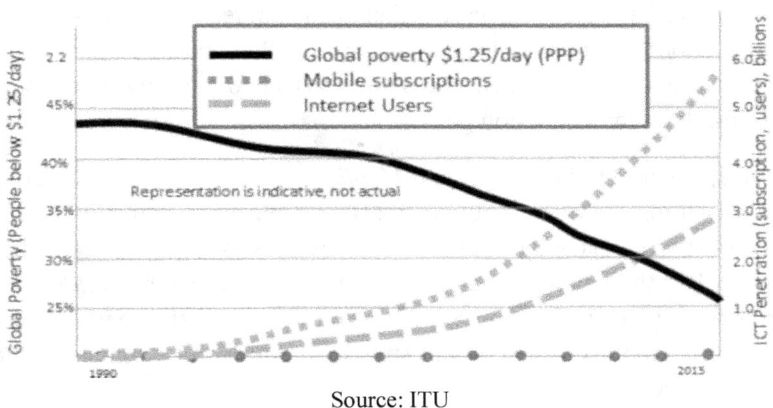

Source: ITU

Global Information Technology Report assesses these parameters in sufficient detail. Here, we will suffice it to say that *ICT is the principal source of new opportunities to foster economic and social prosperity in developed as well as emerging economies.*

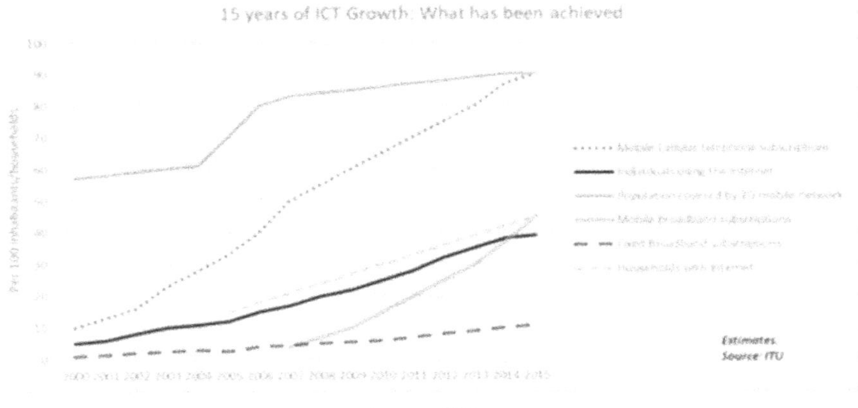

Source: ITU

With courtesy of the ITU report on ICT facts and figures, we are privy to some interesting data that supports the theory of increased adoption with the evolution of technology across all regions of the world. All the major factors for technology-driven business growth are right in place and the trends are positive. There was never a more opportune time to leverage the combined power of business and technology to create a positive impact across the economic spectrum.

Since economic growth is inextricably linked to ICT, it is clear that developments in ICT will not just foster new opportunities for business, but will also bring Business and IT closer together so that they can no longer be independent of each other. We have also seen earlier that growth in technology has resulted in increased *adoption* of technology by business and for business. In the current context, success depends on Business and IT (technology) operating together, as two-in-a-box, for a common goal.

Of course, the growth in *Internet* and *Mobile* penetration is a primary driver of ICT and, in turn, Business-IT alignment. But we must accept that in the current environment, these have become far too ubiquitous to foster differentiation on their own. It is the innovative use of these technologies as the *building blocks* for constructing enterprise-centric advanced solutions that imparts the crucial edge to contemporary business and stresses the need for stronger alignment between Business and IT.

In 2017, there are over 5 Bn unique mobile subscriptions globally, corresponding to a penetration rate of 66%, up from 14% (738Mn) in 2000, while no. of mobile connections in 2017 is over 7Bn.

Mobile broadband is the most dynamic market segment. Globally, mobile-broadband penetration reaches 50% in 2015, an increase of almost 13 times since 2007

Average monthly per capita consumption of mobile data among internet users globally has grown from 356MB in 2013 to 3049MB in 2017

Between 2000-2017, global Internet penetration grew 8 fold from 6.5% to over 50%

Internet enabled mobile devices like smartphones have increased from 1.9 Bn in 2013 to 4.5Bn in 2017, an increase of 140% in 4 years.

Data centric wireless technologies like 4G will surpass voice centric 2G technologies globally by as much as 8 times by 2021 in coverage.

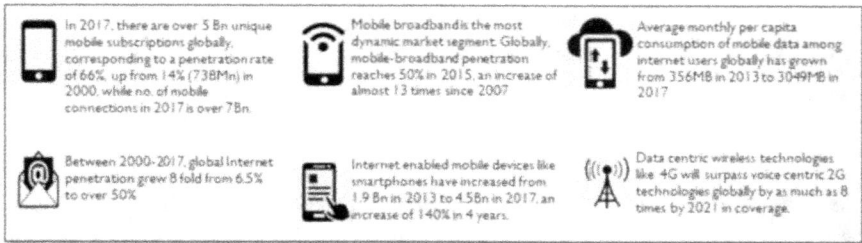

We shall briefly look at some of these new solutions in this chapter. Let me remind my readers here that while these have immense transformational potential on their own, the moment we contemplate their *intersection* with other, often unconnected systems, entirely new perspectives and solutions emerge. This is a vast subject which is the theme of much contemporary research.

While ICT is all around us, it does not cease to amaze. We all have those 'aha' moments with technology even today. It does not have to be a highly complex interplay of advanced technologies – simple ideas using everyday devices put to intelligent use can have as profound an impact. A company I was working for was the first to launch a product called the school-bus tracker. It is common for parents, mostly mothers, of small children to be at the school-bus stop much before time – come rain or sunshine – to be there when the child steps out of (or in to) the bus. This school-bus tracker tracks the bus through GPS and sends automatic messages to the parent on where the bus is at a given time and a special ringing alert when it is at the previous stop – at which time the parent may leave to collect (or drop) the child. A small step for ICT, but a huge gain for anxious parents!

In early 2015, I was asked for my views on the technology landscape of the future by the venerable Voice & Data journal. As precisely as I could, I argued that *intersection* of existing technologies, and not necessarily the emergence of radically new technology, is going to define the future.

A Year of Digital Leap?

The intersection of technologies, not necessarily their convergence, is going to emerge as a value-multiplier in the coming years.

Over the past decade, we have witnessed new technologies converging with the old to drive large scale evolution in the telecom space. The lines between Information technology and Network technology have blurred considerably and continue to do so. The advent of virtualized core networks NFV (Network Functions Virtualization) and SDN (Software Defined Networking) has come as the fresh wave in this sea of convergence. On another level, IP-based communication applications and OTT (over-the-top) collaborations signal sharper convergence of IT and Telecom.

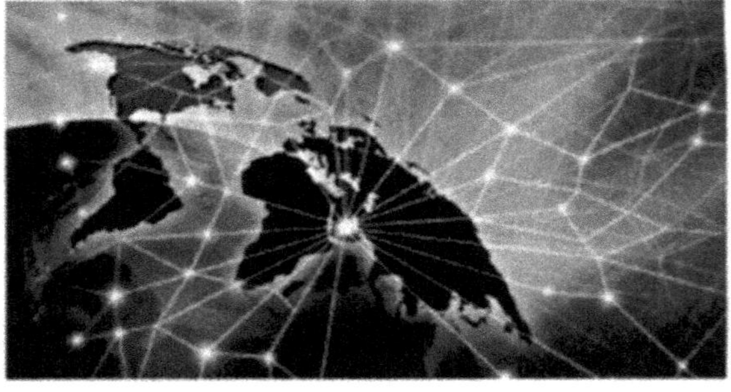

However, convergence alone is not going to be the only driver of growth in products and services. Technologies now need to merely intersect with each other to open up new domains. For example, while Big Data has immense potential on its own, but the moments we conceive its intersection with say, Internet of Things, new perspectives instantly emerge. Take any set of technologies, intersect them, and you will most likely get a similar answer. This intersection of technologies, not necessarily their convergence, is going to emerge as a value-multiplier in the coming years.

And the advancements are going to be a lot more rapid than in the past. The communications world is an adherent of the Half-Life theory according to which every new technology takes half the time to mainstream as its predecessor. For example, the adoption of smartphones in Tier II and III cities has happened very rapidly with the advent of high-speed networks. This trend is not likely to abate.

Growth Trends

The world will continue to gravitate towards mobility, which requires that you make yourself independent of networks, platforms and devices. This spawns three distinct growth trends in 2015: increasing cloud adoption for access to content and applications, abundance of bandwidth and up scaling of the information security infrastructure.

On its own, Big Data will gain a firmer foothold in telcos as hyper-competition drives them to strengthen their data management and analytics capabilities to drill deep and wide for gaining better insights to enhance customer experience at every stage of interaction.

As much as technology, the regulatory environment will drive the development and growth of new trends. There are many advances that are ready for launch in 2015 from a technological perspective and that have the potential to revolutionize. Take IoT for example, it should gain pace, at least in vertical segments, in 2015 but this is subject to various other non-technological factors.

Smart Cities are another example, as is the mass adoption of Mobile Financial Services, Mobile-Health and a host of other Mobile Value Added Services. The year 2015 may well see the arrival of these and more if only the environment can catch up with technology!

Year 2015 can be an year of technological leaps that will introduce India to the new world of communications that the telecom and IT convergence is enabling.

Ashish Pachory
The author is Chief Information Officer, Tata Teleservices

vndedit@cybermedia.co.in

In the remainder of this chapter, let us discuss some of the new technology trends that are making waves in today's business world – what these trends are, how they are helping in shaping the future of business, and importantly what it means for Business-IT Alignment or BITA.

Before getting to the new technology trends that are going to dominate the foreseeable future, let me make a bold statement here. Many of my readers would have, to their exasperation, come across terms bandied by technologists that make no sense to anyone but technologists. They use these terms with a flair that implies that anyone not familiar with them is somehow inferior. Prime among such terms is *Platform*. Others in the category include *Framework*, *Virtualized*,

Abstracted, *Protocol* etc. If you get somewhat confused by these (and other such) terms, you are not alone. More importantly, you are in no danger. The Digital Age will replace the confusing jargon with new and more relatable concepts, which would be universally understood. Terms like Cloud Computing and Social Media, for example, are no longer jargon, but everyday terms that the average person recognizes as applications that simplify his or her life.

1. **Cloud Computing**

Cloud computing has finally emerged from the folds of experimentation to becoming a real-world business enabler. For people and enterprises of the new-age digital world, the cloud is the new plaza. It is the go-to place for apps and data, a shared platform for content and preferences.

Cloud refers to a *remote* cluster of *computing resources* (servers, storage, applications, and data) accessed by the user over a secure network or the Internet, as a logical extension of the user's device. The practice of using the cloud, rather than the local device, to store, manage and process data is called cloud computing. Thus, if your data and applications are on a cloud, you make yourself independent of the device. This allows us to view computing through an entirely new lens, with profound implications for the way information is accessed, retrieved, processed, managed, stored and displayed.

Cloud-based computing resources are typically hosted by a Cloud Service provider (CSP) and are made available to the user *on-demand*. The user may be charged by the CSP based on usage, quite along the lines of utility services like electricity and water. This is a paradigm shift from the earlier system where you 'owned' computing resources, and these were dedicated for your use alone. Depending on the model you subscribe to, cloud computing can be a very efficient way of utilizing computing power. One of the reasons cloud computing has gained traction with enterprises is the freedom it allows from having to procure capital equipment and the associated infrastructure (like real-estate, power, cooling, etc.), and instead leasing the computing resources *as a service*. As some would say, the cloud is a 'capex-to-opex-converter' which allows you to get what you require without the concomitant worries of support, obsolescence, depreciation, capacity-planning etc. There are some concerns over security as most companies are yet to come to terms with the idea of keeping their critical data on a third-party's (CSP's) server. I think there would have been similar concerns when banks first started, and people were faced with the option of keeping their hard-earned money in their custody. These concerns will be tided over by time, but caution about the privacy of data is always a good thing. In my own view, the cloud is no more or less secure than a private data-center – though the types of security concerns are different here.

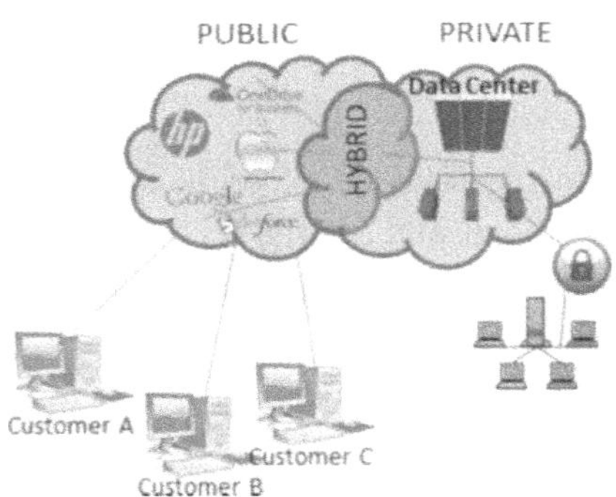

Cloud can be **Private, Public** or **Hybrid**. As the name suggests, a **private cloud** is exclusive, or unique, to an enterprise. All resources within a private cloud operate with the sole purpose of providing a distinct and *secure* environment to a specific company *only*. This is akin to an in-house **data-center** - which is a facility with an organized set of servers, storage and associated hardware and software components that collectively function as the "IT Powerhouse" of the company. The private cloud can also be hosted (or co-located) for a client company by a remote third-party *Infrastructure-as-a-Service (IaaS, a form of cloud)* provider who takes care of the management and routine operational overheads on behalf of the client for a fee. In either event, a private cloud is a *single-tenancy* cloud computing environment. By contrast, a **public cloud** is a *multi*-tenancy cloud computing environment, where each client shares the computing resources with several other clients over the Internet. Many of the personal cloud-based services (like iCloud, OneDrive) that we use are examples of public cloud while (large) enterprises mostly prefer the private or the *hybrid* model. A **hybrid cloud** is a cloud computing environment which makes use of a *mix* of existing private cloud infrastructure and available public cloud services, such as Salesforce.com, with orchestration between the two cloud environments to render the best of both worlds.

The benefits of cloud computing are now well known and accepted which is why it is gaining ground in all spheres. These include freedom from devices and networks, predictability of costs, reduction of operational overheads, disaster recovery, scalability etc. However, cloud computing plays another very vital, but often ignored, *strategic* role in promoting Business-IT Alignment. This is best explained with another real-life example.

I recently participated in a panel discussion with a rather dark theme: 'The Death of the CIO'! As a CIO myself, it is a no-brainer that I chose to argue against this prophecy. The idea behind the theme was that with the advent of cloud computing, there would be nothing for the CIO (read internal IT function) to do, since all the servers, storage, networking gear, applications and data would be managed by a third-party in some unseen location. So, the reasoning went, the CIO and his flock would become a redundant entity (hence dead metaphorically). It was a tricky spot because I am a strong proponent of the cloud but not of the CIO's death!

I argued that cloud would indeed free the CIO of some of the routine operational issues, but in its place, a more *strategic* role would evolve. Most CIOs today spend far more time in just keeping the show going, than on issues that matter to the business. Cloud is, therefore, a boon to the CIO who can now pair shoulders with the business to advise and drive *strategic* solutions that would be of far greater value to the business than the monitoring of the uptime of IT servers. Secondly, migration to enterprise-class cloud is not a fork-lift operation. It is an opportunity to re-evaluate, consolidate and revamp your IT architecture to better suit business needs and save costs in the bargain. This requires elaborate and ongoing planning in consultation with business. Thirdly, the CIO has a better opportunity than before to qualify and prioritize new business requirements, filter and bundle them consultatively and interwork with the cloud service provider to deliver on time, cost and quality targets set by the business. The whole cloud operation, which is run by a partner, must be systematically managed with high efficiency and throughput, which places demands of its own on the CIO.

To conclude, the cloud is perhaps a metamorphosis of the CIO but certainly not the death of the CIO. It is a redefinition of the CIO as a more strategic enabler of business success through better-aligned Business and IT priorities.

Obviously, Cloud computing requires very close Business and IT interplay. Many of the critical business applications that are used by the internal teams (like salesforce.com) as well as customer-impacting applications like CRM, Self-care portals etc. are now cloud-ready. A lot of medium-sized enterprises are relying entirely on cloud-hosted applications even for routine activities like email.

With IT bringing in the domain and management skills to run cloud-based services internally for the business and externally for its customers, a strong alignment between Business and IT becomes a pre-requisite here. Given the speed of business today, the cloud also imposes a high need for synchronization between Business and IT. A strong BITA in the Cloud-enabled world can bring many differentiated offerings to customers quickly. In a company that I worked for, there was an imminent requirement of the business to launch a mobile payment service. The Business and IT teams worked together to identify and evaluate a cloud service provider for this. The CSP agreed to customize an instance (a version of the Mobile Payments application) as per my company's requirements, and we were ready to offer this to the market in 4 weeks. During this period IT worked diligently on assuring the right interfaces with backend applications etc., while business tested the main functionality iteratively in live scenarios and performed quality audits. This is not an isolated, industry-specific example. As we go forward, such interworking will become the norm to bring cloud-based services quickly to customers and take the lead in the market. This can only happen with strong and sustained Business-IT Alignment.

There is Hollywood film called *Transcendence* with a rather scary scenario related to cloud computing. It attempts to ask big questions on how far technology can go. Its lead character, a scientist dabbling in Artificial Intelligence, comes close to uploading all of human intelligence (and consciousness) on a Cloud of his creation, thus ending up with a supercomputer that's fully sentient! The plot thickens as the movie progresses, but this much is scary enough though fortunately beyond current human capability. Still, an interesting theme, as long as it stays in the realms of sci-fi!

2. **Big Data**

Incidentally, this book is not only for IT specialists (or geeks!) who may find my conceptual introduction to contemporary technologies too simplistic. The purpose is to introduce IT and its current manifestations to the non-IT folks as well – students and people in business, finance, HR, supply chain etc. Perhaps I should have named this chapter 'IT for non-IT folks', but that would have excluded the tech fraternity – to which I too belong – who could perhaps pick up from this theme to conduct awareness programs on BITA in their own organizations.

Let's talk about Big Data – another new technology that is very relevant to the times for reasons we shall see and hence making rapid strides into our business world. Big Data means precisely that – when *data* becomes very *big* in its volume, variety and velocity (i.e., the throughput and speed of processing), it becomes, quite predictably, *Big* Data. True to this, we define Big Data in terms of these three Vs. There's actually a fourth V for the more meticulous reader, which is Veracity – but for the most part, Big data refers to the **v**olume, **v**ariety and **v**elocity of data. We shall return to three Vs shortly, but for now let us look at data *creation* in the current age which is in fact, at the root of Big Data evolution and growth.

The rate at which data is being created and transmitted today is well beyond our capacity to comprehend. There is an exponential growth in social, enterprise and machine generated data in the last five years, and the rate of growth is expected to only increase from here. It is not just the volume of data which is staggering, but also the variety – from text messages (structured) to high definition video (unstructured). A lot of information on human preferences, behaviours and trends can be garnered from this stream – but the question is, *how to do it* given the high volumes, staggering speeds and wide variety? This is where Big Data comes in.

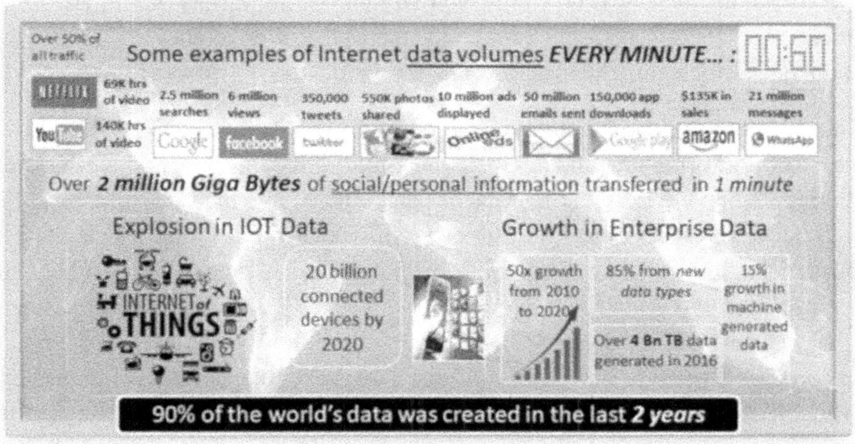

The Vs that we referred to earlier are very briefly defined in the adjacent figure. The best way to understand them would perhaps be to consider the *changes* in the three Vs in our lifetimes:

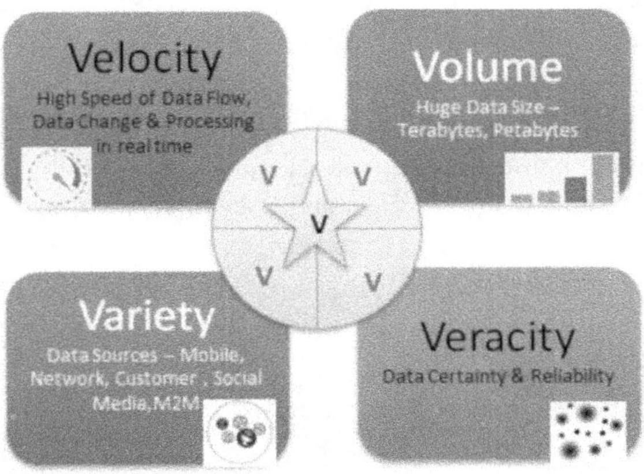

A. Velocity – Batch → Periodic → Near-Real-time → Real-time → Data "Hose" (e.g., incessant Twitter feeds in a wide survey)

B. Volume – MB (Remember the good old 40MB disk-drive?) → GB → TB → PB → EB

C. Variety – Table → Database → Web, Photos, audio → Video, Unstructured →Social → Mobile → Mix of these

The V in the center of the diagram here represents *Value*, to unleash which we require special techniques that can handle huge Volumes (there is no defined size threshold for Big Data), high Velocity and large Variety, simultaneously. Of course, Veracity is critical too as it measures the jitter, latency and ambiguity in the data which can enhance or erode the Value.

Data (Big or not) is meaningless if it does not lend itself to analysis, transform into useful information, and generate meaningful insights that support decision making. While we are creating tons of data, do we have the tools and the skills to process (i.e., read, decipher and classify) such huge volumes of data in reasonable time-frames? After all, a business can no longer wait for days to get a response to a query on say, a customer's proclivity to churn. Processing of Big Data – like the 3 Vs – is also one of its defining characteristics. You do not process Big Data the same way that you do regular data. Techniques are available that allow us to *fragment* the data across multiple nodes for parallel processing thus resulting in a much faster response. I may have alienated some of my readers by suddenly straying into unfamiliar territory so let me explain this with a simple example, that surprisingly pre-dates Big Data by over a decade, but beautifully captures the essence of how we process Big Data today.

In the year 1999, the University of California at Berkeley conceived of a project that was nicknamed SETI@home. SETI, of course, is Search for Extraterrestrial Intelligence which is the collective name for scientific activities undertaken to search for intelligent extraterrestrial life. To search for intelligent signals in the vastness of deep space required several giant telescopes that could scan the skies, detect even very weak radio emissions with remarkable sensitivity, and send them to a centralized computer which could record all of them and analyze them. Quite possibly, somewhere amid all the radio noise, there could also be a signal sent by intelligent beings light years away! Unfortunately, finding this needle of a signal in the enormous haystack of data required almost unlimited computing time (and power) even on the largest and fastest computers in existence. The folks at the

UCB stuck upon a rather bold but brilliant idea to solve this problem: Why not turn to a massively underutilized computing resource: the millions of *personal computers* (like your laptop) sitting on desks and offices the world over, spending much of their time running mindless screensavers. Anyone with a PC could enlist as a participant in SETI@home, and the process was completely unobtrusive. This combined computing power was harnessed to process the mountain of SETI data thus solving much of SETI's computing problem at a stroke. That is, they embarked upon the idea of fragmenting the vast received data and assigning it to multiple nodes (the vast number of PCs the world over), processing it in parallel and finally feeding the *processed* data back to the centralized computer over the Internet. Brilliant indeed!

This is also how Big Data is processed. That is, fragment the huge blocks of data into smaller chunks, process them in parallel across multiple nodes (as PCs in the SETI example) and finally collate the processed information. This cuts down the total processing time from weeks to hours! I have run Big Data projects and seen this for myself. At first, it almost seems like a miracle.

Once data is processed, how do you analyze it to generate meaningful reports for business users and other stakeholders? This is where Analytics comes in. Unfortunately, a fundamental limitation of Big data is its inability to lend itself to relational databases and desktop statistics/visualization tools. The size, structure and speed of Big Data are a variable mix depending on the need and capabilities of the organization managing it. The key here is that it is not Big data alone, but its intersection with Advanced Analytics that can give a fresh insight into a completely new worldview. When you cross this intersection, you enter the world of *Big Data Analytics*.

Analytics is the process of deriving information from data. This information can be presented in the form of dashboards, tables or text depending on the requirements of the end-user. This, in turn, can lead to useful insights which support business decision making. The world of Big data analytics is, however, quite different from our known and familiar world of desktop analytics. Traditional algorithms for processing data require the data to be in main memory, accessed through a *single* CPU. In Big Data Analytics, the sheer size and diversity of data do not allow it all to be in memory at the same time in a single system, and hence it calls for *distributed processing* across a host of systems, using tools like Hadoop for processing, and Pentaho for analysis. This is a very specialized discipline which has given rise to a new branch of study called *data science* and whose proponents are called, as you guessed, data scientists – a much-coveted discipline today.

Big Data is fast becoming a primary lever for gaining a competitive edge in a world that is increasingly dominated by data. It has become very relevant for marketing campaigns to leverage insights uncovered by Big Data, which can then effectively personalize communication to individual customers of the brand. In addition to analyzing all the transactional data generated by businesses, it is important for companies to assimilate all the relevant information shared on *social media sites*, to provide solutions that are tailored to fit individual needs.

If brands want to reach a specific audience, they need to carefully analyze the adoption, usage, payment and service-satisfaction trends of consumers of the brand. This trend, or behavior, analysis of various customer segments is one of the leading pull factors for the enterprise adoption of big data analytics as the gateway to smarter marketing campaigns and better management of customer experience.

For successful adoption of big data, cooperation between leadership teams across Business and IT is crucial. The focus of CIOs today is on identifying opportunities to streamline business processes through investments in data management. The CIO must recognize the importance of managing customer expectations at each stage of the lifecycle which in turn must spur the deployment of IT tools and processes to garner deeper customer insights. Ensuring requisite skill-set in the organization to derive gains from big data is another critical battle that CIOs need to win.

With the advent of Big Data technology, data has become an undisputed business asset as it is now possible to dive wide and deep into the ocean of data and generate useful business insights, like individual customer preferences for targeted marketing. Coupled with this is the fact that Big Data is emerging concurrently with a host of complementary trends such as Cloud computing, Social media, Enterprise mobility and In-memory computing to name a few. We may see a very new kind of convergence which brings these trends together, to create THE enterprise architecture of the future. When this happens, can anyone seriously afford for Business and IT to be NOT aligned perfectly? Let me point this out straight and square: it has happened *already*. Now, where would you rather be?

3. Enterprise Mobility

Somewhat contrary to popular thinking, Mobility is not about *movement*. It is about *freedom*. Freedom has a direct impact on an individual's agility, which makes Mobility both liberating and transformational. It is no surprise therefore that Mobility is making rapid advances into every arena of human endeavor.

In the enterprise context as well, Mobility means *freedom* from devices, platforms, networks and of course, geography. Simply put, it means that access to what I hold important (e.g., a Document) is not restricted by the device I am holding in my hand, or where my data and applications are hosted (e.g. data-center, private or public cloud) or by the network I am connected to (e.g., within the office LAN or on Public network – Wi-Fi or cellular) and certainly not by which part of the globe I happen to be in!

A lot of times people equate Mobility to BYOD (Bring Your Own Device) as BYOD enables you to have seamless access to office and personal data without having to switch devices, and you can do so from your living room or your office cubicle. True, this is Mobility but only *one* of its many use cases. While some organizations totally disallow BYOD as their security concerns override the anticipated benefits, many are still taking a cautious approach to it, and typically allow email and some employee apps (like leave, travel) only. There are however several smarter organizations that have built robust authentication and access control systems to embrace Mobility in a much bigger way and reaped considerable benefits in productivity and employee morale.

Who are the biggest adopters of Mobility?

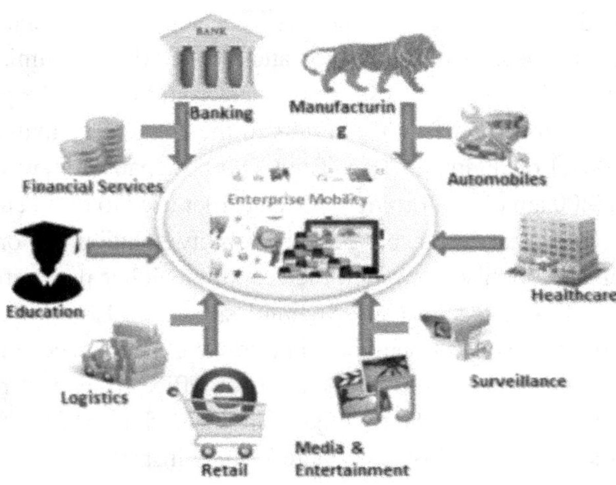

The proliferation of mobile devices like smartphones and tablets has been a catalyst for Mobility. Availability of abundant bandwidth across the length and breadth of the country has been another boost. However, the biggest driver for Mobility has been the *hunger* for information anywhere and anytime. With the basic device and network infrastructure in place, it was only a matter of time before smart business applications arrived on the scene to leverage Mobility for business benefit.

A communications company I worked for had a vast countrywide network of distributors and dealers engaged in providing mobile connections and associated services to the populace. Traditionally, the company's territory sales manager (TSM) responsible for a patch routinely visited various distributors and dealers gathering information on sales, channel performance, forecasts etc., while assisting them in promotions. The data collected by the TSM was fed into a web-based application back in the main office as and when the TSM could visit – which was not very often given the requirement to be on the 'street', and the remoteness of some territories from the nearest office. The calculation of sales commissions across the hierarchy of distributors, dealers, sub-dealers (who could even be a grocery shop owner or the village milk-man!) were frequently delayed for this reason. It was also not possible to track sales or achievements against sales targets on a frequent basis. Management was unable to review territory-wise sales and plan timely interventions. They finally took to *Mobility* as the solution. Each TSM was provided with a tablet that ran the Mobile instance of the web-enabled application (earlier available in the office only) so that he could input data *on the spot* (or from the nearest network zone), and thus track and report sales by distributor, dealer and sub-dealer. This application instantly provided the territory sales performance to the TSM. It enabled all data to be captured in a near real-time fashion and allowed daily commissions, sales data etc. to be available on request. The system could collate the performance of all TSMs in a zone and feed the results to the zonal sales manager, and so on up to the level of regional COO. The COO now had a report on previous day's sales at 9:00 am each morning – which earlier used to be an end-of-month activity. This is a clear instance where a Mobility solution not only boosted internal efficiency but also increased the scope for higher penetration into the market, and trade satisfaction (faster commissions). It also allowed the sales managers to do lightweight operations, like travel expense reporting, while on the move (avoiding the need to check in at the office instead of being in his market territory). Most importantly it gave an insight into where he stood with respect to achievements against sales targets at any instant!

In fact, Mobility is perhaps the single biggest game changer in the enterprise world today. As we said, Mobility is enabled by a dynamic device ecosystem, abundance of bandwidth and an array of applications – some custom built and others bought off the shelf – seamlessly coming together to satisfy a growing hunger for information anytime and anywhere. It has changed behaviors across the organization and brought in a new culture – be it the average employee using BYOD or the territory sales manager with his mobile enabled device and application or even the company CEO, as the following example illustrates.

The CEO of a well-known Indian software services company was on a visit to Japan where he was to meet one his most important clients. This meeting was to be with six members of the senior staff of the client company including their MD. The importance of their time and the need to be up-to-date to make the best use of the 30 minutes allotted for the meeting was not lost on the visiting CEO. While he was on the 45-minute car ride from his earlier meeting to this one, he used a Mobile enterprise app to get a complete dossier on his tablet PC, giving the profiles, with photographs, of each client delegate and who from this CEO's organization met him/her last and when. Some data priming, of course, had already been done by the local office for their CEO's visit! Next, a quick status of the key projects, billing information, major complaints and resolution state *as of that morning* was populated through the app on his tablet. Thus, when the CEO arrived for the meeting, he knew everyone by face, name, function, preferences and grievances. I imagine the meeting went quite well, as everyone, and not least the Japanese, appreciate a good preparation and astute management of time.

Mobile solutions (like in the examples above) offer better communications, faster and more accurate decision making, and better customer service, all of which lead to a competitive advantage for the business. For example, an employee at the client site may be able to access any required information on the company's products and solutions from the cloud storage through his device (laptop, tablet, even smartphone) to show what his customer *needs*, as he is no longer confined to stuff that is on his laptop! He may even connect remote experts through online chat or video to resolve customer complaints while on the site. That is good for customer service.

Enterprise Mobility is an intelligent offshoot of the existing mobile-data ecosystem. You can offer rudimentary (i.e., with *limited* ability to manage and control what you are rendering) services leveraging the existing wireless network infrastructure, a server somewhere that hosts data, a few mobile applications (applications that are capable of being downloaded on mobile devices), and all the available smart handheld devices out there. To give it a tinge of robustness, however, you need a mobile security management and authentication system for preventing misuse and unauthorized access. To offer more enhanced services to the user base, you need a **Mobile Device Manager** (MDM). The MDM is a client-server system which enables end-users to benefit from plug-and-play data services irrespective of the device they hold. The MDM server is a centralized component, hosted by the service provider, which sends out various management commands to the mobile device. The MDM *client* here is a piece of software running on the end-device itself. How many times have you had to call the service provider's desk to configure a new device you have acquired? All that the service rep does is to send you a link and ask you to 'activate' it from your device. This essentially installs (downloads) the client on your device, and the MDM takes over from there, insulating you from complex configuration procedures. Another instance of MDM at work is over-the-air download of software updates on your device. Some versions of MDM server also take care of accounting and authentication of the user.

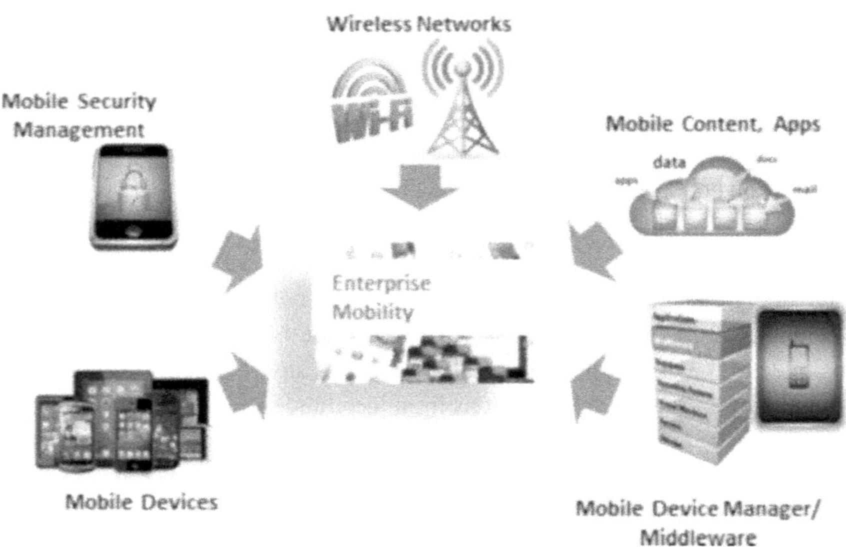

One of the biggest benefits of Mobility is the level of engagement it enables the customer. The availability of information wherever and whenever you want does give you an edge that is hard to beat. Ability to provide better customer service remains a primary driver for adoption of Mobility by enterprises.

We have daily examples of better customer service through ready availability of information on the move. One such could be an insurance surveyor being able to upload photos of the accident site and provide a spot approval for the claim – which would normally have taken 3 or 4 working days. This certainly boosts customer satisfaction and in turn, customer loyalty. Banks are offering mobile solutions (like payments on-the-go) which are not just a matter of convenience for the customer, but also save the banks countless person-hours. So with airline/railway ticketing – services that some of us may remember tying us down to fixed spots or long queues before the Mobility revolution took over.

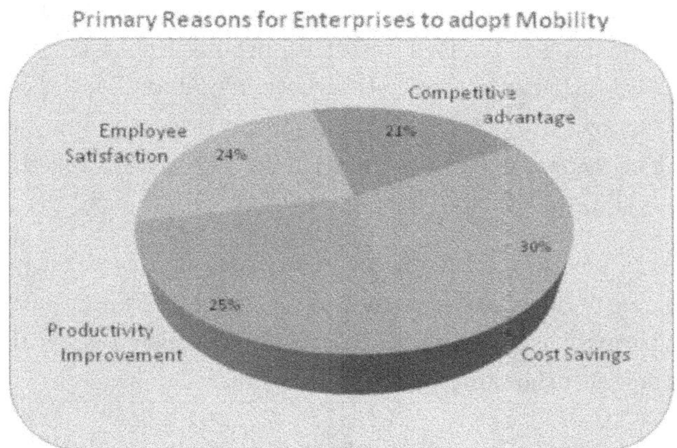

In the end, let us remember this –

The enterprise world today seeks increased sales and better customer service (competitive advantage), lower expenses, improved productivity and happier employees. It so happens that Mobility provides *all* of these benefits and more. A recent global survey focused on the primary reasons for enterprises to adopt Mobility confirmed this. Cost savings emerged as the dominant reason, but the others were not far behind. This is highly significant for the present and future of enterprise business. The earlier you adopt Enterprise Mobility, the faster you can achieve these goals. Of course, this adoption is strongly contingent upon close step-locking between Business and IT, and therefore organizations with strong BITA have a much higher chance of benefitting from Mobility.

4. Social Media

I will be very surprised if you, the esteemed reader of this book, are not a part of any social media network. It requires no introduction. Social Media (SM) has crossed all boundaries of age, race, status, income and nationality. It has made the world a smaller, better informed and more connected place. Some amongst us have firmly held views on the extent it should be allowed to penetrate our lives at the cost of 'human' connections. While this is a tenable point of view, we will not enter this debate for now as this discourse is about how SM is impacting the business landscape and about SM being a key element of the redefined IT ecosystem. It is another constituent that depends on a strong BITA to leverage its potential as a driver of business growth.

As we know, SM collectively refers to tools, channels and applications that allow creation, sharing and exchange of content – messages, information, pictures/video, files etc. – between people over the Internet. More pertinently, SM is a collective term for mediums that promote online collaboration between communities. Social Media is a result of pre-existing technology building blocks, like IP-centric networks, web-servers, cloud, devices and applications coming together to fulfill an inherent human need to mix and mingle. As the sociologists like to say, it is more an art than a science – but this is another debate we will skip for the time being.

Social Media is just about everywhere. Websites and applications dedicated to a wide range of collaborative activities are among the many types of social media that surround us. While all these cannot be listed here, the following table depicts some of the more prevalent ones.

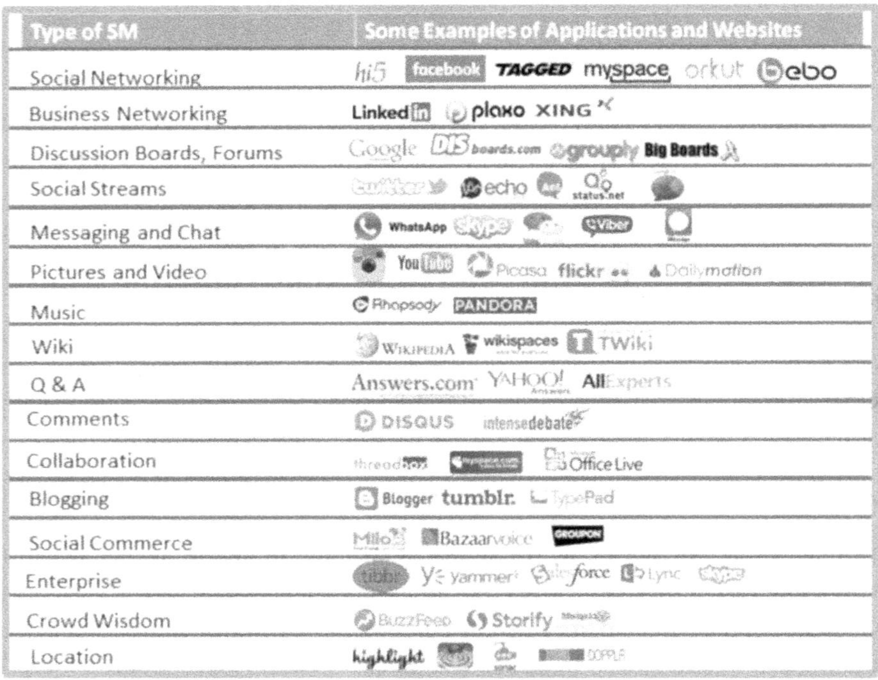

Type of SM	Some Examples of Applications and Websites
Social Networking	hi5 facebook TAGGED myspace orkut bebo
Business Networking	LinkedIn plaxo XING
Discussion Boards, Forums	Google DISboards.com grouply Big Boards
Social Streams	twitter echo status.net
Messaging and Chat	WhatsApp skype Viber
Pictures and Video	YouTube Picasa flickr Dailymotion
Music	Rhapsody PANDORA
Wiki	Wikipedia wikispaces TWiki
Q & A	Answers.com YAHOO! Answers AllExperts
Comments	DISQUS intensedebate
Collaboration	Office Live
Blogging	Blogger tumblr. TypePad
Social Commerce	Bazaarvoice GROUPON
Enterprise	tibbr yammer salesforce Lync skype
Crowd Wisdom	BuzzFeed Storify
Location	highlight DOPPLR

Again, this is not the entire social media universe – neither in terms of types of SM nor applications and websites against each type. Further, let's not forget that it is an expanding universe.

As CIO of a multi-billion-dollar enterprise, one of my aspirations was to connect, at least on a quarterly basis, with the IT users (read all employees, partners) across the organization, dispersed across 70+ offices in the country. For most people IT, like oxygen, is noticed only by its *absence* – you feel choked when it is not there, but take it for granted while it is! I felt that there was a strong need for open, interactive sessions with all users to deliver an update on new developments in technology, listen to and address user grievances, get a firsthand feel of how things were shaping up on the market front and take suggestions on how IT could better support the business in the field. And as a corollary, remind the folks that IT was active behind the scenes *even* when things are going well! The problem was, how to simultaneously and interactively cover all employees without going into the elaborate arrangement of video cameras, HD TVs, microphones, speakers, tons of bandwidth, assembly halls et al. I also did not want employees to take time away from their work for these sessions. As a solution, the CIO-Online virtual chat room was created – a product of Social Media. The CIO Online session projected my audio-visual on all participating-employees' laptops, who could see and hear me as well as type in their questions and viewpoints for me in the message box. Though the users were not visible to me or each other, their names, location and messages were. I would read out these views or questions and provide my response for everyone's benefit. We used a popular version of an enterprise messaging platform, a client of which was embedded in every laptop provided by the company. Thus, we could have a secure interactive session, give the users –particularly the remote ones – direct and exclusive contact with management, achieve two-way learning and ensure that any pending grievances were addressed. All this at virtually no cost, achieved without anyone having to leave their work-stations! The sessions were immensely popular and went a long way in boosting collaboration between IT and users.

Since SM allows instant communication with many constituents, it is an excellent tool for campaigns and promotions by companies. As you would have seen, a lot of enterprises are talking to their customers on Facebook, Twitter and similar platforms, both on a collective and individual level. However, a lot more creative instance of SM usage is the *reverse* communication channel. That is, *consumers,* sharing information on the product or service with the vendor, or

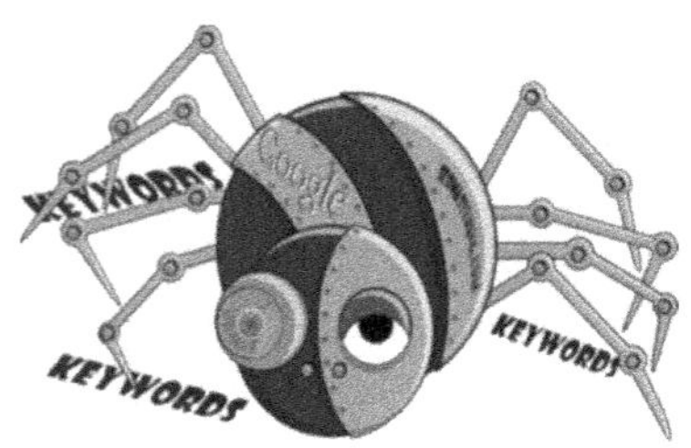

amongst themselves. By using special programs like Web Crawlers, companies can get crucial data which offers insights into the sentiments expressed by customers on social media, analyze these, and use the results to make timely course corrections. In fact, 'sentiments analytics' is emerging as a field on its own, given its relevance to companies and consumers alike. It was once said that the voice of one disgruntled customer could reach ten others. Well, social media just made it a million others! It is not hard to imagine the profound impact of this on companies and their reputations. And revenues, of course.

Given the rising impact of social media on business, it is not uncommon to find a distinct *social media strategy* being implemented by many enterprises. A few examples: DELL used SM as a channel for generating sales – perhaps one of the first examples of leveraging the power of social media. Comcast used SM to reach out to customers in need of support. Starbucks used social media to give a voice to their customers to propagate new product ideas. All these (and other) examples ride on the unprecedented reach enabled by SM and the opportunity provided by SM for businesses to interactively embrace their customers at last.

Using SM as part of business strategy makes sound sense given the payback. The two-way engagement path enables you to *measure* the reach, influence, traffic and transactions relating to your market audience. This, in turn, allows you to analyze the results for timely insights into preferences, sentiments, views and ideas relating to your offerings. SM underlines the need for strong integration between Business and IT to derive these insights and use them for enhancing sales and customer experience.

5. Customer Experience Management

Like Social Media, Customer Experience Management – or CEM, as it is popularly called – is not a technological evolution by itself. It is a system that uses some of the building blocks of modern technology to fulfill the core business need to engage, and stay engaged, with customers.

The core premise of CEM is that customers do not buy technology. They buy experiences. Thus, CEM is focused on the management of the complete *lifecycle* of the customer. The customer's view about a provider is influenced by various touch-points that the customer comes across – right from the pre-purchasing stage to post-sales support – and CEM views each of these touch points as an opportunity to improve the customer's experience and build loyalty and advocacy – the ultimate goals of CEM.

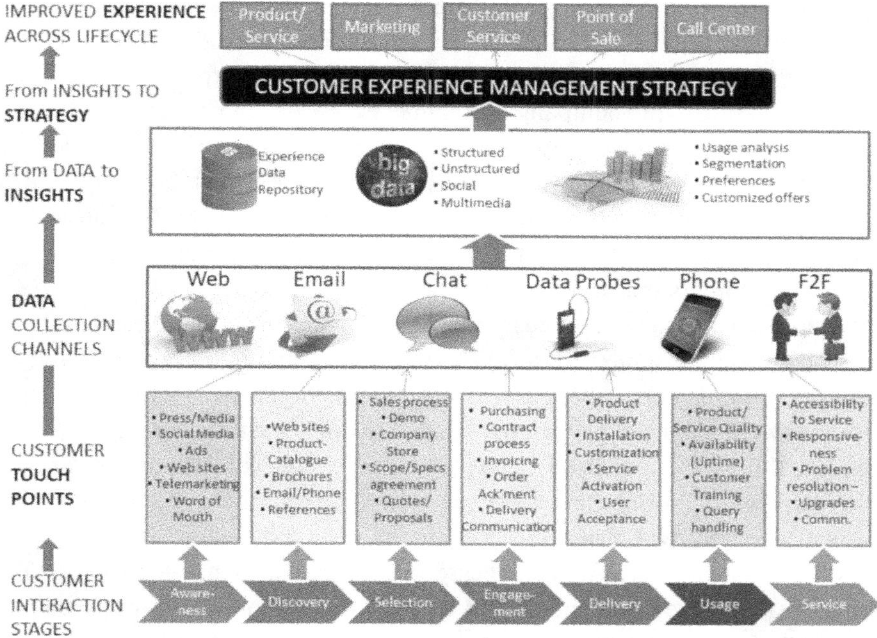

The pictorial representation of a typical CEM framework may not look very simple at first glance, but if you give it a second one, you will find it is quite straightforward. It's the best (simplest) I could construct to depict the full CEM cycle across all touch points in a single sequential flow.

In a nutshell, the figure highlights how CEM makes use of IT tools and infrastructure to convert customer *data* into meaningful *insights* that can be leveraged to create an effective customer strategy, which is then embedded into all the various touch points across the lifecycle. The process is cyclic and hence enables *continuous improvement* – which is quite useful, as customer expectations are always progressive and keep going up a few notches with every positive experience!

Given that a big part of my experience has been in the telecommunications business, I hope I will be pardoned for citing many of my examples from this industry. One of the problems every telecom operator faces is customer *churn*, especially with the advent of mobile number portability (MNP). An operator typically gets both churning-in (which is good) and churning-out (which is bad) customers in a given month, and the strategy is obviously to increase the in-churners and minimize if not eliminate the out-churners. Before CEM, it was not possible to get accurate insights into the reasons for churn, so there was not much that companies could do about it. One of the telecom operators I know of was particularly perplexed about the churn situation. This company had launched a very compelling customer loyalty and retention program, driven down its call rates to one of the lowest in the market, improved its customer service levels, but despite all this, it found the churn rate still increasing month on month. Curiously, it scored among the highest on the customer satisfaction scores! Then why should customers churn out? The company (let's call it X) adopted CEM to gain deeper insights into customer behavior to solve this mystery. What it discovered was quite insightful. As we know, India has a predominantly *pre-paid* mobile subscriber base. A few years ago, the trend had picked up for many folks to keep *two* phones instead of one. Due to lower on-net (i.e., within the same operator's network) calling rates, customers preferred their SIMs (including family members') to be from the *same* operator. It was discovered by X that a substantial part of its subscriber base used two distinct phones, each having SIM card from X due to the above reasons. Of late, however, the trend had picked up for *dual-SIM* phones as opposed to two phones per subscriber. People now preferred that the two SIMs on their one phone be from *different* operators, to safeguard against any network problems, and to avail of the best of calling rates between operators. This was more relevant to users than the diminishing differential in the on-net vs off-net call rates. Due to people with two SIMs with X now moving one SIM to another operator, X had a higher churn-out. It was indeed an elusive root-cause, something that was only stumbled upon through deep diving into the customer behavior aspects. As of writing this story, X is still working on an effective strategy to counter the situation, and if they found it, I am not aware of it. But knowing the root-cause is half the battle won!

Another example, this time from the banking world, could further explain the importance of CEM and help cement the concept. Whether CEM was deployed here is not known. However, the scenario demonstrates the relevance of CEM in aligning more closely to customer expectations at any given stage in the lifecycle.

I happen to be a privileged customer of a renowned private bank in India, fortunate to be endowed with relationship banking. At the time of expiry of my Debit Card, the bank promptly dispatched another one, along with a PIN number in a separate, sealed envelope. When I tried using the new debit card with the received PIN number, I was told the PIN was invalid and was perfunctorily thrown out by the ATM after the allotted three attempts. I called my relationship manager who was courteous but could not tell me why the problem had occurred, other than hinting that I may have typed those four simple digits wrong three times in a row! Anyhow, she promised to get back to me having reluctantly conceded that I may after all not be that dim! She came back next day to say that the problem was that the PIN validity was five days from creation to first-use (four of which were consumed in the parcel delivery) and since I used it after that period, it was invalid even before I started! She also mentioned that this problem was being faced by many customers as per data received from call-centers and other relationship managers and hence the bank was soon revising its policy about the initial PIN. I am sure this will come as a boost to the bank in reducing complaints and less frustration to its customers. This is how acting on feedback based on direct customer experience – which is what CEM is about – makes a great deal of sense for all participants in the value delivery chain.

For driving customer loyalty, operational efficiency and new revenue streams in an environment characterized by evolving technology, changing expectations, and hyper-competition, customer experience management plays a pivotal role. Customers are justifiably demanding more of their service providers today, and managing customer experience as a discipline goes a long way in improving every interaction throughout the lifecycle. This includes interactions and experiences at all stages, including purchasing, call-center communications, payments and other touch points across the organization, and even outside, as through social media. Most customer-focused organizations achieve this through the deployment of tools and processes to garner deeper customer insights. But more importantly, this environment requires a responsive customer services organization and a dynamic information technology eco-system working seamlessly together to implement the CEM strategy.

As evident from the above examples, CEM is focused on understanding customers' preferences and expectations based on their behavior *through the lifecycle* and using these to calibrate the customer service strategy. Its focus is not merely on problem resolution or incident management – which is usually the purview of a customer *relationship* management, or CRM, solution.

Big data is expected to play an increasingly important role in the institutionalization of CEM. Big Data enables us to reach the bottom of the pyramid and target the right group of customers for, say a new campaign or service. Today the focus of every service organization is on customer loyalty and retention. And retaining a customer requires you to be able to differentiate your offering from the rest. Which in turn means providing an individualized and special experience to each customer tailored to his/her preferences. A strong alignment between Business and IT is thus at the core of CEM and organizations with a higher BITA index have a clear edge in attaining a loyal customer base – indisputably the biggest asset for any business.

In this chapter, we have introduced some of the many new technological developments that are already well-entrenched in modern business and are expected to play an increasingly dominant role in the business of the future. These are the building blocks using which the technology-driven business edifice of the future will be constructed. As this happens, technology will play an enhanced role in driving business success, creating an environment in which technology and business will be inseparable from each other. The illustration below depicts the gradual convergence of Business and Technology over the ages until they *fuse* with each other in the Digital Age.

There are, of course, many other trends emerging, or have already emerged, which we have not touched upon here. These include Internet of Things, Artificial Intelligence, Machine Learning, Merged Reality, Blockchain et al. on one level, and advanced encryption and data privacy, packaged applications, mass out-reach programs (like Education, Health, Governance, Location-based services, etc.) on another, all driven by intersection of existing and future technologies with and amongst each other.

The sun will soon set on some of the established systems especially the proprietary or bespoke ones. Desktop PCs, voluminous local disk storage, home-grown applications and stand-alone (not interoperable or networkable) devices among others do not appear to have a bright future. *Consumption* devices like smart-phones, tablets, book-readers will be distinct from and more prolific than *creation* devices – like laptops, stand-alone cameras, and 3-D Printers.

Telecom companies, being key players in the ICT game, will no longer be content with being providers of dumb ‘pipes’ (euphemism for communication channel). They will migrate from being connectivity providers to becoming *service* providers. Thus, there will be an increased collaboration with the so-called ‘over-the-top invaders’ to create a more seamless eco-system and smarter

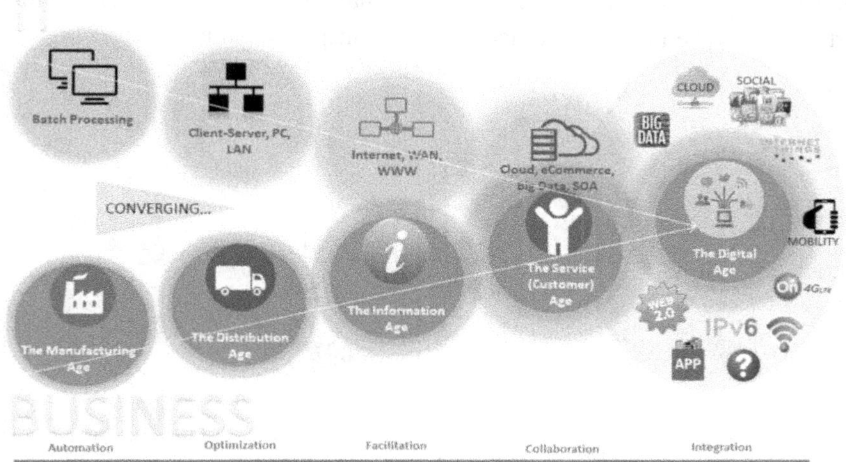

telecom networks. The performance of optical communication networks will continue to grow by a factor of 8 to 10 times every three years, making bandwidth more abundant. On the wireless side, new generations of technology – both cellular and Wi-Fi - will continue to evolve. While they may not actually catch up with optical networks in the bandwidth department, they will more than make up for this by enabling even more seamless mobility. As a corollary, this will spawn new device eco-systems and application landscapes.

On the IT software side, we can expect a higher prevalence of *object-oriented* technology (like Java) which enables the development of self-contained units of software that can be shared. Non-standard software interfaces, architectures, applications will be set aside as standardization will become the norm since it ensures portability.

On the infrastructure side, alongside increasing dominance of Cloud computing – particularly SaaS and IaaS – we should see phasing out of the era of dedicated machines (servers) and the new architectures will be increasingly based on *virtual* machines which are emulations of (real) servers for hosting applications dynamically. This 'virtualization' will lead to far more efficient utilization of resources and is already gaining prominence in data-centers.

With the sun rising on a host of new technologies while setting on others, it is clear that the future is going to be more different from the present, than the present is from the past – considering a 20-year horizon both ways. From what we have covered so far in this book, that's indeed saying a lot! The boundaries of technological growth have been, and will be, drawn only by human imagination. Perhaps no one could have said this better than William Arthur Ward, the famous American writer of inspirational maxims:

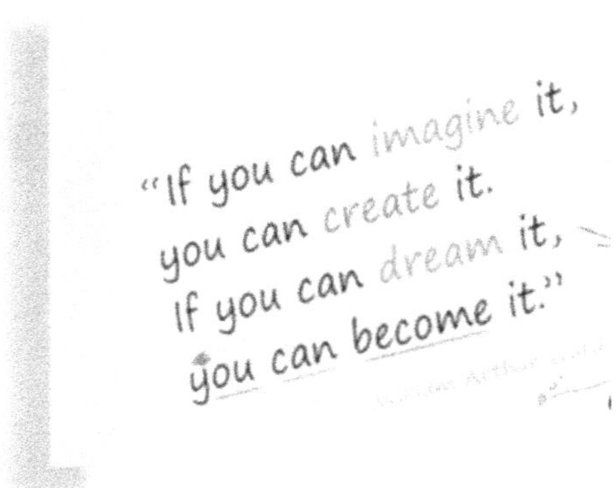

"If you can imagine it,
you can create it.
If you can dream it,
you can become it."

Clearly, IT has come a long way since centralized mainframes, batch-processing minicomputers and Y2K. So has business. Established systems have been demolished to pave the way for a new order. The preceding figure depicts the journey of Business and IT through the ages to a final state of full convergence, heralding the dawn of the *Digital Age*. Here, your speed determines your survival. If trends are anything to go by, the advent of each transformative technology will emphasize the need for **stronger** BITA. The core principles of BITA, which we discussed in chapter-2, will, however, continue to hold in the altered Business-IT landscape. Companies and individuals who are strong on BITA through its early infusion in their belief systems will clearly have far higher growth – and survival – prospects in the digital economy, which is what we shall discuss next.

4 The Digital Economy And What BITA Has To Do With It

Businesses traditionally define themselves by their *core competence*, with technology being at best an enabler. For example, a progressive retail business may view itself as a *merchandising* company that uses technology. Let's shift our perspective for a minute. Can this business be viewed as a *technology* company that does merchandising? If the answer is yes, this business is almost certainly a part of an emerging new world order. In fact, much before the advent of this new order, the above viewpoint was aptly stated by FedEx: "We used to be a trucking company that used technology. We are now a technology company that uses trucks." Now think about *your* business in these terms.

Digital technology has permeated the creation, distribution, trade, and consumption of countless products and services across the globe. In other words, *the eco-system of digital computing and communication technologies has engulfed economic activity*, giving rise to what has come to be known as the Digital Economy. While point technologies like Cloud, Big Data, Mobility, Social Media, etc. are essential components, it is the coming *together*, or a seamless *union,* of these technologies that has resulted in the thriving eco-system that is the Digital Economy.

We explored in some detail the history of Information Technology in the first chapter. If we take a quick peek into the history of *business,* we see that early economic activity was driven primarily by the twin engines of *production* and *distribution* of goods, and hence was bounded by raw material (natural resources), labor and capital. The value of intellectual property and by extension, technological innovation, was ignored entirely. Ironically, it was when Businesses invested in technological innovation or collaborated with research institutes on technology projects, that real transformation occurred, leading up to the evolution of digitally enabled business.

When digital technology first made an appearance, it was only in isolated pockets, creating what came to be known as the digital divide – an *inequality* regarding access, use or impact of information and communication technologies (ICT). For a business to thrive in the digital economy, the first condition was the abolishment of the digital divide. While its complete elimination is a rather lofty goal and something the world cannot wait for, the twin revolutions spawned by the Internet and Mobile technology have considerably narrowed the digital divide as we noted earlier. This has created the right conditions for the digital economy to thrive.

Incidentally, the digital economy is not just about trade and commerce. It's a *way of life* in which digital technology blends seamlessly with business, leisure, education, health and almost every sphere of human activity. Let's look at a few familiar examples.

Photography: Until a few years ago – around the late 1990s or early 2000s – photography was quite different from what it is today. Not everyone had a camera. Those who did were not always carrying it on their person. Taking a picture was thus rarely impromptu. It required elaborate preparation. Even then, it could be weeks before you saw the result. The process involved buying the right kind of film reel at a store to load into your camera, take pictures (typically up to 24 or 36 per reel), wait for the entire reel to finish before giving it at the studio for processing and development, select some pictures for enlargement, cropping, extra-copies etc., and finally send them by snail-mail to friends and family. How different from just pulling out your mobile phone and pointing it at your target and clicking, then sharing it next instant over social media with virtually anyone in the world – all in a matter of seconds. Incidentally, the old generation of photography had also omitted to provide for the 'selfie' option, which I am sure many today would find ludicrous!

Banking: Remember the days when every time you needed a bit of cash, you had to go up to the bank (within the working hours) queue up in front of the (human) teller, submit a requisition and get the cash handed to you over the counter through a small window in the glass? More 'involved' transactions like transferring money to another account, getting a statement of accounts, ordering a new cheque book etc. could take up a lot more time (and forms and queues). Banking was never fun and very seldom quick. Things have changed with ATMs and more recently internet and mobile banking as we all know. This is enabled by having all relevant constituents of a banking system – customers, branches, ATMs – on a digital network which is readily and conveniently accessible at all times and in all zones, using computing technology to render services online.

Shopping: Shopping is a matter of individual preference. We sometimes do it just out of impulse, while at others we do it out of necessity. Two forms of shopping exist today – the mall or mom-and-pops where you can buy stuff instantly across the counter, and the online stores where you may get a wider choice but must wait for at least one day for the product to get delivered to you. I think both forms will co-exist in the future as well. Shops are not about to become extinct! Even if you choose to do your shopping at the good old brick-and-mortar store, digital technology is at work to make your experience richer. First, you walk in as a much better-informed customer having done the due research on product specs, variety, and pricing on the Internet. You are provided with a choice of payment options through networked payment machines which are linked to your bank. At the back-end, your purchasing trends have been analyzed to inform you of special offers on products that may be of interest. Lastly, the depleted inventory level at the store is automatically updated to trigger next re-ordering so that stock-out situations are rare. If, however, you are still not sufficiently immersed in the digital experience, you always have the option of buying stuff online while never leaving the comfort of your sitting room.

Transportation and Navigation: When I was younger, venturing into a new territory almost always meant stopping passers-by for directions. Route planning for long distance travel was a manual and often cumbersome exercise. For example, you could never be sure how much to stock up on fuel and supplies since there was no way of knowing the location of filling stations, restaurants etc. on the way, even if you could figure out the route. It was quite common to carry folded maps and stop at junctions to rediscover your bearings. Some might say that there was thrill and adventure in all this, but then the pace of life was different too. Cutting to the present, we all have map software on our phones or tablets and are therefore rarely 'in the woods.' We also know traffic patterns and alternative routes to get to our destination in the quickest possible time. This is enabled through the blending of satellite imagery with mobile data network and intelligent application software. In fact, as you would perhaps be aware, the map software on your mobile phone will work even when you are not covered by a cellular network, as your phone communicates directly with the satellite to get your coordinates. You would, of course, need to preload the maps to get the right context. This is ICT at work again to literally and figuratively alter the way we view the world around us.

An extension of the above example can be found in fleet management systems that are used by fire-trucks, ambulances, taxi services, delivery vans etc. to find the fastest way to get from point A to point B.

There can be many such examples from our day-to-day experiences that emphasize the role of digital technology in transforming our lives. Just reflect on the way we now call for taxis, pay our utility bills or book tickets for movie shows, as compared to ten years ago! Even governments have forayed into the digital space through various e-governance initiatives. It has become so ubiquitous that for many of us ICT is like oxygen – ever present but not noticed, except by its absence!

Let's turn our attention next to the business dimension of the Digital Age and see for ourselves how it can expand horizons and make the world a smaller place at the same time.

The Digital Economy – also frequently referred to as the Internet Economy or the Web Economy – is built on a foundation of **Technology** (ICT) with the Internet at its core. As depicted in the accompanying graphic, the other essential constituents of the Digital Economy are **Partners** (Ecosystem Partnerships), **Influencers** (External Environment) and **Markets** (Market/Consumers). Strong interplay between these constituents of the digital economy is, of course, key to its sustenance and growth.

Before we go further, let us look at another example from my personal experience which essentially illustrates the profound impact of the Digital Economy on all walks of business. I have an apartment in a condominium about 30km outside Delhi. The commercial infrastructure is under development even as families continue to move in into the large number of apartments in this locality. A person who used to work as a driver with me decided to cash in on the emerging opportunity and rented a shop here to sell vegetables and fruit to the new residents in the area. He gets vegetables from the wholesale market early in the morning and starts his shop around 7.30 am every day. He accepts phone orders for home delivery as well and takes payments by cash and mobile wallet. Though it is still early days for him, business is good. A few days ago, he met me to get my views on an idea that had struck him. He said he wanted to offer people the convenience of ordering vegetables through a mobile app. Vegetables being a perishable item, any unsold inventory at the day's end is a write-off, and his plan was to increase the off-take by offering more channels, especially considering that much of his clientele was away from the locality most of the time. I advised him instead to become a 'supplier' in the value chain of one of the established

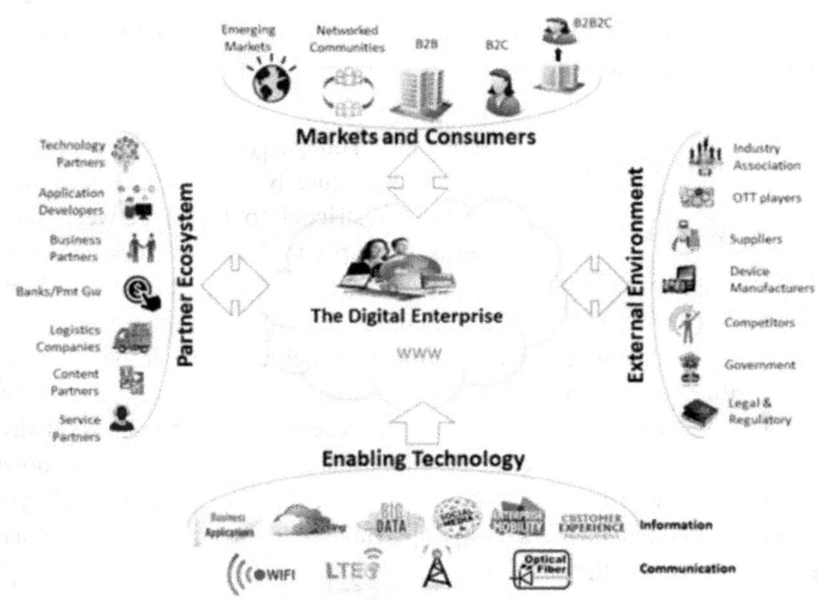

retail e-shopping firms, with exclusive rights for that area. Depending on the success rate, he could completely move over to this model and close his shop which came at an exorbitant rent. His idea certainly has merit and speaks of how businesses of all hues can potentially benefit from digital transformation. The point here is that the digital wave is spreading to every walk of our lives and all sections of our society. It is not just about large, technology-driven enterprises anymore.

Even in this small example, we see that all the building blocks of Digital Economy that we spoke about are at play. Perhaps unknowingly, by hitching up with an e-retailer the vegetable-seller is making use of the **technology platform** [communication network, business application (perhaps hosted on Cloud), Mobility], the **external environment** [regulatory framework (laws governing sales, taxation etc.), the local vegetable-sellers association for spot pricing info], **partner eco-system** [e-retail firm, mobile service provider, payment gateway, bank, app developer], and **markets/consumers** [B2C customer base in an 'emerging market']. In this sense, he is a true digital enterprise and a part of the growing digital economy. The web is replete with examples of medium and large enterprises going digital and transforming themselves in the process, using these building blocks. A few cases in point are Starbucks, Nespresso, Disney, T-Mobile and Fujifilm amongst many others, which the interested reader may like to study. Another example, which may resonate with many of us in India, is presented below.

During my younger days, travel within the country was mostly by train. Flying was generally restricted to travel between large metros, primarily for business/work. Traveling by train required reserving your seat or berth (if overnight journey) in advance. The process meant going to the city reservation center - which could be at the other end of town, filling up a form, queuing up before the ticket window for up to two hours and finally presenting the form to a flustered clerk who almost always had an air of 'take it or leave it' about him/her, and was typically not known for being very helpful towards the teeming crowds. At the end of it all, you may well be told that no seats/berths are available, so you may need to re-plan the travel and repeat the process! It wasn't fun.

I have seen the system change from the above completely manual process where there were physical registers with date-wise entries for every train, to a more automated version which enabled the same clerk to now punch information into a client terminal at his window and hence speed up the process. In time, this gave way to a system that allowed internet-based bookings by the clients through a networked PC, and finally to a mobile-enabled system that lets you reserve your seats on the go. Instead of a paper copy, you can now travel with just an image of the ticket that is instantly delivered to your phone! It is not only that you can make your bookings online. The way the train options and availability information is presented makes it very convenient to plan and undertake train travel. Most people in India are now familiar with this system, which has a somewhat curious name – the Indian Railways Catering and Tourism Corporation web site, or simply IRCTC.com.

What's so great about this, you may ask. Doesn't every travel service (airline, train, bus) offer basic reservation service and status information? No denying this. But consider some facts about IRCTC:

- It handles well over a million ticket bookings on an average day.
- It is the biggest e-commerce service in India, more than double of the next one in volumes handled.
- The system is highly complex. It has to deal with about 13000 trains of different types; seven or eight classes of travel; various types of reservation/ ticket statuses – Confirmed, RAC, Wait-listed, Special Quota and Tatkal; Concessions (senior citizens, students, disabled, armed forces etc.); seasonal changes at short notices; journey breaks and onward journeys, among others.
- IRCTC as a *public* body had to win against massive bureaucracy, funds shortages, cultural bottlenecks and a lack of political will to create one of the *world's largest* e-commerce sites.

Nowhere has the impact of technology on daily life been higher – in terms of where we were to where we are than in the Indian Rail Reservation system. If we take a quick peek into the technologies that have made IRCTC possible, we would see:

Web technologies –	Server-side programming (ASP.net, Java) Client-side programming (Java) Mark-up languages (browser interface) (XHTML n.0) Embedded style sheets, cookies, encoders etc.

Security and Authentication –	Encryption apparatus (HW and SW) for prevention of unauthorized access and misuse by intermediaries, brokers.
Analytics –	Google analytics to get detailed stats about visitors to the website
Advertising Network –	Adsense, Amazon
Payment Gateways –	Multiple

The above is built on the core technology foundation of server farms, data storage, etc. in a Private Cloud and seamless connectivity over terrestrial and wireless networks. The system uses a strong *technology foundation* including Big Data and Mobility. It leverages a *partner ecosystem* of banks, telcos, App developers, advertisers and others. It also meets the requirements of the *external environment* of government regulations and policy, industry practices, supplier networks et al. All this is geared towards delivering B2C (mostly) and B2B service to its vast *customer base (market)*. It thus leverages all four dimensions of the digital ecosystem that we introduced earlier and offers a great example of how technology can transform an enterprise, regardless of volume, traffic and complexity considerations to simplify life for the denizens of a digital world. Leaves one wondering – if Indian Railways could do it, what's stopping the rest of us?

In varying measures, all digital businesses follow this model which calls for seamless adoption and interplay of the four building blocks. For most businesses, these are the minimum that is needed for hitching a ride on the digital wagon.

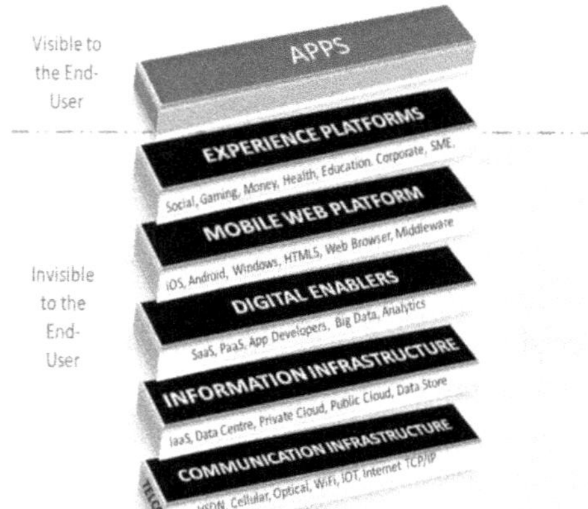

As the spread of Digital increases, you come across more and more *Apps* becoming available. 'App' has become a popular term to describe a digital service. In reality, these Apps sit on top of a layered 'stack', most of which is invisible to the end-user. When you download an App, you are inviting a whole *range* of disruptive forces to participate in your digital experience. The App is only the tip of the digital iceberg.

While the B2C and B2B models find a parallel in the traditional economy as well, the Digital economy has also spanned the C2C (consumer to consumer) model. Here, anyone can become a buyer and/or a seller. Many examples exist (like renting residential premises), some of which are quite inventive.

Just the other day, as my wife and I were busy packing for a road trip to Nainital (a hill-station about 6 hours' drive from Delhi), our nephew came in and suggested a mobile app which I could use to 'advertise' my trip. This would enable, he said, another couple somewhere in Delhi who may be scouting for travel options to Nainital on the same day (and using the same app) to connect with us and use the unutilized capacity of our car for their own journey. In the bargain, we would get paid enough to recover the cost of fuel and more! Plus, we could make good friends, he insisted! While our response was a No Thank You (this didn't quite fit in with our holiday plans), I found it quite amusing. The Digital Economy and C2C are sure opening new ways of making a business out of anything – such as the unoccupied seats in my car!

As C2C is typically between perfect strangers, *secure* payment transactions must be assured. This has opened new options like C2B2C (where B is a 3rd party payment gateway), and in future, Blockchain – for secure peer-to-peer transactions. Endless possibilities…

Very few of us would doubt that if there is one thing quite certain about the future, it is digital dominance. Enterprises beating an early path to digital are therefore at a clear and unbeatable advantage.

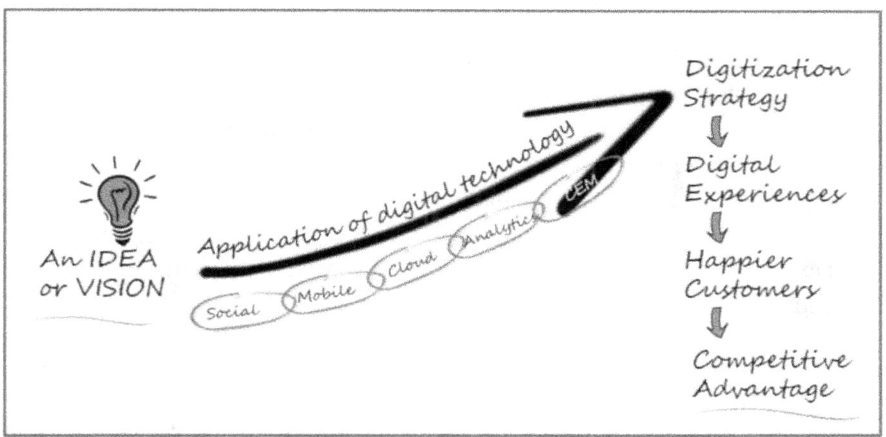

The Digital Transformation of an enterprise is a well thought through a process that typically germinates in an idea (or vision) around the innovative use of digital technology and culminates in a clear competitive advantage to the business, as shown. Simply put, digital transformation is about boosting your business by leveraging new advances in digital technology – be it the vegetable seller, the Indian Railways, or anything in between. It applies universally and certainly to *your* business. Think about it.

Digitization is clearly transforming the economy, and businesses that do not embrace it quickly enough are at grave risk. But isn't digital transformation easier said than done? Well, it is not as hard as you'd think. It is important, however, to pay attention to these fundamental and oft-ignored aspects to assure that you begin the journey well:

☞ The biggest inhibitor to digital adoption in an organization is surprisingly not the stage of its technological evolution but the state of mind of its people. Overcoming this may consume crucial months or years during which your competition may get an unsurpassable lead. As a first step, therefore, make sure that *everyone* on the bus shares the digital vision, believes in it, and is passionate about its accomplishment. This always works top down and must be reinforced by the top management at every opportunity.

☞ For businesses and enterprises in the digital economy, *a strong BITA is the new normal*. We shall see how your own enterprise measures up on the BITA index in a subsequent chapter, but even without doing an actual measurement this should be obvious by now as the digital economy DEMANDS a strong BITA. Business has become so closely intertwined with technology that lack of alignment between business and technology is the surest recipe for disaster that you can brew.

☞ Perhaps the biggest threat to established enterprises aiming to go digital is the lowering of entry barriers by the digital wave. New entrants often exhibit greater flexibility and can ramp up much faster and at considerably lower costs thus threatening the very existence of legacy enterprises. This stresses the need to be very nimble and fleet-footed. Time is not on your side if you are a large monolithic player striving to achieve, or retain, supremacy in the Digital Age.

☞ The digital economy places a very high premium on intellectual property, being driven by Innovation. The innovation can come from a mix of new products, services, distribution channels, payment methods, security and authentication, business models, etc. It may not be possible, or feasible, for one company to have expertise in all these segments. The digital value chain may, therefore, require plug-and-play of many participants, who may also in other circumstances be competing. This "co-opetition" is not an exception but a norm in the Digital Age, with a single offering carrying several integrated elements to deliver a comprehensive experience to the consumer.

☞ Digital Transformation is not a destination but a journey (how often have you heard this?). Each innovation may propagate a series of radical new possibilities, and the cycle repeats itself. The point here is that once you come up with a digital strategy and business model, and launch yourself as a digital enterprise, you cannot rest on your laurels. The need is never to stop seeking fresh ideas and keeping your ears tuned to the customer's voice. More companies have failed due to complacency than owing to an unviable product idea or poorly designed business model.

There is, unfortunately, no time-tested standard flow that works for all enterprises seeking to embark on the digital journey. Like people, enterprises are unique and at any point are at different stages of their digital evolution. For example, the Indian Railways would have a far different journey to digital than say, a local taxi service. However, there are certain items that every enterprise on the route to becoming a digital one must check off as it undertakes this crucial journey. Here is a quick rundown of these items.

Establish a sense of urgency

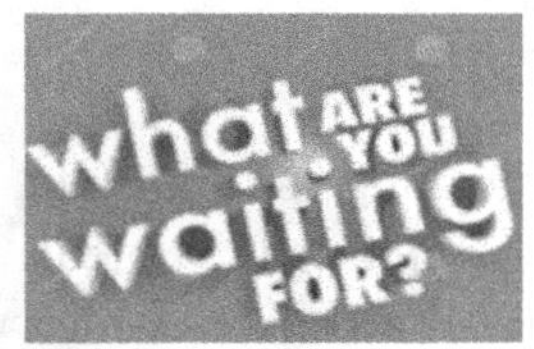

The start of the digital journey is not something you put in your three-year business plan. The time is NOW. This sense of urgency is not required only in the CEO, CIO or the company's 'Digital Champion.' There must be a visible and palpable wave of excitement *sweeping the enterprise*, generated (and reinforced) through constant motivational communication by the leadership. Good orientation programs may help to usher a shared sense of urgency.

Create a shared vision for the Enterprise

A digital transformation is about journeying into the future. You cannot start the journey without envisioning that future. *Everyone* who is on the journey must *share* this vision of the future. Thus, the vision must constantly be reinforced through town-halls and internal campaigns like emails, screensavers, posters etc. but most importantly by "walking the talk." To be shared by all, the vision should be believed and understood by all. It must project a simple, yet inspiring image of the future. Remember, technology, or ICT is *not* the purpose for which the enterprise exists. It is only a means to achieve it. Hence your vision statement should *not* be "We will provide online access to cloud-based portfolio information over high-speed communication channels to empower our customers to get the maximum from their investments", but the rather more mundane but purposeful, "We will help our investors achieve the best returns on their portfolio in the quickest time."

Define your Digital Transformation Strategy

A strategy is nothing but a plan to achieve your vision (What and How?). While defining the digitization strategy for your enterprise, it is important to pick the right questions which the strategy attempts to answer. Typical questions would be:

- In what way will digitization impact our current business model?
- How does it affect our positioning in the value chain?
- How will it help us identify and enter new business areas?
- How vulnerable will we be to disruptions from new entrants?
- Which new capabilities are needed to become an industry leader?

Identify your Digital Transformation *Objectives*

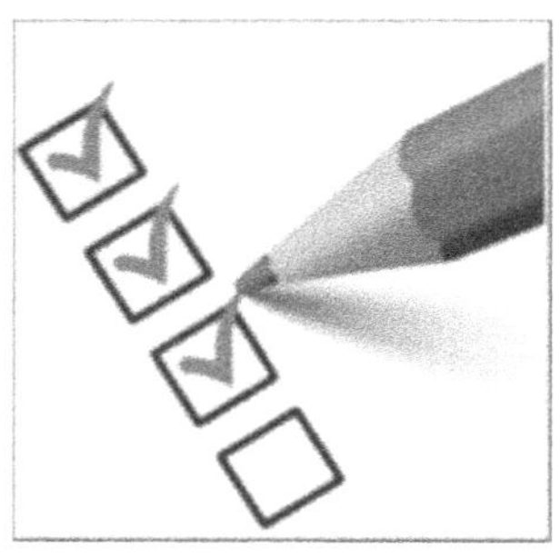

Even the best strategy is meaningless if it is not *executed* well. Hence it is important to break the strategy into SMART objectives which serve as milestones in the transformation journey. Though there is no universal set, it may be useful to build your transformation objectives around the following, with the over-arching goal of achieving a sustained competitive advantage.

- **Customer loyalty**: How can I improve customer loyalty through enhanced digital experience?

- **Market Differentiation**: What's my plan to create clear market differentiation through digital innovation?
- **Cost Reduction**: How can I achieve better productivity and asset management through the use of digital technology?
- **Higher Efficiency**: How can I achieve efficiency gains in operations and service delivery through digitization?
- **Agility, Speed-to-Market**: How do I leverage digital technology to optimize my business processes for higher agility and speed-to-market?

Refresh your Information Technology charter

The IT function and its leadership in a digital enterprise can no longer be defined by their ability to execute projects, maintain IT assets and generally *run* the business (operations). Digital transformation calls for an IT leadership and organization that can realign the IT people, processes, technology and information to *transform* (change) the business creatively and consultatively. In a digital enterprise, IT is an equal stakeholder in the creation of business value (*outcome-based IT* – see chapter 2), and this must reflect in the renewed IT charter, which should now include:

- Onboarding of business savvy IT leadership and people
- Redefining IT KRAs to include ownership of the customer experience
- Developing the plan and capability for new technology platforms like mobility and e-commerce solutions in line with business roadmap
- Embedding content and brand management strategies in the overall IT plan

Design an adaptable IT Architecture for digital business

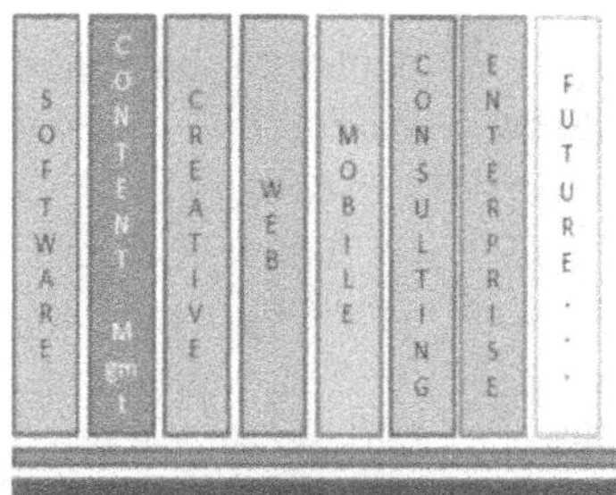

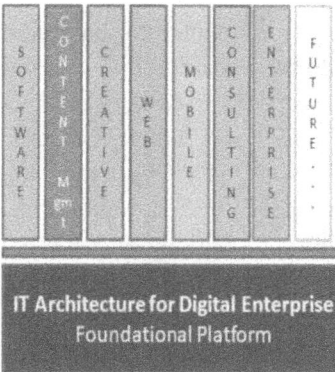

Digital business requires a very robust foundational IT platform, on which new services may easily and quickly be constructed to achieve targeted business outcomes. Your organization may need the services of an IT architecture consultant for assessing and rebuilding the IT foundation. The essential aspect here is that stacks for the various business services (or business units) must be dynamically reconfigurable to suit the changing landscape of the digital enterprise.

Depending on the size and state of your organization you may choose an entirely cloud-based solution or a hybrid of cloud and on-premise solutions, but your logical construct may still conform to the above.

Develop the right Structure for Digital Business

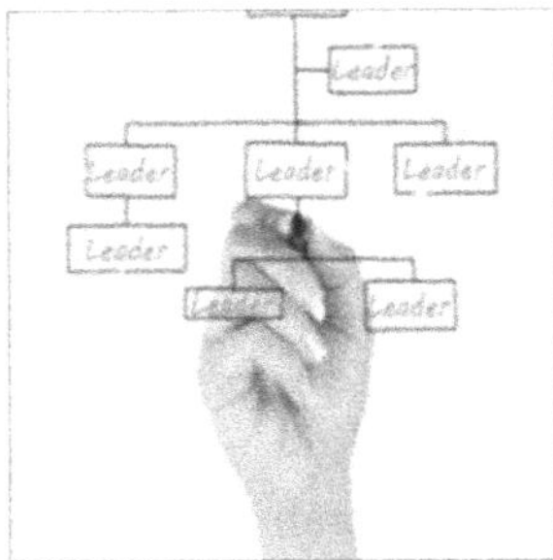

Structure follows strategy. For a digital enterprise, the mindsets and competencies required for success are quite different. People need to reinvent themselves, and those ensconced in tight comfort zones often do not find a place. For the digital organization, it is important to onboard people who, apart from being competent in their core function, are

- Customer-centric to the point of obsession
- Continuously looking to innovate
- Agile (quick to change), data-driven, challengers of status quo
- Business folks with strong aptitude for technology
- IT folks with a strong aptitude for business

Digital transformation requires a strong leader with ownership and authority to make changes in the organization, implement current and future digital initiatives, and own the customer experience. This leader may be from the technology or business/marketing organization, i.e., an empowered CIO or CMO. In some organizations, this position is now held by a *Chief Digital Officer*, or CDO, with a clear focus on digital strategy and its outcome delivered jointly by the Business and IT teams.

Boost your BITA power as you prepare your digital launch

The stage is now set for your launch into the digital space. Remember, you do not transform into a digital enterprise overnight. The capacity to work in a *hybrid* environment spanning legacy and future platforms, infrastructure, applications etc. is thus another key determinant of your success as a digital enterprise. The 'digital' edifice is not built entirely on the *ruins* of legacy: some legacy survives. Through close interworking, Business and IT need to take calls on legacy elements that may be retained, revamped or retired. While the transformation of IT delivery processes and infrastructure is underway, Business and IT work interdependently in an agile, iterative cycle to shape the enterprise's digital future in which they fuse together to deliver an enhanced user experience. This functional harmony, or BITA, is the backbone of digital transformation and early benefits to customers.

With the day not far away when every enterprise will be a digital enterprise, your blueprint of digital transformation is your most important tool to craft your future. The best time to start, if you haven't already, is now. Run the transformation as your highest priority project with clearly defined milestones and a system of measuring the progress in your journey. In my experience, companies that get their project blueprint "bought-in" by all stakeholders early in terms of deliverables, schedule and funding have the best chance of executing it successfully. Thus, it may be worth their while for your senior leadership - from the CEO to the heads of IT, Marketing, Finance - to embark on this posthaste. Sometimes it helps to engage external consultants, especially if there are thick walls between departments, to facilitate the baselining of the transformation goals.

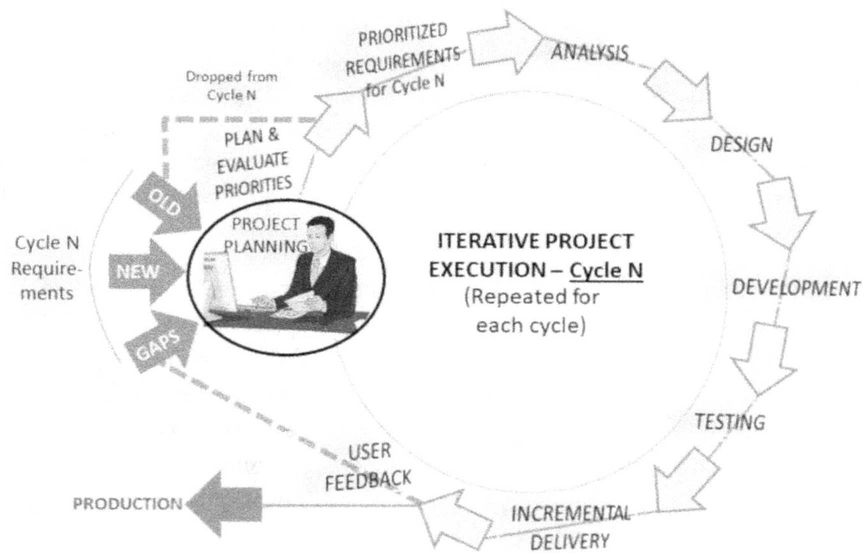

A system to *measure* the progress with respect to the agreed goals is important. It is also very important to note that a digital transformation project is run in an agile, iterative mode. This means that it must factor in frequent changes in business requirements – as opposed to a traditional ('waterfall') project where requirements are frozen *before* the project kicks off, and the next stage only starts when the previous one ends. Thus, a flexible approach which allows for *incremental* deliveries is best suited for digital transformation. This also helps with fine-tuning the output by feeding any quality or performance gaps back into the next-stage requirements. It is somewhat beyond this book to go into the description of the iterative project methodology, but I am just presenting a conceptual drawing here to illustrate this for context.

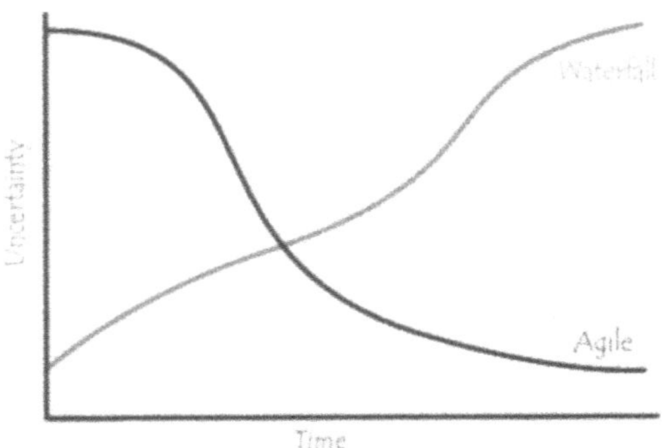

Obviously, the iterative model, which is based on continuous feedback and interaction between users and executors, reduces uncertainty in the final delivery, though there is often some confusion initially with less clarity on precisely what is to be prioritized for delivery.

While we have touched on a few essential aspects of transforming to a digital enterprise, let me re-emphasize here that digital transformation does *not* happen by merely adopting new technology. You may implement the most advanced technologies, but would still not become a digital enterprise unless the entire organization transforms itself to take advantage of the potential unleashed by these new technologies. It's a bit like putting the latest smartphone in the hands of your grandmother and expecting her to exploit its full potential even while she is happy with her button-phone and does not aspire to anything beyond! It's the same for enterprises - *people must be ready first.*

There are many great examples of successful digital transformation by companies. I had an opportunity to meet with some of the digitization champions, mostly the CIO, CMO or CDO, at organizations (including the companies where I have worked myself) that have successfully transformed their businesses and it was inspiring to hear them speak very passionately about their experiences. While their paths were different, I found some common ground that everyone had encountered in their journey. They all adopted each of the steps for digital transformation that we mentioned earlier to varying extents, depending on their stage of maturity. It also emerged that in all digital enterprises each business process in marketing, sales, manufacturing, accounting, and customer service is designed, modeled, and optimized with deep involvement of the IT team in an impressive show of BITA.

Sifting through my notes from these meetings, I find that almost everyone mentioned the following in one form or another. I, therefore, have good reason to believe that these are important pointers for companies aspiring to become successful digital enterprises.

1. The ultimate goal of digital transformation is an unwavering connection with the customer
2. Digital Transformation depends heavily on a *shared* passion for achieving the company's vision
3. It is a journey which takes new turns every day, opening up exciting possibilities. And challenges
4. It does NOT require doing away with your existing IT infrastructure, though some consolidation must be done. In fact, it was now possible to get *more* out of this infra than ever before
5. Listening to the younger generation has been very useful in enhancing the business model. Most large companies are not doing this enough
6. Engaging an external transformation consultant helps, but only as a conscience keeper and facilitator. The real impetus comes from the passion shared by the entire workforce.
7. Alignment between Business and IT was never a greater need than it is during and after the transformation. It must be built and nurtured as an asset.

One of the leading wall-paint companies in India has had a very remarkable metamorphosis from a manufacturing company to a digital service enterprise. Of course, it still *manufactures* but at the core now is its renewed vision to improve the experience of its retailers and customers at every touchpoint, using digital technology. The company's retailers can now devote quality time to helping customers, rather than sort transactional issues internally. Customers have also been given a choice to browse product catalogs on the web and make their selections at home, where the paint is to be applied in the end, instead of at the retail shop. Retailers can submit their customers' orders through a centralized call-center which provides better service by tapping into the many depots scattered across the country. The centralized order taking freed up the company's own salespeople from the cumbersome and time-consuming order collection process and enabled stronger relationship building with customers (and retailers). The salespeople leveraged mobility by carrying tablet devices so that relevant information is always available at their fingertips. The company expects customer loyalty as well as the demand to get a boost through this initiative which in turn will reflect in a healthier balance sheet, and of course an edge over the competition.

The company achieved all this through a transformation of its core IT systems and processes. It created an online B2B portal for quick and easy access by its subcontractors and retailers and set up a Customer Relationship Management (CRM) system for further improving the service levels and order fulfillment process. At the backend, a more precise view of the orders and forecasts enabled the creation of highly automated plants tuned to demand. These plants were connected through an ERP system to automated warehouses across the country, allowing more efficient servicing of customer orders.

The digital transformation enabled the company to sell *services* instead of products – a complete shift in the business model and market positioning. Instead of *selling* a can of paint, they now offer the *service* of a painted wall. This enables them to better meet customer requirements, including guidance to customers on the proper application of higher-end products, and launch new ranges of high-end paints. The company could also better understand customer preferences and potential demand – which helped create more targeted offerings. The benefits are many and varied and go much beyond revenue. Importantly, now there is direct engagement of the end-customer in the planning process. Traditionally, end-customer involvement in the paints (or most manufactured goods) business was very low. Digital has changed that.

The above called for a high a degree of commitment to a shared goal by all parts of the company – IT, Business/Sales, Supply Chain, Manufacturing, Retail, and others. Without the passionate participation of all stakeholders, a transformation of this kind would remain a vision. The company needed, of course, to invest in strong IT capabilities derived from the renewed business model and processes. We find in this example that all the steps we spoke about – most importantly the transformation of IT systems and processes in tune with a change in the business model – have been applied. It's an inspiring story.

The need for a strong Business-IT alliance in the digital economy is, of course, a no-brainer. In my experience to date, I have not come across a single successful digital enterprise that did not attribute strong alliance between its Business and IT functions among the top three reasons for achieving its success. Not even one. In the next chapter I will briefly present the results of a very objective survey that I did amongst business and technology teams in various organizations, including some that have not yet achieved the status of a digital enterprise but are trending towards it.

The world of digital business is a lot different from our familiar world of traditional (or *analog*) business. I cannot over-emphasize this. The quirks of the digital world would be unimaginable a few years ago. Here, the largest taxi service in the world does not own a single taxi! Yes, I am talking about Uber – a quintessential digital enterprise. There are more examples. Skype provides one of the world's largest communication services without owning a single piece of telecom infra! Some of the world's biggest retailers – like Alibaba – hold no merchandise in their inventories. Even the world's largest movie house, Netflix, does not own or run a single cinema. Facebook does not create content yet is one of the largest media owners on the planet today. If it's not capital or infrastructure, what has powered the phenomenal rise of these – and countless other – successful digital enterprises? Well, the answer lies in the ability to leverage technology for business in very innovative ways. These enterprises have all germinated from a *business* idea (or vision) backed to the hilt by digital *technology*. In short, a strong *BITA*.

Having gone through the arguments and stories presented in this chapter, the reader probably does not require a further elaboration on the importance of BITA in attaining success in the digital world. It is a world where Business is IT and IT is Business. In other words, Business and IT are indistinguishable from each other as both play an equally active role in driving business success. There are still folks, and even companies, who are skeptical on this point. Well, good luck to them. If *you* do believe in BITA, it says a lot about your aspirations of going digital. Now is the time for you to move from the aspirational to the operational level in attaining your goals. Mastering the seven dimensions of BITA which we will introduce in chapter 6 will help not only in achieving a stronger BITA but also in creating a greater overall impact as a digital enterprise.

Before we go into measuring and improving specific dimensions of BITA for your organization, let me briefly present to you the results of a survey I conducted among folks from various organizations on the digital path, and show how BITA is placed relatively amongst other significant factors that contribute to enterprise success in today's world. This is the topic of the following chapter.

5 *BITA: An Outside-In View*

How does the world view BITA? While few would still doubt the need and importance of BITA in the new economy, gaining an insider perspective on BITA from a cross-section of viewpoints may be an excellent barometer to ascertain its place among the myriad of concerns and priorities afflicting a typical enterprise. In the earlier chapters, we discussed the evolution of BITA as a driver of enterprise success in the Digital Age. Now let us look at how some real organizations view BITA and the factors influencing it.

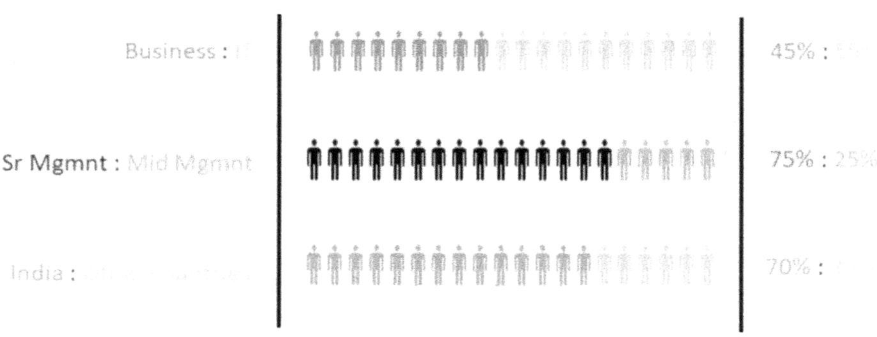

I approached a select but insightful set of people from both business and technology backgrounds with a detailed questionnaire seeking their views on critical factors influencing business in the digital economy. This set was constituted of folks from different industries. I contacted individuals from the senior and middle management rungs of Business and IT streams in organizations which have already made significant forays into the digital world. I am committed to confidentiality with respect to names and companies of course, but some broad distribution parameters are as shown.

In this chapter, I am presenting the consolidated view of the responses received. Personally, given the profiles of the people who responded, I consider this a reasonably accurate and tenable assessment which can be extrapolated to represent a comprehensive and credible picture. I have only considered responses from individuals who are deeply associated with driving digital initiatives and have achieved a certain degree of success in their ventures. Even within this set, I filtered out the most extreme responses on both ends to make the results more accurately reflect the consolidated view.

The charts simply rank the various attributes in their order of importance as scored by the respondents, and there is no attempt to slice and dice the data to derive inferences which may be open to interpretation. I am presenting the questionnaire that was used in this survey later in the chapter, and *I encourage you to run this amongst the key people in your own organization to create similar charts for your unit.* This may provide some useful hints that may help as you work your way up.

These charts are not intended as a rigid benchmark to be necessarily aspired by your organization. They are statistical derivations and we all know the pitfalls of taking statistics too seriously! At best, they can provide you broad guidelines. Your individual situation may well be different and yet be good. In the end, it all depends on how you have set your organization's goals and priorities. That said, I do believe that if you are reading this book, you probably place a high importance on BITA. So, if you find BITA near the bottom of the rankings, you may need to introspect and see how you can pull it up. In later sections, we have dealt with this in some detail, but I hope for now that the findings of this survey help you in adjusting your sails with the fast-changing winds.

What Creates Market Differentiation?

The first part of the survey was to determine the critical differentiators in the new economy, before attempting to *rank* them in any order. Surprisingly, the usual suspects that one would associate with differentiation in the old economy, namely Speed, Brand (reputation), Service and Pricing also emerged among the top differentiators in the new economy. Features like geography/coverage and logistics were considered too tactical (and location-specific) while people-practices and ethical business conduct were considered too foundational to be included, and hence were dropped from the list. In the end, we had six key differentiators which included three *new* entrants: *Innovative Offerings* (which includes R&D focus), *Customer Experience* (which replaced Customer Service) and of course, *Business-IT Alignment* (which as we saw did not figure in any significant way in determining the course of business in the old economy). It emerged very clearly that BITA played a significant role in ascertaining the success of the Business strategy and it could no longer remain an invisible and uncertain factor.

The respondents, from both Business and IT streams, were asked to give a score of 1 – 10 against each of the six attributes in terms of its potential for creating market differentiation, 1 being No-Impact-At-All and progressively increasing in order of importance up to a maximum of 10. It may be noted that the responses here are from an *internal* company perspective and not the end-customer perspective.

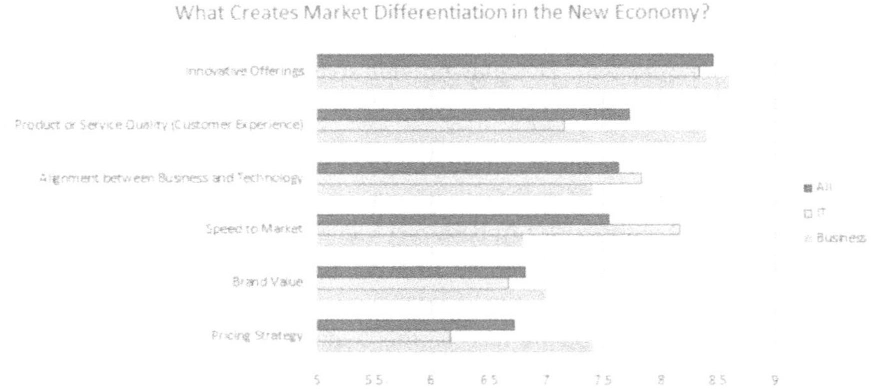

As with all surveys, we did get some surprises. For example, consistency and quality of *Customer Experience* were rated significantly higher by the Business than by IT in terms of their potential for creating market differentiation. While IT may consider Customer Experience a *hygiene* factor, Business places higher importance on this attribute as a *market differentiator.* On the other hand, IT puts much higher emphasis than Business on *Speed-To-Market*, at least in spirit. Whether it gets translated into aggressive delivery schedules is not clear from the survey, but at the very least this points to a heightened sense of urgency in IT to deliver quickly, and that to me is a positive sign.

It is no surprise that Innovative Offerings is rated as the most important differentiator in a rapidly changing business world which is increasingly dominated by technology. Business-IT Alignment is ranked as the *third* most important factor for creating market differentiation in the new economy, coming narrowly after Customer Experience. In my view, this says a lot about the pace at which the contribution of technology functions in ensuring business success has grown in a few quick years.

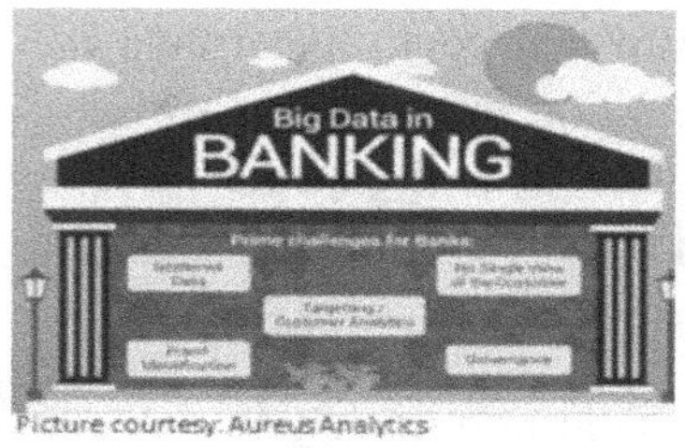

Picture courtesy: Aureus Analytics

The power of BITA to create market differentiation is a lot more pronounced in the new economy as IT-enabled solutions like Big Data, Mobility, etc. come to rule the business landscape. One of my respondents to the survey, a banker, had an interesting tale to exemplify this. The bank (or Financial Institution, FI) we are referring is a diversified entity which is into personal banking, insurance, home loans and credit cards for the individual customer and a host of merchant banking services for the business customer, like many financial institutions today. The diversified entities of this FI, however, might as well have been different companies – for there was no common denominator in their business operations. The customers of one unit were complete strangers to the other units. There was no common thread that tied together the experiences across different units or a way to offer promotional incentives to customers of other units in a bid to attract them over. Someone who availed insurance for their car from this FI and expected to be recognized, let alone be rewarded, when they applied for a home loan was in for a big disappointment. Other than earning the displeasure of the customers, this was also causing the bank to miss out on a substantial cross-selling opportunity. Everyone knew about this problem, but the cry that rang through the portals was a dismissive 'what can we do?'

This issue eventually came up in one of the board meetings, and it was decided to take a crack at the problem. The leaders of the IT and business units were summoned. As a first step, a common 'governing' group on technology was created, tasked not with operations but with leveraging cross-unit potentialities through technology. I think this was an excellent first move. The group recommended standardizing some aspects of the data structures (I will not go into the technical details) across the various units so that the data could be amalgamated. The process of requirements finalization for 'project unify' included IT teams spending a great deal of time with business and customer reps *in the field*. The 'intelligence' gathered was instrumental in grouping customers into demographic segments to support sales, promotions, and campaigns across units. This was achieved by collecting and analyzing all available data and using Big Data technology to mine for intelligence from underlying data.

The close interworking between the Business and IT teams did not end here. The teams next worked on targeting new product and service offerings to the *right* customers by implementing software that could understand the customers' preferences for communication, selection and buying of services. The system was also open to inputs in the form of social media feeds to analyze customer sentiments and opinions and identify key influencers across the lines of business.

At the time of writing this, there is not much field information available to quantify the competitive benefits of this initiative, but there is a visible wave of excitement and optimism among the internal stakeholders that it will set this bank apart in its market. I tend to share the optimism, having been at the receiving end when approaching banks for different types of services. I will, therefore, be very keen to know the results of this innovation in bringing differentiation for this bank. Time will tell.

BITA is the hidden force that is behind many a success story in the digital economy. Even a relatively simple project like putting a new feature, or changing the user interface, on a mobile ticketing application – run collaboratively between customer teams and IT - could produce vastly improved business results. I am therefore entirely in agreement with our survey on the high importance of BITA as a factor for creating clear market differentiation. Are you?

Why Does Business-IT Alignment Matter?

There was a consensus among everyone I met that in the new economy Business-IT alignment was not something one could overlook and still expect business growth. As "Business Growth" would be a somewhat over-generic term to describe the key motivation for BITA, I decomposed this into common

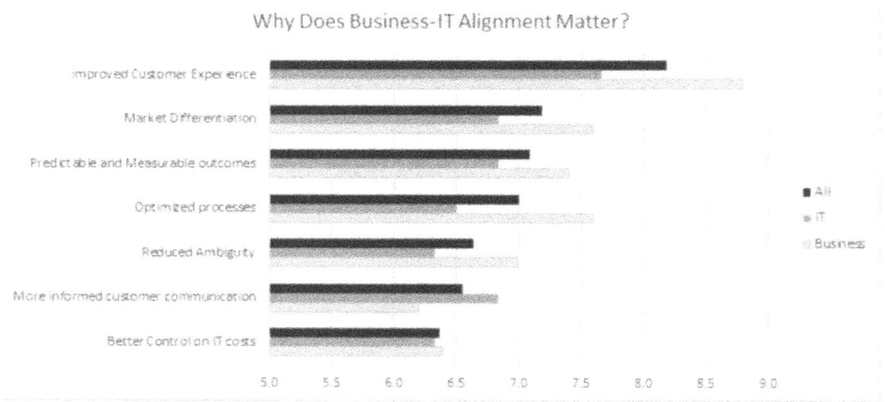

constituents that could lead to this outcome. I then asked the respondents to score them on a similar scale of 1 to 10, where 1 signified the least impact of BITA and 10 signified maximum impact. There were wider variations between Business and IT on this question, but both agree overwhelmingly that the impact of BITA on *improving customer experience* was the highest. No surprises here. Overall, Business was more upbeat on the impact of BITA on almost all the selected parameters than IT. Significantly, the "old economy" attribute of cost-control ranked the lowest among the motivations for embracing BITA, and on this specific parameter, there was a very close agreement between Business and IT. This does not mean that cost optimization is *not* expected to result from BITA, but that it is not the primary reason people are promoting Business-IT Alignment within their organizations.

During the survey, I interacted with folks from several industry domains. This incident was narrated by a senior IT Projects Manager from a very reputed software services firm (let's call it SSF). A year ago, one of their overseas clients had visited their development facilities as part of the assessment process, accompanied by the business account manager of SSF. SSF was one of the four shortlisted companies whose centers were being visited by the client-team during the week. The day started at 10am with the arrival of the client at the facilities where the traditional Indian welcome of garlanding and lamp-lighting was accorded. The client team was cordially escorted into the swanky facilities which had a space-age conference room laden with refreshments of a wide variety. No detail was overlooked, however trivial. The client team, led by the director of engineering, was here introduced to the top leadership of SSF, which brimmed with an eagerness to serve and an unshakeable bonhomie. After this, the client team patiently sat through some fantastic power points on SSF's people and processes, success rate, client testimonials, the works. Lunch was lavish.

After lunch, the client made an unexpected request which threatened to deviate the proceedings from the choreographed routine. This client had recently acquired another company (let's call it AC2) which was also a client of SSF. The director of the client company asked if they could visit the dedicated development center – also-called offshore delivery center, or ODC – that SSF ran for AC2, and interact with the team members there. Some murmurs ensued regarding lack of notice, client security and confidentiality etc., but in the end, the request was ceded.

What followed was an exemplary show of good conduct that brought a major twist to the story. As the client team walked in amidst the AC2 offshore delivery team – which had not been alerted formally – there were some curious and surprised glances, but otherwise, it was a bustling, busy delivery center going about its business as usual. The director of the client team stopped at a corner desk where a young lady was contemplatively sitting at a workstation with two screens. He spoke to her directly. Asked her first about who she was, her experience, role in the project, etc. It turned out she was two years out of college and was an Associate Software Engineer assigned to the AC2 project. The client asked her a series of questions relating to the project and how her work fit into the larger picture. She gave a detailed and accurate answer to each question and spoke about AC2 the company, its mission, the various touchpoints, and the processes for staying in sync on the deliverables and dates. As the client later confided, he was completely taken in by this young engineer's in-depth and contextual understanding of not only the project, but the business of AC2, perhaps beyond her designated charter, and this swung the deal in SSF's favor.

All the sales and marketing effort, swanky facilities, affirmations of top-management and impressive track record of SSF were rendered trivial before this display of close alignment between the company's IT (engineering) and customer's (business) organizations, which was apparent at the working level. The new ODC set up by SSF for this client mandated a culture of close alignment between the technical delivery team and customer's business and support teams. This was closely monitored by the senior management. Quite expectedly, repeat orders and good recommendations followed. As the customer wrote later in his testimonial: "The sense of urgency that the SSF team displayed across the board not only fixed problems for us quickly but prevented a lot of them from surfacing. This team worked with minimal supervision and knew exactly what our customers expected. We had no hesitation at all in going back to them when we embarked on our expansion project lately. I commend their business and IT teams for step-locking with us all the way, going outside their charter to understand and help enhance our business." The grandest sales effort can only bring the customer to your door. But an emotional connect that culminates in building a spirit of trust is squarely the preserve of BITA.

The impact of pervasive BITA in influencing the customer's overall perception of the company is apparent here. Regardless of the size and nature of your business, *BITA is your best bet* in the digital economy.

What drives BITA in an organization?

The third question of the survey was directed at determining the factors that need to be institutionalized in an organization aspiring to a high BITA. In arriving at the list of choices, we excluded intangibles like mindsets, business/IT competence, attitudes and situational behaviors, simply to retain objectivity in the evaluation, and not because they are considered any less important for BITA. In the following chapter, we will introduce the seven dimensions of BITA which cover *all* aspects that matter for BITA and their ramifications in some detail. Later we will discuss the role and importance of each dimension in driving assured and sustained success for an enterprise in this digital era.

The agreement between Business and IT was the closest in this question, on almost all the listed factors. Both Business and IT gave equal importance to *Leadership Example and Role modeling* as the factor with the maximum potential to enhance BITA in the organization. It is indeed hard to imagine a BITA-powered environment under a listless leadership. As we have said before, BITA must be driven from the top, reinforced at every possible opportunity and led by example.

Closely following this, and quite on expected lines, was Business-*aligned IT roadmap*. I know of companies that have invested a great deal in intensive workshops, sometimes involving expensive consultants, to arrive at their technology roadmap. Entire technology teams go to offsite locations, frequently exotic ones, in the hope of finding the most optimum IT roadmap to guide them for next two, three or five years. Few of these workshops, if any, invite business participation, other than at a very superficial level. The teams rely on their own knowledge of the business and make idealistic assumptions about business, frequently leading to a widening gap between the business and technology

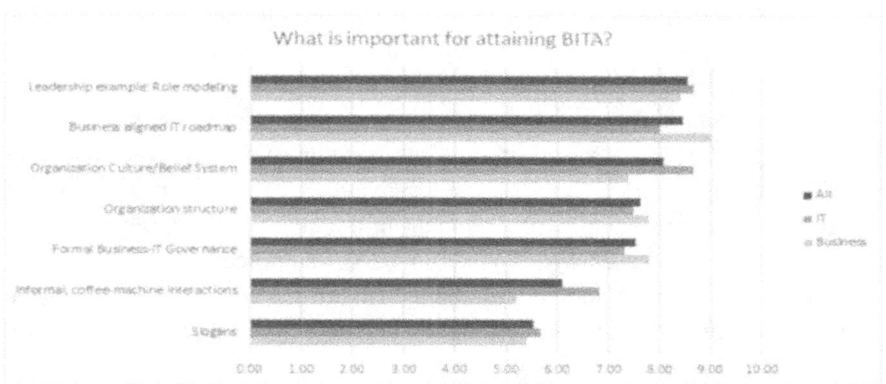

roadmaps over time. All it takes, however, to arrive at the best IT roadmap is to use the business strategy as its foundation and develop the roadmap using this as the starting point. The IT roadmap must encompass the business strategy and focus on making it simple for business to become successful. No element of the business strategy is untouched by IT. Many IT organizations make the grave mistake of postulating that certain aspects are outside of IT. Not in this digital era, as the results have confirmed. We dwelt on Business-IT roadmap alignment in Chapter-2, and this result is a corroboration of the points that were made earlier.

The Digital India movement is a case in point for illustrating the impact of Leadership Example and Role Modeling. India has a precious natural resource of technical talent which is routinely tapped by global corporations (leading to a thriving Indian IT industry), and a strong communications network backbone. On the demand side, there is a mounting necessity to streamline the availability of government services – including records and documents – to its citizens, through digitization and high-speed internet connectivity which the Digital India project aims to provide, particularly to large sections of the deprived population in rural areas. The DI project also envisages rendering e-health, e-education, surveillance, and e-Banking services to millions, which would benefit communities as well as businesses through higher empowerment, and finally an opportunity to re-skill the youth to drive digital literacy and create more options for employment. All in all, Digital India project is firmly on the critical path of India's progress. Some would say survival.

It was only on being articulated and reinforced by the top leadership of the country – no less than the Prime Minister – that the rubber hit the road. If the PM and his senior ministers did not emphasize this initiative at every available opportunity, driving home its advantages to all and sundry, the project in my view would have been a non-starter. As I write this, a lot is taking shape on this front. I hope to see in my lifetime the benefits of this program reach all parts of the country, including its most disadvantaged sections, bringing about a significant and measurable improvement in the quality-of-life index and the level of empowerment enjoyed by all. The most significant factor behind its eventual success would undoubtedly be the role of the country's leadership in focusing the attention of the government machinery, industry bodies, institutes of learning, and the common man alike to make this a personal mission.

If leadership example and role modeling can energize a nation of 1.25 billion, think of what it can do to your own organization which has a much higher proportion of highly erudite folks routinely achieving the impossible! Given that the awareness of the implications, the cutting-edge talent, commitment to excellence, and the energy levels to convert plans to reality are so much higher within your enterprise than in the nation as a whole, wouldn't a spark from the leadership go much farther in igniting the fire of digital transformation across your organization? Of course, it would. Unfortunately, the converse is also true. The fire would fail to conflagrate *without* that spark, and the enterprise would quickly degenerate into cold embers, only useful for future case studies that caution against following its example.

SURVEY QUESTIONNAIRE (As it was sent to respondents)

In the current times, the importance of Business-IT alignment cannot be over-emphasized. I would like to collect some views on important aspects around Business-IT alignment for an important project that I am working on. I need your help on a few basic questions on this topic which would help me immensely in presenting a well-rounded view on the subject.

In this respect, I would greatly appreciate if you could take a couple of minutes out whenever convenient to quickly respond to the below. **The response is purely numeric. You only need to put a number between 1-10 against each line, i.e., give marks out of 10,** based on your judgment/ experience.

(1 is least in importance, 10 is highest in importance)

1. Rate each of the following on a scale of 1-10 on their potential for creating market differentiation in the Digital Age
    - Speed to market
    - Pricing strategy
    - Innovative offerings
    - Product/Service quality
    - Brand value
    - Alignment between business and technology (IT)
2. Why does Business-IT Alignment matter? Rate each of the following from 1-10 as a motive for improving Business-IT alignment
    - Market differentiation
    - Improved customer experience
    - Better control on IT Costs
    - More informed customer communication
    - Optimized processes
    - Predictable and measurable outcomes
3. What is the importance of each of the following in attaining a strong level of Business-IT alignment (Rate each on 1-10)
    - Organization structure
    - Organization belief system
    - Leadership example/Role-modeling
    - Formal Business–IT governance structure
    - Informal, coffee-machine interactions
    - Business-aligned IT roadmap
    - Slogans

4. In your view where would your company be today on its Business-IT alignment index (1-10)? [ ]

5. What is a realistic target level of alignment after one year for you (1-10) [ ]

This is for statistical analysis only, and all responses will be treated in strictest confidence. Still, if you choose not to answer any particular query, it is fine.

I value your opinion and hence seeking it.

Thanks in advance,
Ashish

6 *What's Your BITA Level?*

In chapter-2 we briefly looked at some of the characteristics that enterprises striving for higher BITA need to possess and display. The question in your mind, however, is how *you* as an enterprise stack up on the BITA scale. While BITA is not a purely numeric entity – much like your quality or customer-centricity attribute – it is possible to get a fair idea of your BITA level through a simple tool that I am now introducing. Of course, the ultimate evidence of a strong BITA is the success you achieve in the digital marketplace through the joint efforts of Business and IT. Some preparatory guidance in determining your BITA level as well as gaps may, however, prove helpful in focusing on the right attributes for capitalizing on the digital opportunity around you.

If you were to be informed by the tool only that you were low or high on BITA, it would most probably be a reiteration of what you always suspected. But you would still not know where to put your emphasis to achieve a better alignment. For this, it is essential to go into the various components of BITA. In this chapter, I will introduce the individual dimensions that make up BITA and a way to measure how you as an enterprise stack up on each dimension of BITA. As with any tool, the integrity with which responses are provided, as well as the specific setting and circumstance of the organization conducting it, will determine how closely the results of the tool match the ground reality and market performance.

The seven tracking dimensions for BITA

We noted in the previous chapter that Business-IT alignment is rated among the most important success factors for a digital enterprise. Its significance as a driver of business value is increasing rapidly. Ascertaining your own position on the BITA scale will help assess your success (or indeed survival) chances in the world of digital business and allow you to focus on the right attributes for enhancing your prospects. The BITA Calculator introduced here helps you do precisely this, by simply evaluating your Y or N responses to a set of statements.

A few months ago, I did a 'trial' run of the BITA Calculator. Surprisingly I found that people equate BITA very tightly to the overall digitization status of the enterprise. That is, people believed that companies high on BITA are mature digital enterprises while those not showing a high enough score are the strugglers of the new economy. This may well turn out be true in many cases. However, it is important to remember that BITA is only *one*, albeit significant, attribute of a successful digital enterprise amongst several others. That said, I do believe that a high BITA score certainly *enhances* your prospects in the new economy and this is what I called-out to the test group. I also asked the group to lean towards the negative view when asked to give an opinion on a topic about which they were unsure. (E.g. if asked "Is your technology roadmap aligned with Business strategy?", say N if you don't know.) It doesn't matter if your initial score comes out lower than you expect. It gives you a higher room for improvement through innovation and thus a greater scope to transform yourself as an enterprise.

Do remember that the dimensions on which this measurement is based are for the estimation and eventual improvement of your *Business-IT Alignment* score, and not your overall digitization index (or DMI). Once you have BITA on your side, you will probably have an easier task of developing some of the other attributes on the path to becoming a successful digital enterprise. BITA is an ideal starting point for the inevitable journey you must embark upon to digitally transform your enterprise.

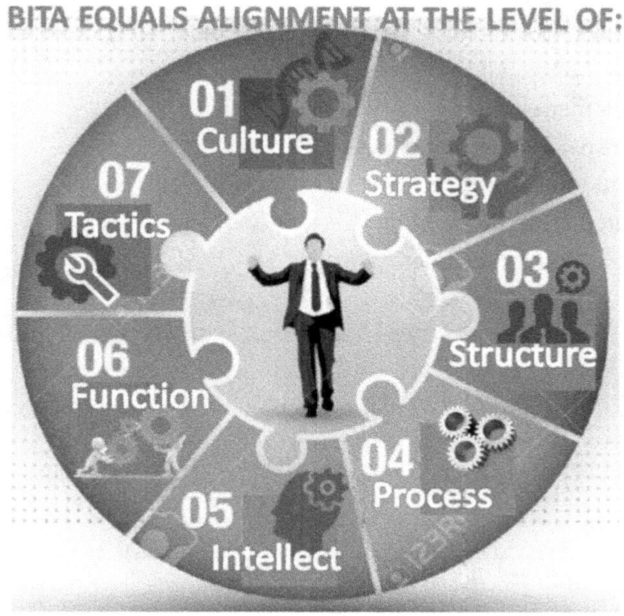

Business-IT Alignment, or BITA, refers to aligning at multiple levels, or dimensions. Before we move to the tool based assessment of BITA Index, let us look at its seven *dimensions*. The term dimension is used here to define each critical factor that matters in the attainment of high BITA. I have chosen to call them *dimensions* because just like our spatial dimensions (L,B,H) these are *all* required for creating a complete model. If I had used say *characteristics, attributes,* etc., it may have implied that they could exist independently of each other. The accompanying illustration shows the seven dimensions of BITA, which are the same across various industries and business segments, enabling uniform benchmarking.

Each of the dimensions is the subject of detailed treatment in the next section. However, a quick primer and some pointers of the individual dimensions here would aid our interpretation of the BITA score.

1. **Cultural** Alignment

Cultural alignment implies that the people in the organization consciously, consistently and collectively live by the same set of values, principles, norms, and policies, frequently emanating from the organization's *belief system*, in their actions, words, and spirit. Some pointers*:

- Well-articulated Belief System
- Shared vision, driven from the top
- Results-orientation (Focus on the Outcome)
- Drive for excellence
- Customer-centricity
- Transparency and Openness
- Continuous learning and development
- Shared sense of urgency
- Intolerance of mediocrity

The year was 2003. I had called a couple of friends over to my house in Bangalore to watch a cricket world cup match. Most TVs, like mine, were the picture-tube (box) variety in those days. To my dismay, when I switched on the TV that morning (the match was in the afternoon) I saw

* *'Pointers' are features that give* ***evidence*** *of the dimension being ingrained in the organization.*

a white horizontal line across the screen and no picture. I had a service contract for the TV and had also met the service manager once, who had spoken animatedly of customer-centricity in his organization and had assured me of right and timely attention. I called the number given to me but was pushed around to two other numbers before I got through to someone who could relate to my problem. They promptly told me that someone would visit me two days later! After many appeals, they reluctantly agreed to send someone on the same day. Well, someone did arrive minutes before the match was to start. He looked rather surly, talked impolitely, and conveyed in no uncertain terms that he was doing me a favor. He took one hard look at my TV, lifted it about 4" above the table and dropped it with a thud! For good measure, he then banged it on the top! Lo and behold, the picture was back, much to my relief at that instant! He then went away, probably with a smirk. But to this day, I wonder what kind of culture was imbibed by the frontline – the customer-facing people – of this company which professed itself to be their customers' champion. I won't be going back to this company again.

Culture is what defines the company, and it's NOT invisible. Even if the outcome is positive, as in this example, culture (behavior) can negate it. If the company's values and beliefs are only known to the CEO and his vice-presidents, they may as well be non-existent. In matters of your belief system, BITA included, there is no such thing as *over*-communication.

2. **Strategic** Alignment

Strategic alignment is about Business and IT deriving their goals and plans from a *common mission*, which is to make the business successful. Some pointers:

- Understanding of business strategy at *all* levels of the organization
- IT Architecture and IT Roadmap alignment with Business strategy
- Correspondence between IT KRAs and Business strategy
- Flexibility to respond to market changes
- Shared vision of the future
- IT readiness to support future needs of the business

It goes without saying that creating the right business strategy is almost certainly the most impactful, and yet a very precarious, aspect of running a business. A strategy that is incongruent with your core competency could be an open invitation to disaster. It is important that the strategy is defined simply and unambiguously, is communicated clearly to all constituents and focuses not only on WHAT must be done but also on WHY it must be done.

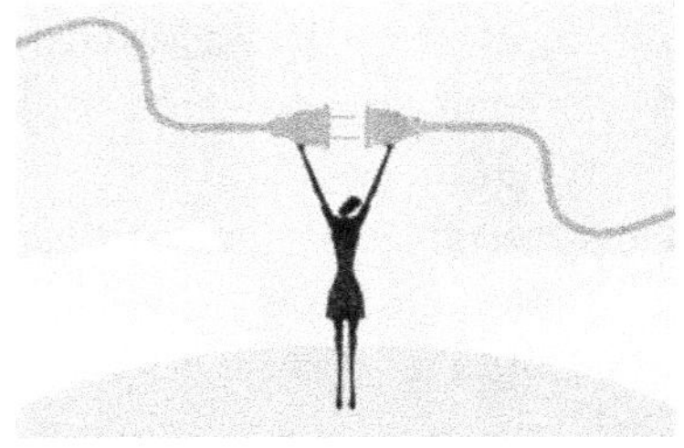

It is quite common to build a strategy around *adjacencies*, like finding new products for existing markets or finding new markets for existing products. Nothing wrong with that, but it requires a lot of preparatory work at all levels. If done hastily it could spell disaster for even your existing line of business. A *telecom services* company I was associated with bet big on its foray into *software development services*, banking on its good name for attracting exceptional *talent,* and on its relationships with OEMs to attract *business* for its new venture. Even with all the investment in getting people on-boarded, setting up facilities, etc. and launching an impressive global 'marketing' campaign, the venture never really took off. Instead of relying on a *strategic fit* the group had entered the venture on the assumption of *quid-pro-quo* deals with telecom OEMs. The core competence required for this venture was quite different from the proven skills it had in its mainstream telco business. To top that, there were established players who could do software development jobs better and cheaper. Unfortunately, the company had to lose money and eventually set itself up for an acquisition. Apparently, the business strategy here was out of sync with the core competence and brand positioning. On perhaps a smaller scale, this is what happens when our business plan is not supported by the IT roadmap. Incidentally, the above company later revamped its mission and strategy to *reinvent* itself as a developer of *software products* for telecom service providers globally – a field much better-aligned to its parent core competence – and achieved a turnaround to become a prime acquisition target of its giant competitors. The lesson here is that it may never be too late in the journey to invest in aligning your business strategy and the technology roadmap, even if you have suffered some knocks en route.

3. **Structural** alignment

Structural alignment is a form of synergy in the *skills, roles, and responsibilities* of Business and IT teams that lead them to accomplish their common mission. Some pointers:

- Business-led IT Organization
- Core competence defined and built
- Clear roles and responsibilities
- Unambiguous interfaces between Business and IT
- Think, build, and operate together

- Skills aligned with business direction
- Flexibility to adapt IT skills to changing business needs

Structural alignment has a lot to do with joint ownership of business outcomes, continuous skill upgradation and collaborative interworking leading to Business and IT complementing each other effectively and always. It is not only about creating congruent organization structures and reporting paths but, as we often observe in team sports, building synergy and solidarity leading to greater strength. Its absence achieves the opposite, as this example illustrates.

As engineering head for my company's delivery center in Bangalore, India, I once submitted a proposal in response to a customer inquiry from Texas, US. In a few weeks, I learned that our proposal had been accepted and that the customer had invited our company for the mandated 'technical-round.' I traveled all the way from Bangalore to Dallas, fully prepared to present our technical proposal and to answer all potential questions that may come from the customer on our approach and methodology. When the questions started after the presentation, however, I was in for a surprise. These questions were not directed at my colleagues or me. Instead, these were directed at the customer's own technology team from their business folks! The questions were as basic as their current IT capability, the share of responsibility between Business and IT, business benefits of the project, budget (who will pay), staff-availability for managing the project and the like. Obviously, the two functions rarely met and had no common interfaces. It almost became a scuffle between the customer's internal teams. We were simply mute, and somewhat embarrassed, spectators. The most surprising part was that this proposed project, for which we had submitted our partnering bid to this company, was to develop a solution for this company's *biggest global customer*! How would this company meet the expectations of its customer in the face of such apparent misalignment between its own business and technology arms? As it turned out, it didn't have to as the end customer scrapped the project which I strongly suspect was due to lack of a cohesive response from its existing supplier – the one that I presented to. While this example may seem extreme, it is not. It is likely that you'll find such examples around you, without having to traverse the globe! If you don't, you are better perched on your path to a strong BITA than many of your peers. Make the most of it – it's a clear competitive edge.

4. **Procedural** Alignment

Procedural alignment corresponds to an agreed set of *processes,* tools, procedures and methods that are directed towards leveraging technology for business success. Some pointers:

- Simple, flexible, adaptable processes
- Customer-centric business processes
- Tools adoption (automation)
- Focus on continuous improvement
- Quality focus
- Process innovation
- Risk control

Procedural alignment is about assuring that the IT delivery and operations processes in the organization stay tuned to the *changing* needs of the business. Let me emphasize this, though you know it already: the *processes* must align with the business, and *not* the other way. Nothing blunts your edge more than processes which remain static in a dynamic business world. This is also evidence of poor change management. It is particularly true of *automated* processes which are considered the Holy Grail in many companies and trump customer experience. Here's an example from the everyday experience of how some inflexible processes may cost the business.

Late one night, I arrived at the hotel I routinely stay in during my frequent business trips to a particular city in India. I was a proud owner of this hotel chain's 'privileged-guest' card. As always, I had a room reservation, and my secretary had duly printed out the reservation confirmation page, which I was carrying. I was shocked therefore when the gent at the front desk, after welcoming me back with a smile, cheerily informed me that I had no reservation. I protested this and showed him the confirmation sheet. The manager was summoned, and investigations started while I was asked to wait in the lobby. After a seemingly interminable period, the manager came to me with the triumphant expression of a man who has just solved a big mystery. It turned out there was a group of four other executives from my company scheduled to check in that evening, and a few hours ago they had *canceled* their booking. Their *system* which was designed to put *all* guests from a company in one bracket, automatically changed my *Confirmed* status to '*Wait-list: PAX Advice pending*' as per some apparently goofy logic and sent an auto intimation to the booking agent (*after* office hours apparently). The hotel manager meanwhile was visibly relieved as it was a big problem off his chest. After all, it was a *system* issue, not his doing: where in the world does one question an auto process? No, he said, I couldn't be confirmed as there were no longer any rooms available that night, but I could try in that other hotel miles from anywhere. It was now midnight. I managed something elsewhere at a rate beyond my approved limit, feeling very disgruntled at the treatment. I made sure that no one from my organization ever used this hotel again. I do hope my experience triggered a change in that hotel's process though I am not going back to find out! Process automation is well and good, but cannot substitute the application of common sense!

5. **Intellectual** Alignment

Intellectual alignment refers to Business and IT being on the same intellectual plane to drive technological *innovation*, *adoption* and *alliances* (with technology partners) to create an ambiance where IT is a *trusted advisor* to the Business on its transformation journey. Some pointers:

- Exploiting new technology for competitive advantage
- Adoption of Cloud, Big Data, Mobility, SM for business value creation
- Tracking new trends and piloting their adoption for business advantage
- Speed-to-market
- Incentivizing ideas and the spirit of Daring-To-Try
- Customer-feedback driven tech innovation
- Future-readiness of IT architecture and capabilities
- Conformance to standards (architecture, interfaces, protocols, etc.)

Intellectual alignment occurs when both Business and IT have a *shared passion* for creating or enhancing the present and future business value through the innovative use of technology. It goes beyond just demonstrating the *competence* to execute on your business strategy (which is a *structural alignment*). Kodak's inability to recognize the market potential of digital photography, which it *invented*, is a well-known and classic example of intellectual misalignment leading to a great company's downfall.

My long experience gives me the benefit of diving deeper into time to come up with relevant anecdotes from the past. I leave it to the reader to discover their connections to present-day scenarios. Back in the day, I was responsible for service operations of mini- and microcomputer systems in a region. The technology (and engineering) was nascent, and customers were unaccustomed to the use of computers, so problem incidences were high. We relied heavily on the availability of spare parts like electronic motherboards, interface cards, mechanical items (like print rollers), sensors, cable connectors, etc. These spare parts were democratically distributed across various offices in the country, in a decentralized fashion. Frantic calls to virtually every office store in an emergency, begging for a missing spare part while customers waited, were quite common! Recognizing the criticality of spares in the customer delivery value chain, there was a strong proposal from the IT support team for a central inventory management system to ensure availability where and when it was needed most. However, in the view of the business, this was a low priority issue since such a system would not be directly visible to the customers, and the manual system seemed to be 'okay' for current volumes, so there was not much sense in making any investment. Remember, this was before the Internet and most communication was through telephone calls. Eventually, our competitor seized this pioneering opportunity and got a lead over our company in service execution. Had there been better trust and alignment between Business and IT we could have become the first with what would have been an innovative introduction towards improving our customers' experience and making our profitability decidedly stronger. We missed the connection and paid the price!

6. **Functional** Alignment

Functional alignment between Business and IT is a harmonization of the priorities that drive their decisions, measurement and actions. Some pointers:

- Measurement of *Business-Value of IT*
- Collaborative prospecting, pre-sales, fulfillment and delivery
- Business-led IT funding
- Tuned to Voice-of-Customer
- *Business*-outcome driven IT delivery and operations
- Quick Time-to-market
- Success of digital initiatives (like marketing campaigns)

Functional alignment leads to *business-outcome-based IT* which we touched upon in Chapter-2 with examples from a few sectors. A simple example here from my own experience goes to demonstrate how unwise I was in basing my function's measurement system on a set of attributes which had almost no bearing on business results.

I was heading the technical support operations for an independent business unit that produced peripherals, mainly printers, for computer systems. It was a close-knit unit comprising the factory operations, sales & marketing, and technical support – which included on-site support. My stakeholders were clearly interested in metrics that provided useful information for them to act upon. For example, factory wanted to know the number and nature of defective arrivals so that they could use this to crank up the QA processes. Business wanted to know about the throughput or the number of days in which the print-head or cartridge required replacement so that they could plan their consumables sales accordingly. They would have also liked some benchmark data on usage trends, part-wise failure rates and the customers' overall satisfaction with our services and product performance. However, what my team and I did regularly present to the business (and factory) teams was data on total number of complaints in Sev1/2/3, average response and turn-around time for complaints, number of calls handled per engineer (productivity) etc. Only later did I realize that this served almost no practical purpose to my stakeholders. Now I recognize the folly of my actions and how mismatched my priorities were from those of the stakeholders, customer included. The saving grace, if it may be so termed, was that this was exactly how everyone else was doing it, so probably it didn't impact our competitive position at the time. However, looked at another way, had we indeed measured and acted based on the needs and priorities of the business, and focused more on the *outcome* than the internal attributes, we would have raced way ahead of the competition in terms of product quality, marketing, user delight and ultimately revenues. But we missed the bus! This example is a wake-up call to IT organizations that are inward focused as opposed to outcome-oriented. Any amount of introspection in hindsight is futile – reevaluate your measurement systems *today* and tune them to the business priorities.

7. **Tactical** Alignment

Tactical alignment refers to step-locking for *executing* the joint strategy through a supportive *service*, *operations* and *delivery infrastructure* designed to ensure an outstanding *customer experience* consistently. Some pointers:

- Successful project execution, e.g., digital transformation
- Supportive IT Infrastructure
- Shared ownership of customer experience (CLM)
- Collaborative change management process
- Delivery Excellence – Time, Cost and Quality
- Confidentiality, Integrity and Availability of business-critical data

For much of their histories, Business and IT have followed diverse tactical paths. The convergence, if any, ended with the overlap of certain items of strategy but as far as tactics were concerned, it was each to his own. The advent of the digital era has changed that. You cannot, for example, launch an app based product strategy (say a taxi-service) without Business and IT intricately collaborating at every step of the development and operations. Tactical alignment implies that Business and IT are complementing each other in the execution of their digitization strategy, particularly in delivering a superior experience to their customer throughout the lifecycle.

I was steering the development of an innovative product that our marketing research had shown would be hugely impactful in putting us on a growth trajectory. Our IT team and partners had done several internal workshops to nail the specs and prepare the shortest schedule for production. It was thus a surprise to see our company's advertisement on the TV one day announcing the product to the market at a date just a couple of weeks away, a *lot earlier* than the timetable available with my team! It turned out that this was the *original* launch date, but it had been *revised* (extended) in the IT project plan due to some new requirements that had come in later, and my team was very sure that the revised plan had been conveyed to marketing. Anyhow, there was no choice now but to bring the product into the market on the publicly announced date and we did. However, this entailed short-cuts in user testing, insufficient time for a pilot run, and an inability to provide sufficient training to teams handling complaints, customer inquiries etc. Even our channels were not fully ready to handle the sales relating to this product. Obviously, the business and the IT project teams were moving in an uncoordinated way. Owing to this lack of alignment between Business and IT through the development phase, we faced a lot of turbulence in the early days. It took us a great deal of effort and cost to stabilize the product, and we probably lost a share of the business and perhaps some credibility in the market. In hindsight, had there been a small investment of time and effort in ensuring that Business and IT worked shoulder-to-shoulder through this critical project, a lot of subsequent grief could have been avoided. Evidently, an unwavering tactical alliance that always keeps Business and IT on the same page on market commitments has no substitute, particularly in this digital era.

About the BITA Calculator

The BITA calculator is a simple assessment tool for estimating your BITA score. It consists of a set of statements, each of which can be responded by a Y if true, else left blank. These statements are designed to estimate your scores with respect to the seven dimensions of BITA and calculate your overall BITA Index. The statements are scattered, i.e., not bunched into dimensions, to avoid extempore responses. Each statement tests your alignment to a dimension, though some statements may map to more than one dimension. It is a first attempt at creating a measuring tool of this kind and I do concede that there is room for making it more situational, precise and entertaining. As I work on refining this, I hope it serves the important purpose of marking your bearings on your BITA journey and sets you in the right direction towards your goal. You can, of course, modify the tool by inserting more statements, deleting or editing some statements, and creating different versions, as you advance on your journey. You can also set your own 'benchmarks' on what constitutes a low or a high score and use these for tracking trends over time.

Method:

1. Appoint a tool administrator (TA).
2. The TA will load the statements on an excel file and distribute this among selected respondents
3. (Paper version using photocopies would do too, with some loss of flexibility, if respondents are few, typically up to 3 or 4.)
4. You can also download the excel version of the tool from *AlignedToWin.Com*, or use a standard survey tool available on the net by inputting these statements (e.g., surveymonkey.com), or even create a small app

of your own to run this widely, but that's entirely a matter of preference.

5. The TA will guide the respondents as necessary in completing the feedback.
6. It is recommended to initially run this tool with a small and experienced group of not more than four individuals – perhaps two each from Business and IT.
7. Ask the respondents to input clear and accurate *Y* (yes) or *blank* (no) responses to each statement and mail/submit this back to the TA.
8. For each Y, the TA will enter a 1 in the *Score-sheet* against the statement number, under the appropriate dimension using the *check-sheet* (scoring guide) as key.
9. Finally, the TA will add up the 1s under each dimension and compute the dimension wise and overall BITA score for each respondent. This simple process is further exemplified below.
10. The composite score of multiple respondents is the *average* of all responses against each dimension. It is a good practice to report scores for Business, IT and Enterprise level separately.

As we go through this chapter, this process will be further crystallized. For best results, I suggest you run the test with several key members of both Business and IT organizations and average the result. Initially, this exercise is recommended to be conducted quarterly to assess (and plot) the trends, and once your benchmark index is reached, you may reduce the frequency to once or twice a year.

An illustration of scoring is given below. It is quite straightforward. Take a blank *Score-sheet* (provided in this chapter) and keep it alongside the *Check-sheet* (which is also provided). The *Check-sheet* is a reference table which is the key to map a statement to a dimension. The check-sheet is not shown to the respondents and is available with the TA only. For each statement that is responded with a Y, the scorer (typically the TA) puts a 1 in the *Score-sheet under the corresponding dimension.* If the response is *not* Y, nothing is scored

CHECK Sheet

St.No.	Culture	Strategy	Structure	Process	Intellect	Function	Tactics
1	1						
2					1		
3		1					
4				1		1	

SCORE Sheet							
Statement	Culture	Strategy	Structure	Process	Intellect	Function	Tactics
1							
2					1		
3		1					
4							

for that statement. For example, let us say we have just 4 statements, and the response is Y against statements 2 and 3. As statements 1 and 4 are *not* Ys, nothing is scored in these rows on the Score-sheet. For statements 2 and 3, which are Y, look at the Check-sheet to determine the *dimension* under which 1 is to be entered. Here, these happen to be Intellect and Strategy respectively. This is helpful as an illustration, but over simplistic. An actual BITA computation depicting the total counts for each dimension may appear as follows (this is an *example*):

	Table-1: ***Example***								
	BUSINESS or IT or OVERALL								
	<Name>	Culture	Strategy	Structure	Process	Intellect	Function	Tactics	BITA
A	Max Y-count (*Fixed-do not change*)	22	18	18	25	22	24	29	158
B	Raw Y-Count (Actual Count)	12	8	10	6	8	5	8	57
C	Score ((B/A)*100	55	44	56	24	36	21	28	**37.6**

The last row provides the dimension scores on a scale of 100. In the above example, the overall BITA score is 37.6 (out of 100). If there are 4 respondents, take the *average* total for each dimension and enter this in Row-B to get the overall dimension scores and the overall BITA. For example, if the totals of 1s under Culture for 4 respondents is 13, 15, 11 and 9, then enter 12 as the count for Culture. Later we will look at what each score value/range signifies, and what should be a *good* BITA score.

To the extent possible, the statements are objective and unambiguous. However, in few of the questions, you may have to use your best judgment. If in doubt, do *not* answer with Y.

We contended earlier that Business and IT must **think, build, and operate** *together* for true and sustained alignment that leads to long-term business value. Following this principle, the BITA measurement tool consists of three sets of statements clustered under the Think, Build, and Operate (TBO) axes. Your quick Y/Blank responses to these statements will therefore not only enable you to ascertain if you need to ramp up your efforts on any of the TBO axes, but also provide a comprehensive view of your score on each of the *seven dimensions* of BITA and the overall BITA level for your organization.

We will discuss the Think, Build, and Operate axes in some detail in the next section, during the discourse on BITA-driven organization structure. Here, I have used the TBO distribution only to group the statements. The definitions of Think, Build, and Operate are included in the box above the tables. I have found it useful to cluster the statements into T, B, O, but let me stress that if you wish, you may focus only on the BITA score on the seven dimensions, and skip the TBO aspects for now.

While getting as many views as possible is always a good idea and results in a more accurate analysis, it adds to the overheads of computation. Hence it may be worthwhile to run this tool with a select but significant set of IT and Business people in your organization. It is recommended to get the CIO, solution architects, IT delivery and operations managers, CMO, Product Manager, Customer Service head and Account Managers on-boarded for this. As an alternative, you may like to have a *dedicated workshop* on BITA with a group of chosen participants and as part of this workshop, this tool can be run to determine your BITA index. As a progressive enterprise, the modality of conducting the assessment is a matter of your preference but it is a good practice to run this periodically in whichever manner suits your organization. Organizations that have a clear view of where they stand on their BITA journey have a far better chance of succeeding in their digital mission.

Let us get started. Keep about 30 minutes for completing each of the three sections (T, B, O). Use the first response (*Yes* or *not*) that comes to your mind after you read the statement. Do not pause to reflect or overthink. I have found that instinctive responses generally lead to more accurate results.

The statements are intended to be responded by both Business and IT people. It is important that the respondents are reasonably familiar with the company's Business and Technology landscape. In an aligned organization, it is *expected* that Business is aware of the direction of its IT and vice versa. In an organization that is aspiring to lead in the digital economy, *all* the team members of both Business and IT organizations should have at least a general awareness of their shared beliefs, strategy, tactics etc. on which the statements are based. Some statements are *designed* to be subjective so that individual *opinions* from folks at different levels (not just CXOs) may be factored in the BITA score. Still, if you happen to be *not* sure of the truth of a statement, you are advised to respond with 'N' (or blank). For example, you are *expected* to know – whether you are from Business or IT organization – if the company's "Long-Term business strategy is the basis of IT roadmap and architecture." If you do not have a clue about this, then consider N (blank) for this statement. Even if at some level this statement is accurate, from *your* perspective it is not. But most statements, hopefully, will not cause such dilemmas!

The list is by no means a comprehensive one for each dimension. For example, the statements mapping to 'Tactics' should not be taken to be a complete list of *all* that is required for tactical alignment. However, I do believe it gives a good sense of the state of alignment under each of the seven dimensions. It should point you to the dimensions that you need to prioritize to improve your overall BITA index and bring out your *hidden* strengths/weaknesses. In more advanced versions, the statements may be tailored as per the organization's maturity, assigned weights according to its needs and priorities, and have graded responses on say, a 5-point scale than a simple 1 or 0.

THINK: Plan- Strategy, Roadmap Design- Innovation, Improvement Share- Knowledge, Ideas, Culture Measure- Trends, Analysis

S.No	Statement	Response
1	I have participated in a belief session conducted by our top management at least once in last 1 year	
2	IT in our organization is not just a support arm for technical services, but also advises business on technology trends and practices	
3	We have a clearly articulated mission, frequently reinforced by the top management, that envisages the use of digital technologies as a vehicle for enterprise growth	
4	Business outcomes (like time-to-market, effectiveness of digital campaigns) are a measure of IT success in our company	
5	We have a supportive IT foundation on which the future business services can be built quickly and efficiently. That is, our IT architecture is not an obstacle to our future growth.	
6	If I have a great technical idea, I feel encouraged to walk up to the CTO/CIO or CMO to discuss it	
7	We have regular Business-IT interlocks to assure that our IT processes and systems are tuned to the ever-evolving needs of the business	
8	One of our strengths is our business savvy IT folks, most of whom understand the competitive landscape, regulations, customer expectations etc	
9	One of our strengths is our technology savvy business folks, most of whom are familiar with concepts like IP, IT architecture, Cloud, Big data etc	
10	Sensing from the present momentum, I feel quite confident that we will meet our digital transformation objectives, in the next one year. (This is my opinion)	
11	I feel empowered because I know exactly how my work is contributing to my company's business	
12	Business and IT often have joint brain-storming sessions to arrive at make or buy decisions, driven by Time-to-Market or Cost considerations	
13	We have many success stories of Business and IT achieving together (winning business, solving customer problems) that I believe could be used to attract fine talent in our company	
14	I can recall at least one offsite event (office get-together, outing, social function) in the last one year in which both Business and IT folks took part (not just the CIO and CMO but larger group)	
15	I have gone through our IT strategy. It is well aligned with the Business strategy. It won't be wrong to say that our IT's mission is to make the business successful.	
16	I have been part of a meeting where Business and IT shared and debated their strategy/roadmap with each other	
17	Our competitive landscape, offerings portfolio, customer expectations and strategy is explained to IT during induction of employees (and/or through subsequent programs) by Business	
18	We understand that market is dynamic. Hence we reassess IT skills yearly on both Technology and Business attributes, if necessary through external consultant	
19	In my experience I have found that senior business leaders in our company directly interact with our tech specialists on business/customer issues. We do not follow a hierarchy-driven protocol.	
20	As a Business (IT) person I have participated in at least one IT (Business) training program as student or instructor in last 6 months	
21	We engage with diverse stakeholders including partners, suppliers and customers for their inputs in charting our business/IT roadmap on the path to innovation and growth.	
22	Our technology capabilities, architecture and roadmap is explained to Business during employee induction and/or in successive programs by IT	

THINK: Plan- Strategy, Roadmap Design- Innovation, Improvement Share-Knowledge, Ideas, Culture Measure- Trends, Analysis

S.No	Statement	Response
23	We periodically benchmark our IT operations performance with the industry-leaders and reset our targets to meet or exceed these	
24	We have an empowered technology council for evaluating new ideas relating to products, services, campaigns etc, which consists of nominated persons from both Business and IT	
25	One of the reasons I am happy to be in this company is the opportunities offered for skill building in new technology domains.	
26	I attended at least one training program on new business or technology trends in last three months	
27	Inititaives towards learning and adoption of new technology, like participation in development programs, matter in my performance appraisal.	
28	Selection of a technology partner for products, services or consulting involves acceptance of both Business and IT teams in our company	
29	I was in a product or technology training program in the last 6 months where both business and IT folks participated	
30	In our last company R&R event, there was at least one award given for an innovative idea around use of new technology	
31	I am encouraged by my company to participate in industry events and seminars on technology trends. I have attended at least 1 in last 6 months	
32	Rotations across Business and IT functions through internal job postings are encouraged. I know of at least 3 such cases.	
33	The motivation and push for investing in new technology in our company often comes from the business team	
34	As an IT person, each performance objective in my goal sheet can be linked to an element of the business strategy. I therefore understand how my work impacts the Business	
35	Enterprise Architecture (EA), eTOM, TOGAF etc are some standard frameworks that aid Business-IT alignment. My organzaition has adopted standard frameworks in its IT architecture.	
36	I have participated in discussions between Business and IT for finalizing the high level design of products or customizations	
37	The speed and precision with which our IT is able to translate new concepts into revenue generating products and services is an undisputed competitive advantage for our company. I can cite examples.	
38	There is an annual Internal Customer Satisfaction Survey conducted in our company to assess improvement areas	
39	In our company no project or investment plan is final until both Business and IT have agreed upon it	
40	We have seasoned Technical Architects in our organization to help the business identify, design and build customer solutions based on emerging technologies.	
41	Over 50% of our IT investment in the year is for developing or supporting business transformation (new offerings, differentiation, digital enablment - SMAC)	
42	Apart from being IT experts, several of our IT people bring in good knowledge of our industry domain and are engaged by Business as thought leaders and strategic advisors.	
43	In the course of routine Business-IT review meetings, it is normal for IT to report on cost savings achieved through various initiatives (like re-use).	

BUILD: Collaborate- Governance, Teamwork Construct- Process, Organization Deliver- Projects, Solutions Deploy- Technology, Best-practices Optimize- Time, Cost, Quality

S.No	Statement	Response
44	My company's performance rules require bottom performers to be resssigned or eased out	
45	As a Business (IT) person, I routinely go for my lunch with IT (Business) colleagues (respectively)	
46	Business and IT celebrate their wins together in our company	
47	As far as I know, before finalizing our IT organization structure our CIO/CTO has discussions with Business Heads for their inputs and agreement	
48	We have Business Analysts (or equivalent) in our company as single-point interface between business and IT	
49	My performance goals and KRAs are dependent on the business achieving its mission. That is, if the business fails, I fail, irrespective of whether I am from the Business or IT team.	
50	Outcome-based IT is a well-entrenched concept in my organization. For example, "Boosting customer engagement via Digital Channels" could equally be a goal for IT as well as Business	
51	Decision to bid for a contract is made jointly by Business and IT (except in case of 'standard' offers)	
52	Our IT strategy and status are part of the agenda of our company's Board meetings (to my knowledge)	
53	We have systems to identify unexpected gaps between Business and IT strategies due to market dynamics etc and make timely course corrections.	
54	We hold a customer meet at least once a year with our key customers (and/or partners) which is attended by leaders from both Business and IT	
55	The processes in our organization, at least those that I am familiar with, are designed to make it easy for people to get things done	
56	IT team members routinely participate in sales/marketing conferences in our company	
57	We are able to respond quickly to business needs because our process workflow, particularly for IT requests, is designed to be fast and quick, with minimum approvals	
58	Business teams share the updated plans and progress with designated members of IT team (e.g. BA) every month in our organization	
59	Our IT organization is quick to align its skills and/or structure with the changing needs of the business. That is, the market landscape drives the IT development programs	
60	I believe that our IT is spending more time and money on 'Change the Business' (transformation and new initiatives) than on 'Run the Business' (routine operations, upkeep, keeping the light bulbs on).	
61	We have launched products or services in the market based on at least one of these - IOT, Cloud, Mobility (apps), Big Data	
62	Our IT processes are well documented and available on a public folder (or Intranet), accessible to both Business and IT	
63	For some IT/Technology positions, it is common in our company for busines leaders to interview (IT) candidates	
64	We have a new product introduction process clearly outlined which requires business and IT to work together on a new market offering from its inception to launch	

BUILD: Collaborate- Governance, Teamwork Construct- Process, Organization Deliver- Projects, Solutions Deploy- Technology, Best-practices Optimize- Time, Cost, Quality

S.No	Statement	Response
65	Our marketing campaign relies on customer data managed by IT. A formal process exists for Business and IT to jointly assure veracity of customer data.	
66	Our change management process for delivering IT products and customizations (change requests) is agreed with Business	
67	The User Acceptance Testing of IT deliverables is conducted exclusively by the Business (without IT intervention)	
68	I count our ability to launch new business services on time as one of our organizational strengths.	
69	Our IT development follows the iterative (agile) model to incorporate changing business requirements without hampering our time-to-market for new offerings.	
70	Business and Technology teams meet frequently and regularly (say every week) specifically to discuss pending and/or escalated customer issues	
71	Business and IT together review (steer) critical or transformational IT projects through senior level involvement (governance)	
72	Customer feedback is the trigger for Business and IT to interlock for the deployment of enhanced offerings like e-commerce platform, cloud based services, mobility etc. I can cite at least one example.	
73	Finalizing the specifications and design for new IT development is accomplished collaboratively with inputs and agreement from both Business and IT	
74	We lay strong emphasis on information security. However our security stance is not an impediment to smooth business conduct.	
75	Business and IT commonly work together in preparing response to an RFP	
76	We have invested in tools to gauge our customers' sentiments through social media and use this to calibrate our response to customers	

Aligned to WIN

OPERATE: Execute- Sell, Service, Install Monitor- Process, Performance, Cost Control- Assets, Policies Support- Customer experience, Enterprise productivity, Data privacy & security

S.No	Statement	Response
77	We promote and encourage BYOD in our organization	
78	The quality of the business outcome (like customer experience, revenue growth, speed-to-market) is a measure of IT performance too in our company	
79	More often than not, I talk to the person who sits on the same floor as me, than send them an email	
80	If my business card described me as a Customer Satisfier instead of my present title, it would do full justice to my role. By Customer here I mean the end, or external, customer.	
81	Our ability to offer personalized customer solutions based on use of advanced technologies like Big Data is a undisputed success factor for the company.	
82	Business and IT regularly review the customer service data (like response time to complaints, escalated problems etc) as a strong indicator of customer's overall perception about us	
83	Business and technology teams routinely particpate together in meetings with technology partners/vendors in our company	
84	IT budget is owned by the business as it has a direct impact on the P&L. Therefore, Business and IT jointly decide on business case for IT expenditure.	
85	Business and IT are also jointly engaged in innovation and transformation in methods of doing business, e.g. proposals, offers, campaigns, bills and receipts, upsells	
86	Participation of the relevant team members from IT organization in business conferences is a routine matter in our company	
87	Our IT team members often visit our dealers/stores to assess the market pulse and experiences of local staff in working with our IT systems	
88	We track Business Value of IT focusing on business outcomes influenced by IT (like Customer Experience, Revenue/Upsells, Cost-Savings) rather than IT-centric metrics like Uptime	
89	Business and IT periodically meet to discuss the feasibility of current IT services - e.g. applications that can be retired, merged, consolidated, enhanced or upgraded	
90	My company has the IT tools and expertise to gather and act upon market intelligence and/or voice-of-customer in a consistent and timely manner	
91	I am part of, or am aware of, the regular forums in which expenditure on IT infrastructure and services (capex and opex) is reported by IT to Business	
92	I have the right tools, connectivity and devices to access the data I require for making decisions that impact my internal and external customers	
93	A mechanism exists in our company to get customer feedback on quality of our service/product and use this to improve the quality	
94	In the last 30 days there have been at least two joint visits by business and IT folks to a customer site	
95	As a Business (or IT) person, I know exactly whom to go to if I have an IT (or Business) problem (respectively).	
96	Our IT systems undergo annual refresh cycles and/or system upgrades and/or capacity dimensioning in consultation with Business to keep pace with the changing business requirements	

OPERATE: Execute- Sell, Service, Install Monitor- Process, Performance, Cost Control- Assets, Policies Support- Customer experience, Enterprise productivity, Data privacy & security

S.No	Statement	Response
97	We have regular (scheduled) forums for presentation by IT to Business on customer operations and delivery performance and trends	
98	In our company both Business and IT are in the 'front end' delivering customer proposals, solutions, service. IT is not a back end function.	
99	We do not launch a new product or service until we have built the capability in IT to fully support it in the market	
100	Once Business and IT have agreed on a plan, I would not hesitate to announce it publicly, including to customers. I have confidence in IT's ability to deliver on their promise.	
101	At least once in 6 months, IT updates business on the capacity of the IT infrastructure (servers, storage, bandwidth etc) to support business needs and decide jointly on next steps	
102	We have an agreed business continuity plan to keep our essential services working in the event of a calamity that shuts down our core IT systems	
103	Customers and business folks can access our customer complaints tracking tool without IT intervention	
104	After the resolution of major customer complaints, IT team provides a root cause analysis report to business team	
105	Our Change Management Process sets clear roles and responsibilities for Business and IT in various stages of the delivery cycle. I understand the process clearly.	

Some of the statements may appear daunting initially, especially if you are from an organization where Business and IT do interwork but are not strongly aligned. This is by design, as BITA is also about Business and IT having an in-depth understanding of issues affecting themselves and each other. Further, not everyone using the tool is expected to be at the same level of BITA, which necessitates a heterogeneous mix.

To create sufficient copies of the statement sets to administer the test, you may do one of the following:

1. Take photocopies of the statement sets and blank scoring sheet from this book
2. Make the one-time effort of entering all the statements and the scoring sheet in a simple excel sheet in the format shown. This has the advantage of allowing you to tailor the statements if you so wish.
3. Download the excel from the website AlignedToWin.Com. This has all the formulas for score computation and generating a radar graph along the 7 dimensions.

These are minor practical issues and matters of detail. The important thing is to rally your organization on the path to attaining high BITA which as we discussed is a matter of survival – and not choice – for all businesses aiming to capitalize on the new opportunities in the digital economy. Do not let any minor hurdle deviate you from this goal as a huge price may have to be paid later for small omissions now.

The Check-sheet to be used for scoring on the individual dimensions is included below. Once the respondent has submitted the completed statement-sets, the statements responded with a Y may be scored as per this check-sheet. There is no score to be given for statements that do not have a Y response. Put a 1 in the Score-sheet (blank score-sheet is included in this chapter) for each statement that is marked Y, *under the relevant dimension(s)* as per the Check-sheet. Please note that some of the statements have two dimensions associated with them. For these statements, a Y response would lead to 1 score under *each* of the two dimensions – say Function and Tactics.

CHECK Sheet

Sl.No.	Culture	Strategy	Structure	Process	Intellect	Function	Tactics
1	1						
2					1		
3		1					
4				1		1	
5		1					
6	1						
7					1		
8			1				
9			1				
10		1			1		
11	1						
12		1					
13	1					1	
14	1					1	
15		1					
16		1				1	
17			1		1		
18			1				
19	1		1				
20	1						
21		1					
22			1		1		
23		1					1
24					1		
25			1		1		
26	1				1		
27	1						
28						1	1
29			1		1		
30	1				1		
31					1		
32	1		1				
33	1				1		
34		1					
35				1	1		
36				1			
37		1				1	
38	1			1			
39		1		1			
40			1				
41		1					
42			1		1		
43						1	
44	1						
45	1						
46	1						
47			1				
48			1				
49	1	1					
50		1					
51						1	
52		1			1		
53		1					
54						1	
55				1			
56	1					1	
57				1			
58		1				1	
59			1			1	
60						1	
61					1		1
62				1			
63	1		1				
64				1	1		
65					1	1	
66				1			
67				1			1
68				1			
69				1			
70							1
71				1		1	
72					1		
73				1			1
74				1			1
75						1	1
76				1			1
77	1				1		
78				1		1	
79	1						
80	1						
81				1			1
82						1	1
83							1
84						1	
85					1		1
86			1				1
87						1	1
88						1	
89							1
90						1	1
91						1	
92							1
93				1			1
94						1	
95			1				1
96				1			1
97				1			1
98			1				
99					1		1
100		1					1
101							1
102				1			1
103				1			1
104				1			1
105							1
	22	18	18	25	22	24	29

THINK. Scoring Sheet *(For Y response put 1 below corresponding dimension. Else leave blank)*

Statement Number	Culture	Strategy	Structure	Process	Intellect	Function	Tactics
1							
2							
3							
4							
5							
6							
7							
8							
9							
10							
11							
12							
13							
14							
15							
16							
17							
18							
19							
20							
21							
22							
23							
24							
25							
26							
27							
28							
29							
30							
31							
32							
33							
34							
35							
36							
37							
38							
39							
40							
41							
42							
43							

BUILD. Scoring Sheet *(For Y response put 1 below corresponding dimensions. Else leave blank)*

Statement Number	Culture	Strategy	Structure	Process	Intellect	Function	Tactics
44							
45							
46							
47							
48							
49							
50							
51							
52							
53							
54							
55							
56							
57							
58							
59							
60							
61							
62							
63							
64							
65							
66							
67							
68							
69							
70							
71							
72							
73							
74							
75							
76							

OPERATE. Scoring Sheet *(For Y response put 1 below corresponding dimensions. Else leave blank)*

Statement Number	Culture	Strategy	Structure	Process	Intellect	Function	Tactics
77							
78							
79							
80							
81							
82							
83							
84							
85							
86							
87							
88							
89							
90							
91							
92							
93							
94							
95							
96							
97							
98							
99							
100							
101							
102							
103							
104							
105							

The scores may be entered as shown in table-1. The actual count of 1s in each dimension is entered in row B (shaded) as below, while Row-A is the *max* possible count, that, is the total number of statements corresponding to that dimension out of the full set. That is, 22 statements correspond to Culture, 18 to Strategy, and so on. You may note that the total number of statements is 105, but the total of Row-A is 158. This is because some of the statements correspond to two dimensions.

The score for each dimension is calculated on a base of 100 by simply taking the ratio of Actual (row-B) and Maximum (Row-A) count and multiplying by 100.

	Table-1: ***Example***								
	BUSINESS or IT or OVERALL								
	<Name>	Culture	Strategy	Structure	Process	Intellect	Function	Tactics	BITA
A	Max Y-count (Fixed-do not change)	22	18	18	25	22	24	29	158
B	Raw Y-Count (Actual Count)	12	8	10	6	8	5	8	57
C	Score ((B/A)*100	55	44	56	24	36	21	28	**37.6**

Plotting the final scores (row-C) on a radar graph as drawn here gives an excellent relational view of the scores on each dimension, and I prefer this graph-type to others, though you may choose your own. The graph tells us here that while the organization has relatively good Cultural and Structural alignment, it needs to pull up its Procedural (Process), Functional and Tactical alignment which is way below, and in parallel, it should also analyze the reasons for the lower level of alignment on the Strategic and Intellectual levels. In the next section, we shall go into the depths of each dimension and discuss ways to improve the levels. As we said earlier, all dimensions are connected. For example, if you align strongly on your strategy, without strengthening the capacity to execute it (tactical alignment), it wouldn't take you very far. Or, if you align on strategy and tactics dimensions but lack the structure (people, competencies) and process alignment required to deliver, the desired outcomes will elude you.

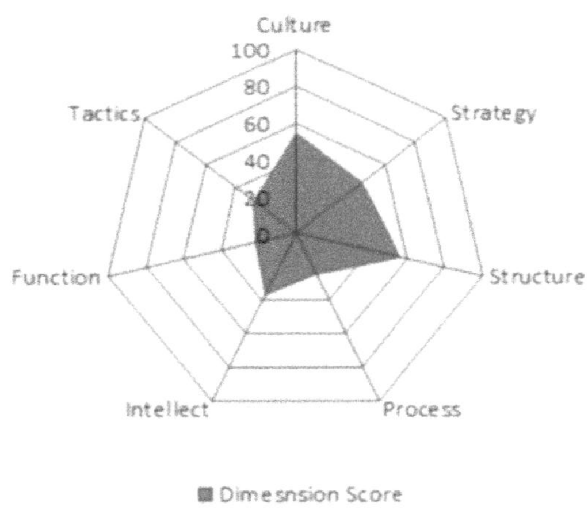

What's a good BITA score?

If you are expecting a centum score on BITA – or even any of its dimensions – you are setting yourself up for frustration and disappointment. Let's face it. There are far too many variables in every dimension of BITA for any one enterprise to achieve perfection in the initial attempt. However, CAN you reach 100 on BITA or any of its dimensions? The answer is YES! But let's not get too ambitious about it and set our goals more realistically.

There are no benchmarks yet available for the BITA scores. Hence, I am relying on my own assessment which is based on the scores of enterprises at different stages of BITA . When I performed the test for that one organization (can't name it) which I rate the highest in BITA among the few organizations that I considered, I achieved an average of 55-60 on each dimension and an overall BITA of 59. Does this mean this is the most one can aspire to? Probably not. It is certainly rewarding to aim higher, and more importantly, to *grow* from wherever you may be right now. For this reason, I may put an organization which has moved from, say, 25 to 40 a bit higher than the organization that is stagnating at 45 in the same period.

On the other hand, another company that I conducted this test for (again, can't name it) surprisingly scored as low as 7-10 on culture, strategy, process, intellect and function alignment while it scored 20 on tactical alignment. Overall, it was at about 12. Having some knowledge of where this company is in its thought process and actions regarding BITA, I think this should form the lower end of BITA scale. Anything lower would indeed make it rather uphill to achieve a respectable score.

Going by my experiments, and I hope to corroborate this with actual data in the coming months, companies with an overall BITA score of over 50 in their first assessment should feel reasonably good about their prospects in the digital economy. Taking this further, the progressive score ranges and the *targeted* semesterly improvement in the scores would be as per this table:

SN	BITA Status – where are you on your BITA journey	Score Range (Overall BITA, Dimensions)	Semesterly improvement Target	Retest in
1	Excellent – Well settled	80+	Maintain	1 year
2	Very Good – Arrived	60 - 80	10%	9 months
3	Good – Almost there	50 - 60	20%	6 months
4	Fair – On the right track	40 - 50	25%	6 months
5	Deficient –Need course correction	30 - 40	25%	3 months
6	Low –Lack momentum	20 - 30	35%	3 months
7	Non-existent – Not started	< 20	50%	2 months

It would be helpful to further plot a line graph for each dimension (and the overall BITA score) to monitor the trends. Any dimension showing a*downward* movement should immediately ring an alert and must become the focus of instant correction.

Variants are possible which may perhaps yield more accurate results. One such could be to rate each statement on a scale of 0 to 4 (Never Demonstrated → Major Strength) instead of just 0 or 1, and calculate the scores accordingly. This will enable monitoring the improvement at the level of each *statement*. There is indeed great scope for innovating as we go to make this tool a very precise indicator of BITA in your organization.

7 Setting the Stage for the Digital Enterprise

Thus far in this book, our focus has been on the importance of Business-Technology alignment in the digital era and its role as an enabler of success for the digital enterprise. We established that as the focus of technology has shifted to *business* outcome, one can no longer separate Business from Technology. In other words, Business and IT are fused together at the level of their culture, strategy, structure (people), process, intellect, function, and tactics (execution). If you have taken the BITA test, you are probably more aware now of your strengths and shortcomings along these dimensions and hence better geared to manage technology as an effective tool for assuring your business success.

Much as Business Management and People Management have been integral to enterprise success, the new economy also requires a strong focus on *Technology Management* as a driver of growth and success. Technology Management – or Managing Technology for Business – is a vast subject which is quickly emerging as a coveted discipline of management study and research. Technology Management does not necessitate in-depth and intricate knowledge of technology itself but requires honing the qualities that lead to its effective use for business. We cannot go into all its myriad aspects in this book but will look at it from a very practical and experiential standpoint and highlight the required traits and behaviors for achieving business success by effectively leveraging technology.

Technology now has the power to alter the business and market landscape of any industry completely. And it has exploited this power to the hilt (see next example)! Alignment between technology and business in this backdrop, therefore, must be a key strategic priority for the digital enterprise. As obvious as this may seem, most businesses have not been successful in driving this alignment within their organizations, as they have relied on conventional approaches and idealistic assumptions. The truth is, be it Business or Technology, people are too focused on their short-term objectives to seriously work on harmonizing their Business and IT imperatives, which 'sounds like a great thing to do, but not right now.' Obviously, an approach that does not rely on re-engineering but instead works on the level of *injecting BITA into the organisation's DNA* is the solution. And this, in turn, brings us back to the seven dimensions we earlier introduced, which we will use as the genetic code to program the successful digital enterprise.

If you search the web, you will find several approaches and frameworks for achieving Business-IT synchronicity, and these are commonly built around harmonizing the Business and IT strategies, processes and organizational structures. This, however, is only a subset that may not be enough to paint the complete canvas. Even after more than a decade that this has been a subject of discussion and action, most organizations cannot boast of having reached the level of alignment required drive their continuous growth in a tough market. Clearly, successfully navigating the ocean of digital business requires a more inclusive and *rounded* approach to alignment which focuses on *each* of the *seven* dimensions that are now familiar to us.

The term 'rounded' is the key here, by which we mean that isolated focus on a set of dimensions (like strategy, process, and structure) while ignoring others is *not* going to get you to your destination safely and quickly. Thus, in the instances depicted below, A is the BITA score we achieved in the example we studied in chapter-6 (inserted here for reference only), and B & C are hypothetical illustrations of higher BITA scores. Here, while B represents a slightly *lower* BITA than C, it is a much more *'rounded'* achievement (i.e., comparable achievements along *all* dimensions), and hence preferable to C which is a somewhat higher BITA score overall but does not stack up comparably on the Intellect dimension. This lack of roundedness in my experience has been the single biggest reason for organizations not achieving targeted long-term

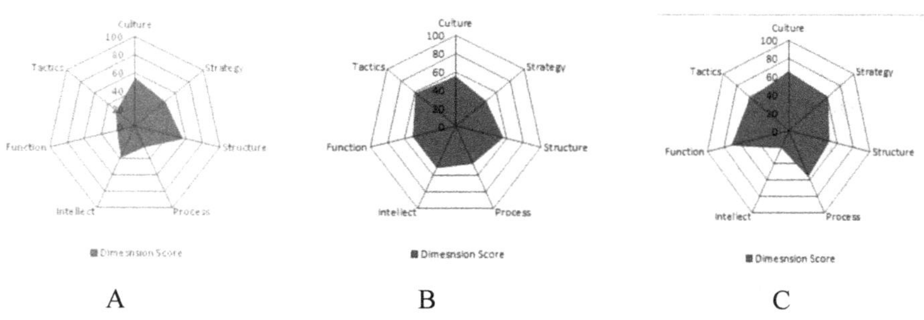

success in their digital endeavors, despite good intentions and effort. In the absence of a tool to measure along every dimension of BITA, an enterprise that prides itself on, say, its strategic and functional alignment may yet rue the fact that business results are not commensurate with expectations. They'd probably take the view that this whole BITA thing is just hype, as they would not know that a *lack of intellectual alignment* is at the root of their travails. By using the BITA tool covering a good mix of Business and IT folks in your organization you should be able to identify such depressions and then work to smoothen them out. Hopefully, this should clear the path for your future growth.

That the digital era is upon us is unquestionable. Yet, many believe that they can brace the winds of change it brings without adjusting their sails, basing this on their record of doing nothing in times of upheaval and still surviving! Their refrain is: 'Haven't there been environmental changes, economic upheavals, increased competition and other barriers in the past? These have not proven to be mill-stones, and our success stories have been unaffected. So why change now? The new upstarts are the ones that need to worry.' Of course, this is not an openly stated position by most companies, but deep down there is a nonchalance, a smugness that this entire thing is over-hyped and that beyond some surface-level alterations, it is pretty much business as usual. How wrong they are! One can only wish that they will wake up before it is too late (many are already lining up the waysides) and take some quick steps in the right direction.

On the other extreme are the new wave digital enterprises (disruptors) riding on a surge of innovation, chiefly technological. They have achieved a great deal of success early in the game and are therefore firmly of the view that their way is the only way. Many of them scoff at conventional business management and organizational practices as 'oh so old-school.' This view is also not sustainable. Neither can one entirely ignore digital transformation, even tacitly, nor can one bypass all established practices of business management and conduct. Clearly, a middle path must be discovered on which both these proponents may walk. Therefore, we stress the need for a *well-rounded* alignment between business and technology, considering all the seven dimensions as of equal significance in attaining long-term business value.

The environment is fast changing to adapt to the mores of the digital enterprise and a digitally enabled world. Consider as an example the upheaval in financial services on the back of the digital revolution. Quite like instant messaging surpassing SMS, new ways of conducting business transactions digitally will surpass conventional banking services.

1. The mobile revolution has changed the way we access and use computers for banking and other financial services. In a mobile internet-based environment, you are always connected. Everywhere.
2. As we move from a cash-based society to a digital community riding on the back of a billion mobile users having access to mobile data through initiatives like Digital India, there is potential to link everyone's Unique ID (like Aadhar card, or SSN) with the mobile number and use this ID to authenticate as well as access a wide range of digital services. The potential is limitless.
3. Electronic clearing services like NEFT-RTGS and IMPS have already overtaken traditional payment systems. When all the billion plus mobile users are provided access to digital banking services through these means, it will be a mega trend which will completely revolutionize the economy. Imagine, every mobile phone will be a veritable ATM with the ability to send and receive money, pay for goods and services, transfer funds etc.!
4. Biometric authentication linked with Aadhar (Unique ID), will enable a billion plus mobile users to have online KYC (Know Your Customer – a system of record for validating customer data by banks and financial institutions), online payment, and online receipts based on a Unified Payment Interface.
5. Your Smartphone will replace all types of debit and credit cards with Mobile payment systems (like Paytm). Physical-cash to digital-cash and digital-cash to physical-cash convertibility will be a game changer. Digital wallet and digital locker will revolutionize the security system. Enabling peer to peer payment system will do away many intermediaries and will reboot the existing infrastructure.
6. This new system will unleash a fresh wave of innovation which will lead to the demise of many existing businesses and the birth of a whole range of new ones. Imagine the amount of data created with a billion connected users transacting online and how this data may enrich us as a society through advanced analytics giving insights into behavior patterns, preferences, expectations, and sentiment of various classes, communities, cities, states, and the country as a whole.

India is gearing up for digital business in a BIG way. So is the world. As the surrounding environment is beckoning to digital business with a resounding 'bring it on', imagine the plight of companies that are not ready for it. Either because they did not ride the *digital wave* well enough due to inertia, or because they lost sight of the *business practices* required to sustain their forays into the digital world. In any case, companies that have not invested in an alignment between Business and Technology will not survive as digital enterprises. A strong BITA is thus the foundation on which a successful digital enterprise is built.

The Characteristics of a Digital Enterprise.

An enterprise that uses digital technology as a strategic tool to gain competitive advantage is a digital enterprise. A digital enterprise follows a business model which envisages the use of digital technology to conduct its internal and external business operations. For example, the sale of goods through online sites, customer self-service through online portals, web-based order booking and fulfillment, targeted digital marketing campaigns, crowd-sourcing of ideas to drive innovation, enabling BYOD in the workplace, using social media analytics for managing customer experience, etc. The list goes on.

Enterprises, including digital, have their own personalities, shaped by their distinct cultures. They may differ greatly in their internal dynamics, business processes, technology deployment, addressable markets et al. All digital enterprises, however, conform to the pattern of a *web-based enterprise* surrounded by an ecosystem of *Technology, Partners, Influencers (external environment)* and *Markets* and exhibit a common set of characteristics. There is always a close linkage between their business and technology units, and hence they depend a lot on the seven BITA dimensions for success and sustainability.

When an enterprise goes digital, it is swept by a new wave that brings with it changes in the way it communicates with its stakeholders including customers, partners and employees. The traditional methods of marketing and running its operations have to be seriously reevaluated. As we have already discussed, its landscape begins to be dominated by new digital technologies like cloud computing, social media, mobility and analytics until these become an intrinsic and inseparable part of its identity. Contrary to widespread perception, however, a digital enterprise is not just about technology. It is also about its innovative use. As central as technology is to its existence, technology is not the essence of the digital enterprise. (Uber, Amazon, Netflix, Twitter and others differentiate themselves by the *services* they provide, not by the *technology* they use to deliver those services. Do you know (or care) what class of web-servers, data analytics engine or media gateways are used by any of these companies?). Business acumen, economic brilliance and common sense are as relevant in a digital enterprise as in a traditional one. This fact too underlines the importance of close alignment between the business and technology in a world where customers are becoming increasingly tech-savvy, sometimes far more so than the sales professional who is trying to strike a business deal with them.

A quick enumeration of *some* of the characteristics that define a digital enterprise is presented in the following table. Of course, not all characteristics are necessarily displayed by any one digital enterprise, but if your organization is actively embracing many of these traits, you are well on the way to becoming a digital enterprise.

Common Characteristics of a Digital Enterprise

PERSPECTIVE	CHARACTERISTICS
LEADERSHIP	Visibly passionate about digital vision
	Reinforces the digital way thru constant communication: Digital is our BUSINESS, not a CHANNEL
	Develops a comprehensive strategy around the digital platform. Ensures it is understood by all
	Makes data-driven decisions
ORGANIZATION AND CULTURE	*Everyone* understands and is able to function in digital environment
	Attracts/hires/assimilates talent from other industries to nurture digital initiatives
	Millennials are well integrated into the org structure and cultural ethos.
	Few layers, fast growth for achievers. Values skill over experience.
	Demonstrates a culture of innovation through internal collaboration
	Information/data-driven environment. Online info on all offerings
	Skills and capabilities to manage direct relationships with customers
BUSINESS MODEL	Creates value thru new (digital) revenue streams and by reducing the cost of doing business
	Built around value chains constituted of ecosystem partners, who may also be competitors
	Embrace innovation and transformation in methods of doing business, e.g. advertising revenue
	Flexible business model and business processes
GO-TO-MARKET	Use of digital channels (web, mobile, social) for engagement with customer thru lifecycle
	Able to shift gears between B2B, B2C and C2C models
	New pricing and payment models. Digital revenue streams
	Multiple agencies collaborate digitally to service customer need
	Customer engagement is at the center of GTM strategy

Drive for Innovation	Customer-feedback-driven technology innovation
	Involvement of customers in innovation and ideation
	Recruit, promote for the innovative bend. Recognize even tried-&-failed (Dare to Try)
Sales and Marketing	Analytics-driven. Use of Big Data for segmentation/target marketing
	Automated digital marketing processes, solutions and activities (e.g., campaigns)
	Adoption of digital channels to transact proposals, offers, bills and receipts
	Use of web-based automated tracker to capture VoC at all stages from sales to lifetime loyalty
Customer Interface	Serving a base of Informed, tech-savvy, mobile, SM empowered consumers
	Able to sense customer stimuli (e.g., to churn)
	Able to handle last-minute customer requests for change with ease
	Personalized customer experience at all stages of customer lifecycle (end-to-end)
	Establishment of CEM for lifecycle tracking and improvement
	Use of digital tools including social media for customer service
	Engagement with customers thru online chat including FB, Twitter etc
	24x7 availability to customers for service, response to queries and assistance
	Uniform experience over multiple channels: web,chat,mobile/ SMS,email, person-to-person
Technology/IT	Aligned with Business (BITA score of 60 or above)
	Leverages new technology (Cloud, Mobile, Analytics, SM) for agility and competitiveness
	Business-aligned technology roadmap and architecture
Big Data/ Analytics	Excellence in analytics: E.g., ability to visualize data using data discovery tools
	Drills down to base of pyramid for deep insights on customer preferences
	Important data sources integrated into a single BI system to facilitate decision-making
	Invests in and manages comprehensive data warehouse. Appreciates importance of data
Cloud/Mobility	Multichannel coordination using SM, Mobility, Cloud

	Use of mobile data for business decision making (e.g. ATM locations for a bank)
	App-based customer interface for all common device types
	A holistic Mobile strategy – for sales, service, employee engagement
	Uses Mobility for customer service using real-time, in-context data
	Uses cloud-based systems and enterprise mobility solutions for sales tracking
Social Media	Uses corporate social media across the network of stakeholders
	Social networking and collaboration to collectively solve problems
Security	Manages security risks in protection of I-P
	Documents risks associated with use of digital channels
	Manages security risks associated with BYOD, Cloud etc.
EMPLOYEE ENGAGEMENT	Encourages BYOD across levels, locations
	Mobile access to Email, calendar, messaging, corp intranet, video conf for all employees
	Routine apps like leave, travel, etc. are available through mobile portal
	Empowered employees thru innovative use of Big Data and Mobility
PARTNER MANAGEMENT	Digital rights and royalties management of ecosystem partners
	Tracking and governance of ecosystem partners through online SRM initiatives
	Ability to work remotely yet seamlessly and securely with partners over digital channels
INTERNAL OPERATIONS	Agile SOPs and development methodology for continuous delivery and improvement
	HR, Legal, SCM, Finance – all departments execute on digital strategy
	Investments in Digital technology cover customer solutions *as well as* back-office operations

A digital enterprise is almost always characterized by *disruptive* innovation. Here are some examples of disruption brought in by simple, but out-of-the-box, ideas aided by cutting-edge technology. No doubt disruptive innovation calls for some bold initiatives, but ultimately it is what drives the digital economy.

We have been used to airline self-service kiosks at most airports for many years. They are indeed a source of great convenience for the hassled business traveler who reaches the terminal usually a few crucial minutes before the flight gate closes. Of late, of course, these kiosks are less used since you could always web check-in even while at office/home or in the cab to the airport. All the same, digital kiosks were a disruptive trend ushered by the digital revolution. A few years ago, car rental company Hertz took the kiosk concept a step further. Initially, they had deployed self-service kiosks for customers to choose their cars, complete the paperwork and then just amble across to collect the keys and drive off. Later they took this concept even further by installing *dual* screen kiosks. One screen was dedicated to providing rental options and transactional support, while the other screen – at eye level –enabled the customer to communicate with a Hertz support rep over real-time audio and video. This resulted in closer engagement and an enhanced experience which frequently translated into loyalty. This is truly going digital, imbibing all the key characteristics, but most importantly listening to the customer and exploiting new technology to the hilt.

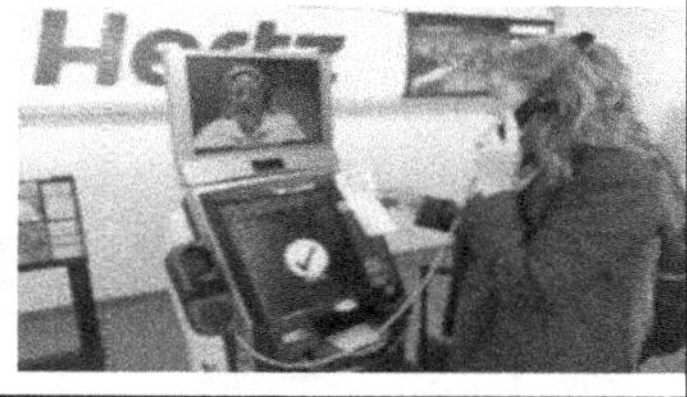

When I walked into the very posh office of the President and India Business Head of a mobile services operator for a meeting last year, I was struck by a large map of India – extending from the ceiling to the floor – on the wall facing him slightly to his left. This map was very unusual. It was not a pixelated plasma screen, but a printed map showing all the key cities and towns of India. LEDs adorned each town and city on the map. Depending on whether, at the end of the last day, that town/city was below, equal (+/- 10%) or above its revenue target, the LEDs were lit red, orange or green, being controlled by a server somewhere that sent appropriate signals based on daily status reports fed to it from sales offices. The map was liberally interspersed with green and orange dots but had a fair sprinkling of red. It's anybody's guess whom the president was on the line with that afternoon! I was impressed by the simple yet effective medium of keeping your finger always on the pulse of the problem – far better than reams of sales reports mailed to you from all corners!

When I expressed my amazement, he told me that I hadn't seen anything yet! He showed me another map of India – this time on the large computer screen on his desk – and invited me to click anywhere. When I did so, a zoomed in picture of the spot I had clicked appeared with a lot of detail.

What stood out was several green and blue spots. On clicking further, I got a better-resolved image of the area. He explained that the green, blue (and some red) spots represented *individual mobile towers* (called BTSs in telco jargon) in the zoomed-in locality while the colors indicated their financial viability. Thus, a green tower meant that traffic (and hence revenues) from that tower adequately covered the cost of its operation and that it was showing profits. Blue indicated that it was close to breaking even, while red meant it was a loss-making proposition. This system enabled him to quickly decide on redeployment of assets by moving loss-making base stations to augment capacity in the more profitable sections of the town, without having to invest in expensive new equipment. The excessive amount of back-end gleaning and churning of information to present complex data in such a simple and intuitive fashion is made possible by Big Data, Cloud, Mobility and Advanced Analytics coming together in a harmonious interplay to aid business decision making. I thought it was a great example of the use of digital technology to stay agile in a competitive market. There is a somewhat similar (and perhaps more familiar) example of the unified portal created for its employees by P&G. This one portal provided access to up-to-date sales data across P&G's various brands, products and geographies to more than 50,000 employees across the world. It helped teams quickly identify issues and take the right steps to tackle them expeditiously. Think about how such solutions could promote *your* business. Digital can make it happen for you.

There are many examples of disruptive trends aiding business in the digital economy. Let's take one more. While most businesses want their customers to stay away from their competition, here is the story of a company that leveraged its competition's strengths to create customer loyalty. Sounds unbelievable? Well, it has happened and produced great results for online retailer Zappos. If Zappos went out of stock on any product, it helped the customer find the item from a competitor – at no extra cost. Instead of turning customers away, this simple – albeit somewhat risky – gesture on the part of Zappos results in most (over 75%) customers coming back to Zappos for repeat business. The reason is simple –Zappos values fulfillment of its customers' expectations at all costs, and the customers appreciate this. While this is not entirely a disruptive phenomenon ushered by new *technology*, it is nevertheless symptomatic of digital enterprises.

It won't be long before we witness the reality of the driverless car. Though I am not yet holding my breath, I do realize the disruptive potential of the trends this will set. It has, of course, a lot to do with technology and at the same time calls for a complete alteration of our views and attitudes towards transportation and most importantly, the transfer of trust from humans to machines in another key walk (or ride, if you may) of life.

The *non*-characteristics of a digital enterprise

In as much as we could draw out a list of some of the *desired* characteristics of a digital enterprise (refer the previous table), we could also list down the *inhibitors* to digital evolution. Of course, not displaying the *desired* characteristics itself would suffice to throttle your aspirations of turning (or being born) digital; for example, if a desired characteristic is "Engagement with customers thru online chat including FB, Twitter etc." then *NOT* engaging with customers thru online chat is clearly an inhibitor. Unfortunately, it is not just a simple game of antonyms. There are some subtle characteristics that could water down your most ambitious plans if not recognized and addressed early in the game. Hence while doing the opposite of the traits mentioned in the previous table would undoubtedly prove an inhibitor, especially if it is rampant across the list, there are some other traits that can block your path *even* if you are conforming to all, or most, of the desired traits. Some of these are very commonly found even in the most enlightened companies and are worth mentioning here.

×INERTIA: Most managers are resistant to change, more so when the change is transformational, as they see the associated risks at cross-purposes with their personal aspirations of job security and growth. They are well ensconced in their comfort zones and resist internally induced disruptions. Many a time, good ideas are not allowed even to reach the top where decisions could be taken about their cultivation.

×OBSTINACY: Given the speed at which markets, technologies and customer expectations are moving, a company whose leadership team sticks too long with the old approaches is at high risk. You cannot transform your technology or business platform without first transforming your mindset and posture.

×BUREAUCRACY: Many companies still have too many layers of decision making which inhibits the speed of response. In other words, they do not have adequately empowered customer-facing teams. This is where companies that are turning digital lose out to digital start-ups (born-digital companies) which are more agile.
×HIERARCHY: A lot of companies are still shackled by rigid hierarchical structures that were created for the industrial era, long before digital technology and information transparency. Digital calls for transforming your structure in line with your strategy. That is, building flexible structures of empowered people always tuned to the changing needs of the customer.
×INFLEXIBILITY: In this era of diverse and progressive expectations, a customer product or service plan that is designed to cater to everyone will almost never work. Each customer must be treated as an individual and personalization must be intrinsic to your offerings.
×CONFINEMENT: Nothing is a greater barrier to your digital journey than silencing the voice of innovation. Sometimes the best, and the most profitable, ideas come from the most unexpected sources which would have gone unheard in a climate where innovation was not openly stimulated. A company that does not encourage the 'dare to try' spirit does not have a great digital future. I have seen that while professing innovation is common, practicing it – which means embracing its risks, making investments – is not.

Sharpening the axe - Gearing up to go Digital

In the next section, we will focus on the seven dimensions of alignment to achieve success as a digital enterprise. Before we get there, let us ensure that the stage is set for this interplay. A digital makeover requires solutions and approaches that are unique to each enterprise. Usually, the services of a consultant are engaged to help establish as (or transform to) a digital enterprise, as you may have done yourself (or planning to do). While each industry, unit, and enterprise has its own brand of business model, technology mix, and process flows, there are aspects which are common to the construction of all digital enterprises: Every digital enterprise is built against the backdrop of strong Business-IT alignment, using a *similar* set of building blocks. We will discuss these common aspects in the subsequent chapter, with the aim of encouraging more informed participation in the digital journey by people across the organization.

A digital enterprise may either be born digital or be turned digital. Taking some familiar examples, Uber, Alibaba, Facebook, Twitter, Grofer, PayTM,

Instacart, Airbnb and Google are examples of enterprises that were born digital. Interestingly, born-digital companies are some of the fastest growing companies in history, and yet many of them do not own (or stock) the goods or services that they 'sell.' For example, Uber does not own a single taxi cab, just as Trivago does not have its own hotels, nor does Alibaba stock the merchandise that it retails. Such is the power of digital technology. These companies rely on a robust Internet and a complex yet efficient supply chain (delivery) system, to reach millions across the globe. They themselves are just extremely thin layers that sit on top of these supply systems. All that they essentially do is *interface* with a huge number of people looking for options at a good price while automating the entire value chain involving supplies, payments, logistics and service. The value center is clearly shifting from the product to the interface. While this is a compelling business model, digital enterprises that take the *opposite* path have also emerged – they own *all* the layers from R&D to marketing and distribution thus having greater control and higher profits but also more overheads and challenges in scaling up. Both these types of digital enterprises, however, are examples of companies that were *born* digital. Then there are companies that *turn* digital. The Indian Railways (ticketing system), FMCG companies like P&G, e-Governments, and Banks are among countless examples of institutions that have *turned* digital to embrace the changing times. The questions to ask right now are – were *you* born digital, and if not, have *you* turned digital yet? Do you have a distinct business model to take advantage of the digital opportunity? An enterprise's digital makeover is a continuous journey. Are *you* on that path yet?

The great thing about digital enterprises is that despite the many different models, markets and ambits, they are all constructed from a similar set of building blocks. These building blocks come together seamlessly in a well-coordinated interplay, creating an inclusive entity that is more than the sum of its parts. A disproportionate focus on technology alone is the commonest reason that many companies fail to reach their potential. It is the seamless integration of technology into a larger ecosystem that is the key to success as a digital enterprise. What are these building blocks, and how do they fit together? To answer this, turn to the next chapter.

8 *The Making of the Digital Enterprise*

There's an American proverb that says, *"The only difference between stumbling blocks and stepping stones is in the way you use them."* It is the same with the building blocks of a digital enterprise. That is, depending on how they are used, the building blocks can be an impediment or an impetus to the evolution and growth of a digital enterprise. Which is why, starting with the same set of building blocks, some enterprises make it big in the digital world, while others struggle. In general, constructing a successful digital enterprise entails harmonious interplay and fine balance among the following facets.

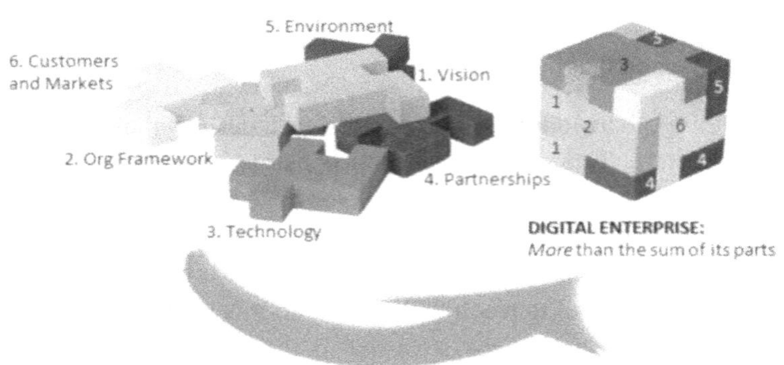

1. Creating a clear digital **vision**, business model, and strategy
2. Redesigning the **organizational framework** of processes and capabilities
3. Setting up a robust **technology** infrastructure
4. Forging strong **partnerships**
5. Blending with the **external environment**
6. Uncompromising focus on **markets and consumers**

These are the basic building blocks of the digital enterprise, and we will discuss each of these in this chapter, with a higher emphasis on Technology. Readers who are indifferent to Technology may skip the related sections without losing the overall thread, though I daresay a perfunctory skim would help.

1. **Vision and Strategy**

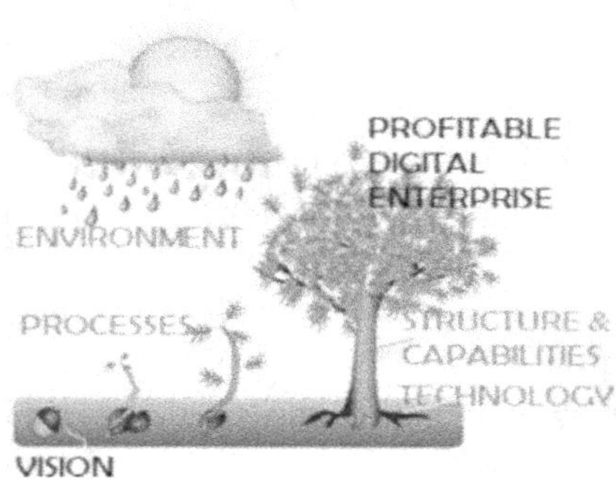

An idea whose time has come is almost always the starting point of a digital enterprise. When the entire organization rallies behind this idea it forms the vision, or the *seed*, which eventually blossoms into a profitable digital enterprise. Of course, a strong foundation of technology, a supportive structure (capabilities), adaptable processes and a conducive external environment are critical to the development of the vision into a mature digital enterprise just as roots, branches, photosynthesis, and sunshine (respectively) are to the metamorphosis of a seed into a fruit-bearing tree.

A seed does not transform into a tree overnight (Jack's beanstalk being the exception). Similarly, the transformation into a digital enterprise does not happen instantly. All the nurturing forces must have the time to act upon the idea (vision) before measurable results are apparent. A word here about '**idea**' and '**vision.**' I have used these terms interchangeably, but differences do exist which it may help to keep in mind when developing a vision.

An *idea* is often born in an isolated setting, perhaps in the shower or on a mountaintop, in the mind of *one* individual. It often comes as a flash from the blue in a most sudden and often jolting way. The *vision*, on the other hand, is created in a *group* working in a collaborative fashion to consciously weave an achievable reality around the idea.Thus, when an idea mutates from a solitary spark to a shared inspiration, it becomes a *vision* for the company. It is always a good practice to have a visioning exercise involving as many stakeholders as possible as this creates greater ownership and alignment. If your vision is 'seen', and *believed*, by your entire organization, it has the power to metamorphose your enterprise in an unprecedented way. Think about it – an entire organization of hundreds, or even thousands, of individuals committed to a single belief about making the future happen. Can there be a greater propulsion?

Here is a hypothetical example of a vision emanating from a simple new idea aimed at superior customer experience and hence better competitive positioning for the company.

Someone in a stock broking company had an idea to move from a 'pull' based portfolio statement delivery for its stockholders (where the client logs in and *requests* for information on his portfolio) to a completely online, 'push' based portfolio management system. The plan was to use digital technologies to alert the client when any of the pre-set criteria are met (like > 1% daily change in the value of a stock). This would enable the client to take timely decisions regarding profit-booking, disinvestment, purchasing, etc. The company adopted this idea to develop a vision which, instead of focusing on new *technologies*, revolved around how the enterprise can enrich the *experience* of its customers through the lifecycle. The vision that this company finally settled on, after involving everyone from its CEO to the stockbrokers, was: "We will be the number one stock broking company in the country by maximizing the return to investors through on-time, accurate and relevant information. Every time." Such a vision is immune to the type of technology used for its accomplishment and hence has a better chance of surviving through newer generations of technology.

The vision, let's not forget, is the enterprise's image of its *future*. Once you envision a future, you cannot soon replace it with another image. If the vision of a cement manufacturer is to achieve global dominance by producing high-grade cement that stands out for toughness, this remains its vision even as it goes through changes and upheavals. New ideas may contribute to *realizing* the vision in innovative ways, without *altering* it. However, it is a good practice to reassess your vision as you model yourself into a digital enterprise. But once a vision is decided, all innovation must be directed at its realization, rather than reformulation. Your digital vision, once articulated, must be immune to methods, technologies, and processes adopted to realize it. The vision changes only when the enterprise collectively reimagines its future.

When crafting the digital vision, it is important to keep in mind the end state of the digital transformation journey. As more advanced technology becomes available for bringing ideas to fruition, the timescales for value creation are shortening. For example, with the advent of Hadoop, incorporating Big Data into your solution is much faster than earlier. With such accelerators at your disposal, the rubber hits the runway quicker, and this must be reflected in your vision and strategy. Else you risk being outpaced by the market.

When the enterprise embarks upon its digital journey, it must do so with the knowledge that there are frequent and unexpected turns on the path. It is important that these do not diminish the determination or lower the motivation levels. The leaders of the organization must continually reinforce the digital vision and its implications for the company. The value to be gained from the use of digital technologies, and the strategies adopted for engaging with customers and stakeholders must be clearly seen by *everyone* in the enterprise as necessary conditions for realizing the digital vision.

As is clear from the above, envisioning the future of the digital enterprise is not just about technology. First and foremost, it is about capturing a compelling image of the future in the hearts and minds of the people in the organization.

2. **Organizational Framework**

The company's vision defines an image of its future, while its mission states the purpose for which it exists. The vision stems from the mission and forms the basis of its *strategy*. The vision, mission and strategy together ensure that the enterprise is no longer rudderless and is moving forward as a unified force in the desired direction. It may have distinct strategies for its various parts, but they are all directed towards accomplishing the company's common mission. Independent, non-converging departmental strategies pull the enterprise in opposing directions, restricting its forward movement.

Your digital journey starts with capturing a compelling image of the future in the hearts and minds of the people in the organization. We made this point to end the previous segment, and I am repeating it here for emphasis. Through the journey, your chances of success as a digital enterprise are largely dependent on the people of the organization standing firmly behind the vision and being fully committed to working harmoniously together to realize it.

I define the organizational framework as the *collective of the structure, capabilities and processes* ***designed to execute the company's strategy.*** All too commonly, companies tweak their strategy with changes in the market, or at the beginning of each business planning cycle, but fail to make corresponding changes to the *organizational framework* to support the revised strategy. This is a very common, though often intangible, reason for businesses failing to accomplish their stated missions. I have seen companies engage expensive consultants to determine the root-cause of failure and often the consultants simply come up with a recommendation to change some business processes or organizational structure to align with the strategy. This is clearly an avoidable expense, and it also entails the risk of keeping the actual executors out of the loop.

The construction of the organizational framework is traditionally done progressively, graduating from one level to the next, focusing simultaneously on the *three* pillars – processes, capabilities and structure. The following table provides a high-level view of the properties for each pillar at different levels of maturity. The pillars are interdependent entities and must be taken *together*. That is, a focus on any one of them while ignoring the other two will not lead to targeted results. Each level incorporates the attributes of the preceding one as well. Thus, Level-4 processes (Metrics based controls) would include level 2 (Repeatability) and level 3 (Standardization) processes as well.

Most successful digital enterprises would be in, or targeting to be in, the levels 4 or 5. These are the only levels compatible with the mores of the digital enterprise. Hence any enterprise that is in levels 1 to 3 may also find itself struggling to stay afloat in the fast-paced customer-centric world of digital business, though of course, those that have reached level 3 would be better off than those still in level 1 or 2. Unfortunately, most enterprises are still in levels 1-3 and probably are not even aware of it. Let me caution here that this migration through levels is neither quick nor trivial, but can be accomplished through consistency of planning and effort to make constructive changes across the three pillars.

Level	Process maturity at	Capabilities focused on	Structure influenced by
1	Initial (Mostly situational)	*Individual* competence	*Hierarchy*, boss-subor-dinate
2	Repeatable	*Project*/Portfolio expertise	*Teams*
3	Standardized	*Functional* excellence	*Departments and Functions*
4	Predictable; metrics based controls	*Customer* (lifecycle) experience	Inverted *pyramid*, Voice of Customer*
5	Continuously & Mea-surably Improving	Innovation and differen-tiation	*Collaboration*, Alignment

[* A quip I heard somewhere amply demonstrates the concept of structure being influenced by VoC: "*Your customer doesn't care how much you know until he knows how much you care.*"!]

As the enterprise moves up on the maturity scale, its capacity to synchronize its organizational processes and capabilities with the strategy improves, and therefore so does the level of BITA. Connecting back with our organizational framework, we already made the point above that the target region for successful digital enterprises, in fact for all enterprises, is in the vicinity of levels 4 and 5. The organization structure in these levels is influenced by the Inverted Pyramid and Collaboration, respectively as shown in the table. While not going into a detailed treatment of these structures, I am presenting here a high level, conceptual view in a self-explanatory way to refresh the reader's understanding.

Inverted Pyramid Structure

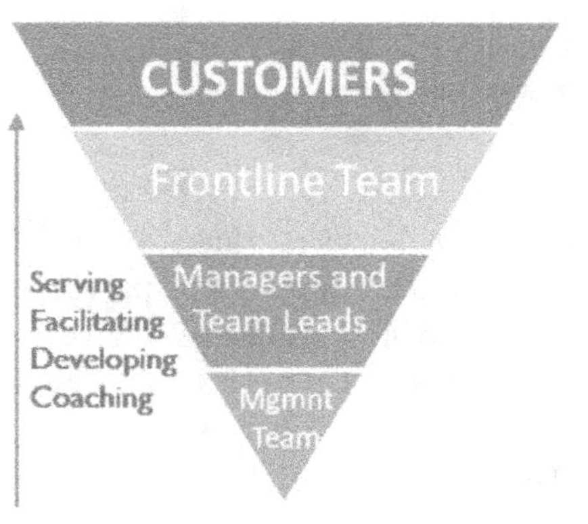

Collaborative Structure

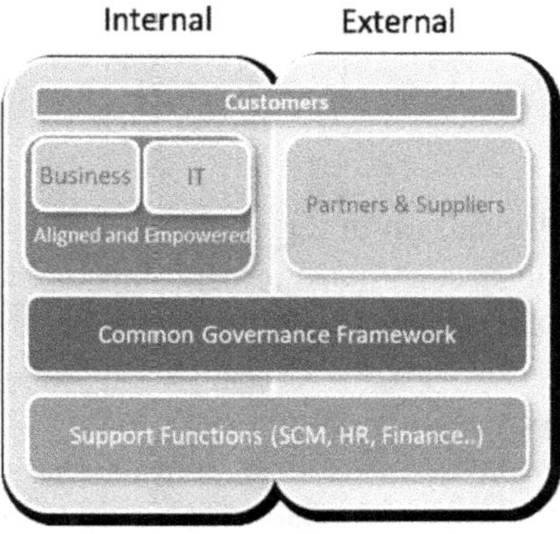

We are in the process of constructing our digital enterprise piece by piece. With this background on Organization Framework, let us move to the next building block of the digital enterprise, viz, Technology.

3. Technology

In chapter-3 we talked about the role of new technologies like Social Media, Mobility, Analytics (Big Data), and Cloud [collectively SMAC] in bolstering Business-IT alignment. In this segment, we discuss the maturation of these technologies as the core of a digital enterprise.

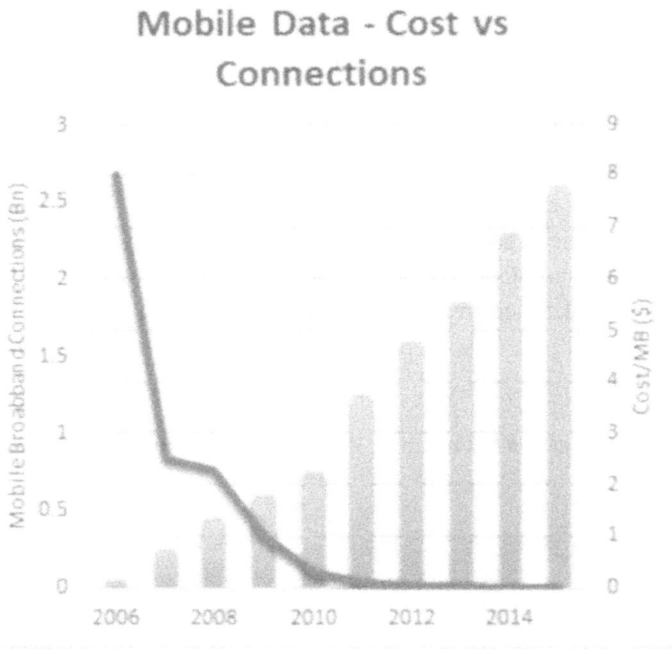

The advent of digital technologies was spurred by telcos as a means to drive up data traffic. For a profitable data business model, the cost of providing data services must be covered by the resultant growth in revenues. However, with rising subscriber connections and falling costs of data, a tipping point was reached around 2009 when the cost of carrying data traffic surpassed the revenue earned from conventional data. The only viable option then was for providers to create new revenue streams by transforming themselves from *connectivity providers* to *full-service providers*, leveraging new technologies to stimulate data generation, access, consumption and exchange over the

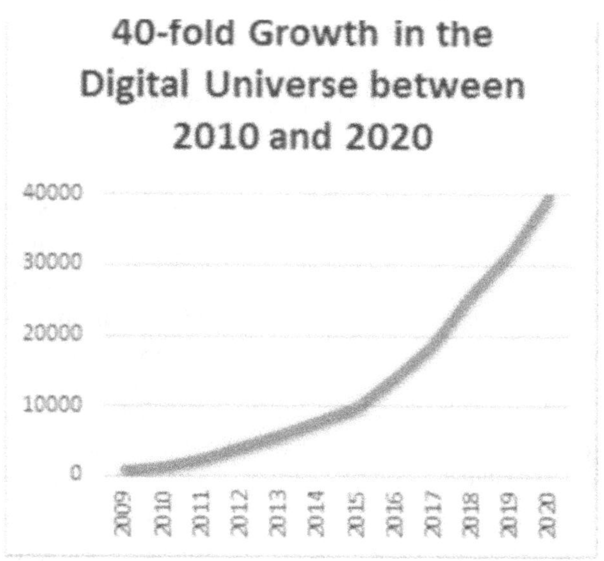

Exabytes

Internet. Though telecom service providers were beaten at this game by the so-called over-the-top players (OTTs) (like Facebook and Google), their network backbone was still used to provide the necessary speed, coverage and capacity for the new data services based on Cloud, Social Media, Mobility, etc. As it turned out, this proved to be a win-win formula for providers and consumers (not to mention OTTs) alike, eventually leading up to the emergence of the digital enterprise. That said, it is quite likely that other, independent forces could also have spawned the digital enterprise eventually. However, as the digital enterprise is the product of an intersection of Telecommunications and Information Technology, the above evolution has ensured that all the enabling ingredients for it to flourish are firmly in place even when it is seeded.

Is Moore's law driving digital transformation?

For my college project in the final semester way back in 1981, I worked on the Intel 8080 microprocessor chip, writing an assembly language program to perform floating point arithmetic. It was a rather tedious project since assembly language programming entailed writing instructions directly on the microprocessor using hexadecimal nibbles made cf 4-bit clumps of 1s and 0s. Nevertheless, it taught me a good deal about the then-emerging field of microprocessors. The 8080 contained about 6000 transistors woven into a single silicon wafer. Sounded pretty impressive and I recall talking rather boastfully to friends about the marvel that this chip was (as if I had something to do with its creation!). Then Moore's law came along, and the 8080 was suddenly left far behind in a fierce race in which successive newer generations recurrently doubled in speed and density of packing, from the 1980s up to the present. Compare the 2 MHz clock speed and 6000 transistors on the 8080 with the multi-core microprocessors of today with their superfast 4 *Giga*Hz clock rate and over 1.75 *billion* transistors packed into a thumbnail size wafer of silicon. To put it in perspective, a comparable growth in other human endeavors would have meant that the tallest structure today would measure half way up to the moon, and the fastest cars would be nudging the speed of light!

Moore's law predicted that the number of transistors packed into a square inch of integrated circuit would double every two years – exactly as experience has borne out since the 1980s – resulting in higher computational power from the improved computing architectures that it enabled. A lot of the advancements in technology that we see around us are a result of Moore's law, including the revolutionary smartphone which packs more power than a room-sized computer of yore. And this is not the end of the road. There is no doubt that hardware will have a profound impact on the *computing architectures* of the future as well. Indeed, without the strides in IC technology, we would have no foundation to stand on. I foresee that as hardware becomes compacter and faster, it will further drive up *computational power*, or the ability to process complex calculations very quickly. Computational power has been the locomotive of IT in the pre-digital era. However, could strides in *computing power* alone have led to the evolution of the digital enterprise? Probably not. While IT continues to surge at the same accelerated pace, its drivers have changed. These new drivers, culminating in the evolution of the digital enterprise, define a shift from Moore's law and raw computational power to **Software**, **Network** and **Emerging Technologies (Next Wave IT)**, while hardware still provides the much-needed foundational layer. A digital enterprise must achieve fine-tuning across all these constituents to become and stay successful.

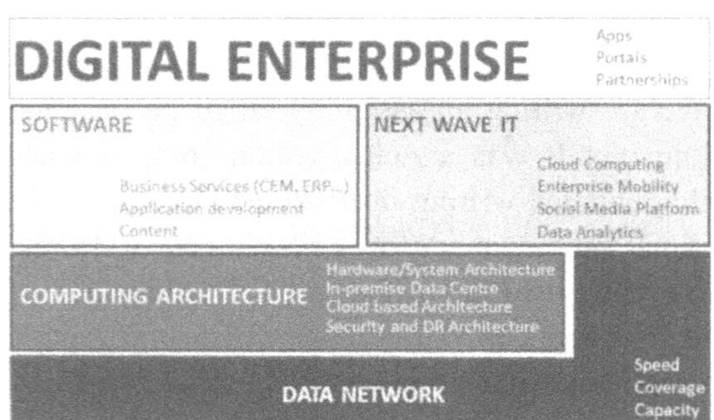

The schematic alongside is an attempt to depict the major technology drivers of the modern digital enterprise, with computing architecture supporting the software and new-technologies stacks. The architecture itself is supported by a strong *network backbone* to seamlessly interconnect the various modules and components (described in subsequent segments) which are typically *non-localized*, and to render mobility and connectivity to the digital enterprise.

Setting the stage...

The essential elements of the digital eco-system, with the digital enterprise at its center, were discussed in chapter-4. In this chapter, we present the inside view of a digital enterprise to introduce the reader to the technology elements on which the business depends, without necessarily getting into the *depths* of technology. In today's fiercely competitive environment, assuring this basic technology awareness is a matter of hygiene. If you are not up to speed with even the foundational aspects of technology, you will be outpaced in the digital race before you know it. This does not mean that everyone must be a technologist in the digital world. I am taking the rather cautious approach here of only inviting you to wet your toes on the shores of the vast technological ocean. With this understanding, you should be able to dive deeper into the subject of your choosing and relevance when the time comes.

Before we proceed further with our discussion on technology, let me make a few important points here, which may seem rather obvious but are still worth emphasizing. Incredible as it may seem, in my work as a consultant I have come across issues having snowballed into catastrophes due to such simple matters having been overlooked.

First, having *access* to technology today does not mean *acquiring* (owning or building) the technology. Which is to say that in the era of Cloud, Virtualization, High-speed data links and Remote Infrastructure, the *proximity* of the hardware components, or their *ownership*, is becoming increasingly less relevant. Hence an enterprise may well start life, or its digital avatar, using a public cloud infrastructure for all the heavy lifting and adopt publicly available instant communication services like Skype or Viber, to roll out its digital venture. Further, the various modules/ components of the architecture need not be physically localized. With a strong network backbone, you can have geographically interspersed components on a single logical plane. This imparts great freedom while designing your architecture. As the enterprise evolves, it will need to reevaluate its stances on data security, privacy, etc. and adopt a mix of public and private resources fused seamlessly.

Secondly, a robust *internet connectivity* lies at the very center of the digital enterprise. Even your most efficient infrastructure is meaningless if your customers, partners and employees have no access to the internet. The web is at the very heart of the digital enterprise and permeates all its constituents. Which is why bridging the digital divide becomes an important goal of the digital economy, and of digital enterprises individually. In countries like India, with a vast population in the rural areas still not having web availability or the means to access it, this presents both an opportunity and a challenge. A modern enterprise may either take the stance that it cannot access this vast chunk of population, ignore it completely and plan around it, or take a more proactive stance and help with ongoing initiatives to bridge the divide and be the first to enter those markets. The following story from an unconnected field is an apt one to explain how a positive attitude can make a threat become an opportunity.

A reputed shoe manufacturing company in Europe wanted to increase its market to emerging territories, as it was already well-entrenched in most developed markets. It formed two teams with a mandate to visit an African tribal area and report on the viability of expanding the business there. The two teams headed out to this remote region and conducted extensive on-ground research into the potential of the market. On their return to the headquarters, they were both asked to present their findings. The leader of the first team came forward and reported: "There is no market in that area. *No one* wears shoes." Then the second team was called, and it reported: "There is a huge market in that area. *No one* wears shoes." Same situation, different perspectives. Who do you think prevailed? I would bet on team 2. These are the kind of situations new enterprises entering uncharted markets frequently come across, and it is their attitude that determines the winners. In this case, you may take the back seat and wait for internet availability, or create your own market by contributing to the ongoing efforts to ensure internet availability. Your choice.

The next few sections delve below the surface of the technology, though not too deep. If you are not a technology aficionado or lack prior exposure to technology platforms, you may gloss over the sections on *Architecture* and *Software,* though a quick read may have some payback. The section on **Next-wave IT,** though, could be a worthwhile read, given its relevance in the digital world. Though the treatment is very gentle and brief, you can always refer to the web for clarity, or consult colleagues, if you find this tangential.

Computing Architecture

The computing architecture is the foundation on which the technology infrastructure of the digital enterprise is built. It is a bit of a challenge to talk about the foundational architecture while avoiding technical jargon entirely. However, I will try to skirt around the complex aspects while preserving some logical flow in the discussion. In any case, there is no common computing architecture that applies to all enterprises, so taking an outline approach is probably the best.

A digital business recognizes information, processes, people, and IT systems as entities that participate equally in creating value for the business. At times, some of these entities may be beyond the control of any *one* company. The architecture serves as a platform for reliably managing the interplay between the participating entities to assure optimum business efficiency. A well-designed architecture ensures that the enterprise remains agile (quick response to change), flexible (add/modify services 'on the fly'), and future-ready while allowing seamless interplay across participating entities. While at it, the architecture must conform to evolving global standards as well. If you are going through life as an enterprise architect, you probably don't have too many dull moments!

Some may ask that if the process of creating the foundational architecture is so challenging, do the 'digital disruptors', who ride on a revolutionary idea to acquire enormous user bases *in a short span*, also need to conform to this, and if yes, how? The disruptors bank on the flexibility of the architecture to initiate the roll-out with modest beginnings, to be scaled over time. S*ustaining* the business momentum, however, depends on a resilient architecture so even the disruptors *will* have to build their distinctive architectures at some point in their journey. Secondly, and this is good news for most companies, the availability of digital tools and platforms like cloud computing reduce the barriers of cost and complexity, so you can have your supporting architecture up and running relatively painlessly. As we said, the modern computing architecture is a hybrid of pre-built and new elements, from a mix of on-premise and remote sources, building up to a seamless platform for speedy delivery of digital services to the end-user.

A good starting point for creating the supporting architecture is to establish some non-negotiable ground rules. What must the architecture necessarily accomplish? A few pointers -

- It must be able to integrate external devices, programs, components as well as partners and their services through standard application programming interfaces (APIs)
- It should comply with international standards of interoperability with legacy and future systems.
- The architecture must lend itself to incremental growth strategy, or scalability, in line with business growth.
- Users must be able to access the business network through maximum possible channels and devices
- It should *not* begin with worst-case load scenarios and yet be able to support peaky conditions (e.g., through cloud-first implementation)
- It should expose interfaces that allow secure connectivity in compliance with the information privacy norms and policies.
- It should have the capability to acquire and act upon user specific data like location, time of interaction, type of activity etc.
- The architecture must allow interworking with a variety of data sources and advanced analytic tools for harvesting contextual information from huge repositories.
- It should allow service creation and easy configurability to support personalization based on user preferences.
- It should enable quick time-to-market by leveraging ready-made solutions. That is, it must promote re-use.

These are some indicative, though realistic, principles which may form a good starting point for designing the right architecture for your enterprise. It does not matter if you are adopting the public cloud, private cloud or captive data-center for your infrastructure hosting. Some ground rules must still be established as a starting point. You may like to have a broader discussion on establishing the ground rules with all concerned stakeholders, *including Business*. If you are in a collaborative structure (level-5 of organization framework), such outcomes come very naturally as part of the decision-making process.

Let us also remember that our discussion here is in the context of Business-IT alignment. A common understanding and agreement on the key principles governing the architecture are essential for a strong and sustained BITA. Many organizations make the mistake of letting only the IT organizations decide the principles governing the foundational architecture of the enterprise. This inevitably leads to future contentions for which the business pays a hefty price. Avoid this. Invest in creating the right computing architecture, as the price of a misstep here could be the derailment of your entire business strategy.

In one of its more common manifestations, the computing architecture for digital enterprises is a conglomerate of distinct *modules*, each having a critical role to play in the delivery of digital services. Representative modules constituting the computing architecture in a typical digital setting are depicted in the accompanying figure, with brief words on the role of each module. This composition into independent modules ensures speedy reconfiguration to accommodate new features or services. That is, changes can be made in any module without disrupting the other modules so long as the interfaces between the modules remain the same. For example, the addition of another channel of *interaction* (like SMS) can be accomplished without affecting other modules, like Information Management, Data Models or Application security. These modules are built on an underlying layer of hardware resources typically working in a *virtualized* environment. That is, abstracting the required configuration using *software enabled virtual machines* that replicate the hardware. This means that available hardware resources are more efficiently utilized as there is now a dynamic allocation of (hardware) resources instead of a fixed one. As we discussed earlier, the computing architecture interfaces with the surrounding systems (Data Network, Software, Next Wave IT) that constitute the technology landscape of the digital enterprise, as also shown here in the architecture view.

The computing architecture varies according to the model, size and nature of the digital business but there are some core elements – like development, integration, security, orchestration, and management– that are almost always present. These

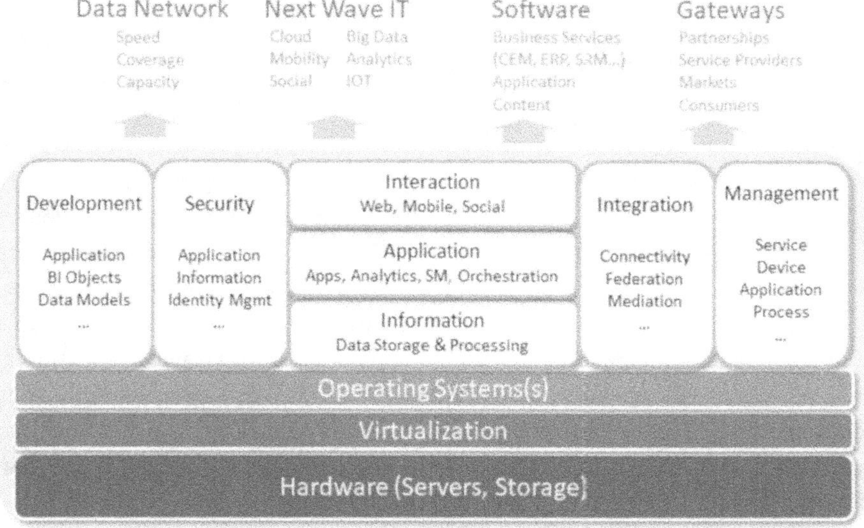

elements are needed to implement the ground-rules of the computing architecture, some of which we mentioned in this section. Intrafaces (between modules) and interfaces (with external world) are also critical from a standardization perspective. You do not have to go into the specific design details of each module that constitutes the IT architecture of your enterprise – unless you are an enterprise architect – but it would be good to familiarize yourself with the overview of the major modules that constitute your enterprise architecture.

The architecture of a running digital enterprise is not only a matter of topography. Of course, sound architecture principles applied by seasoned enterprise architects, business analysts, technical architects, dimensioning engineers and others working in tandem are critical to its evolution but are not a guarantee of its survival. The architecture must also be built for scalability, reliability and resilience. Once built, it must be carefully monitored by experts using specialized tools to achieve exacting performance SLAs on availability. The business depends on it. It must be ensured that redundancy, disaster recovery and physical security are adequately factored in its construction. Close monitoring of Network, Servers, Applications & databases, and Data storage elements is mandated on an ongoing basis with comprehensive logs on performance and precise reports on usage, availability and other trends generated to achieve improvement. What are the major performance bottlenecks in the architecture? What are the top 3 components or issues that are causing, say 70% of all glitches in a month? How could performance be improved by 20%? There are intelligent tools that conduct an in-depth analysis of performance and incidents to answer such questions, and it is highly recommended to embed these in your architecture.

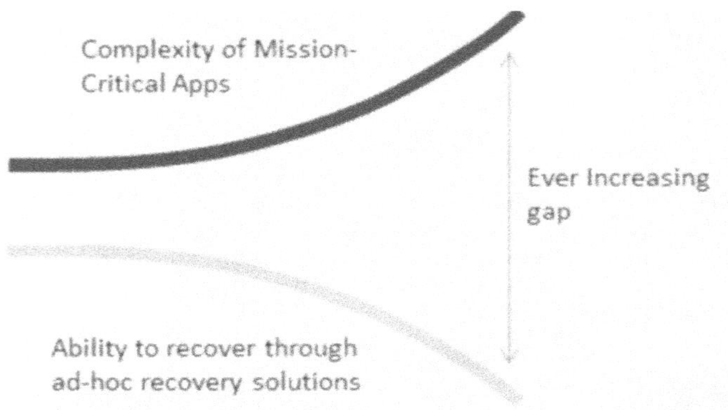

As technology has advanced, architectures have grown to be increasingly complex, even as the user interface has become more simple and intuitive. Implementations today involve a complex interplay of network elements, 3rd party Cloud platforms, data warehouses and remote applications. As a result, the gap between technical complexity and the ability to recover from problems using *ad-hoc* solutions is widening, thus putting the business at risk. This is an area of concern for both business and technology teams. It is imperative to ensure that required skills, tools and recovery solutions are in place *before* the architecture is rolled out and to certify their currency periodically, either through in-house technical experts or through outsourcing to specialized agencies. A lot of companies that have otherwise been on strong trajectories have discovered this to their peril and hence I cannot over-emphasize the need for a systematic approach and intuitive tools to monitor performance and diagnose problems. The first goal must always be *service restoration* and **not** *problem resolution.* Hence workarounds, fallbacks, redundancies, re-routing, DR, etc. should be carefully planned keeping business continuity in front.

Software

The term Software always conjures up different images depending on by whom and from where it is viewed. In the view of the microprocessor or VLSI designer, the machine language program using the unique instruction set that controls the behavior of the microprocessor is the software. For a custom IC (Integrated Circuit) developer, the programs that are *embedded* into the chip are its software. For a computer programmer, the code written to implement a functionality – be it for business process automation, app development, gaming, or simulation – is Software. For most of us who are not computer professionals, the business applications (like CRM or ERP), productivity tools (like Word or Excel) and the apps downloaded on our devices are Software. Why for my wife the controls on the microwave oven are its software! The fact is, everyone is right. Software is a rather generic and over-used term today. But that does not diminish its power to impact our lives profoundly. In fact, with digital taking over every walk of human life, the share of software in our lives is now bigger than ever before. And increasing.

The term Software is often used interchangeably with Computer Programming. However, the fact is that Software includes, but is not *confined to*, Computer Programming. It extends to operating systems (or system software), information systems (data and content, their analysis and organization), user programs (computer code written in a programming language) and tools, utilities, and drivers like compression, disk cleanup, print manager etc. (which are not programs but scripts, or commands). In short, anything that is understood by a computer and can interact with it, and in turn provide users like us a means to exploit its capabilities and perform tasks, is Software. As we all know, hardware and software are both indispensable parts of a computer system, and each is incomplete without the other. In fact, the current trend is for hardware to become increasingly commoditized while software provides the differentiating functionality. Custom hardware is a fading prospect. An example (from telecom world) is the trend towards software-defined network elements, where radio functionality is abstracted from advanced software running on standard hardware servers. Most of the routing function for the Internet is implemented on standard servers (running software) and not specialized routers. The days of dedicated hardware like core switches and routers, base stations etc. are surely numbered, thanks to leaps in software.

There is nothing more maddening than a lengthy discourse that rants on about topics already familiar to us. It's an affront to our intelligence. I believe that a discussion on the meaning and relevance of software in today's world would fall into that category. I will therefore not go further into the generalities of this vast topic here. I do strongly advise folks who need to refresh their understanding of this topic to check out the relevant Web sources (like Wikipedia) which provide useful information on the subject of Software.

Many types and forms of software exist. We use them every day. Our search for software products (tools, applications etc.) in our personal and business setting begins with identifying the type and *purpose* of the required software. We then look at the available *options* for that type. The table on the following page is a compilation of useful *business* software categories with common examples of each. These are chosen for their increased relevance in the context of the *digital enterprise*.

I wish I could provide a complete and comprehensive list of the software universe here, but this is outside the realms of practicality. In any case, the software landscape is a changing one and is also best defined by the unique situation of the individual or enterprise.

One of the most critical tasks that an enterprise would undertake in its maturation is defining and implementing its software landscape. It is not a task that can be done and dusted away in a single effort. The software landscape is a *series* of changes, new implementations, upgrades, consolidations and re-assessments that go on throughout the lifespan of the enterprise.

The sun keeps rising on new applications as it sets on older ones. This calls for migrating and transforming vast volumes of data to conform to the changing landscape. Traditionally IT organizations have been doing this almost single-handedly, but in the digital era, this process involves both Business and IT equally. The overhead of undoing and redoing is too high for a digital business to bear, and BITA is your safety net against this. Organizations where software planning, design, development and implementation follows a disciplined approach involving both Business and IT are thus far better poised to take advantage of the digital opportunity than their counterparts who rely solely on IT for this.

Software Category	Example
Analytics	Cognos, Tableau
Antivirus	McAfee, Symantec, Dr Web
Architecture	TOGAF, IEEE 1471, Zachmann
Audio / Music program	iTunes, WinAmp
Configuration	CASE Tools, Data Modelling
Cloud Computing	SaaS, PaaS, IaaS
Data Management	Hadoop
Business Intelligence	Data Mining, Data Warehousing, Visualization, dashboards
Database	Access, MySQL, SQL
Device drivers	USB
File Transfer	FTP
E-mail	Microsoft Outlook, Public email - Yahoo, Gmail,
Enterprise Services	ERP, CRM, Human Capital Management (HCM)
Gaming	World of Warcraft, Need for Speed, Battelfield4
Information Security	Identity Management, Authentication, EPS, Firewall
Internet browser	Google Chrome, Internet Explorer, Mozilla
Messaging and Communication	Lync, Skype
Mobility	MDM, Mobile App Development
Movie player	Real Player, VLC, Windows Media Player
Navigator	Google Earth, Apple Maps
Operating system	Windows XP, Mac OS X10, Unix, Linux
Photo / Graphics program	Adobe PhotoShop, CorelDRAW
Presentation	PowerPoint
Programming language	C++, HTML, Java, Perl, Visual Basic (VB)
Scripting	VBScript, Jscript, Perl
Simulation	Flight simulator, SimCity
Spreadsheet	Excel
Testing	Test Manager, QA tools
Utility	Data Compression, encryption, disk clean-up, backup/restore
Web Development	Java, Netbeans, HTML editor, Frontpage
Word processor	Word

There is no established formula for creating the most optimum software landscape. It is a function of the present state of IT systems and processes in your company, the future direction of the company, investment capacity and market dynamics, among others. What is certain is that the implementation must follow.sound BPM principles, and that deep commitment and involvement of all stakeholders, with IT steering the enterprise around bottlenecks and inefficiencies, is a must at every stage.

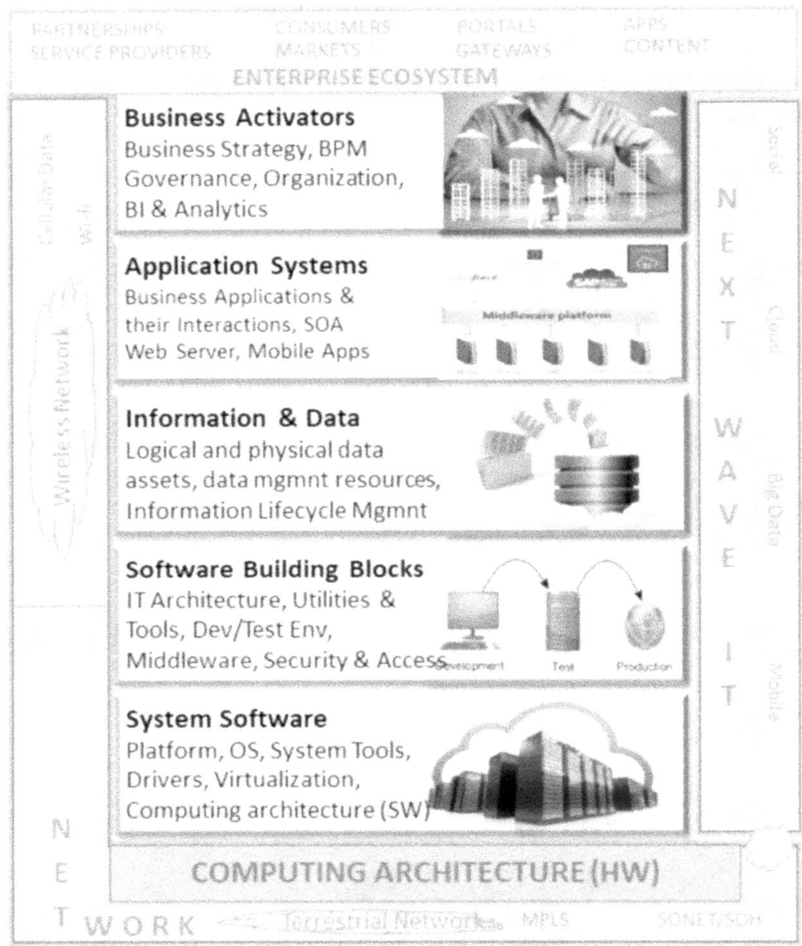

The graphic here is an attempt to illustrate the major software constituents in a typical enterprise. I have endeavored to depict this in a way that traditional enterprises can relate to it. As we said above, there is no one-size-fits-all concept here. The software landscape designers must work on at least five different levels as depicted in the central boxes shown in the graphic. Each box calls for a different set of competencies and focus. The boxes must be designed such that they fit together seamlessly and smoothly and are also able to interact easily with the surrounding environment consisting of the network (both wireless and terrestrial), computing architecture including the hardware platform, and the emerging technology ecosystem consisting of (for now) cloud, social, mobile and Big data and perhaps IOT, Web2.0, IPv6 and others down the road. Software is nothing if not scalable and adaptable.

A technical discussion covering all the myriad aspects of software engineering involved in constructing the enterprise landscape would be neither possible nor justified here. However, a brief introduction to software considerations governing *mobile applications* would be useful since these are the mainstay of digital enterprises and are still relatively new on the block. Basic familiarity with these concepts may not make you stand out, but *not* being familiar with them certainly would!

Most simply put, mobile application development has two aspects – the front end (FE) and the back-end (BE). A developer can write, test and deploy FE and BE mobile applications using several available platforms which provide the components and tools to design, develop, deploy and manage the apps.

The FE is the mobile *user interface* which is designed to provide inputs for manipulating the capabilities of the enterprise system from a hand-held device in an intuitive and friendly manner, taking into consideration the users' screen size, platform (Android, iOS, Windows), context (location) etc. Several popular platforms are available for developing FE apps for both "native" and "cross-platform" deployment. Native refers to applications that can be deployed on *specific* platforms like Android, iOS or Windows while cross-platform applications, built using the new markup language HTML5, are *independent* of platform. The supremacy debate between Native and HTML5 is an interesting one. Eventually, one of them will prevail, but for now, it is split in the middle. Proponents of HTML5 flaunt the ease (as HTML5 is a markup or browser-based language) and speed of developing and updating web-based mobile apps since they rely on a *single* codebase that could be run in *any* environment – browser, platform, device. On the other hand, advocates of Native apps argue that even though the cost and time to build and maintain applications on multiple platforms is higher, the ability to exploit the strengths of each OS led to superior aesthetics and performance than their browser-based counterparts.

FE Mobile apps typically use HTML5, C#, C/C++ or JavaScript as the programming language using an Integrated Development Environment (IDE) which could be MS Visual Studio, Android Studio, Eclipse or NetBeans, among others. Various tool combinations exist to achieve the most optimal environment for FE apps development.

The Mobile Back-end (BE) apps pick up where the FE left off. BE applications provide integration, authentication and reusable business logic to enable users to access enterprise systems through the FE apps. BE functionality is supported by mobile app servers and SOA infrastructure.

The tools used to develop BE apps differ from the ones used for FE apps. Here again, several combinations exist for developing the right tool environment to support the design, development, management and deployment of BE apps. Unlike FE apps, BE apps are installed on back-end *servers*, either on-premise or cloud-based, running on Windows, Linux, Unix, Mac OS etc., to support mobile devices running Android, iOS, Windows Phone 8, HTML5 browser-based client etc. Java is commonly used as the programming language for BE apps though sometimes other languages like C#, C/C++, Object-C, JavaScript, and even proprietary (native) SDKs are used to build BE apps. The BE programmer can choose from a range of IDEs for building, editing and debugging code, but most commonly used ones are Eclipse, IDEA and NetBeans.

Aside from Mobile apps, the enterprise software consists of traditional software components with which the mobile apps must interwork. As we noted above, the FE mobile apps are used to get user inputs while the BE mobile apps provide access to the enterprise systems, some of which may be legacy. Thus, building your software landscape for the future does not require sun-setting all your legacy systems. It is an incremental or phased, approach wherein elements are retired and refreshed in layers. Invest time in planning this well, and you will discover that it is entirely possible to coincide your new acquisitions of software and hardware with the End-of-Life time-line of your legacy systems (which would anyway have necessitated an upgrade or a refresh). That way you spread your costs over a length of time and avoid a deep dent in your budget.

A common question companies ask themselves is whether to buy the software off the shelf or to build it as per internal requirements of the company. Most commercially available software is customizable to individual requirements, and I strongly advocate that where possible, *go for COTS* (Commercial Off the Shelf) software. The kind of interface challenges and hassles (e.g., keeping up with future requirements) entailed in *bespoke* software are not worth the comfort of 'tailored' development in most cases. The following example will explain my reasons for this proclivity.

A couple of years ago I was part of a working group to assess the reasons behind a group company's repeated slippages of time-to-market commitments for new launches, and consistent failure to bring products that could sharpen its competitive edge. The company was falling behind in its ability to fulfill customer orders, deliver committed levels of service, and bill customers for the new range of services. After a lot of internal deliberations, it was concluded that a major root-cause was the lack of sync between the IT and Business functions. An independent assessment was called for, and this working group was created with a mandate to diagnose the exact cause.

The company's IT systems were implemented about six years ago. Barring some user applications like office productivity tools, email etc., its entire software architecture was made up of bespoke (custom-made) systems that were uniquely adapted to the company's business environment of six years ago. What was not entirely homegrown was so heavily customized that it was difficult to distinguish it from homegrown development. All too often, business requirements would either change or give way to completely new ones. In such events, business would approach the IT team with 'Change Requests (CRs)' mostly capturing at a high level what business had in mind. Based on these CRs, the IT team would either develop or (rarely) buy new software and customize it to fit in the environment. Each completed CR was tested for its functionality as well as for regression (i.e., if it had impacted a previously existing functionality). This system had been perfected to an art form in the company. As many as 100 CRs were being implemented each month!

What we, the working group, discovered was that six years later the system was crumbling under the weight of these CRs. The overall performance had become sluggish, and for the last two years, the system was on the brink of collapse. There were many islands of CRs working *outside* the main architecture. There was also no standard integration across the incrementally (CR by CR) built modules. Version mismatches abounded which inhibited interactions. Elements were somehow 'glued' together to interwork, even when they were non-compatible. In many cases, OEM support was not available due to heavy customization. Documentation for the countless CRs was inadequate. There was heavy dependence on the original coder, who was always elusive. Bug-fixes and patches overlaid the code almost entirely. These problems had reduced the software architecture to a parody of its original avatar to the extent that it was no longer able to cater to 'routine' business requests for performance and functionality. When we presented the detailed findings to the management, I still remember that there was pin drop silence in the room for about 30 seconds. Then the CFO spoke up, 'can we do anything now or we have to close shop?'

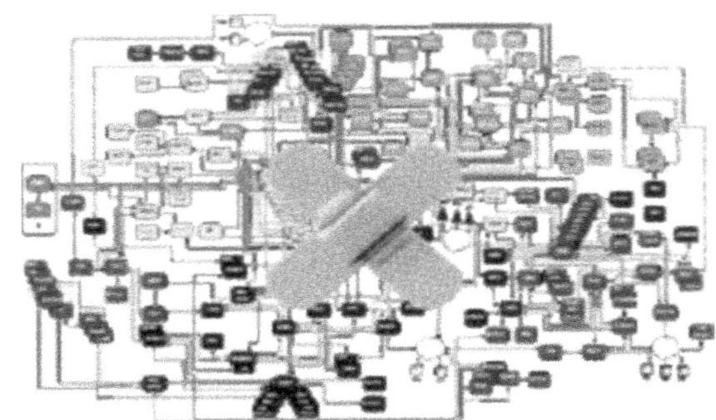

Well, we did have our recommendations on redesigning the IT landscape and bringing in a better, more modular structure to the IT systems, but the dominant lesson for everyone was that overdependance on homegrown software, in the long run, was disastrous. Unlike COTS, homegrown software does not lend itself to automatic upgrades and migrations to keep itself current, nor does it offer the level of standardization that is required to interface with the external world. If you are a closed system unto yourself, like a NASA rocket mission to Saturn, you can go the bespoke way. But for a business enterprise in a dynamic environment and catering to a plethora of external agencies, I always recommend the COTS route with carefully planned and minimal changes to the original code. Changes that can be accomplished by altering the *configurable parameters* in the software are fine. But those that require *changes to its code* are an invitation to disaster in the long run.

Transforming your software and systems to meet the evolving requirements of the digital enterprise is a carefully planned and monitored process. Applications and software need to be transformed in accordance with the business landscape. The term **Digital Transformation** is commonly used to describe the enterprise's journey from the traditional to the digital. It is a non-trivial exercise involving the conversion of software architecture from the patchy and non-standard specimen like the one described in the previous example, to a more decentralized and modular one in which the various modules are independent and interactive, like SOA. To conform to the changed architecture, and to bring flexibility and agility, your old, or legacy, *applications* also need to be modernized. This could require a revamping of the source code to modern platforms such as C# and .NET. Some applications may need to be re-engineered for new functionalities, and new and friendlier user interfaces may have to be built that are supported across different platforms and devices. If you have a sizeable IT infrastructure, it is best to engage a digital transformation consultant to advise on the quickest path which may entail not just modernization of your applications and architecture but also seamless interworking with newer age IT solutions that are defining the digital landscape in the modern business world. Let's see how.

Next Wave IT

I thought long and hard for a term to use for all the new technological advancements that are becoming a part of our lives and yet cannot be uniquely classified under the existing building blocks of technology like Software, Network, or Computing Architecture. We are familiar with Social, Mobile, Analytics and Cloud, collectively known by their acronym SMAC, and I toyed with this. But the field is emerging so fast that soon we may have other, more powerful technologies becoming dominant to which the term SMAC will not do justice. Take IOT for example, or 3D printing. Or for that matter IPv6, Smart-everything (Smart devices, homes, cities, planet), AI, Robotics etc. I am very sure that these – and their intersections – will become as much a part of the digital ecosystem as SMAC over time. I finally settled on the term **Next Wave IT** to describe all such new advances in technology, built from familiar blocks, but profound and pervasive in their impact. Much of our current discussion on digital enterprises may still focus on SMAC, but it is important to be mindful that the digital ecosystem is an expanding one.

A question very often asked in the context of emerging technologies is about the specific role of these technologies in the construction and running of the digital enterprise. It is impossible to answer this question comprehensively. Every digital enterprise envisages a new way of leveraging these technologies to suit its business model. The following use case is probably the *simplest* illustration of this.

I am very fond of reading books of all kinds, and this has been a passion with me since childhood. I am also quite old-fashioned in the way I do my reading. The smell and feel of the paper version (or *PBooks*, as opposed to *EBooks*) for me are unmatched. I haven't quite warmed-up to reading whole books off an electronic screen, however 'paperized' it is. I buy my own PBooks and have built a little library at home. It's my favorite spot in the apartment. Now I am running out of space to keep books but not my interest in reading. I tried to find a library in my neighborhood to *rent* books. Sadly, I could not find one, though such places abounded when I was a kid. The only option, my daughter told me, was to become a member of an online library service. I found one in Gurgaon where I could create an account and for a fee, get chosen books delivered to my home in two days, and return them when I was done with them. It was a convenient system but inadequate, as the PBook selection was rather limited and my home did not lie in their delivery 'zone.'

Most books are read but once, and spend an overwhelmingly large part of their lives lying untouched on bookshelves. Can these unused books on your shelf become an asset? I have a great collection of fiction paperbacks from **A**rcher to **W**odehouse, and books on many non-fiction subjects ranging from spirituality to string theory. I am sure somebody would have already done it before me, but it occurred to me that I could catalog these books, create a growing community of other *like-minded* book lovers who could also individually catalog their collections, and we all publish our catalogs at a shared space on a public cloud, accessed through a simple mobile app with our individual IDs. We could choose books from this larger catalog and fix a day and place in the week – through a link to a common calendar app –to meet for the exchange. It entails no cost and provides an ever-expanding opportunity to access interesting books with candid feedback from those who have read them – unlike at the time of buying books over the counter. It is also an excellent platform to make new friends to talk about our common passion over weekly coffee or beer rounds.

In the above simple example, we have several elements of SMAC at play. There is a **cloud** storage where all the catalogs are published by individual members, there is a **social** interaction between the members using a messaging platform (an existing social app), and there is **mobility** which enables access to information from everywhere, using a *mobile app* run on smartphones. The process even entails **aggregation** of multiple suppliers (in this case, group members), another digital concept which has led to the success of many new age enterprises, including Uber and Airbnb.

This is a very elementary case, but representative of how a small idea can seed a full-fledged digital enterprise – with demand/supply management, markets/consumers, and delivery logistics incorporated – using emerging technologies or *Next Wave IT*. The only missing component was money exchange!

The above is a simple example of how social media, mobility, and cloud can come together to ignite the enterprise spirit and boost collaboration. The only private ingredient required above is a Java program to implement a basic mobile application hosted on a home computer connected to the Internet, which doubles up as a web server. The obvious question that begs to be answered here is then the following: If all it takes to create and run a digital enterprise is Next Wave IT or SMAC, then why invest in complex IT systems described earlier in this segment? Unfortunately, life, and business in particular, is not as simple as the above example. A typical enterprise of even medium size would need systems to manage its internal workflows (like the ERP), run customer service operations (using CRM and other IT tools), manage its order processing, payments/collections and fulfillment streams, run marketing campaigns and manage its internal operations involving people (HR), supply chain (SCM), Financial planning and such. There are of course myriad other considerations ranging from productivity tools to management reports, tight integrations between modules, foundational computing power, data warehouses etc., which involve IT systems. In larger enterprises, the IT substrate penetrates even deeper. For a thriving digital ecosystem, the computing architecture and the software must integrate and interwork with Next Wave IT and together create enhanced value for the business.

A lot of us think of digital enterprises as ones that interact with its customers only through an app or portal, while its people remain faceless and anonymous. When was the last time you *spoke* to someone at Amazon? Indeed, one of the characteristics of digital enterprises we mentioned was "Use of digital channels (web, mobile, social) for engagement with customer thru lifecycle." However, it is important to emphasize that this is only a subset of the digital enterprise. There are high-tech enterprises, large and small, that stress *people-to-people* relationships and yet fit firmly in the digital cast and leverage Next Wave IT to the very hilt, enabling their clients and stakeholders to ride the digital wave.

A few months ago, I interviewed a business manager of a multi-billion-dollar software services company on the adoption of Next Wave IT for selling and delivering services to a global client base in a clearly high-tech high-touch scenario. Here is the gist of what he passionately shared with me:

- As the first step, his company established innovation centers for incubating digital technology solutions *collaboratively with customers*. The innovation center focuses on bringing the benefits of technologies like Mobility, Cloud Computing and Big Data to enterprise customers across industry segments.

- Next, this company has built unique capabilities in digital space based on its extensive experiences globally, spawning a distinct practice *to help customers with their digital and social media strategy, marketing analytics and experience management.*
- The company has further invested in building breadth and depth of capabilities in the Next Wave IT and its application, which go beyond technology to include strategy experts, business analysts, digital marketers, user experience designers, and data scientists, which are available to its customers onsite or in the company's offshore delivery centers.
- As a global player, it has also fostered local and global *alliances* with technology partners to enrich its offerings and enhance its capability to offer end-to-end digital solutions.
- Apart from cultivating skills and partnerships in the Next Wave IT technologies, it has built its own cloud-based offerings (PaaS and SaaS) which offer customers quick and cost-effective solutions in a multi-tenancy mode.
- All through these initiatives, the over-arching aim is to enable customers to reimagine their businesses and help them seamlessly transform to digital.
- Over the last two years, they have emerged among the most trusted technology partners globally for enterprises going digital.

Sounds like a sales pitch, doesn't it? Well, it probably isn't, going by the track record and customer references. Anyhow, the point is that this is a large company that is enabling digital transformation by itself *practicing* what it advocates and implements for its customers:

The internal environment here buzzes with high-tech. BYOD is strongly encouraged, and most of its Intranet is accessible over the mobile. Its employees routinely log in to their work or leisure activities in the company-run Wi-Fi enabled buses on their way to/from work. Most of the company's data and programs – like its ERP, Financial systems, HCM etc. – are hosted on a hybrid cloud which incorporates solutions from its technology partners. It leverages big data and analytics to provide real-time information to employees and stakeholders on a range of issues of interest in an incredibly intuitive fashion. There is a thriving social network of its own which is at the fingertips of each one of its over hundred thousand employees across the globe. It helps employees connect on issues ranging from sharing of accommodation to help on customer problems through focus groups. Even the process of account management is digitized with online information on customer's entire portfolio, people and projects. They are also building an Artificial Intelligence layer to supplement some of their back-end shared services. When a prospective client scouting for a digital transformation partner visits their facility, the deal is half done while just walking through the aisles.

The above examples bear testimony to the fact that irrespective of the type, size and category of the digital enterprise, Next Wave IT is critical to its success.

Despite its transformational potential, many aspiring digital enterprises are often uncertain about the adoption of Next Wave IT due to its disruptive nature. They are averse to risk and wonder if they could transform themselves *without* embracing SMAC. Well, if you were on a treasure hunt, would you dive into the deep end of the ocean without your SCUBA gear because you imagine that you look silly in that outfit? Perhaps you would. But would you survive? Now that's another question entirely! Sidestepping your essential survival kit – be it SCUBA or SMAC– is the biggest of all risks.

There are four primary reasons behind enterprises embracing SMAC for business. The first is *connectivity,* or the ease of networking among ecosystem participants. The second is *collaboration*, or the ability to come to a common platform for transacting business and sharing experiences. The third is *freedom,* that is, not being dependent on a specific device, platform, network or location for engaging in a business activity. And the fourth is *empowerment* or ready and direct access to relevant information by those who need it, when they need it. Underlying these advantages is the enormous convenience that SMAC offers to the participants of the enterprise ecosystem through simple, new and exciting ways of doing business.

In chapter-3 we covered the various components of SMAC while defining the new IT landscape. In the backdrop of our discussion on the digital enterprise in this chapter, this would be a good place to very quickly reassess the impact of SMAC components on business, individually and collectively.

Social: Be it socializing or social networking, social is in the human DNA. At no point in history have social traits shown a declining trend and this is not likely in the future as well, with technology making things more expedient than ever. Social is about engaging people in something they care about, and digital businesses have leveraged this human trait brilliantly to expand their reach. Businesses are now using Social as an indispensable source of insightful data on customer behavior and sentiment for their marketing and design purposes.

Mobile: We are a people on the go. With the proliferation of mobile devices and ubiquity of wireless networks, we are no longer subject to the restrictions of time and place to conduct our business. As we said, Mobility is not just about movement. It is about *freedom*. With more mobile devices than people in the world and with over 3 out of every 5 of those devices having 'smart' capabilities, businesses must necessarily transform themselves to enable this freedom for their consumers. Or perish.

Analytics: We talked about the data revolution earlier. There are startling statistics on the speed, size and types of data that we as a populace are generating and consuming each day on Social and Mobile platforms. This data is now recognized as an indisputable *business asset*. Our ability to analyze this Big data – irrespective of its volume, velocity and variety – and garner deep insights into preferences, behaviors and sentiment will decide, in ever increasing ways, our survival chances in the digital economy.

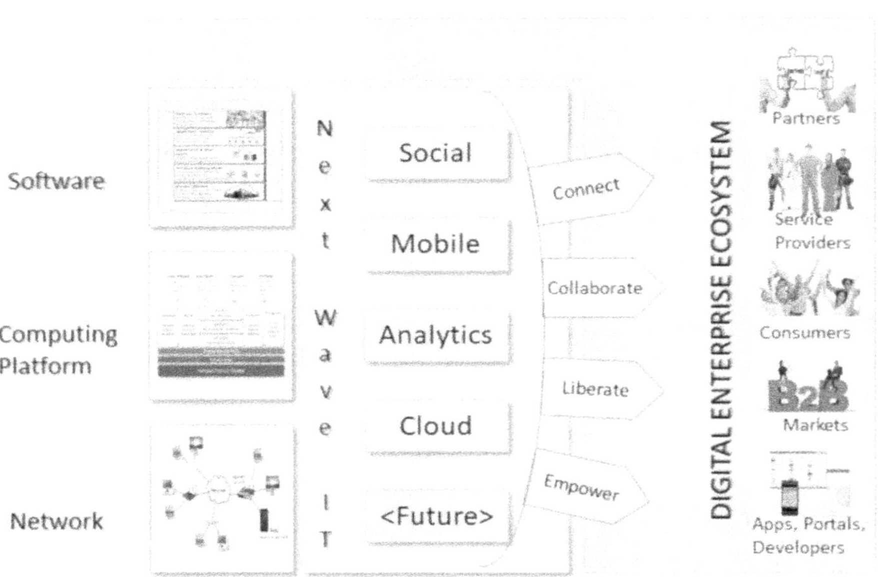

Cloud: From the point of view of consumers, Cloud implies that all the heavy lifting – running complex programs, storing huge volumes of data – is no longer the burden of their device. A 100-dollar smartphone can 'run' almost any program and access unlimited content. And you can switch to any other device at any time and still get the same experience with no loss of processing-power or content. For the enterprise, cloud means avoidance of substantial investments in premise-based equipment and technology, freedom from maintenance, and the ability to offer quick set-up times (reduced TTM) to the business.

As we have seen above and before, each element of SMAC has compelling advantages for business. However, the real breakthrough happens from their coming *together* as a stack or as *intersecting elements*. Enterprises can maximize their impact through the innovative use of these elements in their business. Some examples: using *big data analytics* to gauge customer sentiments about the company's products over *social media*; using *cloud-based* content to enable seamless experience for *mobile* users when they are in another city, country or continent; accessing *cloud-based* data to get user information and combine this with preferences derived through *big data analytics* to recommend places of his interest in the vicinity, like book/CD stores, restaurants etc.

Look at a digital enterprise as a symphony where the individual SMAC elements are the musical instruments, each of which can produce a beautiful rendition of its own, but when they come *together* as an ensemble, magic happens. It is up to you, the conductor of the symphony, to orchestrate the digital concert and set the right rhythm and tempo which will keep your audiences enthralled.

I find it quite amazing that even in this day and age, there are questions like "Would Next Wave IT or SMAC, really help <u>my</u> business?" coming from even enlightened quarters. It is probably their inherent reluctance to change being projected as uncertainty. For the sake of my hesitant friends let me enumerate here just five of the many distinct advantages of SMAC for business.

- SMAC offers global reach – Companies that adopt SMAC can tap into new markets more easily
- SMAC promotes collaboration – It provides limitless opportunities for enterprises to engage with customers, understand their preferences and offer custom solutions
- SMAC enhances customer experience – By analyzing behaviors and trends, SMAC makes it possible to personalize offerings and preempt problems, thus promoting customer loyalty
- SMAC is a great leveler – SMAC levels the playing field for enterprises and customers alike. Every business has access to all customers, and vice versa

- SMAC boosts productivity – With the level of empowerment, freedom and access to information enabled by SMAC, enterprises that adopt SMAC achieve far greater workforce productivity

Next Wave IT can be built incrementally, i.e., investment of time and money in building the Next Wave IT infrastructure can be aligned closely to the business growth, and thus there is hardly any risk of going over-the-line with your costs.

You may not know it, but it is likely that you are already leveraging Next Wave IT for your business. There are many cases of ad hoc, crisis-driven use of SMAC to meet short-term business commitments. Two employees engaging with each other over WhatsApp (SM) on a business issue, or a manager using Skype to do a candidate interview, in a sporadic, self-initiated manner is not the most optimum use of SMAC. It may not bring sustainable enterprise-wide gains that SMAC can deliver. But it is a step into SMAC territory.

Like all enterprise initiatives, Next Wave IT must have a clearly stated goal for its existence. For most organizations, this goal is to *enhance business value through a collaborative, instantaneous and comprehensive engagement with stakeholders* (markets, customers, employees, partners et al.) Once your goal is defined, study where you are today to determine, as granularly as possible, the gaps that need to be filled to reach this goal, and prioritize these. Each 'gap' is an action item that must be tracked and completed. There may be certain dependencies (like cost, skills) in closing certain actions which need to be planned for.

Companies that best leverage SMAC are ones that can manage their customer information, interfaces and experiences in the most optimal way. They can capture customer data through multiple channels (SM, IVR, CRM etc.) and keep the information current and relevant. They set up systems and processes to avoid recapturing old information with every interaction. [Every time I call this company that works as an agent of my Health Insurance company, I am asked to provide all details of my medical history, personal records etc. – even when I simply wish to pay my annual policy renewal premium! It's extremely infuriating. They always explain by saying they are doing it to verify my credentials and assess the suitability of my coverage plan, but I suspect the real reason is they have no systems to track their customer's history. They may soon be a customer short. I am looking for options.]

In adopting Next Wave IT for your company, a *dedicated* team to assess its potential, and focus on maximizing its use in your environment would be a better idea than spreading the responsibility too widely. It is also recommended to keep scouting for best practices of other successful organizations and plan to blend these into your environment. There is still evolution happening in this field, and hence there is great scope for learning from peers.

When we started out on our segment on Next Wave IT, we mentioned that it is built of SMAC and *other* disruptive technologies which have great potential that we are only beginning to tap. These are the technologies that are waiting to take hold of the 'Future' box in the previous diagram depicting Next Wave IT. Let us consider one such in a short example and then reflect on its consequences on business when this intersects with some existing technologies.

We are familiar with the digitization of *information* in today's world which essentially means reducing text, images, sound and video into a string of binary digits (1 or 0) which can be stored, processed, analyzed, transmitted, and regenerated in same or different form. Look at the revolution this has brought. Loosely speaking, the impact of digitization is felt by two human senses – sight and sound. Now think of digitization not just of information, but of matter itself! That is, the possibility that you can store, process, analyze, transmit and regenerate *physical objects* (that also cater to your senses of touch, taste and smell) using the same software principles that were applied to information! **3D-Printing**, as digitization of matter is referred to, is poised for a tremendous impact on the future of business and society. It is no longer about simple toys and tools. It is expected that the first 3D-printed car will be on the road by 2022. Even more astonishingly, the first transplant of the 3D-printed liver may happen as early as 2024! With 3D-printing, you can do your own personalized object design and production, thus closing the gap between product creator and user. Instead of waiting for an ordered item to be delivered to you, just press Ctrl-P and presto, it is there – made for you! There are of course some sinister and worrisome aspects of 3D-printing as well – some may use this to mass produce weapons and counterfeits, even spurious human organs. New forms of security, control mechanisms and ethical protocols will no doubt evolve to counter this threat. There are many profound questions that 3D-Printing raises: What impact will it have on mitigating conditions for the less privileged sections of society – not just prosthetics but in addressing disease, hunger etc.? Will it help reduce waste and boost recycling? How will it impact the global economy? Will it lead to many industries going bust (or obsolete)? Etc. Here, we cannot answer all the questions. However, as a technological breakthrough, it is indeed a giant step. And it is only one amongst several contenders (think IOT, Smart planet et al.) for the 'Future' box in our Next Wave IT depiction. Exciting times ahead.

It is very common for people to ask at this stage if technology will replace humans as the world becomes increasingly digital. Or at the very least, will technology, at some point, take over most jobs that are around today? In my view, the answer is No. Technology, in fact, has recently created *more* jobs than any other discipline and it will continue to do so. The amount of displacement – or the difference between repetitive roles *eliminated* and new ones *created* – will always be in favor of humans. However, I will say this: while technology will not replace people, *it is certain that people who understand and can use technology will replace those who cannot.*

4. **Partnerships**

In my several years of working with digital enterprises at various stages of evolution, I have not come across even one example of a digital enterprise that did not rely on partnerships to conduct its business. Clearly, as a digital enterprise, you cannot go it alone. It does not matter if you are big or small. A digital enterprise is not a company but an ecosystem. It rests on the premise that one company is not the undisputed champion in every area of its business operation and therefore to leverage the expertise of other companies – even those that it may be competing with – in their specific expertise domains makes sound business sense. In fact, we have many examples of companies having no core competence in the area that they dominate their markets in, but their ability to manage networks of partners and weave them into their business model has spelled their success. They are called aggregators.

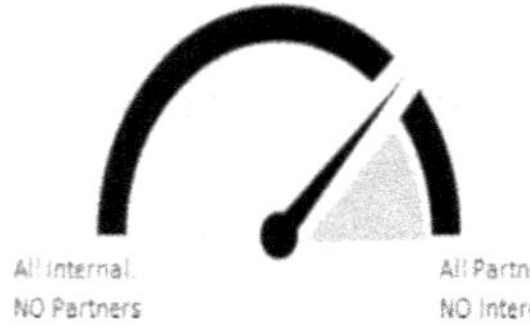

Aggregation is not the only form of partnership known to digital enterprises. Depending on the size and nature of the enterprise the partnerships may differ. Almost every element of the digital enterprise is amenable to partnerships as after all, a digital enterprise stems from an idea or vision and that is all that is truly integral to the enterprise. But it is best to keep a balance. With value chains becoming more complex as customers expect complete solutions from one source, the extent and role of partnering are becoming an increasingly core aspect of strategic planning in digital enterprises. In other words, partnerships are a matter of corporate strategy and cannot surface (or submerge) randomly.

Partnerships require nurturing and management. Your business depends on it. It is not just a matter of putting controls and management dashboards. There is also *trust* to be invested from both sides. The whole process of partner management is usually quite complex though many companies believe it to be trivial. It is *never* safe to assume that one can 'partner and forget.' A partnership is an extension of your own enterprise which does rid you of certain routine overheads but also brings in uncertainties which need to be managed transparently. It is very important to remember that *your partner is invisible to the external world.* You must own the consequences of any deficiencies in service, legal infringements etc. and their impact on your hard-built reputation. No customer (or court) will accept the plea that it was your partner's fault. Therefore, in managing your partnerships, avoid suspicion but never drop caution.

The following graphic illustrates the most common kinds of partnerships constituting the *extended* digital enterprise. It is not comprehensive, but representative. Managing these partnerships is the lifeline of the digital enterprise. Generally, each partnership comes with its own contractual frameworks, key result areas (KRAs), and service level agreements (SLAs) which need to be closely monitored.

The <u>Extended</u> Digital Enterprise

Typically, mobile companies are not at their best when it comes to stocking and dispensing *music* to suit the individual tastes of their millions of users. On the other hand, users today are no longer content with the canned set of ring-tone options that come with their device. Take the case of my driver, a rather spiritual person. When he receives a call, there is a shrill but soulful rendering of Sanskrit shlokas that suddenly fill up the room (or car). When I call him, I hear a Bhajan (Hindu religious poetry) in my earpiece until he picks up the phone. Of course, tastes vary, and instead of bhajans, there could be limericks! This bhajan that I hear is the CRBT – or caller ring back tone, while the shlokas are the ringtone here. Whom do people turn to for fulfilling these wants? Yes, the mobile service operator. Though this is a seemingly trivial requirement, every operator must be able to fulfill it to stay competitive. So, operators turn to partners for rendering this service. These partners build the required logic for delivering the selected music to the individual user, host the service on behalf of the operator and provide necessary integrations to enable provisioning, de-provisioning, charging etc. Further, these *service* partners rely on a different entity called the *content* partner for providing a continuously updated supply of music choices to the user. This is a familiar instance of a seamless, invisible chain of partnerships enhancing the delivery capability of a larger, more visible, customer-facing enterprise (the Mobile Operator). The customer-facing enterprise - in this case, the operator - must take ownership of the quality and conduct of the invisible partners. It may be noted that the same partner may be working across competing operators here, which no one minds as it results in uniform content and quality.

Strong partnerships are the invisible driving force behind the digital enterprise. They make the enterprise more wholesome and attractive. A digital enterprise is essentially a *network* of companies blended together, presenting a single window to a whole world of exciting options.

5. External Environment

We live in a highly regulated environment. Almost every industry – telecom, retail, insurance, banking, and healthcare – is governed by a set of regulations that it must comply with. The regulator can – and does – demand regular as well as exceptional reports on a range of parameters relating to the company's operation and its compliance to the commitments based on which it sold goods and services to its clients. The digital enterprise is not excepted from regulation. It must, therefore, conduct a detailed assessment of the regulation and the steps required to comply with those regulations in a demonstrable way. Unlike with partners, most enterprises have an arms-length relationship with regulators. Here the determinant of success is not collaboration but compliance.

Almost every enterprise must interwork with its peer companies in the industry. For example, banks work with other banks for inter-bank transactions, telecom companies have interconnect settlements for roaming and call completion, etc.

All companies connect to a common *gateway* through which the inter-company transactions are routed. A digital enterprise must expose standard interfaces to the requisite gateways to assure its subscription to the industry network, and thus avoid isolation.

It is usual for industries to have associations consisting of individual companies as members. These associations are powerful bodies that formulate the rules of engagement and are a guard against unfair practices by one of its own members or outside forces. They play an indispensable role in guiding and influencing government policies for the industry. As digital enterprises are in an emerging stage, some of these practices are in a relatively fluid state at present. There are few, if any, active countrywide associations of digital enterprises belonging to an industry. However, over time there will be greater regulation, Government involvement and public participation, which would necessitate strong industrywide associations of digital enterprises as well. For example, the various taxi aggregators may need to form a unified association for a common representation of their concerns, while the existing associations (for example of Banks) may expand their coverage to include digital initiatives.

With the advent of social media, customers have a new way of expressing their opinion about any aspect of an enterprise. It is easier for negative sentiment, or bias against one company, to transcend the one-on-one communication between the company and the customer and reach 100s of other customers. These customers may, in turn, come together against the enterprise and collectively escalate the matter resulting in undue negative publicity. In order to protect their reputations, digital enterprises must have access to impartial nodal agencies to look after their interest, singly and jointly.

There are many such instances that call for a seamless merger of the digital enterprise with its external environment. The enterprise must align with its competitors, customer forums, govt. bodies etc. to reach consensus on pricing, quality, service levels etc. and therefore it is essential that it stays 'plugged-in.'

Lastly, an enterprise, digital or not, is part of the larger community to which it owes its existence. This larger community is the canvas of educational institutions, hospitals, utility services, non-profit organizations, environmental lobbies, and society in general from which the enterprise has benefitted and to which it must give back. This may be in the form of various contributions including monetary donations, participation in development work, espousing a charitable cause, extending aid etc. A digital enterprise can be said to have truly 'arrived' once it recognizes that as much as it exists to generate business and profits, it has an equal responsibility towards the society of which it is a part.

6. Markets and Consumers

Some things do not change even with major economic, technological and social upheavals. To exist, businesses need customers. In other words, the creation of a customer is the only true measure of a business's success. That was true before the digital era, and it is true in the digital era. Some might argue that *profit generation* is the prime goal of a business. This only reinforces the argument that the customer is the raison d'être for any business. Profit is the difference between money inflow and money outflow, and cannot happen without a *sale*. To a *customer*, who else!

People have needs which are very fundamental. For example, a hungry person *needs* food. To satisfy the need for food, he may *want* a pizza. When the want (or desire) is backed by a capacity to pay for it, it becomes a *demand.* A customer is someone who has the power to *demand* what the company is offering, and the *set of all customers with a similar demand (not just need) and all sellers who can fulfill that demand, constitutes a market.* A simple example: I *need* transportation. I *want* a private jet to meet this need. Can I *demand* a private jet? No. So I am *not* a customer – even though I have a need and a desire – and therefore I am not part of the *market* for private-jet companies.

Many of the essential tenets of marketing behavior are unaltered by digital technology, which at the end of the day, is only a medium for accessing markets and enabling the instantaneous exchange of information between its constituents – albeit a very potent one. The advent of digital technology has spawned the field of *digital marketing* – a common term used to describe the innovative use of technology to understand and influence consumer buying behavior. I find it quite amusing that digital marketing is itself being marketed as a discipline to be taught in classrooms! I belong to the school that believes in the company's marketing and technology teams putting their heads together to find the best way to exploit existing technology for maximum business advantage, rather than a generic external course. In other words, *a strong BITA equals a sound digital marketing strategy*. Let us consider the next example to understand how the digital marketing strategy is unique to an enterprise and is a function of its technological prowess and vision of the future.

This example is an illustration of how a sound digital marketing strategy is formulated by starting with a clear vision of the future of the business, assessing the current situation and gaps, and identifying the technological capability required to achieve it. A leading industrial conglomerate in India which was into diverse lines of businesses, each of which operated as an independent, autonomous company, created a vision to exploit cross-sell opportunities across its businesses by using technology to transcend organizational and industry barriers. For example, it asked itself if customers that used its high-end hotels could be targeted for travel-related products (like rented luxury cars, airline tickets etc.)? The trouble was, the hotel business was clueless about the customers of the travel business, and had no visibility into the critical marketing inputs such as net worth, spending power, personal profile etc. of its peers' customers. The conglomerate has 70+ autonomous companies under its brand, so the permutations – and hence the opportunities for cross-selling to each other – are mammoth. The company engaged a leading global agency to help with a more unified marketing strategy across the group, to come up with a plan that would help its millions of customers across dozens of business lines get a more uniform experience from the single brand that they had put their trust in.

Now, it cannot simply integrate all the customers of all the businesses into one massive database and share it across the group for everyone to dive into and use as they pleased. That would be quite a chaotic approach as is easy to imagine. A task force was created consisting of a technology expert and a marketing expert, from each of the participating companies. This task force was asked to segment their customers clearly according to a set of common parameters. These included net-worth, current relationship, disposition etc. Using intelligent programs, customers in each segment were classified on their future potential for adopting products and services from the group's *other* lines of business, and a focused campaign was triggered. This required deep **analytics** capability and exploiting **Big Data** for extracting a *segmented* common database of targetable customers across the group in a central repository created on a **private cloud**. The project depended heavily on close interworking between the technology and marketing teams of about six dozen companies having a combined base of over 50 million customers. While all the intricacies of the project cannot be visited here, it turned out to be one of the best examples of the use of digital technologies (mainly **Big Data analytics**) for targeted marketing, using **social media** and Call-center platforms. Naturally, the project required ongoing execution and is today run through a dedicated team in the corporate headquarters which has streamlined the process of data gathering, assimilating, segmenting and analyzing to improve business performance across an ever-increasing base of corporates and consumers. In my mind, this is also one of the best demonstrations of the power of digital marketing.

The future belongs to those who can use the power of digital technology to reach their markets and customers faster. Sounds the obvious thing to do? Well, it is not that obvious to some, as the following example brings out.

I was asked to join a meeting with a client who was a sizeable financial services company. The meeting was arranged with the company's COO and IT leadership at their headquarters in Mumbai. At the outset, the COO made it clear to us that the problem was their failure to capitalize on the power of technology to promote their business, while their competition had been able to do just that. This came as a surprise because this company was a market leader that one associated with sophistication and expert use of technology. Sometimes perceptions can be very far removed from reality! Anyhow, they asked us to partner with them in salvaging the situation and helping them get the business back on track. As technology consultants, we are always expected by customers to pull them out of the vortexes they ended up creating for themselves. But for all the trials and challenges encountered, there is still a lot to learn from these experiences.

Over the years this company had been gathering data from their customers through transaction records, CRM interactions etc. and had various IT systems in place to capture and store this information. The problem was that the story ended here. This data had never been accessed, save for some mandated deep diving into a customer's history in cases of legal dispute, and no one quite knew what to do with it. Meanwhile smaller companies in competition with our customer recognized the asset value of the data they generated and used it for more personalized service to customers. What was even more frustrating for our customer was that two years ago, there had been a request for investing in advanced analytic systems, which had been turned down as an extravagant measure and the funds were used to install a telepresence system (as if *that* is not extravagant!). Had this company recognized the power of big data and advanced analytics at the right time, they would have been in an entirely different league today, certainly not struggling to stay ahead of competitors once considered inconsequential. They accepted our findings and resolved to change course. The story will hopefully have a good ending because as I write this, there is earnest effort underway to deploy the right technology tools to exploit the power of big data, training has been imparted to both Business and IT folks on the use of analytics, and the reach of data gathering has been extended to social media. Still, they will probably never be able to recover the opportunity lost due to their failure to recognize the power of digital technology on time.

Unfortunately, there is no dearth of examples of the kind above. I am tempted to relate one more, which again exemplifies the urgency to adopt digital technology as a means of ensuring survival.

This example will come as a surprise because it is about a company which is itself into high tech (IT) products and solutions! It used to be a well-known company, and many of my past colleagues and friends have worked here. One such friend, who was now associated with this company as a transformation consultant having been employed there earlier for three years, sought my views (as a consultant myself) on his charter to reform the company. He had been asked to determine the root-cause of the downward trajectory that the company had been following for the third year in a row, in spite of no measurable degradation in its product and service quality as per latest customer survey. It had also noted that the falling business had resulted in some of its best people leaving the ship (my friend among them). There was a vague notion, after an analysis of competition data, that somehow the company had not sufficiently leveraged digital technology to do its marketing and outreach, but no one was quite sure. That is why this friend sought me out to get a confirmation of his own assessment.

The company was organized in a hub and spoke structure where the spokes were the all-powerful arms and the hub was rather lifeless. That is, it had a multitude of regional and area offices across the country each of which ran its own operations such as new business acquisitions, customer operations etc. and interacted with the HO only for factory related supplies and periodic sales reporting. Each office even maintained its own customer records and order data. An employee in office A had no direct access to data in office B. Each office was running as a universe unto itself. Obviously, a consolidation was required to keep business-critical information in a cloud-based architecture such that information was readily available when and where needed, imparting freedom and empowerment, or mobility, to the marketing frontline. After all, customers are mobile today. They also have affiliates in other locations. And they operate in a boundary-less mode. A localized, premise-based (not on cloud) database is grossly inadequate to meet the needs of modern business. It also does not allow mobility, which is a must for survival of the field workforce, notably sales, marketing and customer teams. No wonder that the marketing team of the company was unable to penetrate the market being restrained in both availability and mobility of information.

Once the root cause is established and baselined, the beauty of technological problems is that they lend themselves to straightforward solutions. At least in theory, as in the above case. The obvious solution here was to consolidate the regional servers and databases into a centralized one, move this to a private cloud for ready access, and develop mobility based solutions (apps) to make the required information always available to those who need it. In practice, however, this was not as straightforward, and because the problem had been allowed to grow over the years, its solution was quite time consuming and laborious. Sadly, this company has slid further into its market position and seen more attrition of its workforce. While the recommendations have been tabled, I am not sure of their stage of implementation. The world of digital technology is a fast-paced and rather ruthless one, and unless this company takes some drastic steps, it will soon sink further and probably never surface again. Technology can be your biggest ally, but if not harnessed in time, it can spell your doom.

The nature of a digital enterprise lends itself to several marketing modes. A digital enterprise may conduct business with another *enterprise* (digital or otherwise), as in the case of a technology company like Microsoft licensing its software products to a bank, law firm or hospital. This mode is the Business to Business or **B2B** in short. What we as individuals most commonly come across is the Business-to-Consumer or **B2C** mode where the digital enterprise conducts business directly with the end customer, often facilitated by an agent. Examples, of course, include you and me ordering the latest paperback from Amazon, or booking a cab through Uber. We also have a mode where the digital enterprise sells to another digital enterprise which

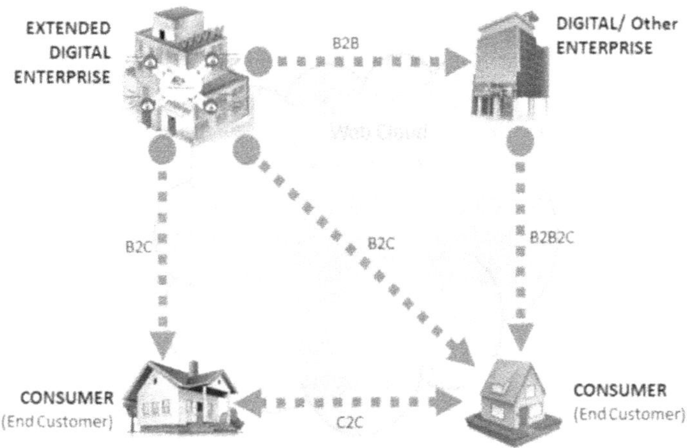

in turn conducts business with the end customer or consumer. This mode referred as Business-to-Business-to-Consumer, or **B2B2C**, is an emerging e-commerce model for reaching new markets and customers. As an example, a product company (business A) in the cosmetic products business sells its products to a retail chain (business B) which stocks and retails individual units to customers in the locality. Or, a global appliances company (enterprise A) may buy user services like lead generation, sales promotion etc. from a *local* company (enterprise B) to promote its business in a territory. A large company that does business through local partners (dealer channel) who in turn sell to end consumers is also an example of B2B2C, though, for the customer, it is perceived as a B2C mode. Lastly, there is the **C2C** mode, where one consumer sells to another consumer using digital channels. In most cases, C2C transactions are facilitated by an unseen empowering enterprise. A common example would be selling off pre-used items through an 'agent' like OLX or renting out your apartment through CommonFloors.

In Conclusion...

Unlike what many technology companies would have us believe, a Digital Enterprise is not a massive powerhouse of complex systems and equipment controlled by experts with pointed ears whom the organization must depend on for delivering some esoteric, magical outcomes. Instead, it is made up of simple *building blocks* which fit together seamlessly. Standing on a bedrock of strong BITA, each block adds unique strength to the digital edifice. A successful digital enterprise recognizes that *each* building block is crucial to its growth and survival, and never loses sight of one for another. This simple, yet powerful, lesson has been at the root of many a digital success story.

This chapter is meant to emphasize the importance of Business-IT Alignment as the future of enterprises goes digital. In studying each individual block of the digital enterprise, you would not have failed to appreciate the growing role of BITA in ensuring enterprise success. Be it strategy, organization, processes, technology, partnerships, or markets – it is no longer Business OR IT but very strongly Business AND IT that is going to make it happen for you. Business cannot go it alone in this environment, and nor can technology. In many nimble organizations, Business and IT are in fact indistinguishable. Some enterprises have even reoriented their organization compass to create roles that merge business and technology into one. In other successful, and larger, digital organizations, business and technology are separate units, but fully synchronized or integrated. In all cases, the cultivation of a strong BITA must be among the organization's foremost strategic and operational priorities.

It is not only a matter of gaining a competitive edge in the future. It's about surviving long enough to witness the future.

The next seven chapters of this book will, therefore, be focused on assuring individual and enterprise readiness to meet the future challenges and survive in an ocean about which little is known except that it is red. It will help you build the right orientation towards working in a new environment where business - success is the preserve of those who have succeeded in keeping their business and technology domains fully aligned at the level of culture, strategy, structure, process, intellect, function and tactics. With this in mind let's march on to the next section for building up to a BITA level that will be our most critical success factor in the digital future.

Part-II:
CONQUEST

9 The Culture Connection

"He will win whose army is animated by the same spirit throughout its ranks."

Culture connects. That is, people align best when they are connected by a common culture. Therefore, let us begin our conquest of BITA with a victory over the Culture dimension.

I know I am treading on thin ice in trying to elucidate the meaning of culture. For most of us, culture as a topic of study somehow doesn't quite grip. Which is not surprising, because becoming "cultured" does not happen by reading about culture or analyzing its meaning, but by being 'out there' and living it. However, alignment starts with creating a common frame of reference. Therefore, I am taking the risk of going ahead with a brief introduction to the meaning and definition of culture in our business context, before we move on to some examples and methods/tools for assessing and improving our cultural environment for facilitating BITA. Hope that works for you.

Culture is the foundation on which the collective identity of a group – which could be a community or a corporation – is built. It is derived from a set of fundamental beliefs which produce common, or shared, traits amongst members of the group. In other words, culture refers to shared behavior patterns, customs and practices, knowledge bases, commandments, code of conduct, arts (literature, music, dance) and other aptitudes, abilities, and traditions that are uniquely characteristic of a group. But what does it mean in the context of business enterprises – digital ones in particular? That's the subject of this chapter. We will avoid going into discourses on the generalities of human culture and focus on culture in the context of its importance in strengthening Business-IT Alignment in the Digital Age.

In Chapter 2 we introduced the meaning of culture in organizations in a generic way. We said that culture is what individuals in an organization consciously, consistently and collectively demonstrate in their thinking and behavior. That is why many companies have a *belief system*, which prescribes a code of conduct – for example, putting the customer first, conducting business ethically, evidencing personal integrity, setting high standards of quality, treating people with respect– that every employee is expected to emulate in word and spirit. *It's the belief system, shared by all the employees, that builds the culture of the organization.* An organization has *character* when it does not compromise on its belief system irrespective of inducements, compulsions or consequences.

In a word, culture is the organisation's DNA. It gives the organization the personality that it is recognized by. Genetic engineering is not my cup of tea, so I am not sure if the *human* DNA changes over the course of a lifetime. The important question that begs itself here is if the *organization's* DNA can change, i.e., can it be rebuilt, or is the organization stuck with an unshakeable set of genes that it cannot ever be free of? Well, it's not quite so gloomy a picture. Culture certainly CAN be built. In fact, it MUST evolve with the changing times albeit with some constants that are immutable. Of course, it requires conscious, organization-wide effort to weave a set of behaviors across its length and breadth, but culture change *can* be induced. Before you embark on the journey of change, however, you must assess your current position and determine the areas that need to be built afresh. We'll devise a simple method in this chapter to help us along in this effort, mainly in the context of BITA.

As enterprises transform to digital, it is common to have concerns over the cultural shift required. People ask: I can upgrade my technology infrastructure, but can I also transform my organizational *culture* to suit the needs of a digital enterprise? After all, we are now entering a new arena with largely the same set of people who are used to an entirely different cultural setting at work. The short answer is, you *can*. Consider this – when we leave home in the morning for office, we are subconsciously transitioning from one cultural setting to another. We all come from different cultures yet conform to a common cultural code while at work together. In short, we transform or adapt to new cultural settings. Take another example: you have to go for a rock concert at the stadium one evening. It's a lively milieu where you dress and behave quite informally. You are in your elements. Next day you may go to another musical program – this time a musical symphony at the opera. Would you dress and behave as you did the previous evening? Of course not, you would be rather solemn and sedate on this occasion. Without even being conscious of it you have taken the leap, quite naturally, from one cultural setting to its opposite. These show that we *have* an innate ability as individuals to cross cultural barriers and adapt to new settings, given the propulsion to do so.

Earlier in this book I had touched upon an example of a company that I was associated with where the strong and indomitable belief in ethical business conduct subordinated every other consideration including business leverage. The belief system was so strong that at no point was an employee of the company in doubt, or fear, about the course of action to be taken in a sticky situation. Even though the corporation extended to all corners of the country, had diversified interests and an ever-increasing number of employees, it was able to stitch it all together with a common thread of beliefs that was unbreakable. How did it achieve this? First and foremost, by example. The leadership constantly related stories from across the corporation, of the belief system being acted out in the most difficult of situations, even if it meant giving up business. These stories were often told at the start of important forums (like quarterly sales meets, annual dealer conferences, employee town-hall meetings, etc.), highlighting the importance of the belief system in the corporation's order of priorities. Even the rare stories of failure to live by the belief system – which inevitably led to disciplining of the concerned persons– were narrated (names being omitted) along with its consequences. Next, it was compulsory for every employee to participate in an annual refresher session on the beliefs by the *chairman himself*, who made rounds of various regional offices specifically for this purpose, and frequently stated that his primary job was to inculcate the belief system and the rest will fall in place as a consequence. The beliefs formed an important aspect of every employee's personal effectiveness goals as part of the performance management system. There were always some questions in the interview for every position to gauge potential adherence to the beliefs, and joiners were made to attend a focused training on the belief system as part of orientation. Managers were expected to highlight stories from their teams that showcased proper conduct. All in all, the company made a considerable investment in building a culture around its core beliefs, and it was clear to everyone that if there was one thing bigger than business, it was beliefs. As was to be expected, the corporation acquired an excellent reputation as an open, honest and trustworthy place that customers felt comfortable doing business with and employees took pride in working at.

Over the years the corporation continued to expand into more businesses and geographies. Its reputation almost always preceded it. Wherever it went, it emphasized its beliefs and its character. It earned the *respect* of stakeholders – one of the toughest things to acquire for a business. The only flip side was that the expectations from the company were always very high and with expanding business, it was challenging to meet every one of those. In such cases too, it was expected of managers to keep customers honest through prior communication, at times from the senior-most leadership. This company has transformed into a digital enterprise with serious alterations to its culture while *retaining its core beliefs*. Where earlier it was a rather conservative company with strict hierarchy and protocol, aversion to risk-taking, clear boundaries, no-frills policies and a formal atmosphere, it was now a thriving digital enterprise teaming with millennials, flat and collaborative organization structure, performance-based culture, technology and innovation-driven environment and a fun place to work. Quite a metamorphosis. If you walk in now as an old-timer who has seen the earlier environment (like me), you will find it hard to believe that it's the same organization. Until you glanced at the *core beliefs* prominently displayed at all strategic points or talked to the employees about the beliefs. They were the *same*, word for word! The message was clear: as you progress, you embrace new cultural mores, but that does not mean sacrificing, or compromising, your *core* beliefs. More on this later in this chapter.

Anyhow, my point of giving the above background is that an energizing culture meticulously kept up over the years packs a punch that is hard to beat as a promoter of your business interests. Just a few years ago, when I was with another company, I was in the US on a project assignment. One day, the business development manager for the region requested me to accompany him to a prospect in another part of the state to help him with the sales presentation. I, of course, obliged. We met the technical director of this prospective customer, and I was asked to give a quick overview of my experience and profile. When I touched upon my work with this company that I spoke of in the earlier paragraph, the TD's entire demeanor changed. I could see that there was a lot more respect in his aspect. He mentioned that he was a great admirer of this company from India and had always wanted to work with them as a customer. It was a bit embarrassing for me, more so as I was accompanying the business development manager of the competitor to that company. Nevertheless, I asked him if he had, in the past, *worked* with that company on some project. He said no he hadn't but was impressed with its *reputation* of a strong belief system and ethical business conduct, tales of which he had heard and read about, and was looking forward to a chance to work with them. And this was on the other side of the globe from where this company is located! Despite my position, I didn't have the heart to refute him as what he said was entirely true. But I realized at that time what a powerful force culture was in not only guiding people's behavior but promoting business interests farther than one could imagine.

Organization culture is like a powerful wave which can lift the organization, that is, the employees surfing it, to new heights. The trouble is, it can also plunge the organization to low depths from which it may be unable to surface. Bad culture mostly goes unnoticed by the company's board until the company's financial performance (or lack of it) can be attributed to it, and by then it's too late. If you are part of a bad culture, it sticks to you, and you reach a point where you are unable to shake it off. Worse, it imparts a 'stink' (pardon me, it's a strong term but the only way to describe over-exposure to a bad cultural environment) which wards off potential customers and employers. It's a vicious quandary from which only the exceptionally talented or the astonishingly fortunate can hope to emerge unscathed. My advice to folks who approach me for career-related guidance is therefore always to do as much research as possible into the *culture* of the company and ascertain how closely it resonates with their personal belief systems. If there is a good match, they can be assured of a healthy and long-term association. All else can be learned, but culture must be *blended* into.

Here's an example of a company that believed it had a cultural ethos where in reality it had only a deeply ingrained ferocity for getting results that compelled its people to behave in ways that were often contrary to their own personal codes. This is quite a common phenomenon. Companies often believe that their control systems somehow manifest as organizational culture and this gives them the false reassurance that they have nailed it. This is not a very recent example but symptomatic of the malaise we are discussing. Several years ago, a couple of sales folks and I were with a prospective customer working on a deal for the supply of hardware (desktop computers and networking equipment) to be installed at their huge factory in North India. It was a large deal in a market that was fiercely competitive and hence had piqued the interest of several companies, out of which three had been shortlisted based on the price quotes. From this point on, it was a level playing field, and the decision would be based on delivery, quality and so on, not price. Before we entered the discussion room, we had an informal chat with some folks from the factory who were known to our sales guys. They told us to be very careful when we went in because the previous company which had come for the discussions had left the purchase committee very rattled. It emerged that this company's executives had opened the discussion with the announcement that they had *already got most of the equipment delivered* the previous day and it was in the customer's warehouse. This shook the committee quite a bit, as they had issued no purchase orders or instructions to the warehouse to accept incoming material. It was seen as a contravention of their policies. Yet this company kept flaunting it as a piece of exceptional service, saying that they had got their deliveries done in *anticipation* of the business and of course, in the extreme unlikelihood of their losing the order, the customer could always return the equipment. Clearly, a method designed to put the ball in the customer's court. The company had clearly assumed that such a tactic would bind the customer to them because having already crossed the price barrier, what better way to demonstrate fast delivery than one that *preceded* the PO! They actually flaunted this as a strength, not realizing that they had unduly interfered in the customer's purchasing process, put unwarranted pressure on the committee, and worst of all – as it emerged later – offered 'inducements' to warehouse staff to accept the consignment in the absence of relevant documents. No wonder it created quite a flutter and (I am not sure of this) termination of the services of some warehouse staff. One thing that did happen irrevocably was the disqualification of this company from the tender process and its debarment from tendering in future.

In the car on our way back to Delhi that evening, we were discussing the kind of 'bring-the-deal-home-at-all-costs' culture that would pervade in that company, overlooking the fact that ethical boundaries had to be transgressed in the process, personal beliefs thwarted, the customers' policies disregarded, just to close the deal. What of the people who went along the shady path and performed these acts? After all, it is the people that showcase the company and its culture. Would we want them in our company, regardless of their sharpshooting skills in salesmanship? Probably never. Over time, this company that had started off quite well a decade ago, shrunk to a quarter of its size and eventually got sold off to a foreign competitor and finally vanished from the scene altogether. A lot of its people were out on the market, no doubt many capable ones among them, but couldn't find suitable jobs. The importance of investing effort and time in building a strong cultural base obviously cannot be over-emphasized, but sadly many companies have been surprisingly short-sighted on this point and proven to be equally short-lived.

Someone recently tweeted a video that left me aghast. I just couldn't believe it and thought it to be a hoax. Only later it emerged that it was a real – and not a staged – event when I read comments from people who had witnessed it. There was a natural outcry, and you have probably heard or seen it yourself. The story is from a certain country in Asia. At the annual company event, a senior manager walks up to the stage and invites ten people, including four women, to join him. He called out their names and then announced to the present audience (probably all the employees) that these are the people who had failed to meet their annual sales targets and therefore brought shame upon the company and themselves. They deserved to be publicly punished, he said. After this he hurled the most humiliating and abusive taunts at them while these people stood with their heads bowed, just getting shamed in front of their colleagues. As if this was not enough, the man then produced a large cane and started hitting these ten people on the rump as hard as he could, still hurling abuses. All the women were openly weeping, and probably the men were in tears too. After this ordeal, the senior manager then announced that this, or worse, was the fate reserved for anyone who would not meet the sales target in the coming year. What a way to give a message! And what does it tell you about the culture in this company? Would you ever, for any remuneration, contemplate joining such a company? I wonder what kind of pathetic people did join this company. A company with a bad culture will only attract one kind of people: the desperate ones. And you don't need them.

As we said earlier, a digital enterprise may be born digital (Digital *native*) or turned digital (Digital *migrant*). Eventually, natives and migrants must conform to comparable cultural codes, but their journeys may be quite different. Typically, a migrant enterprise would need to cross over from a legacy culture to a digital culture while retaining the *kernel*, or the *core* beliefs. In doing this, it will have to let go of some 'established' norms like deep hierarchies, centralized decision-making, resistance to change, aversion to risk-taking etc. and acquire new ones like drive for innovation, emphasis on outcomes, risk-taking et al. At the same time, if the enterprise stands on a strong foundation of say, ethics and fairness in business dealings, or unrelenting organization-wide focus on customer experience, quality or service, it must be careful that in migrating to a digital environment, it does *not* in any way compromise these *core* beliefs.

As an analogy, think of your car wheel. It consists of the central hub and the tyre surrounding it. The tyre must be changed when it gets unfit for the road, while the hub remains. Migrating to a digital culture is somewhat similar. You retain your core beliefs – like the hub – while you change your peripheral behaviors – like the tyre. The trick, of course, is not to confuse the hub-beliefs with the tyre-beliefs, or vice-versa.

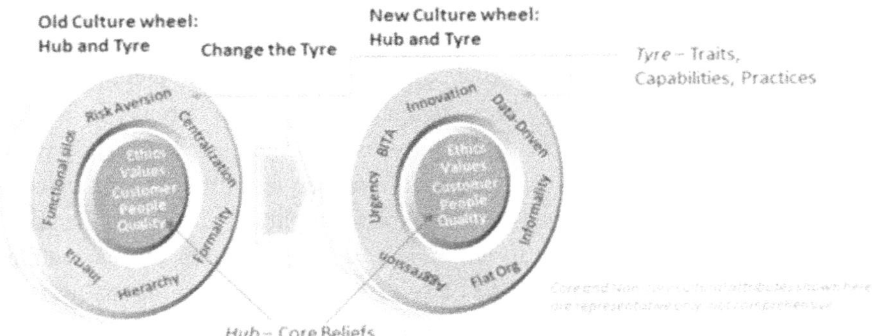

To be fair though, bringing about lasting cultural change is a bit more involved than changing a car tyre. Culture change does not come about because of a nicely-crafted memo from the CEO or a well-articulated speech delivered in the town hall meeting (though these may help). Trying to convince people of the merits of digitization – or BITA – through external reinforcements just won't do the trick. It must be carefully and sensitively injected into the enterprise environment through leadership example, rewards, encouragement, role modeling and constantly focusing and guiding people on the right way. It takes time to seep into every nook and corner of the enterprise. Your *existing* culture can have a strong constraining or liberating effect on generating the change you need. Build on the pre-existing behaviors that support the desired changes and reinforce them continuously but sensitively.

Culture gives an organization its personality which in turn determines how the world sees and experiences it. Culture can, therefore, be broadly classified to have internal and external attributes. Internal attributes of culture refer to a company's intrinsic environment which includes its people, processes, priorities, and practices while the external attributes refer to how it is seen by the outside world including its customers. In the table below, I have attempted to enumerate the differences in culture between an outmoded traditional enterprise and a new-age, BITA led digital enterprise taking both internal and external attributes.

Going back to our analogy, the attributes listed in the table 8-1 correspond to the *tyre*. The core beliefs – or the *hub* – may well be similar in the two cases though their conduct on peripheral attributes is quite dissimilar. In other words, vastly different sets of behaviors may surround the same core.

Table 8-1: Cultural Characteristics

SN	Traditional (Analog) enterprise	BITA driven Digital enterprise
	INTERNAL ATTRIBUTES	
1	Layered, slow decision-making based on rigid workflows and designated authority	Rapid decision making by an empowered front line with access to relevant systems and data
2	Multi-level hierarchical structure where your behavior is predicated on who is N or S of you	A flat hierarchy where levels don't matter. Abilities do
3	Emphasis on Teamwork (i.e., what are we going to do?)	Emphasis on Alignment (i.e., Who do we intend to become?)
4	Formal relationships, constrained by strict protocol	Informal relationships, liberated by shared ideas
5	Discouragement of risk-taking (openly or covertly)	Encouragement of risk-taking (openly)
6	Emphasis on tasks, methods, processes, policies - you can blame failure on these	Emphasis on the outcome. Innovate, find a way around constraints
7	Technology is a back-end productivity enhancer. Select few understand technology	Technology is a front-end business driver. Being tech-savvy is required for every role
8	Inertia and acceptance of status quo characterize the environment	Continuous innovation and challenging the status quo characterize the environment
9	Age and experience matter. Progression is a function of seniority and grey hair	Only ability and potential matter. Progression is a matter of performance and grey cells
10	The organization exists in silos. The only way to communicate across silos is 'cc to boss.'	Open and transparent organization. Frequent, informal cross-functional interactions at all levels
11	Business and IT, at best, work in *agreement* mode on case by case basis	Business and IT are fully aligned at all times and share a common cultural ethos
12	Lack of accountability beyond own functional area ('your problems do not resonate with me')	Shared sense of urgency pervades the organization

EXTERNAL ATTRIBUTES		
13	Mindset: "The customer must buy what I produce."	Mindset: "I must produce what the customer buys."
14	Decisions impacting customers and business partners taken internally in isolation	Customer and business partners participate in generating ideas that impact them
15	Focused only on fulfilling current needs of stakeholders	Focused equally on anticipating and meeting future demand from stakeholders
16	Supply-driven. Focused on purchasing, manufacturing, distributing	Demand-driven. Focused on fulfillment
17	Service refers to incident management	Service means customer experience management over entire lifecycle

Exercise: *Looking at both sides of Table 8-1, tag the characteristics that most closely reflect the culture in your own company. What do you conclude? Are you leaning towards an analog (left) or a digital (right) culture? List down the top 5 characteristics from this table, in the order of priority, that your company must espouse for gaining improved respect of its employees and customers. What has prevented this from happening so far?*

The above table lists only some of the *changeable* cultural attributes for acquiring and sustaining a high level of BITA. The cultural *core,* meanwhile, remains largely unaltered. As you step up your BITA level, it is this core that gives the enterprise its grounding. It is *not* situational. This core has probably been the result of years of conscious effort starting from the founding fathers of the company. If you look at large global conglomerates like IBM, GE, and Tata they have all cultivated their unique personalities based on the core cultural ethos they have espoused, which they have not given up for digitization. Digital natives like Google, Facebook, Apple among others have also built their distinctive personalities as companies that listen to customers, create great products (offerings) and have a work environment to die for. Many young and successful digital startups too – while still not having unique personalities – have created their own cultural identities that set them apart from their peers. Unfortunately, there are also examples of companies devoid of a cultural core that remained focused on relentless pursuit of short-term gains by any means. These shall remain unnamed here, but I am sure you, the reader, can easily cite examples from your own experiences. I would be very wary of investing in the stock of such companies.

What is this cultural core? Does your company have one? Think about it – what are the three (or more) values or beliefs that have remained unchanged for at least last seven years (or since your company started) and that you are sure will *not* be compromised in future as well? If you cannot answer this question off-hand, look at table 8-2 below and tick off at least three values on which your company would *never* compromise, irrespective of the consequences. Easy enough? What about you as an individual? What are the values that would prompt you to jump ship if compromised?

This is a random list of some attributes that form the cultural core. See if you can add to this from your own experience at your present or past organizations.

Table 8-2: Core beliefs

Integrity	Transparency	Accountability	Diversity
Customer-centricity	Respect for people, trust	Ethical conduct	Innovation, dare-to-try
Emphasis on Quality	Emphasis on Service	Emphasis on Safety	One company
Intolerance for mediocrity	Fairness (Impartiality)	Simplicity	Openness to change

There's a company I know which started off over two years ago as an internet-based aggregator that could pull items out of various apparel catalogues (of different brands) to create personalized wear - down to combination, style, color, size, etc. through a single interface. I never quite understood the exact business model, but I presume the idea was to be an end-to-end outfitter, reducing the need for customers to go to several stores (online as well as real) to complete their ensemble. I know one of the founders, and he had walked me through quite an impressive website where you could upload your picture, physical measurements, etc. and it would create a 'model' of you on the screen, and then you could choose various clothes to 'try on'! Anyhow, the visual aspects aside, I knew this founder was a principled individual and was confident that his company would do well. And it did. At the end of its first year of operations, it had gone up from a staff of just the three founders to a sizable office in an uptown building employing about 30 people, and by about 18 months from inception, they had acquired customers in all parts of the country and doubled their employee count. They even went to some reputed colleges during the campus hiring season and picked up some bright youngsters to add to their strength.

When the company had started, the founders had clearly articulated a vision for the company to guide it for next three years. The company also stood out from most start-ups as one that had a strong and clearly articulated belief system that emphasized excellence in customer service, as well as respect for people.

As the company was completing two years of operation, the business trajectory started flattening and in the next few months was on a downward spree. The initial excitement was apparently over, and the company had not sufficiently scaled up to keep their hold on the customer base through more innovative offerings. It had no choice but to retrench people at short notice. Unfortunately, the matter was handled quite insensitively – which was very uncharacteristic of the company as it had a culture that stressed respect for people – leading to several unpleasant episodes with the departing employees. A lot of these employees claimed that its culture was only a façade and even called the company inhuman.

The question is, can business exigencies subordinate the belief system or its *practice*? In the above example, business pressures clearly forced them to go against the 'respect for people' belief to somehow keep the business afloat. In hindsight, it is easy to say that rather than firing later, they should have gone slower on their hiring. But that wouldn't be entirely fair. The point, however, is that business pressures can undoubtedly call for difficult measures, but it is at such times that the culture is put to its real test. Businesses can, and often do, turn around, but if you let go of your beliefs you would have lost your character, and that certainly is a lot tougher to rebuild.

Luckily, the venture capitalists were still optimistic about the company and it got more funding, which was utilized to upscale and expand, and I hope they now have a long and stable run.

(If you need a more extreme example of how an ostensibly good culture could fall flat when the ride gets rough, think of Kingfisher Airlines. Even if the airline were to revive under the same management in future, I doubt that a lot of the earlier staff would willingly come back to work for it again.)

Culture does not lend itself to some standard formulae to give it a fillip, or to any form of metrics for measurement. It is intrinsic to the organization's spirit.

We are treading on extremely thin ice therefore when we talk about assessing the cultural grounding of one enterprise as compared to another. In our BITA Calculator, we did include certain statements on the Culture dimension, but that was in the overall context of BITA measurement and contained only a set of 'observable' aspects of culture. I hope that this tool has helped you with an approximate idea of your organization's standing on the cultural dimension. In general, I have found this to be a fair indicator of an organization's strengths and weaknesses on the cultural dimension if carried out over a healthy and well-represented group size.

Let's take this a bit further, staying focused on the cultural dimension only. We will try to devise a more contextual (i.e., pertaining to *your own specific environment*) procedure to ascertain the factors, or cultural attributes, that are characteristic of a robust BITA, and discover which of these *you* need to build, or nurture, for sustained alignment.

This is a simple exercise which has no pre-conditions or requisites except that it asks you to come in with an open mind. In general, organizations respond best to such exercises in a 'workshop' mode, facilitated by an external, neutral agency. However, that does not preclude running it on your own with one person from the group playing the role of a moderator. This is also a matter of culture, incidentally!

Remember, perceptions rule when it comes to assessing culture. If it is not *perceived* to be part of your values or behaviors, it is *not* happening. Intents and claims do not matter. So please go with your spontaneous response in this exercise.

Step-1. Form a group of experienced people who are able and willing to participate in this exercise. The ideal group size is 8-10 comprising an equal mix of **Business** and **IT**. It may take up to 3 hours of their time. Communicate the brief purpose of the session at least 3 days in advance.

Step-2. On the appointed day, meet in a relatively quiet setting where disturbances and interruptions are going to be minimal. The room should have a whiteboard, a flip-chart stand with about 20 charts, markers, writing pads for each participant, a laptop, and overhead projector.

Step-3. The person appointed to be the 'moderator' will take the whiteboard and write down: "What constitutes good culture?"

Step-4. Give the group about 10-15 minutes to individually jot down as many ideas as possible on what, in *their opinion*, constitutes good culture. It is important to remember that this is independent of the culture in *your* company. It is just to get a general view of the *desired* attributes that people *think* make a great culture. (Participants may at some point be shown Table 8-3 for clues, but should not *restrict* their ideas to this.)

Step-5. At the end of this period, the moderator goes to the flip-chart and asks for inputs (one at a time) around the table. Each person contributes one idea in his or her turn, and the moderator writes down all the *unique* points on the flipcharts. S/He does not give 'expert comments' on the inputs. Just takes them down so that at the end, there are at least *40-50 unique attributes* on the list. [A sample list is included in Table 8-3.]

Step-6. It's time for a 15-minute break. But not for the moderator. During the break, the moderator quickly types out the inputs on a word or excel file which can be displayed from the OHP.

Table C1: Values

SN	Definitely not stated or implied in our Values	Not sure if implied in our Values	Definitely stated or implied in our Values

Step-7. After the break, the moderator displays a blank table (Table C1 here) on the screen:

Step-8. The aim is to call out each item from the desired attributes list and place it in *one of the three columns* here, as per the inputs from the group.

The term "*Values*" is used to collectively describe the organization's values, belief system, rules and code-of-conduct that guide the behavior of the people in the organization. Note that this includes the core (unshakeable) beliefs as well as the non-core (changeable) cultural attributes that constitute the set of *prescribed* behaviors in the organization. This is not a literal but a representational term.

Step-9. Before going further, the moderator explains to the group the meaning of the 3 columns so that everyone is on the same page:

Table C1a: Values

SN	Definitely not stated or implied in our Values	Not sure if implied in our Values	Definitely stated or implied in our Values
	# Finds no mention in stated belief system	# Articulated only in customer meetings, induction	# Guide to behavior
			# Stressed in team meetings
	# Management hardly ever brings this up in their communication	# Posters, screen-savers, co. website proclaim it but not stressed by management	# Clearly stated in the belief system
			# Never questioned
	# Not shared in employee orientation and other programs	# Known cases of the belief and its opposite being stated	# Included in induction and orientation programs
		# Often questioned as no one is sure	# Role modelling by mgmnt
	# No examples set for reinforcing the belief		# Pervades the spirit of the organization
		# Articulated only during good times	

(This is only a guide. The group may debate and add/modify the rules.)

Step-10. If for example, 'Common Courtesy towards people' is one of the attributes in the 'desired' list which is *generally* felt by the group, going by the above rules, to be NOT part of the values of the organization, this will go in column one.

On some points, there may be a debate on the column to be used (most commonly in attributes like Accountability, Empowerment which could be position dependent). In my experience, if there are even two dissenters, that value is not ingrained, and the attribute should be listed in column 1 or at best 2. Do not attempt to be too democratic.

Step-11. The moderator populates the Values table in real-time as each desired attribute is called out until the entire desired-attributes list is exhausted. At the end of this part of the session, you have a fair view of where your company stands vis-à-vis its values. It's usually quite insightful to look at the three columns, as an indicator of what people do recognize as values and what is desired, but missing or ambiguous.

Step-12. Having a set of beliefs, value system or code of conduct is rather meaningless if it is not *practiced* across the organization in a demonstrable way. The moderator now takes the group's attention back to the raw list of desired attributes. This time he asks for the group's view on the **practice** in the organization concerning each desired attribute.

Step-13. The moderator now displays the following table (Table C2) on the screen:

Table C2: Behavioural Practices

SN	Never (or very rarely) practiced	Sometimes practiced (situational)	Always practiced (Never or rarely compromised)

Step-14. Once the group is clear on the difference between Values and Practices, the moderator again proceeds to guide the group on the meaning of each column in the above table.

Step-15. Taking the items from the desired-attributes list one by one, the moderator invites the group's view on the correct column of the Practice Table to place them in. The interesting part here is that you may get a long list of items in the column-3 (Always practiced) even if the company has a non-existent or weak set of articulated values. Or for that matter, a strong value system may not necessarily lead to a strong practice system across the organization. The Practice table is about 'Walking the Talk.'

Table C2a: Behavioural Practices

SN	Never (or very rarely) practiced	Sometimes practiced (situational)	Always practiced (Never or rarely compromised)
	# Breach is tolerated withou consequences	# Practiced only in specific situations (e.g. in good time	# leads to recognition & rewards
	# No time, budget, resources invested for implementing	# Cases of consequential action for default are rare	# Guides behavior in crisis periods
	# No role models	# No recognition for demonstrating the practice	# Role modelling by mgmnt - lead by example
	# Not linked to employees' personal effectiveness goals	# Belief is proclaimed but n budget/resources given	# Resources readily allocated for reinforcement
	# No reinforcement from top		# Practiced even when no one is looking
			# Overrides business priorities

Step-16. Having completed the Beliefs and Practice tables, you may like to draw inferences on the extent to which values are put into practice in the company. The workshop ends here but not the work of the moderator (be careful before you nominate yourself to be a moderator – it is hard work!)

Step-17. At the end of the workshop, when the workshop participants have gone back to their calling, the moderator prints out the two tables that were laboriously created during the day. The next phase is analysis. Though the exercise has probably been insightful, you still don't have much to take back to your management.

The moderator creates another excel in which he makes four lists, under which he enters the attributes from the two tables as follows. Once an attribute is entered in a list, it is struck off from the tables.

List-1: Attributes that are found to be strong in both Values and Practice [common points in column-3 from each of the two tables].

List-2: Attributes that are found to be strong (i.e., in column-3) in the Values table, but weak (i.e., in columns-1 or 2) in the Practice table

List-3: Attributes that are found to be weak (i.e., in column 1 or 2) in the Values table, but strong (i.e., still in column-3) in the Practice table

List-4: Attributes that are found to be weak (i.e., in column 1 or 2) in the Values table, also weak (i.e., in column 1 or 2) in the Practice table [common points in columns 1 & 2 of both tables]

Having created the four lists above, the moderator now proceeds to create the **Culture Map** as below, listing the relevant attributes in the appropriate quadrants:

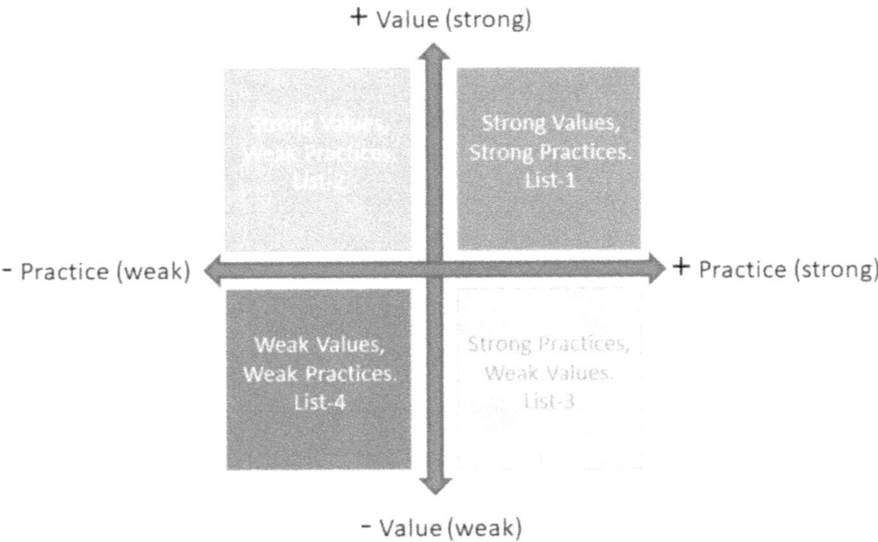

The moderator shares the culture map with the group members on the following day (while the matter is still fresh in mind) and seeks their concurrence. In the event of any strong differences (which normally doesn't happen as this is only plotting the agreed views of the group), it may be best to have another quick meeting to reach concurrence.

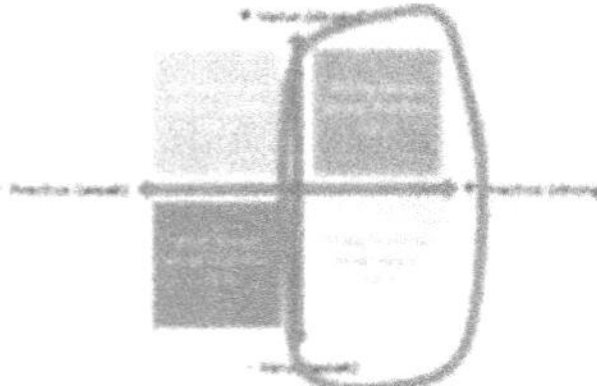

The attributes listed on the right of the y-axis are your cultural strengths – some of which (in the top right quadrant) are prescribed in the value system while some (in the bottom right quadrant) are the good and desirable practices that prevail despite (not being articulated in) the value system. It is normal for every organization to have good practices outside of the prescribed values (bottom-right quadrant). You may consider enhancing your value system to incorporate some of these prevalent practices. Good behavior and culture do stem from the prescribed values, and these are non-negotiable, but organizational maturity lies in demonstrating best practices even when they are not specifically dictated by the value system. To this extent, therefore, the bottom right quadrant is an indicator of the maturity of your organization. If you find an extended list of attributes falling in this quadrant, rejoice. They are your bonus points! Of course, the top-right quadrant is the best of all – the set of points here indicates that your value system is alive and thriving, both in spirit and action, at least with respect to the attributes included in this quadrant. In summary, all the attributes on the right of the axis are your strengths, and these must be preserved over time. Nurture them, most importantly by avoiding complacency.

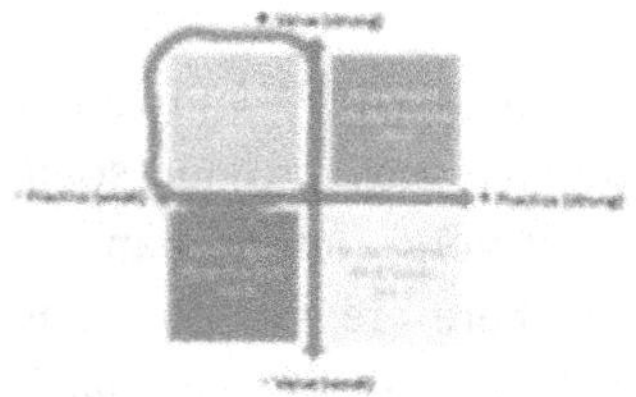

In as much as the bottom-right quadrant discussed above is an indicator of organizational maturity, the top-left quadrant may be said to be an indicator of the degree of *immaturity* in the organization. Let's remember, this quadrant is from the list of attributes that in the collective view of people who participated in the culture mapping exercise are the most DESIRABLE ones for the organization to have. On top of this, all the attributes in this quadrant are included in the prescribed VALUE SYSTEM of the organization. Yet there is no evidence, or even perception, of their inculcation in the organizational *practices*. If you have a long list here, it is indeed an unfortunate state of affairs, pointing to lax attitude and *absence of culture*. Immediate steps must be initiated to dive deeper in the root-causes and put in place serious measures to implement and monitor corrections. Not easy, but got to be done.

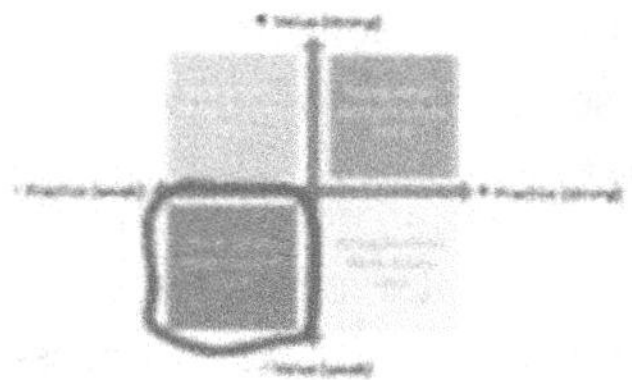

The bottom-left quadrant lists the desirable attributes that neither find a place in the articulated value system nor in the organizational practices. It calls for a more detailed impact analysis to ascertain if these missing traits are reflected in the organization's failure to retain talent, and win the trust of customers and partners. This is a longer-term exercise that may require supplementing the organizational values depending on the results of the impact analysis. Unless it is an unduly long list or has traits that are *significant* in some important context, put this on the slow and steady. In my view, focus on the top-left quadrant is of much more immediate concern.

Behaviors take time to weave themselves into the larger cultural fabric of the organization. Don't expect quick-fixes to work here. Ordinarily, the pattern of the culture-map will be slow to change, despite concerted efforts to bring this about. The next run of the culture mapping exercise should be done at least a year later, and preferably the composition of the participants should be changed in the next round.

After the final concurrence of the group members, present the culture map to your top management along with the list of improvements required and seek their approval on the action plan for raising the culture bar. In most cases, your astute senior management would be already cognizant of the pattern you are presenting. At least that's my experience. But they may be missing the details so go in with good preparation, particularly on recommendations and the precise support – including the budget for training etc. - that you seek from them.

Based on my own experiences and interactions with high BITA companies, I have prepared a 'master' list of cultural attributes that may provide some pointers during the brainstorming session to construct your culture map. Of course, given the myriad manifestations of culture, there are far too many variations to have a comprehensive list, so this should be taken only as a *sample* list of exhibited cultural features collated from several companies with high BITA levels. As a time-saver, you may conduct the culture workshop with this list in the backdrop.

I would have liked to enumerate a "must-have" list of cultural attributes that would apply to *everyone* aiming for a high BITA, but this would be a futile effort as culture is very intrinsic to each company and rather abstract. It should, however, be possible to cull out your own "must-have" list– especially in your evolution as a digital enterprise – as a corollary to the culture-mapping exercise. This should be consultatively drawn from the list of items that need to be *nurtured* (right of the y-axis), as well as from those that need to be *built* (left of the y-axis), the former being the low-hanging fruit.

Let me re-emphasize here that while the new age digital enterprises are characterized by a sharper focus on technology and innovation, strong Business-IT alignment, customer experience enhancement etc., some *core cultural values* are still as relevant in the new age as they were in the past. The maturity of the enterprise lies in retaining these attributes even in their haste to garner a greater share of their market, as companies have discovered both to their joy and peril.

Sample List of Cultural Attributes Collated from Some High-BITA Enterprises

Core(**C**) = Entrenched since inception (Hub)

Non-core (**N**) = Developed/ Changed with time (Tyre)

Table 8-3: Attributes of good culture

(This list is not in any particular order)

#	Attribute	C/N
1	High standard of **honesty** and **integrity** in conduct	C
2	Across-the-board **Customer-centricity**	C
3	Uncompromising **ethical business conduct**	C
4	Passionate about the **Vision**, driven from the top	C
5	Well-articulated **belief system**	C
6	Business and IT are 2-in-a-box (high on **BITA**)	C
7	**Respect** for the *individual* (not *position*)	C
8	**Impartiality** (fairness, lack of bias)	C
9	**Diversity** (Gender, Age, Ethnicity)	C
10	No compromise on **quality**	C
11	No compromise on **service**	C
12	No compromise on **security** and **safety**	C
13	Drive for **innovation**	C
14	Continuous **learning** and **development**	C
15	Intolerance for sexual harassment (**POSH**)	C
16	Intolerance for mediocrity (**excellence**)	C
17	All employees see themselves as '**customer satisfiers**'	C
18	In-built culture of **reliability** (in commitments, offerings, dealings)	C
19	Demonstration of **empathy** (mutual understanding)	C
20	**Go-getter** attitude – find a *way*, not a policy to hide behind	C
21	Emphasis on strong **relationship-building** with customers and partners	C
22	Awareness and demonstration of **social responsibility**	C
23	Respect for time (esp. of other people) and rules/policies – **punctuality** and **discipline**	C
24	**Achievement-oriented** culture – sanctity of goals and performance against goals	C

25	Displaying **common courtesy** towards people regardless of role or function	C
26	Displaying **sensitivity** to the situation of others – new joiners, interviewees, vendors	C
27	Atmosphere of mutual **trust** and **credibility**	C
28	**Transparency** and **Openness** (e.g. open door policy)	N
29	**Flexibility** (Willingness to change)	N
30	**Simplicity** in work processes	N
31	**One company** – no silos, functional boundaries	N
32	**Accountability** for results, outcomes	N
33	**Empowerment (trust**) at all levels	N
34	**Technologically charged** environment (BYOD, Mobility etc.)	N
35	Shared **sense of urgency**	N
36	**Freedom** to express disagreement	N
37	**Pride** of belonging	N
38	Information sharing – open and frequent **communication**	N
39	Attitude of **eagerness to serve** internal customers (employees of other functions)	N
40	Emphasis on **loyalty**, not just meeting needs	N
41	**Customer-oriented** frontline (**empowered** to serve)	N
42	**Minimal supervision**, i.e., no micromanagement	N
43	Appetite for **risk-taking** (dare-to-try spirit)	N
44	Emphasis on regular **soft-skills**(behavioral) development	N
45	**Value-driven**, not cost-driven, in decision making	N
46	Taking direct feedback to **include customer views** in design and creation	N
47	**Solution driven**, not product driven	N
48	Promote **collaboration** – both internal and external	N
49	Emphasis on building and nurturing **strategic alliances**	N
50	**New ideas** and **initiative-taking** is encouraged	N
51	**Sharing** and **cooperation** – generating options, solutions *together*(inter-functional)	N
52	Keeping customers **looped-in** at all times	N
53	Keeping colleagues from other departments **plugged-in** on developments, priorities	N
54	**Data-driven** and **fact-based** conclusions drive decisions	N

55	**Listening** to the voice of employees, customers	N
56	**Value information** (hard or soft) as a critical business asset	N
57	Focus on impact to business rather than RoI, uptime etc. (**outcome-based IT**)	N
58	**Responsive**, not reactive	N
59	Spirit of **out-doing the competition** (emphasis on market intelligence, TTM etc.)	N
60	**Functional integration** – absence of organizational silos	N
61	Abundance of **data-bandwidth** (availability of communication channels)	N
62	**Lack of fear** in taking customer problems to management	N
63	Encouragement of **questioning** the rationale behind decisions, policies, processes	N
64	The **devil-is-in-the-details** approach; getting to the root-cause to eliminate problems	N
65	**Fun at the workplace** – attractive environment for millennials	N
66	Focus on the **long-term** – anticipating the future	N
67	Reliance on **digital channels** for customer reach out	N
68	Adoption of **SMAC** for business	N
69	Making it **easy to get things done** due to absence of bureaucratic culture	N
70	Focus on **Employee engagement** to boost productivity, motivation	N

At first glance, it would appear that ALL the cultural attributes are a 'must-have' in the company's set of required behavioral practices. And to an extent, these all are indeed demonstrated from time to time in all companies, and by most individuals. However, it is not practicable to evolve a code of conduct that encompasses everything. In fact, this may become counter-productive since no one will be quite clear on what specifically is needed to be focused – you can't be all things to all people all the time! It is therefore perfectly normal to have a *few* values and practices that define your 'personality', but it does not preclude good behavior on the other attributes. In fact, the chances are that if your organisation's culture is strong enough to have a well-ingrained value system that is dutifully practiced, there is a sense of order and discipline in the company that embraces the other good practices, regardless of the value system.

Culture is a unique organizational characteristic that pervades its length and breadth. What is good for BITA is therefore good for the company, and vice versa. Everything we have talked about in this chapter applies equally well to Business and IT together as a subset of the larger organization. A *common cultural root* becoming the foundation for both Business and IT ensures parity in values, behaviors and actions, and hence is a potent ingredient for alignment. Without alignment at the cultural level, that is, having a similar stance on the *values* and *practices* in the organization, it would be a waste of effort to attempt to reach alignment on the other dimensions. When you perform the culture mapping exercise, you define a desired and viable set of values and practices that both Business and IT agree are the required foundation for achieving success together. Sustaining a high performing culture, or ensuring the solidity and strength of this foundation, must remain a continuous endeavor of Business and IT, never to be taken for granted.

The culture map consists of the list of cultural attributes that are most desirable for the enterprise in the combined view of Business and IT. There are often ideas that are suppressed to keep conflict at bay. For example, 'Adoption of BYOD for all employees' may be a point of contention, and hence not included due to lack of consensus. Such missing attributes could later manifest as glitches in BITA which could be difficult to detect. For a credible culture map, a climate in which people are not intimidated from vocalizing their ideas is essential. Table 8-3 is included here as a sounding board for this reason.

It's always easier to exemplify than explain, and probably more absorbing for the readers too. Let me illustrate this with another familiar example.

This is a story about how cultural gaps can erode customer loyalty with the teams involved having no clue on the root-causes of their failure to win and retain a customer. I was associated as a technology partner with a company which was itself a thriving large digital enterprise in the high-tech solutions business. Things were initially going well between the company and this customer – who was an existing corporate client. The customer was not a large enterprise, but a medium-sized one – an aspiring digital enterprise – with about 60 employees in two locations. But they served a sizeable customer base with their merchandising business, centerd on sourcing and distribution using digital channels. This customer had a requirement for a lightweight customer relationship management (CRM) system so that it could not only better service its customers but also build, over time, a repository of invaluable information on customer preferences, buying patterns, sentiments etc.

The customer approached this company for a solution. The area business manager mailed the IT team to propose a suitable solution. This customer was a remote one, i.e., not in one of the metropolitan areas, so the IT team suggested having a teleconference with the customer to understand the requirement. This was duly arranged, and in due course, with Business and IT working together, a cloud-based CRM solution was devised and proposed. The customer was all for it, as being of a digital disposition, he preferred the cloud to bulky on-premise servers. So far so good.

The business manager conveyed the customer's expected timeline for the project to which the concerned IT architect agreed. When the requirements were analyzed, it emerged that there were several parts of the project, like customizing the user interface in accordance with the agreed scope, performing back-end integration with the customer's existing IT infrastructure etc., that were beyond the core competence of the IT team. Also, the core product (CRM) had to be sourced from a vendor with whom the company had not yet renewed the reseller agreement. The poor IT architect was taken to task for making a commitment without consulting his management. While all this was happening, the customer was not kept informed, and he was happily basking in the belief that all was going according to plan. That is because both IT and Business assumed it to be the others' responsibility to inform the customer! Anyhow, the teams kept at it on a best-effort basis, but could not steer the project back on track.

When the customer was eventually informed that there's going to be a delay, he was quite shaken. His business was a relatively small one, and it depended heavily on this project. The business team meanwhile was more concerned about their quotas and were busy chasing other customers. The matter was left to IT. In a discussion between the customer and IT, the customer suggested a simpler version for the initial launch, but this was not accepted as it would have meant changes to the work already done. The customer wrote a harsh letter to the president of the business unit who summoned the CIO. A team of technical specialists, accompanied by the area business manager, was rushed to the site for a firsthand assessment of the situation. The specialists called in the business VP to suggest a costlier, but quicker-to-deploy, alternative solution than the one earlier included/costed. With margins already eroded in this delayed project, this request was summarily turned down. The team then was left with no choice but to make the cardinal mistake of asking the customer whether timeline was more important to him or features, one of which would necessarily have to be sacrificed to salvage the project. By now the customer was apparently of the view that if any sacrifice was to be made, it would be of his current vendor! He calmly informed them that rather than re-ignite the project with a company that had betrayed him, he would cast his net afresh to find a better company to work with. And he did. This company had obviously been too complacent to believe that even an existing (satisfied) customer had the option to go to the competition. They lost this customer for good.

Sounds familiar? It's not surprising if it does. Many of us do pass through such experiences not because we lack the proper intent, but due to an inability to cope with multiple, and conflicting, demands and priorities. We find ourselves at a loss. And that is where culture can be your savior. If we consider the above story, there are many practices that were disregarded, even though the cultural ethos dictates them. Going with the list of attributes that was presented earlier in this chapter (Table 8-3), we find that at least the following cultural attributes were overlooked, to varying extents:

- Across the board Customer-Centricity
- Business and IT are 2-in-a-box
- Transparency and Openness
- Flexibility (openness to change)
- Shared sense of urgency
- Inbuilt culture of reliability (of commitment)
- Emphasis on loyalty, not just meeting needs
- Go-getter attitude – find a way
- Value-driven, not cost-driven, in decision making
- Emphasis on strong relationship-building with customers and partners
- Feedback loop involving customers
- Emphasis on strategic alliances
- Spirit of out-doing the competition

It is quite clear that these cultural gaps were neither recognized nor acknowledged in the company, which prided itself on its strong cultural bonding across its functional units! Some lessons in life are reserved to be learned only the hard way!

As we move to the next dimension of BITA, let us only remember that for Business-IT alignment to become your differentiating edge, culture is your most potent weapon. The world is replete with stories of great companies almost always characterized by a great culture. I researched a lot to include a story where I could illustrate a company that was admired by its employees and customers even though it did *not* have a terrific culture. I couldn't find any. With culture comes character, that invisible force which compels you to do the right thing in all situations.

Culture cannot be externally reinforced or thrust upon a company. However, it is important to discover the subtle and not-so-subtle characteristics which could inhibit or accelerate your progress on a rough road, and I hope this chapter has been of some little help in this discovery.

If you think you are now on a strong cultural footing, or at least are on the right course towards it, it is time to turn our attention to the next BITA dimension. If your culture has given you character, your **strategy** will provide you the *direction* to guide you in your journey.

10 The Strategy Statement

*"Every battle is won **before** it is fought."*

In the olden days, the term strategy was chiefly used in the context of military and warfare. It was a plan of execution centerd around one goal: to DEFEAT the enemy. At the time, strategy was broadly a two-step process – first, an assessment of the relative strengths and vulnerabilities, and second, a plan to exploit them to vanquish the enemy. The battle maneuvers and tactics, like equipping the soldiers and motivating them to a frenzy directed against the enemy, stemmed from the strategy.

History is brimming with accounts of triumphs that resulted not from greater strength in numbers or superior weaponry but better strategy. The battle of Thermopylae fought around 500BC is the story of a relatively minuscule number of Greek warriors, equipped only with spears and shields, holding off a massive Persian attack – according to some scholars one of the largest armies in the history of medieval warfare – through the courageous attitude of its warriors and a sound strategy. This strategy required, among other things, positioning the troops on the mouth of the Pass of Thermopylae – which was on the only known path through which the massive Persian army could pass to invade. It worked. They could hold off the attack for a full week before being annihilated due to betrayal by a defector who revealed to the Persian army another path, allowing it to attack the Greeks from behind. Of special note here is the courage and bravado of the 300 Spartans, distinguished warriors of the Greek army, who defiantly fought the Persians to their very last. The movie '**300**' is a very engrossing, if somewhat graphic, account of this ancient battle, immortalizing the Spartan warriors. Do watch it, if you haven't yet.

The above story has a striking similarity to today's BITA-led world of digital business. The marketplace is the new battleground. Companies, small and big, are faced with the challenge of defending their turf and gaining ground against very fierce competition. In such a scenario, the attitude of its frontline Business and IT employees and their alignment to a common purpose are the company's lifeline. Along its way, the company also needs to be on its guard against disruptive forces (like the defector in the story) bent upon its downfall. In the above story, the greatest emphasis was on strategically deploying fearless troops to take on a very formidable enemy. This process evidently started much before the battle, with drafting individuals who could become, eventually, Spartan warriors. Similarly, in the context of digital business, picking people with the right business *and* technology orientation, a never-say-die attitude, and ability to work interdependently is vital to the success of the strategy.

The *strategy* is a map that tells you *how* to get from where you are to where you want to be. In other words, it's the blueprint that guides you in the accomplishment of your mission. *Strategic alignment* occurs when different strategies pursue a common mission.

A strategy is not a directive. The first and the most important part of evolving a successful strategy is to ensure that people who are responsible for executing it have a say in formulating it. Top-down strategies are passé. Regrettably, in many companies, I have experienced that a lot of people in the low and middle order go about their daily jobs without having a clue of how they fit into the larger game plan or big picture. If you ask them to state the goal or purpose of what they are doing, they look confused and go into a deep reflective stance trying to *remember* their purpose! Day after grueling day, they just "turn the wheel", content with being mindless instruction-followers. Taking an analogy from Covey's 7-Habits, they see themselves as aimless stone-crushers, rather than as members of a team building a cathedral! It is difficult to imagine any strategy succeeding in this backdrop, esp. in this Digital Age.

A strategy is not developed only for the CEO, his D-Rs, and the Chief Strategy Officer, with the sole aim of presenting to the Board. If a strategy does not include the frontline people or the people who are working with external or internal customers (which means everyone in the company), it is not a strategy at all, but a pretense doomed to failure from the very start.

It is more common for larger corporations to have a strategy which is not well disseminated or 'bought-in.' The best way to avoid this is to have representation from *each* function in the core strategy group to ensure buy-in to the *business* strategy. The functional representative, typically the Function Head, in the

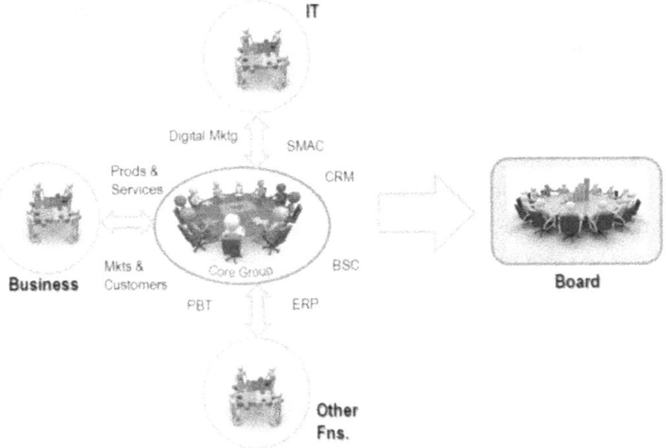

1. A good strategy has inputs and buy-in of all its stakeholders, not just the core group.
2. Functional strategies must CONVERGE into the unified organizational strategy.

business strategy meeting comes to the meeting after taking inputs from *his/her* team on the strategic priorities of the function. Once the larger *business* strategy has been *collaboratively* decided at the group level, each function head then must assure its dissemination in his/her team and derive the *functional* strategy from it. The overall strategy, once approved and accepted, is cast in concrete and is no longer open to negotiation, barring some extreme circumstances and with approval from the Board.

Let's return briefly to our theme of terrestrial warfare to highlight another important aspect of strategy. In a war, the mission of every unit – ordnance, artillery, engineers, signals, etc. – is to enable the frontline (infantry) to advance. Even the most powerful army in the world would be trounced if its different units had conflicting strategies, not aligned to the mission, which pulled the army in different directions. Convergence is key. In the corporate world too, the strategy of every function must converge into the overall business mission of the company. An IT strategy (or any functional strategy) that is not convergent with the business mission is untenable and meaningless. Such a 'strategy' is only an internal plan of action to get around functional bottlenecks that are of no concern to anyone outside the immediate group of people tasked with them. It's also against the outcome-based model of IT, being focused on input parameters rather than the business/customer-facing output parameters.

An overarching *statement of purpose*– or mission – is crucial for convergence, as this example from my own experience illustrates. If everyone in the team is aligned to this one (or few) statement(s) from which the strategy emanates, the task of acceptance and personal ownership becomes a lot easier.

As CIO of a large technology company, I was often asked what the IT strategy of my company was. My answer was always the same, and it was quite uncomplicated: The purpose of IT is to make the business successful. Therefore, the IT strategy is simply a plan *to achieve the business mission*. Everyone in the IT team was tuned to this fact. There was no ambiguity in anyone's mind, and the purpose was clear to even the newest recruit in the team. Every single element in the IT strategy and every single KRA of each person in the IT team had to answer "Yes" to the question: "Does this contribute in a measurable way to making the business successful?" If a person was not clear on how a KRA or strategy statement was accomplishing this, he or she was encouraged to discuss with me and during the discussion, I would either explain the rationale or work with the person and his/her manager to redraft the KRA. But in no event would I accept lack of clarity on the strategy or goals. Across the different vertical arms of IT, including the external partners, I found that having this unambiguous mission helped to unify the team into a single cohesive one.

As in the example above, a strategy is derived from the *mission* of the company. However, a mission is typically somewhat all-encompassing and rather sweeping in its articulation, and cannot be directly translated into a strategy. For example, the business mission could be *to anticipate customer needs and provide lasting value through outstanding software products and services built to help our customers stay ahead.* How do you accomplish such a mission? You break it down into achievable aims, like understand market pulse, develop new products and customizations (to a timeline), improve quality, enhance customer experience, establish competitive pricing while ensuring profitability, etc. Each of these is a *strategic goal* towards accomplishing the larger mission. The mission is also the basis of the long-term aspiration as a company or the *vision* of its future. All this can be a bit confusing as there are many terms – vision, mission, goal, objective, strategy, plan – constantly being thrown around, and they all have overlapping, yet distinct meanings. I am sure you have a fair idea, through your earlier experiences, of what these terms mean but just for a quick and ready reference, here is a concise table clarifying these terms:

Vision	The **future** that you would like to create for yourself, E.g., to be on the cover of Forbes as the most admired company of the year in terms of customer value creation.
Mission	The statement of **purpose** that defines *why* you exist, E.g., to make a positive difference in people's lives through timely, reliable and secure information technology solutions for the BFSI sector.
Strategic Goals	The mission broken down into a set of **aims**, or intended actions - like enhance customer experience, achieve growth in revenues, conduct business profitably, etc.
Objectives	The strategic goals supplemented with **measurable** parameters like timelines, numbers etc. (like, achieve a revenue growth of 15% over last fiscal, achieve 20% PBT etc.)
KRAs	The Specific, Measurable, Attainable, Relevant and Time-bound (SMART) objectives assigned to **individual**s in the group in conformance with the strategic goals of the function
Action Plan	The set of specific **actions** for achieving each goal – must have owner, timeline, and measurement
KPI	**Metric** to indicate measure of success against each objective, like revenue achieved in first 4 months in the current year, vs. previous years' actual for the same period
Strategy	The **roadmap** for getting from where you are to where you want to be. That is, a plan to achieve the goals derived from the company or business mission.

Let's not get too much into the subtler points of difference between the various heads above. For BITA, let us only remember that *strategic alignment* refers to convergence at *all* stages of the strategy, from mission to KPIs (see figure alongside).

Strategic alignment does not mean that Business and IT have the same goals and plans and go about doing the very same things. That would only create a rather gooey mixture of uncertain charter. Aligning does mean that Business and IT derive their strategic goals, priorities, action plans and KPIs from a *common mission* (and vision). Every objective, KRA and KPI of IT should be traceable to the same mission from which Business derives its objectives, KRAs and KPIs.

Strategic Alignment
Why do we exist?
Mission
At Company level
What do we want to be?
Vision
At Company level
What must we achieve?
Strategic Goals
Specific to Function
What are the measurable outcomes?
Objectives
Specific to Function
What are the planned actions and results?
KRAs, Action Plans
For each individual
What is the measure of success?
Measurement (KPIs)
At every level

As we said, Strategic Alignment requires aligning at *every* stage of the sequence, *from Mission to KPIs*. What does this stage-wise alignment mean, particularly in this Digital Age? Let's look at this briefly.

Mission Alignment: Business and IT are on *one* mission and the strategy of both is to accomplish this common mission. Though this may seem the obvious thing to do, in a lot of companies, old and new, the mission statement is a mouthful of platitudes and no one gives it much thought during strategy formulation – or thereafter. As a first important step towards creating a meaningful strategy, and strategic alignment, it is important to assure that the organization is serious about its mission, articulates it clearly and ensures its dissemination across its length and breadth.

BUSINESS
TECHNOLOGY

Let's take the case study of a company that provides wireless and terrestrial communication services to retail (i.e., personal) and enterprise (i.e., corporate) customers. Let's call this company Aligned Communications Ltd, ACL in short (no bearing to any company with a similar name, if it exists). ACL has an extensive cellular and fiber network in its country and is known for its wide range of digital telecommunication services. Like your own telecom service provider, it strives to bring innovative offerings to its customers before its competition. Of late, it has tied up with services companies (in software, mobility, cloud spaces) to become a next-generation *service* provider and move out of the 'label' of being a communication pipe provider, or a utility company.

An example of a mission for ACL could be as below. ACL has invested time and effort in ensuring that this mission is clear to all its employees and partners and that they can relate to it:

Our mission is to empower our customers by offering a superior experience across a wide range of communication services. As a preferred service provider, we will create lasting shareholder value while being a great place to work and a responsible member of our community.

For now, I urge you to not go into the merits of the statement. For sure it can be polished and improved. The idea is to show that a mission statement is an articulation of the reason for your existence. If your mission is not reflecting the organization's real purpose or is not clearly understood by its people, you've lost the race even before you have begun! The mission is the seed from which the goals, strategy, objectives, and KPIs emanate – not just for the business function but IT and other support functions as well. If business draws its strategy from this mission, and the strategy of IT is *to make the business successful*, IT is, in effect, upholding the larger mission and is aligned with the business.

Vision Alignment: When you have a clear mission that states your purpose, do you really need a vision for the company? Well, yes. The purpose of vision is to *inspire*. The vision rallies the organization behind a collective dream of building the future together.

As Stephen Covey says in the 7-Habits, Vision is *the ability to see with your mind what you cannot yet see with your eyes*. So very aptly put. And there are many cases of companies exemplifying this definition in their vision statement. Like the prophetic Microsoft vision in the 1990s: 'A computer at every desk running Microsoft software,' or the inspiring Intel vision: 'This decade we will create and extend computing technology to connect and enrich the life of every person on Earth.'

Like mission, the vision must be shared across the company. Different functions or groups within the company cannot be guided by divergent views of the future of the company. That is, in our BITA context, both Business and IT are inspired by a *single* vision for strategic alignment.

Returning to ACL, let's say its vision is *to be the trailblazer in the evolution of a smarter planet by enabling affordable, secure and reliable internetworking for the next 5 billion devices by 2022.*

This vision, as we see, is independent of function, role or level – as a vision should be. It applies to and is an inspiration for, *everyone* working directly or indirectly with the company. For Business and IT to align at a strategic level, they must share, and be inspired by, the *same* vision of the future.

I have been asked variously about the Technology vision of my company. The best way to answer this is to simply point the questioner to the company vision (like ACL's) and say – *that's* the vision for Technology in my company. This vision will guide us on which technologies to phase out and which ones to embrace in future. While one strives to stay step-locked with the global technological trends, the vision influences their adoption, not the other way.

Goal Alignment: As we said earlier, alignment is not equivalence. This means that an alignment of Business and IT does *not* impose an identical set of goals, even as they both pursue a common mission and are inspired by the same vision of the future. In our earlier depiction, we have shown a branching out after the Vision stage implying distribution of goals at a *functional* level, unlike the mission and vision which were at a company level. Of course, some of the goals may overlap across functions in pursuit of the common mission, but in general, goal sets are functional.

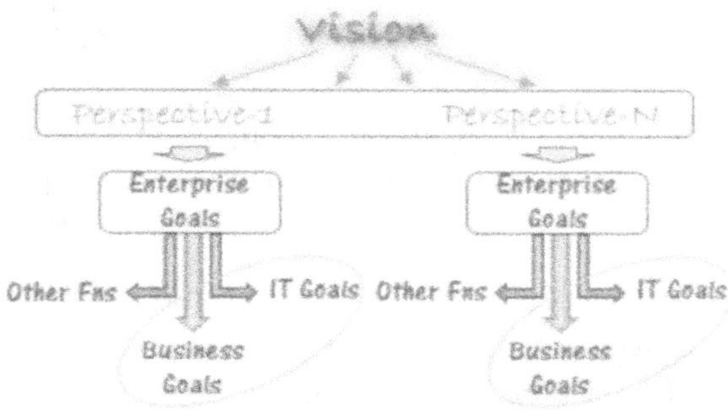

It is customary to segment the strategic goals and objectives along a universal set of *perspectives* that are common to each function. A typical set of perspectives may be – Fiscal, Client, External (Market), Internal (Process) and Development (Human Capital). The goals are classified under these common perspectives to facilitate alignment. Here is an example of a set of *business* goals for our company, ACL, along five chosen perspectives.

Function: *Business/Enterprise*

Perspective	Strategic Goal
Fiscal	Increase revenues from new products, customers (acquisition)
	Reduce churn levels – Prioritize HNI base(retention)
	Optimize operating costs
	Achieve PBT growth
Client	Deliver improved customer experience at all touch points
	Invite customer participation in product innovation
	Segment customer base for differentiated and personalized experience
External (Market)	Sustain brand advantage. Strengthen brand in Eastern India
	Reinforce network of sales and distribution channels
Internal(Process)	Align Technology architecture with business roadmap
	Improve key internal processes – SCM, Rev Assurance, Asset Monitoring& Control
	Consolidate information management across functions (Company MIS)
	Streamline compliance and governance
Development	Assess and strengthen BITA (competitive advantage)
(HC)	Implement effective KM system (empowerment)
	Institute rewards & recognition for innovation in thinking and behavior (culture)

The above system of classifying objectives is a fallout of the *Balanced Score Card* (BSC) method which stresses that enterprises also focus on goals other than financial for their all-round and sustained development. Classifying goals from different perspectives helps in clustering related goals together and enables sharper focus. Both Business and IT formulate their goals from the same perspectives.

The above set of strategic goals is designed for the *Business* function, or could even be at an enterprise level as an over-arching set of goals to guide all functions in their strategy formulation. The IT function derives its goals to harmonize with these Business goals. As an example, let us consider the first goal under the Fiscal perspective – *Increase revenues from new products, customers (acquisition).*IT may not carry this goal exactly as articulated, but may derive the following goals from it – (1) Assure fast time-to-market and operational readiness to support new products in line with business plan, and (2) Build capacity for supporting new customers without loss of performance. Similarly, *every* goal of IT must be traceable to a business goal for perfect alignment. Some of the correspondence may be subtle and implicit, but still traceable. If you go back again to the above table of business goals, you will be able to formulate in your mind an IT goal for *every* business goal included. Try to do this as an exercise now.

A company that I was associated with as a consultant prided itself on its heavy emphasis on Business-IT alignment. Their CEO informed me that its IT managers carried a goal with up to 20% weight "to align with business." As would be clear to my readers, that's *not* how it works. BITA means alignment of *mission*, i.e., at the level of *every* strategic goal, rather than one sweeping "align with business" goal. And it must be carried by every employee in the team, not just the managers. It took us several workshop sessions and redrafts to finally get them to see the light and change the IT strategic goals. Suddenly there is a renewed vigor in its approach to business and customer issues. Now *that's* a matter of pride.

Objectives Alignment: Strategic goals are a great way to set you in the right direction. They are like a beacon that you follow to stay on course. But to ensure that you don't just keep drifting forever, you need a bearing on how far, or where, you must go (a target) as also on how soon you must get there (a timeline). That is, to achieve specific results, you aim for tangible outcomes that you can measure and monitor. In other words, you need more *objectivity*. A goal that is supplemented with a clear and measurable end-result and a timeline becomes an *objective*. For example, while 'increase revenue' may be good as a strategic goal, it doesn't really fire you up as much as saying that 'increase revenues by 15% Y-o-Y.' In case your previous year's revenue was INR 1000 Crore, you are clear that you must achieve 1150 Cr, which you may then proceed to distribute across product lines, regions, etc.

Alignment requires that for each strategic goal, Business and IT have *complementary* objectives. Thus, if a strategic goal has two objectives under Business and two under IT, together the four objectives lead to its achievement. They *reinforce* each other. This is only an *example* that cites one possible way of deriving aligned objectives for Business and IT. You may create your own based on your specific situation. The objectives are defined at the *Function* level here, from which they can be progressively broken down into regional and territory level, as well as into product categories and specific product level, depending on how you are organized.

Perpsective	Strategic Goal	Weight	Business Objective			IT Objective		
			Goal	Target	Timeline	Goal	Target	Timeline
Fiscal	Increase Revenues over the previous year	5%	Achieve Y-o-Y revenue growth	15%	EOY	Timely & defect-free delivery	95%	As per TTM
			Share of revenue from new customers, products	12.5%	EOY	Higher capacity in IT sys with nil perf loss	25%	End of Q1
	Reduce Churn levels. Prio-ritize HNI base	10%	Retain Start-of-Year base of HNI customers	95%	EOY	Segment and tag HNI cust-omers. Reduce incidents	50%	Ongoing
			Retain S-o-Y base of non-HNI customers	85%	EOY	Reduce cycletime for pre-paid charging & incidents	20%	End of Q2
	Optimize Operating costs	10%	Reduce Opex (over prev year): Subcontracting	15%	EOY	Reduce Opex (over prev year): Outsourcing	15%	EOY
	Achieve PBT growth		Increase in PBT Y-o-Y	20%	EOY	Optimize Y-o-Y capex. DC to Cloud migration	20%	EOY
Client	Deliver Improved Cust Exp-erience at all touch points	10%	Cycletime improvement thru customer lifecycle	25%	EOY	Measured Improvment in cust exp at FA&B stages*	25%	EOY
	Invite customer participa-tion in product innovation	5%	Set up product innovation lab with dev & test fcility	Q	End of Q1	Set up product innovation lab with dev & test fcility	Q~	End of Q1
	Segment customer base for differential experience	5%	Establish rules for segmentation	Q	End of Q1	Implement rules for segmentation	Q	End of Q2
			Personalized campaigns, offers per segment	30%	End of Q2	Use of Big data & adv anal-ytics for campaigns,offers	50%	End of Q1
External (Market)	Sustain Brand Advantage. Strengthen brand in East	5%	Develop & implement brand promotion plan	Q	Ongoing	Benchmark IT with #1. Par-ticipate in industry fora	#1 or #2	EOY
	Reinforce network of sales & distribution channels	5%	Strengthen cross-country channel nw per S&D plan	90%	EOY	Design & build channel mgt sys for partner access	As per specs	End of Q2
			Equip co. reps with Mobile soln for channel support	95%	End of Q1	Extend Tablet based acc-ess for mobile salesforce	As per specs	End of Q1
Internal (Process)	Align Technology Architec-ture w/ Business roadmap	10%	Develop & share 3 year business roadmap	Accuracy, Clarity	End of Q1	Modular, standard & scalable IT architecture	Busi RM Algnmnt.	EOY
	Improve key internal processes (SCM, RA etc)	5%	Optimize critical processes for maximum impact	10%	Ongoing	Integrate process optimiz-ation in Change Mngmnt	TCQ	EOY
	Consolidated information management across fns.	5%	Define Business critical dashboards for MIS	Output	End of Q1	Implement tools & sys for data capture & reporting	Timeline, Accuracy	EOY
	Streamline compliance & governance	5%	Regular Business-IT reviews and follow-up	Frequncy, Quality	Ongoing	Regular Business-IT reviews and action closure	Frequncy, Quality	Ongoing
Development	Assess and strengthen BITA	10%	BITA Assessment (tool based) & improvement	10% overall	Bi-annually	BITA Assessment (tool based) & improvement	10% overall	Bi-annually
	Implement effective KM system	5%	Promote re-use (technical proposals, contracts etc)	20%	Ongoing	Cloud based info reposit-ory. Re-use (code, sols etc)	20%	Ongoing
	Rewards & Recognition for innovation	5%	Institute spot and annual awards for 'dare-to-try'	10	Ongoing	Institute spot and annual awards for 'dare-to-try'	10	Ongoing

[* Fulfillment, Assurance & Billing | ~ Qualitative parameters | RM: Roadmap | TCQ: Time, Cost, Quality]

The preceding table, though hypothetical, does give important pointers on deriving Business and IT objectives that are in conjunction with each other. You may notice that some important IT-related objectives like Operations SLAs, Security posturing, Delivery TCQ, etc. are not apparent at first glance. These are implicit objectives that are required for *supporting* the larger objectives and would form the basis of IT function's *internal* tracking systems and individual KRAs. The primary emphasis is on defining congruent and aligned objectives that guarantee business success.

KRA Alignment: KRAs are not too different from objectives, except that in our context, we refer to objectives in the *team* or *functional* context whereas

KRAs are referred in the *individual* context. Typically, a team objective is at a relatively high level – for example, achieve revenues of $380mn in the current fiscal, whereas a KRA would be a smaller derivative of this objective. As an individual in the sales team, my derived target may be to 'achieve revenues of $25mn in the current fiscal' from my assigned territory or product group. Likewise, other members of the team may have their own targets such that they all sum up to at least the company target of 380m. Similarly, various objectives for the IT function – relating to diverse perspectives and goals – are divided amongst individuals and sub-teams in a distinct but synergistic fashion.

For a good BITA, Business and IT team members in a *smaller* group –which may correspond to a geographical territory (say National Capital Region (NCR)), or customer segment (say SME), or product class (say Wi-Fi, for our company ACL) –would have KRAs that overlap more liberally. Smaller teams typically demonstrate stronger cohesiveness. For my KRA of achieving $25mn in sales from my territory, the integration with the local IT team members would be tighter than at the corporate level. It is thus a lot easier to align at a sub-group level than at a corporate level. It must be ensured, of course, that this alignment is maintained as one broadens the perspective and moves higher. This is an important point –while KRAs are percolated from top to bottom, their *alignment* happens from the bottom to top. If a piece at the bottom is flawed or incomplete, it may cause a collapse unless other 'pieces' rally around to share the load.

Strategic alignment between Business and IT is not a matter of choice. Building alignment in small groups is particularly crucial because without this, aligning at a broader level would be a lot more challenging. It's also *simpler* to build alignment in smaller groups. Hence the right approach is to assure this at all costs. If required, incentives like linking bonuses to common outcomes may be used, though it may not substitute an inborn exhilaration of being on a joint expedition towards shared goals.

KPI Alignment: The principle of KPI alignment is based on a simple but powerful premise: If you are *measuring* the same things, you are *managing* the very same things. This is crucial for alignment, as we touched upon during our discussion on outcome-based IT. We said that Business has no concern about (or patience with) IT's internal matters, like uptime of servers, incident turnaround time, defects in unit-testing, efficacy of tools, and work-force skills. These are *hygiene* and it is *expected* of IT to quietly find ways around them, instead of making them an issue for the entire organization to be concerned with.

However, most IT organizations still obsess with internal measurement and controls, instead of focusing on issues that have a more direct impact on the business outcome. For sure, it is required to track the uptime of a server as it, in turn, affects the availability of critical systems. But this must be an internal matter of IT, to be confined to the concerned group and the relevant vendors. Business expects, and rightly so, the server to *be* available and making it so is nothing exceptional. It's like you *expect* an airliner to take off and land safely – it cannot be an *exception*! If you (as an IT function) are reporting these metrics in business forums as matters of universal concern, you need to seriously reevaluate your alignment with Business. I have found that IT teams that are pre-occupied with internal trivia almost always fail to prioritize business concerns and lag in alignment.

A village situated between a river and a tropical forest received a warning of imminent floods that would wipe off their homes and belongings. The villagers decided to leave en masse for safer pastures on the other side of the thick forest. Before embarking on the journey, the village council met and hastily put together a plan to facilitate the crossing. Two teams, let's call them Alpha and Gamma, were created. Team Alpha (in the lead) was tasked with *cutting* the thick and prickly foliage, while Gamma *cleared* the way of roots, branches, stones, etc. for the village folks, cattle, wagons, etc. to move. Now, as they moved ahead, Alpha reported to Gamma on the critical indicators, like how much distance had already been covered by Alpha, the rate of progress so far, the remaining distance to be covered, expected time required, quality of terrain, and anticipated bottlenecks ahead. These inputs were very useful to Gamma in their own planning of resources and effort, and the progress was generally smooth. Imagine for a minute now that Alpha instead reported to Gamma on the skills and tools it took to cut some branches or the number of times their machetes had to be sharpened, or for that matter what percentage of branches were cut in one swing of the blade, vs. multiple swings. This would be of no use to anyone outside Alpha and would have hindered rather than facilitated progress. It is the same with IT passionately reporting KPIs that do not matter to the Business, and in the end, they too hinder the accomplishment of the joint mission.

KPIs are important. They are the mirror in which the company's performance is reflected, based on which future actions and course corrections are planned. Without KPIs, your employees, management, and other stakeholders would be clueless about developments and therefore powerless to act. Hence KPIs must be carefully designed based on the key priorities of the organization. Often, functions report what is *possible* to measure. It must work in reverse. Define what you want to measure and monitor, then *make* it possible to report it.

Returning to our company, ACL, an aligned set of IT KPIs that keeps business outcome at its center would include:

1. The total time from customer's order registration to activation of his connection
2. The end-to-end time from a prepaid recharge request to its recharge confirmation message
3. The number and nature of service-request calls from HNI (high net worth individuals) customers
4. Monthly churn, segmented into customer types, their age on the network, etc.
5. Average data consumption by customer segment (for targeted data campaigns)
6. Impact of brand promotion schemes (new acquisitions under the schemes)
7. Timeliness and accuracy of bills, analysis of usage trends
8. Call/data traffic analysis - revenue per tower, call-completion rate, interconnect billing, etc.
9. Regulatory compliance reports, trends
10. Business projects delivery reports – time, cost and quality estimates to completion

These are just a few KPIs among many. Contrast this with providing unnecessary reports to business like customer calls handled per engineer, first call effectiveness, performance of DC servers and network switches, primary vs. secondary data links utilization, stage-wise bugs captured in software development, et al. At best, such reports may be required during deep-dive sessions for root-cause analysis of catastrophic issues, but on a regular basis they do not help the business. The simple test of a KPI's efficacy is to ask yourself the question: Why? If you get an answer that directly meets a *business* objective, go ahead. Else, table it for your *internal IT index* measurement, but not for business reporting.

A word about Technology Strategy

From the foregoing, it is easy to conclude that the *Business* strategy is all that matters, and every function must derive its strategy keeping this in mind. Is there no place then for a Technology strategy in its own right? Dare a company like our ACL for example, plan for new standards like 5G and technologies like IoT in future, and if so, what does it need to do *today*? Well, in a business-aligned IT organization, it is the job of IT to keep the business apprised of the opportunities that are opened by new technological advances and integrate these into the *business roadmap*. But there is no justification for investing in future technology that is *not* weaved into the business roadmap by common consent. This highlights the role of IT as a *thought-leader* in interlacing relevant emerging technologies in the business roadmap, by drawing attention to the importance of future technologies in enhancing business value and competitiveness. A technology roadmap that is insulated from the business roadmap is an open invitation to divergence and eventually, failure.

Aligning the IT Strategy to Business

If the very purpose of Technology (or IT) is to make the business successful, as it indeed should be, there can be no debate that the business strategy must drive the IT strategy. In companies which differentiate themselves on the merits of their technological prowess, this fact can sometimes get overlooked. That is, the technology strategy may begin to dominate the business strategy. Some influence of the technological strength of the company in its business strategy is healthy, but not dominance. Finally, it is the customer who, through the business function, sets the course and IT should adjust its sails accordingly. I am making this rather obvious observation here because in my experience I have come across technology functions becoming all-powerful and endeavoring to *lead* the business, esp. in product-led services companies and software consultancy firms.

While it makes sound sense for technology and business to work in tandem to improve their common customers' experiences, there are also instances of one function becoming unduly dominant and enforcing unreasonable demands to the detriment of business and customers.

This is precisely what I experienced in a company I was associated with. This company had a mixed reputation – no one doubted the technological superiority of its products, but its standing as an *implementer* of customized solutions around them left much to be desired. The technology delivery team and the business team here were separate islands. What prevailed here was a *'handover'* system and not a partnering model. The only alignment which existed was short-lived bursts of enforced cooperation.

The upshot? Projects were often delayed, sometimes suspended midway due to sudden, unilateral diversion of resources. Customers were incurring additional costs due to the delayed projects. But this did not bother the company because despite this discomfiture, demand for its products was strong and there was a healthy recurring revenue stream from maintenance. In general, a great situation to be in of course, but this company, unfortunately, did not capitalize on it.

Relations between the business and technology delivery teams were not at their harmonious best. They worked independently of each other and often at cross-purposes. Due to the long implementation project cycles and lifetime support requirements, the delivery team was pivotal to the customer's experience. This led the delivery team members to believe that they were calling all the shots. They openly blamed business for their own lapses, attributing these lapses to unrealistic commitments made without technology team's 'consent'! Arrogance clouded the vision of technology delivery teams. They wanted a bigger say in business decisions and planning. It was a matter of time before the strategy of the company was dominated *not by market and customer expectations,* but by *delivery limitations*. In a lot of accounts, business account managers lost their grip on their customers.

Meanwhile, customers were sensing the change in the stance of the company. One large client was so incensed by a mid-stream demand for additional money to complete a critical project that he asked the project to be suspended and ousted this company, rather unceremoniously. This customer happened to be among the company's largest global accounts, with whom the company had been entrenched for a decade. Competition moved in on this opportunity. The reputation of the company started falling as other customers learned of this episode and related it to their own experiences.

Matters reached such a point that the company had to seriously restructure itself, including several changes at the top management. While technical delivery was still the backbone of the company, it could not be allowed to undermine the business role, and from a 'horizontal' function, it was made into a demand-assigned 'vertical' under the business account. Customer advocates were nominated, both from business and technology, who championed the customer internally. Many meetings were scheduled between the company's top management and the customers to apprise the customers of its efforts. The company is yet to regain its former glory in many markets but is now a lot more business driven. It is also a lot more open to listening to customers, surprisingly even small customers in emerging markets. At the time of going to press, the company is in the process of reinventing itself as a BITA driven company, a concept that it would have scoffed at three years ago.

In chapter-2 we introduced the cycle of interdependence between Business and IT. We need not revisit the same in detail here but for context let us reiterate the main inferences. The key point is that the cycle begins and ends with the Business strategy:

- Business strategy drives IT strategy
- IT strategy defines IT architecture
- IT architecture enables IT strategy
- IT strategy influences business strategy

I strongly suggest the reader go back to this segment of chapter-2 for a refresh. In summary, it is critical that IT strategy and architecture are tightly bonded with the business strategy. The IT architecture is required to be agile and scalable to stay step locked with the business roadmap through changing priorities, plans, and market dynamics. This must be at the core of a business-aligned IT strategy.

A business-aligned IT strategy must be enunciated in the form of a *reference* document which is intently followed as a basis for plans, actions, and measurements. This is not as simple as it sounds. In real life, Urgent often wins over the Important, ultimately leading to crisis management subordinating the strategy. Even CIOs, unless they are careful, get pulled deep into the quicksand of crisis management. This, of course, leads to the rest of the IT organization too scampering to douse fires. IT priorities are no longer in sync with business priorities in this crisis-driven scenario. Strategic alignment becomes, at best, a platitude. The *reference* document helps in this situation to adjust the sails. By the way, crisis too is inevitable and needs to be managed. By its very nature, it cannot be ignored. The ability to manage, minimize and recover from even catastrophic situations *without* compromising on strategic focus is one of the biggest challenges for managers of both Business and IT. One must ensure due apportioning of time and mindshare, muster an empowered and skilled workforce, maintain proper oversight, etc. while also taking all preemptive measures to stem the crisis before it spreads. All the great leaders that we have read about and are inspired by had mastered this to an art form. For the rest of us as well, it is vital that we take every possible step to prevent being *consumed* by crisis handling, without *ignoring* it.

A strategy document must be created in a format that is simple and relatable by all constituents and must be at a sufficiently high level. It is a good practice to start with the company's mission and vision statements on the first slide (page) followed by the business goals of the company. The IT strategy document is usually a well-turned-out Power-point or Word file covering the following descriptors for *each* strategic goal of IT.

1. The BUSINESS GOAL that this strategic goal of IT maps to, and how it helps achieve it. Remember, one Business goal can spawn several IT strategic goals.
2. A breakdown of the goal into individual objectives and targets (including timelines)
3. The name of the individuals (or regions, sub-functions) responsible for achieving each objective
4. Dependencies outside the function. These could be internal (as in Business, Finance or HR function), or external (partners, etc.). Note that managing the risks and dependencies is part of the function's *own* charter and these cannot be cited as 'beyond control'
5. High-level action plans (including action owner and timeline) for each objective. Actions may include agencies outside the function
6. Governance structure for oversite
7. KPIs: report on actual results vs. planned in pre-agreed format.
8. Qualitative comments (innovation, corollaries, short-term gains, long-term impact, etc.)

(Go to next IT strategic goal and repeat steps 1-8 until all goals are covered.)

In the end, you will have a comprehensive document that must be tabled for periodic review with stakeholders, with relevant updates against KPIs, qualitatives, risks, dependencies, etc.

Let us close with an important reminder. One may have a sound business strategy or a sound IT strategy, but if it is operating in isolation, no value is created. For real business value to be created, the Business and IT strategies (along with key functional strategies) must be aligned and work in unison.

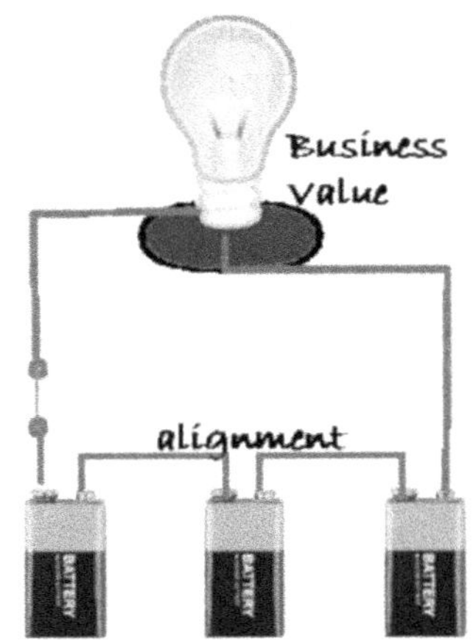

The Business and IT strategies are the powerhouses that form part of the *same* circuit for the creation of business value. Thus, if any one strategy is not firing to potential, it diminishes, sometimes even destroys, business value. It is easy to relate this to a simple battery - bulb circuit. Take out one of the batteries, or replace it with a dead or exhausted one. Will the bulb light as bright even if the other two batteries are at full power? Your guess.

11 The Structure Story

"The war is not won with bayonets, but with effective ***organization.****"*

In a survey at a leading banking and financial services corporation recently, respondents were asked to identify the biggest problem that they faced in dealing with the technology department. Options included technical competency, understanding of the business, ability to prioritize, future-readiness and a shared sense of urgency. The result: *NOTA*. Surprisingly, what came out on top was 'finding and getting to the right person' in the IT function. While the extent may vary, this is a common gripe across companies. In my interactions with business folks from various organizations, I learned that most people were aware – vaguely – of the CIO's name and perhaps a few others, most commonly the helpdesk guy who showed up to fix problems, but IT as a function was a black box to them. When I met the related IT folks, they showed surprise that their organization was not as transparent to the business folks as it was to themselves – no rocket-science here, they said, maybe business just didn't try hard enough!

This has some severe implications for BITA. If Business views the IT function as a formless entity ensconced behind a dark and mysterious door that has no handles or hooks, there is no place for Business-IT alignment to even exist, let alone thrive. In such a scenario, IT as a driver of business success is a total misnomer. At best, it is a weak apologist for office productivity extender.

Bad as the above situation is, what makes it appalling is the unconcerned attitude of both Business and IT towards each other's potentialities, and often the lack of any attempt to reverse the situation. In my estimation, over 70% of the corporates believe in letting both Business and IT do their own bidding, independent of each other, unmindful of the latent *combined* potential which would enable them to tap into the vast opportunities opened by BITA, especially in this Digital Age. What a waste!

To present a joint business-technology front to prospective clients, some high-tech companies do have their own expert (pre-sales) teams that assist with the technical pitch to potential customers. Such teams are part of the core business (sales) organization, while the delivery and support functions are in IT's ambit. Most often the IT arm is not part of the business interactions with customers in the pre-sales stage, even in these high-tech companies. Isn't this amazing, considering that the product/technology under advisement is going to be rolled-out, customized and supported for its lifetime by the IT teams? These are companies that place their trust in "hand-overs" from Business to IT, not *alignment* between Business and IT. In sectors like banking, utilities, retail, airlines, hospitality and a host of others, where there is typically no technical pre-sales arm; the IT team is the sole technology expert in the company. But here too it is rare to see IT being leveraged for business, even in today's digitally dominated world where business hinges heavily on solutions around Cloud, Mobility, Web services, Big Data, etc. I would attribute this only to steep functional barriers which clog mindsets. For a business to succeed in today's digital environment, irrespective of the sector in which it operates, such barriers must be comprehensively demolished.

A few years ago, a large multinational company in the high-tech software products domain – of which I was an existing client for one of the flagship products – approached me to discuss the migration to a more advanced system than my existing one. I had been thinking of upgrading this system, as it was already a decade old and cracking at the edges, and had in fact spoken of this to a couple of other vendors too, who had shown interest in participating. However, given that this company I spoke of was already entrenched in our environment, it obviously had the upper hand. I asked them to present the details to my team asap.

After they gave an outline of the architecture, features, and capability of their new system to a few of my senior colleagues in IT, I arranged for them to make a presentation to a larger group including business people from our company. On the appointed day, a team of sales and technical pre-sales folks arrived for a two-hour presentation to us on the virtues of their new system. It was a great product pitch with some innovative slideware, designed to dazzle even the most skeptical among its audience.

Towards the end of the presentation, I asked them a few fundamental questions: The system was undoubtedly worthy, but did it take our specific environment into account? Had anyone ascertained the pain-points in our current implementation, and how this new solution would address them? More to the point, I asked if they could present a slide which showed *our existing architecture* with its gaps and pain-areas, and then explain how their solution helped fill *these* gaps? After all, that was what we were looking for as customers. It turned out that all they had was this beautiful but canned product presentation which made no attempt to map itself to a customer's unique environment. None of my questions were convincingly answered, and the meeting closed with some mumblings to the effect that they will do a bit more groundwork and convene again some days later.

This is a classic example of the business (including the technical pre-sales) team of a high-tech company making no attempt to engage their own support and delivery (i.e., IT) teams in the customer presentation for making a sale. Had they done so, my questions would have been quickly answered as this company's delivery folks were working with us for years on change requests, enhancements, bug fixes, version upgrades and the like and knew as much about the gaps as any of my own people.

This is also an illustration of the functional barriers that I said must be demolished for better alignment between Business and IT. Incidentally, the company above lost the deal to a competitor, which did engage its delivery (IT) team to do a short gap analysis project before making a directed pitch to us.

A few corollaries: (1) A product, however alluring, will have an appeal for the customer only if it solves the customers' real problems, and not some imagined or 'case-study' situations that most sellers dwell upon. (2) A cohesive front to a customer enhances your deal prospects manifold, (3) If such gaps can exist in a supposedly high-tech, digitally immersed company, the relatively low-tech companies are a lot more vulnerable if they do not demonstrate perfect alignment between business and technology functions.

It is not easy to attribute business failure to the absence of BITA. When a root-cause analysis is done to determine the sources and impact of an order loss, BITA is frequently glossed over. This happens because most companies do not consider BITA to be a vital enough cog in the machinery. No one really *expects* BITA to work a magic in the first place, so how can failure be attributed to it? Clearly, a lot of the industrial-era thinking is yet to be eradicated. Deep down,

this attitude has its roots in the company's siloed organization structure. Silos prevent the pooling of ideas, skills, and knowledge, and probably are the cause of more damage through missed opportunities than any other single factor in the organizational framework. Evidently, there is a pressing need to bridge the Business and IT functions into a connected body capable of leveraging the opportunities opened by the digital economy. We'll try to establish ways of achieving this in the rest of this chapter.

In a reputed software company whose products touch millions across the globe, there was an opportunity to close a large deal for a cloud-based enterprise solution. This would have assured good recurring revenues for the company. The client was in touch with the company's account manager who was internally championing the deal (he narrated this incident). Before placing the order, the client wanted to understand how the technical issues around integration of the product with his existing environment would be handled. The account manager told the customer that this information would need to be obtained from the technical support center and that he would follow up with them. Of course, the process required detailed study of the existing systems, APIs, etc. and the client asked to get the technical folks flown down to the site for a spot assessment. This would not be possible, the hassled account manager had to explain, since the technical support kicked in only AFTER the deal, and not before. They would not work on, or travel for, pre-deal work. The technical support team was obviously in a silo that prevented them from looking at anything outside their own cast-in-concrete charter. Approvals from upstairs might have worked the trick, but would have entailed lengthy justifications. A nimbler company, with a good but lesser known product, was quick to seize the opportunity and walk away with the deal. Customers have little patience with vendors' internal bottlenecks. They have options, and your reputation can only help you thus far. If you don't get it right the first time, customers take it to mean that you never will.

Someone once said to me that BITA is undoubtedly a handy tool in sales closure – both for showcasing the alignment to customers, and supplementing your technical edge in presentations – but that its importance in other aspects of the business charter was less clear. While BITA certainly enhances the efficacy of the sales effort, this is a minor (albeit important) part of BITA. The relationship with a customer starts well before the closure of a deal and goes much beyond it. BITA plays a key role in enhancing the *lifetime value of a customer*, by fostering an increase in customer loyalty which leads to upsells, repeat orders, referrals and ultimately business growth and expansion. But even those are mere ancillaries. A strong BITA is not just about creating an edge in the market but ensuring survival. If culture is the bedrock and strategy the blueprint, structure is the *framework* on which BITA is built. A well-aligned structure thus provides the stability needed to stay relevant and strong.

Why is it that in some organizations IT is in lockstep with business in enabling revenue growth, innovation, and positive customer experiences, while in others it is perceived to be a backend overhead earning the contempt of business leaders for staying detached from market realities? The answer, as we argued above, lies in the ability to leverage BITA for business value creation. An absence of BITA often leads to (or perhaps is a result of) an atmosphere of mutual suspicion, mistrust, blame, angst and disrespect – all of which, in turn, lead to the organization becoming more vulnerable to external forces, including competition. On the other hand, organizations that are built for BITA approach their common mission with a shared sense of urgency in an atmosphere of mutual trust and collaboration, and can consistently deliver substantial customer (and hence shareholder) value. The question is, how does one 'build for BITA'? The answer, of course, lies in *developing* exceptional talent, *organizing* it for high performance, and *aligning* it with a common mission. We will explore these facets in some detail in this chapter.

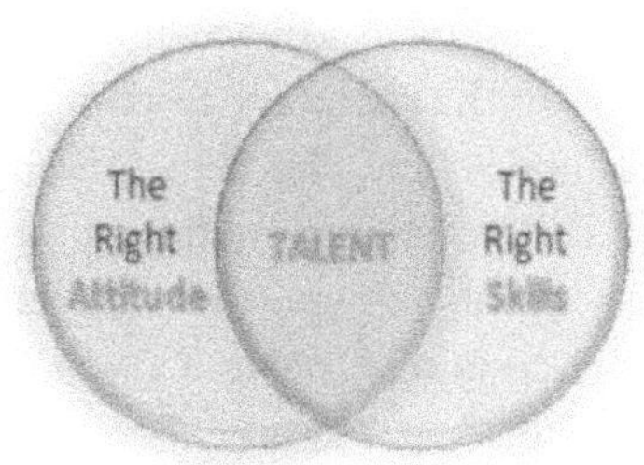

The importance of *talent* in deciding the fortunes of a company cannot be over-emphasized. *Talent exists at the intersection of fitting SKILLS and a winning ATTITUDE.* It is this *combination* of Skills and Attitude that enables some companies to perform unflinchingly through the storms of change, ambiguity, and complexity. The best analogy of this winning combination can, of course, be found in team sport. With all the wonderful facilities, meticulous planning, the best coach etc., do you stand any chance of your team (cricket, football, ice-hockey…) making it in any competition even to the first round if it lacked the required *skills* OR the *attitude* to win? It is the same with business, though we often seem to overlook this in the dazzle and distraction of other facets. As business has metamorphosed from the industrial age into the Digital Age, the contours of talent have also undergone a sea change. Someone who was a great success in an earlier era may find himself or herself quite at sea when immersed in the current digitally dominated environment. (The converse is also true, but irrelevant).

[*It may rightly be argued here that the third attribute of* ***Knowledge*** *is not considered here. That is, Talent must be defined as the intersection of Knowledge, Skills and Attitude. True. But for the sake of ease and simplicity, I have considered knowledge to be embedded in the general definition of Skills required for the job. Thus, Skills in our context refer to the brain and body, while Attitude concerns itself with the mind.*]

As Jim Collins said in his epic *Good to Great*, to build a successful organization, the best leaders first get the right people on the bus. That is, people with the abilities *and* temperament (in one word, *talent*) to brave the journey. They also get the wrong people *off* the bus, and quickly. Finally, they assign the rights seats on the bus to the right people.

Let us begin with the new age *attitudes* necessary for BITA. Attitudes, unlike skills, are not shaped by functions and roles and are regarded as inherent. A given set of attitudes pervades the organization as its *culture*. Today, what you can do is a lot more important than who you are. Your ability and drive to deliver results matters far more than your function, role or level. Organizations must, therefore, strive to ingrain the right set of *attitudes* that characterize Digital Age professionalism for driving business value.

So, who are the right people, and what are the attitudes they bring? We'll look at that here in the context of BITA and the Digital Age in a moment. First, let me make the point that contrary to popular belief, attitudes are not inborn, and *can* be acquired. True, we are born with certain characteristics in our DNA, while others are deeply etched through our upbringing, etc. But it is certainly possible to *build* certain attitudes, given the right climate. The rub-off effect works well in transmitting or uncovering, attitudinal traits. Take achievement-orientation as an example. If we are in a high-energy zone where everyone is passionate about results, we tend to acquire a sense of urgency, which may not have surfaced earlier in a different, less demanding setting.

As important as it is to acquire, or *build*, the right attitudes for achieving success in the Digital Age, it does not diminish the importance of *picking* the right attitudes through a careful process of onboarding. A mix of the new and the old is characteristic of any workforce, digital included. Pick or Build, do not compromise on the attitudes you are looking for in the team. If you must, compromise with skills, they can be acquired. Attitudes are much harder to develop. There is no universal set of attitudes that one must look to maximize, but certain traits do play an important role for a healthy BITA, as we shall see.

Sometimes, a positive attitude compensates more than adequately for even the biggest blunders. I was on a 2-day business trip to Chennai in South India and was staying at a hotel where most folks traveling from my company routinely did, though it was a first for me. The story goes far back in time before mobile phones were part of our lives. We had had a particularly intense meeting at the office that had gone on well past dinner time, and I was quite tired and beat when I hit the bed that night, hoping to catch a restful and undisturbed sleep. It was not to be. Promptly at 4.00 am, there was the sound of the doorbell, accompanied by knocks on the door, which woke me up. It took me a while to get my bearings and walk groggily and unsteadily to the door. On opening it I found a smartly dressed waiter, somehow looking fresh and crisp even at that unearthly hour, smiling ear-to-ear, deftly holding a tea-tray laden with a kettle and cup in one hand, and a rose in the other. In a sing-song voice, which showed no strains of fatigue or sleepiness, he wished me a cheery good morning. "This is your wake-up call, sir. I hope you have a pleasant flight back and a great day ahead." (or things to that effect). Now, I had given no wake-up call, nor had any flights to catch until evening that day. But his whole demeanor was such that even after the obvious discomfort of having my sleep interrupted, I didn't have the heart to chastise him or disappoint him by refusing the tea. I took it from him, thanked him sleepily, and went back to sleep. Had it been a less positive attitude, it would not have drowned my irritability. I would have undoubtedly raised the matter in a strong voice with him, and even more strongly with his management, and generally, the day would not have gone too well for him. But his attitude changed mine.

It was only on waking up at about 8.00 am that I realized that the price for this early and sweet exchange was probably paid by an unfortunate soul somewhere in the hotel who missed his flight that morning, owing to the wrong person having been woken up by the enthusiastic waiter! It was too late to do anything about it, and I just let it pass, but with a little twinge of guilt…

On the other hand, people tend to take a less charitable view towards those who possess sharp skills but do not have an attitude to match. Again, best explained with an example.

This is a more recent example from my experiences. We had commissioned a Wi-Fi network at a prominent public facility in the city. The system was designed to offer Wi-Fi as a convenient alternative to cellular data at this large facility which was frequented by thousands every day. According to the management of the facility, this helped in keeping visitors engaged during wait periods and added to the footfalls. Anyone could log in free for the first thirty minutes and thereafter was given the option to extend the service by making an online payment. The service became very popular, and traffic soon peaked to full capacity. But at these high traffic loads, the system performance became somewhat erratic, and many user complaints started coming in relating to poor experiences. Overall satisfaction levels plummeted. When news of this reached the CEO of the institution, he summoned us for a discussion on the subject. A team consisting of our business unit head, the account manager, our technical expert and I trooped into the CEO's office where he had a few of his own operations folks waiting for us. When the CEO started relating the problem, which was well known to us, our technical expert suddenly became vocal and launched off into an intricate technical sermon which consisted of terms and concepts that no one could relate to. He was clearly of the view that by flaunting expert knowledge he was creating a positive impression and earning some respect. After a few minutes the CEO stopped him and plainly said that he didn't quite understand the jargon. To which our guy smugly replied that people who deploy technology must first make an attempt to understand it!

To make matters worse, our 'expert' then suggested a series of causes that pointed the blame to the *customer*. He thought it was his duty to deflect the blame from his company and put it across to the customer! Protestations from the customer's operations guys present in the meeting only amplified the charges. A point was reached when the CEO could take it no longer. He called an end to the meeting and asked us to leave, while also instructing his team-members present to find an alternative to us quickly. Our business head somehow reasoned with them to allow us to stay and find a solution together, as terminating this meeting would not accomplish anything by way of progress. The CEO relented but insisted on this 'expert' being shown out of the room, which he was. Luckily for us, we could arrive at a course of action which resulted in the current problems being satisfactorily addressed, and staying in the reckoning for the nationwide expansion project that was in the offing here.

Now this 'expert' was indeed a master of his game. Highly skilled, he had technology at his fingertips, but like many of his ilk, this gave him a supercilious rather than a humble attitude. He honestly considered his conduct in that meeting to be 'professional.' Hadn't he 'batted' for the company and left the customer in no doubt that we were experts in our domain, and shouldn't that give the customer comfort, he argued.

The sad fact is that there are many like him in technical streams of companies, and they are among their most valued people. But skills without attitude are like yin without yang – incomplete.

Attitude is tough to generalize and we all have our own brand of it that we share with no one. Still, BITA calls for some very characteristic traits that were perhaps quite alien to, say, the industrial age. Of course, there is a *foundational* base of primeval traits – unchanged with time – that the new age work attitudes are built upon, like uncompromising work ethic, excellence orientation, customer-centricity, etc. But these must be *supplemented* by an entirely new set of attitudes unique to the digital enterprise. The talent pool that is going to steer you to success in the new economy will be defined by all the following attitudes, however alien and improbable it may seem from your current standpoint.

- Youthful (in spirit if not in age)
- Insanely energetic
- Value creativity
- Take risks (dare-to-try)
- Positive spirited. Take failure in their stride
- Go-getters. Stretch themselves for accomplishing their mission
- Love new technologies
- Believe in direct and unambiguous communication (both ways)
- Openly ambitious
- Get bored in a static setting
- Self-starters. Do not like to be supervised
- Always on the lookout for new challenges (May quit their jobs sooner)
- Agile and unbounded. Not restrained by functional boundaries and office decorum

For the striving digital enterprise, this is clearly the set of attitudes worth dying for! Does this define you?

Let's turn to the other ingredient of the talent pie – the SKILLS. These are somewhat easier to mold and cultivate than attitude but are no less important. Here too, a foundational stratum is required, on which new-age competencies are constructed. The skill foundation as well as the stack above, however, is realm and function dependent. Let's look at the *skills* that would assure high BITA and hence enable you to stay ahead of your competition in today's climate.

At the bottom layer, of course, are the unique **occupational** skills – like programming skills for software developers, PMP certification for project managers, accountancy for banking professionals, trading acumen for investment advisors, network planning for telecom engineers, and so on. There is nothing transformative about occupational skills. From the ancient ages to the present, they have been central to the vocational agenda. Apparently, while these may be necessary, they are not *enough* for distinction in the new age.

Skills must be progressive. No doubt demand continues to be vibrant for MBAs who can crunch numbers, lawyers who can craft contracts and programmers who can crank code. But if this is all that will ever define you as a professional, I am afraid your career ladder is going to be a rather short one. In this Digital Age, progress is not a function of years of unvaried experience, but of the order of your skills. As you progress, the needle must move from skills that emphasize repetitive tasks (like coding and testing) to skills that emphasize higher order abilities (like analysis and perspicacity). At the very top, the emphasis is on *human ability* that is *beyond the power of computerization or automation to replicate.* Therefore, skills like imagination and creativity, pattern recognition, trend spotting, storytelling and synopsizing, empathy and discernment (*meaning*

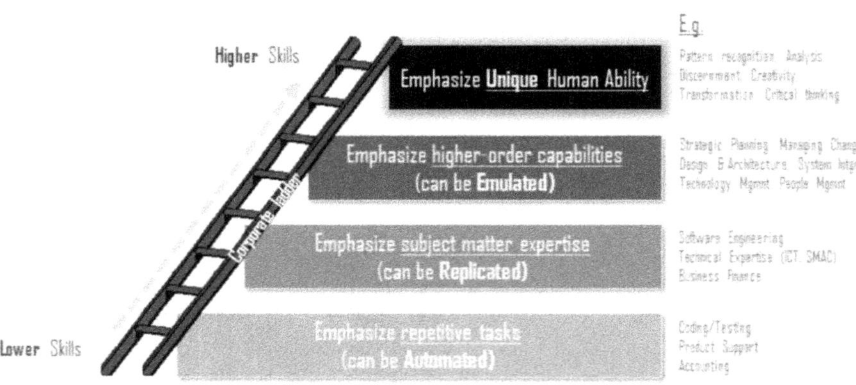

making) are among the real *differentiators* that must be fostered in the digital era. These and other *human* skills will acquire much greater significance as information and intelligence will increasingly become the domain of *computers*.

Exercise: *Specific to your own industry, identify the most desirable skills in each of the four boxes shown against the corporate ladder, from the lowermost skills to the highest skills. Where do you see* ***yourself*** *today on this ladder? In 5 years? Which of these identified skills are currently your* ***organization's*** *(1) Strengths, (2) Shortcomings?*

Any attempt at achieving and sustaining BITA in the organization without instilling the new age skills and attitudes is a futile endeavor. The main propulsion for BITA comes from its people, who are defined by the skills and attitudes that they bring to work. Therefore, compromising on these while focusing on the other dimensions would be like attempting to run a swanky car on an empty fuel tank.

In my experience, I have had the opportunity to be part of the hiring process for professionals at every level. It has also been my privilege to lead some of the most talented teams in the business, and I believe that the right focus during the hiring process had a lot to do with it. Picking the right team, as I have said earlier too, is among the most – if not *the* most – important tasks of a leader. A leader who compromises here is setting himself or herself up for other big compromises later, that is going to cost a lot. No short-term gain is worth having a long-term liability. However, to be fair, it is not always easy to pick the best based on job-interviews, and mistakes happen. Some can be addressed through counseling, training, rotation, etc., while others have less agreeable remedies. It is possible to minimize the possibility of hiring error if your focus is on multiple dimensions, resulting in more comprehensive assessment. Most mistakes occur because we hire based on technical (or subject) knowledge alone, perhaps giving some fleeting importance to visible traits like demeanor and deportment, etc. If my experience is anything to go by, your assessment must cover *all* the following attributes, especially for full-time hires – who will be looking for opportunities to grow in due course.

Domain Competence	Strategic Thinking	Execution Excellence
Business Orientation	Technology Orientation	Interpersonal Effectiveness
Learning orientation	Teamwork and Alignment	Lateral thinking (innovation)

Before you hire, do ensure that the following are in place:

1. A business-aligned organization blueprint or structure (discussed below)
2. Detailed JDs (purpose, qualifications & experience, skills, requirements, reporting, deliverables, etc.)
3. Factors to be emphasized (from a list like the above table) for the position, on a 1-10 scale
4. Sample questions to enable assessment of each attribute

The specific domain competence and experience may, of course, vary depending on the function and level, but broadly the set of attributes above apply to *every* position in the structure. For example, whether you are hiring a financial analyst or a software programmer, 'teamwork and alignment' would be critical. As one moves up the ladder, the *non-domain* attributes assume progressively higher significance, though the importance of domain competence is not diminished.

Most enterprises have their own institutionalized processes of organization building and the less they are tampered with, the better. However, some aspects that are essential from a *BITA* perspective while building the *IT organization* are enumerated below. An important point of note here is that alignment must be built into the organizational framework at the evolution stage itself, as it is much harder to inject as a later enhancement.

1. Size up the **business structure** – particularly the lines of business, SBUs, Product Segments, Customer Accounts and Regions. The IT organization is but an extension of the business structure
2. Create a **business-aligned IT *structure*** along Think, build, and operate principle (discussed ahead)
3. Make detailed **job specification sheets** stating the purpose, requirement, competencies, etc. for each position in the structure, and how it supports the business
4. Identify channels for hiring – internal job postings, referrals, portals, consultants, etc. Ensure that everyone, including recruitment consultants, involved in the hiring process understands the **purpose and requirements** of the position being hired
5. Conduct an exhaustive **hiring exercise** (could be internal or external) that spans all the attributes that you hold important. Involve others, particularly from *Business*, who may be able to add value to the process

The function of IT

As we are talking about the organization and structure in this chapter, this would be a good place to revisit our definition of IT. For most people, IT is just the 'helpdesk' and that nebulous part of the organization that deals with all the technical stuff around. Certainly, IT does provide technical help to people in need as part of its charter, but it is a bit unfair to define it only in these terms. In the digital enterprise context, the functions of IT fall into two broad categories -*Run the business* [R] and *Change (or transform) the Business* [C], with the primary goal of ensuring the success of the Business. These could include the following (this is not exhaustive):

- Design, architecture, deployment, and operations of Information System (Enterprise Systems, Communication Network, Data-center/ Cloud, Information and Data security, etc.) [R]
- Managing the company's data and information as an enterprise asset [R]
- Deployment and support of Business & Operations Support Systems (like Billing, CRM, Retail Management System, Ordering and Fulfillment System, Salesforce Management System, etc.) [R]
- Customer experience management [R]
- Implementing new technology in support of business operations, like Mobility, SM, and Big Data to support marketing function [R]
- Enterprise Resource Planning – use of IT systems to connect business functions including sales, product management, marketing, HR, Finance, SCM [R]
- Software design, development, implementation and support [C]
- Improving processes by collaborating with business to define BPR strategy and achieve cost-savings [C]
- Planning, execution and delivery of customer projects [C]
- Technical solution consulting – internal (e.g., pre-sales) and external [C]
- Thought leadership to the business on technology direction and potential, as a strategic advisor [C]

When we refer to the alignment of IT with Business, we imply that all IT functions, including the above, are operating in synchronization and harmony with Business.

Business Structure

Here is a very quick dip-stick check to test the alignment between Business and IT in your organization. Ask a few of your IT team members to explain to you the broad structure of the business organization in your company. In all likelihood, you will find that most people will be unable to give a satisfactory answer to this seemingly simple question. You will probably get similarly vague answers if you ask the same question to Business team members about the IT organization. Even though it is true in most organizations, this is rather disturbing from a BITA perspective. How on earth can two organizations that do not even recognize each other's form and function ever hope to align?

An understanding of the Business structure is not a matter of choice for the IT team. The business structure, in fact, is the very basis of the IT structure. An organization that builds an IT structure disconnected from the business will find the going quite rough on its digital journey and at some point, will go down the ravine. Yet we see many organizations doing just this.

Hindsight becomes a great teacher, given sufficient time. Looking back on this experience that I am about to relate, it is easy to prescribe a solution now, a few years after it happened, even though it was quite confounding at that time. Sadly, the company concerned is no longer in existence, so it is rather late to go back with a prescription.

We were associated with this company as implementation partners, to cover areas in which the company did not yet have expertise since it was newly formed. The company did a lot of hiring of good talent for creating a sound foundation on which to build its customer delivery structure – programmers, solution architects, project managers and a few senior leaders to be appointed as function heads. I am not quite sure how, but this company had a few good projects in hand from US-based customers early in its evolution. That is why we were taken as partners, to fill the talent gap by bringing in domain expertise. Being closely involved with the company, I could see that a lot of effort went into hiring strong technical delivery professionals. In hindsight though, I could also now spot the first big mistake made: The people were hired *before* the delivery structure had been created. That is, the company just hired people based on their fitment into certain broad criteria it had drawn up, without regard to the purpose they were going to serve or how they fitted into the big picture.

Anyhow, once there were people in sufficient number, supplemented by folks from partners like us, a technical delivery organization was announced. A rickety one to start with. Up until now, there had been no involvement of the *business* teams in the process. But it did not occur to anyone to complain, as no one saw this as a grave problem. The business team meanwhile was busy responding to global RFPs, having set up offices in India, Europe and the US. The business had expectations of pre-sales support from the technology team to help with RFPs, technical presentations, etc. However, the technology team had a very hazy view of the domain and charter and hence was neither able nor willing to help. The business structure and priorities were nowhere reflected in the technology structure. In such a scenario, there was no concept, of course, of Business and IT being 2-in-a-box, as BITA required. With time, the rift that was created between Business and Technology at the very inception widened. In one case, business team hired another company to deliver a critical customer project, while the company's own people were 'benched.' Our own association as partners to this company ended a few months later, but when I heard the news that the company had shut its operations, I could guess why.

In hindsight, it is easy to see that had the organization been built collaboratively involving both business and technology, things would have been different for the company. The technology team would have done well to align itself with the business in its planning stage itself and thus be in the loop on the business plans – like geographical territories, markets and customers, products and solutions, future roadmap, etc. But again, hindsight is always 20/20, and it is easy to criticize in retrospect. I would urge my readers to take a cue and assure that BITA is made a key priority *early in the game*. As we saw, divergence in Business and IT structures can be a threat to the very survival of the enterprise.

The above narrative, while alarming, is by no means an isolated one. Think about it. How many technology people in a bank, FMCG company, telecom service provider, or manufacturing unit have any idea of the skills and competencies that would help their business grow? Or even if they have an idea, how many really invest in building those skills? Or for that matter, how many technology/IT folks truly understand the business organization and its various divisions, product lines, functional areas (like Business Finance, Channel Management, BI/MIS, marketing), regional focus, key accounts, etc.? Not many, I am willing to wager. Hence, at the cost of repeating myself, I would ask that a little effort is invested in this critical but simple act of knowing each other, the rewards of which would be reaped over years to come.

Unfortunately, there is no "standard" business organization and hence no fixed business structure. Depending on whether you *produce*, *distribute* or – as is becoming common in the Digital Age – *aggregate* goods and services,

BUSINESS ORGANIZATION							
Business Lines		Business Functions		Business Regions		Business Channels	
Industry Verticals	SBUs	Marketing	Sales	Markets	Accounts	Direct	Distributors
B2C	B2B	Finance	BI	Hubs	Sub-Areas	Partners	Web

you may have business structures that are widely different. Similarly, your structure would vary to reflect whether you are an enterprise focused on a single centralized operation or a regionally/globally distributed operation.

The essential point is that for BITA to exist, the IT organization must invest in understanding the organization's business structure. That is, the key *strategic focus areas* like lines of business (SBUs), major functions, geographies and channels. The understanding must include knowledge of the key people, processes and priorities. While the greater the depth of understanding the better, it may not always be possible for the IT organization to master all nuances that make up the business organization. This is fine. If a general understanding of the above pervades the IT organization, BITA should work.

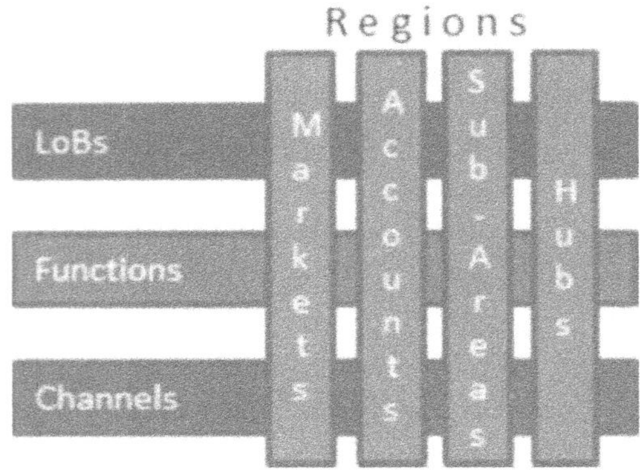

The preceding diagram about business organization, while instructive, is rather simplistic and high-level. In one of its possible enactments, the Business Regions may be organized as 'verticals' and other blocks as 'horizontals' supporting some or all the verticals. The endeavor of the IT organization must be to have clarity on the structure, processes and plans of *each* unit to be able to engage more closely and drive alignment. For example, who are the key people associated with the function of BI, what are the processes, tools and systems that are currently important to them, what are their immediate and longer-term priorities? For this reason, good IT organizations have *Business Analysts* that go *deeper* into the business organization to drive the integration between Business and IT, while the rest of the IT organization may have a more surface level understanding of the business organization.

IT Structure

Like Business, IT does not have a standard mold in which all structures fit. That said, an IT organization that aims to align with its business starts with certain distinct characteristics that it does not relinquish through its journey, in smooth times or tumultuous.

A business-aligned IT structure is based on the premise that for achieving success together, Business and IT must **think, build, and operate** as one. This must manifest in the structure and not just be confined in spirit. It sounds a simple enough idea, yet most enterprises must make a concerted effort to achieve it. This is owing to historical reasons. We have discussed in this book earlier that for most of its history, IT has been a tool for achieving office productivity gains and automation of linear processes. Its role as a business enabler is only now evolving, though it is still largely ensconced in the realms of idealism.

IT started off in business enterprises as a shared service for providing common infrastructure like LAN, email, etc. to create a productive work environment for employees. It had no direct role in the growth of business. In the next stage (stage-2), IT becomes an agency for *automating* certain business processes, where it develops (or *Builds*) software programs for Business, though still a lot of area is uncovered in terms of *optimizing* processes because Business and IT are still not *Thinking* together. Nor are they *Operating* in concert, save for some IT operational support to business by way of maintenance.

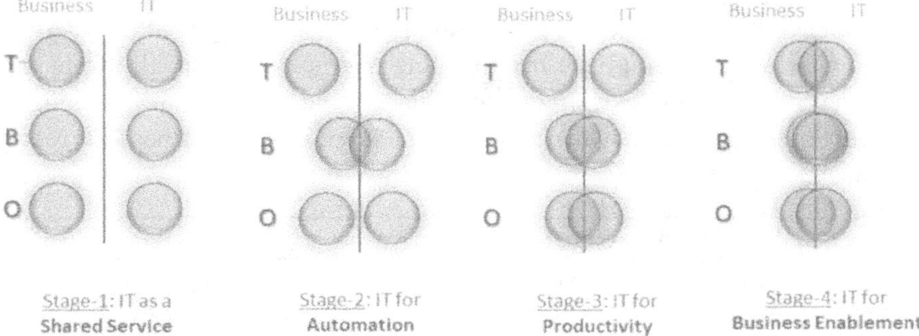

Next, in stage-3, IT evolves to become a productivity enhancer for the business. IT and Business still think independently but are closer aligned in their approaches. IT is no longer responsible simply for automating existing processes, but also for *tuning* those processes to achieve greater efficiencies. IT also shares more space with Business in the operations sphere, by extending direct technical support to customers and other stakeholders, enabling a secure and productive environment for business and helping it to launch better and faster solutions to comply with stated time-to-market requirements.

Things get interesting once you approach stage-4. Here, Business and IT cross over the boundary into each other's territory to think, build, and operate together. It is here that BITA happens. Business and IT are now equal stakeholders in the creation of business value. In this stage, IT as a thought-leader does not just implement business defined solutions but is one with business in imagining and creating solutions that would help the business *and its customers* stay ahead – now and in the future. Business has visibility and influence over the IT architecture, while IT is tuned into the competitive landscape to derive its priorities from it. Business and IT have equal participation in the development of solutions as they share their objectives with respect to time, cost and quality of builds. IT understands the business processes and is an advisor to the business on their optimization and enhancement to outdo industry best practices. We have discussed many facets of Business-IT alignment in the earlier sections of this book. All these facets find expression in stage-4, in which there is overlap in the way Business and IT think, build, and operate, with some room left for independent activity. In my view, a *complete* overlap – like a total eclipse – would overshadow either Business or IT and severely restrict individuality. Therefore, for alignment, a reasonable overlap is sought, leaving room for independence of thought and action.

At this stage, it may be a good idea to pause and reflect upon elements that constitute Business and IT thinking, building and operating together in your own organization. If you have been reading this book sequentially from the start, you may recall our definitions of Think, Build, and Operate introduced in Chapter-6. Let us stay with the same, which are reproduced here for ready reference.

Aspect	**Associated Attributes**
Think	**Plan**- Strategy, Roadmap | **Design**- Innovation, Improvement |**Share**- Knowledge, Ideas, Culture |**Measure**- Trends, Analysis
Build	**Collaborate**- Governance, Teamwork, Partnerships| **Construct**-Process, Organization | **Deliver**- Projects, Solutions | **Deploy**-Technology, Best-practices | **Optimize**- Time, Cost, Quality
Operate	**Execute**- Sell, Service, Install |**Monitor:** Performance, Cost, Process| **Control**-Assets, Policies | **Support**-Customer experience, enterprise productivity, data privacy & security

If you have taken the BITA test already at a group or functional level, you would be having a fair assessment of where you stand on the T, B and O axes. Using the above list of attributes, it shouldn't be too difficult for you to construct an approximate picture of where Business and IT in your organization overlap in their T, B and O aspects. From the above table, an overlap in the **Plan** attribute would mean that Business and IT have an unwavering practice of *jointly* deciding and delivering on the *strategy* and *roadmap* and are aligned on the responsibilities and implications that it entails. And similarly, for the other underlined attributes too. In short, there is an interdependent and harmonized approach towards thinking, building and operating for business success.

Our next task is to assure that the organization *structure* conforms to this Think, Build, Operate paradigm. As there could be several manifestations of IT, each with its own variables and outcomes, there cannot be a single, universally applicable hierarchy or organogram. The unifying factor is the underlying intention to think, build, and operate with the business. I will consider here the commonly applicable scenario where Business and IT exist in the organization as distinct but interdependent functions.

The terms think, build, and operate are connotations employed only to uphold alignment between Business and IT. They are not units or functions in themselves, nor do they ascribe specific behaviors to individuals. Thus, there is no position called 'Think Manager' for example, and it is not that only people assigned to the Think band do the thinking, and others don't! A TBO structure is one which promotes and emphasizes Business and IT thinking, building and operating *together* for a common purpose, and that is to make the business successful. The roles and functions ascribed to the

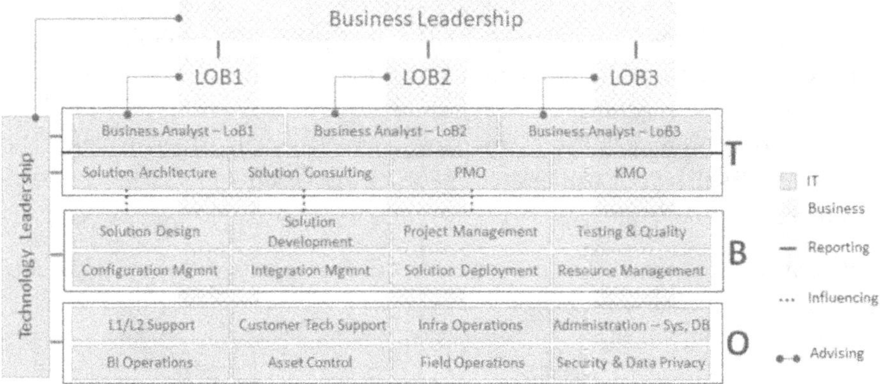

Think band are chosen for their aptitude to interwork with the business on *planning* what it takes to achieve success together. The roles and functions of the Build band are chosen to *develop* together per this blueprint, while the roles and functions in the Operate band are chosen to *sustain* the alignment for long-term success.

There is no such thing as a universal structure, either for IT or for business. To be sure, my intention here is not to invent a universal structure, but to present a business-aligned IT structure. Our diagram here is a depiction of one possible *business-aligned IT organization structure*. The essence of this structure is that it enables the different lines of business (LOBs) to leverage all the functions of IT through a dedicated interface, which is the Business Analyst, as shown. It splits the IT functions and roles into bands to enable Business and IT to think, build, and operate with a common mission while upholding the modularity of the structure. You can, for example, replace specific roles and functions in this structure without disturbing the other functions or the overall alignment with business. Similarly, if the business expands to include more LOBs, it does not require a material change in the supporting IT structure.

In a more general sense, a LOB refers to a strategic business unit. For example, in the case of a banking business, a LOB could be the merchant banking division, the retail banking division, the loans division and so on. In the case of a software development company, the various LOBs could be designated by the different industry verticals that the business targets. For example, the BFSI vertical, the Telecom vertical, etc. Certain businesses are not diversified into sharp vertical segments, like airlines, for example. Here, an LOB may be replaced by say, geographies, or revenue streams – like passenger, cargo, etc. In some environments, a LOB represents a large customer account, or group of accounts – as in the case of telecom (or IT) equipment vendors, or consulting firms. To sum up, a LOB is a distinct but synergistic unit of business within a business, having its own market and strategic focus. As a first step, *the IT organization needs to clearly identify and understand the LOBs* in operation within the company. Think about it. Do you know the various LOBs that your company is made up of? Or do you see the company as one monolithic entity?

Let us walk through this band structure quickly to adapt this to a specific environment, such as your own.

THINK

The THINK band is primarily concerned with keeping the IT plans and priorities in sync with Business plans and priorities. Key roles here are Business Analyst, Solution Consultant, Solution Architect, Program Management Office (PMO) and Knowledge Management Office (KMO). A Business Analyst is typically assigned to *each* LOB in a dedicated way as an ambassador of IT while being a champion of his LOB within IT. That is, the BA is the single point of contact for the Business, who pools the combined strength of the entire IT organization in support of his LOB. This effectively addresses the prime business concern of '*whom to contact*' for an IT matter. In some companies, the BA is referred to as the Business Information Officer, or BIO. The Solution Consultant (SC) plays a key role in translating customer needs into a solution design in the pre-sales stage and in converting the solution design to Business Requirements (BRs) in the post-sales stage. The BRs are used by the Solution Architect as the basis for the development or procurement of the solution. The PMO function has a critical role to play in institutionalizing governance and Business excellence (best practices, process adoption, project steering, etc.) apart from managing the IT program within the budgeted costs. Finally, the KMO has the task of ensuring that knowledge and ideas are efficiently captured and shared for business enablement, as also identifying key competencies and tools required for business value creation.

This is, of course, a very high-level description of the key functions but hopefully, it provides a broad basis for constructing the organization design and charter for the THINK band. The table below lists some of the key functions of the THINK band and maps these to specific roles.

Table-10A

Function	Role				
	BA	SC	SA	PMO	KMO
Single interface to Business	✓				
Strategic Roadmap Alignment	✓	✓			
Technical sales consulting		✓			
Solution Design	✓	✓	✓		
Convert Solution Design to BRS*		✓	✓		
Solution architecture			✓		
Trends Analysis	✓				
IT Governance				✓	
Budget & Financials				✓	
Business Excellence (IT program)				✓	✓
Knowledge sharing & mgmnt					✓
IT Capability management					✓
IT Tools planning &adoption					✓

* Business Requirements Specifications

As a short but helpful exercise, you may like to prepare a more wide-ranging list of functions in the THINK band relevant to *your* organization and map them to specific roles – as above – as a prelim to preparing detailed (and interrelated) job-sheets. Remember, roles are not rigid, and unlike rules, may be bent.

BUILD

The Build band represents the region where ideas get materialized into products and solutions that are of value to the enterprise and its customers. The new age digital environment is a dynamic one, characterized by changing customer aspirations and technological evolution. Further, it is not an environment where 'one size fits all,' and requires several parallel, personalized versions of a solution to be developed. In such an environment, it is obvious that the THINK and BUILD bands must work in tandem to develop market facing solutions. These are the primary reasons for new age digital enterprises adopting the *iterative* or *agile* model of development, in which Business and IT are required to be always and fully intertwined. In some businesses, like a software development company, the BUILD overlap extends beyond the company's own business group to its customers.

From a structure perspective, this means that the BA, solution consultants, and architects create a strong bridge between the business sponsors/leads and the IT Delivery team to assure tight integration through all the phases of IT delivery, and a common view of the timelines, specifications, etc. This is an excellent display of Business-IT alignment at work as the participants are bonded together not by reporting lines but by their common mission. Projects get into trouble when, after the initial estimation, everyone except the project delivery team is hands-off, leading to nasty surprises in the end.

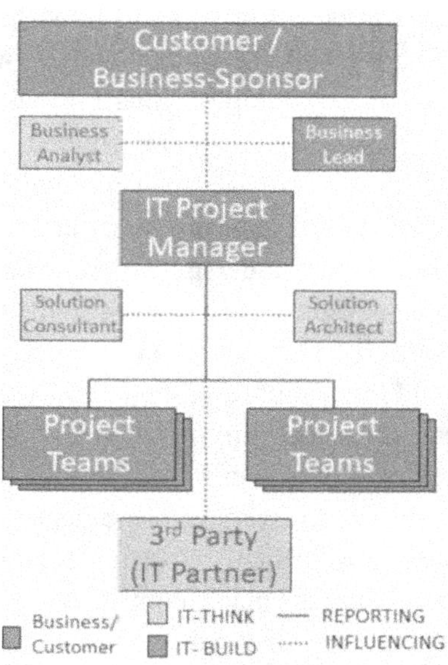

It is again worth doing a short exercise to list the different BUILD functions in your company, and map them to roles:

<u>*Table-10B*</u>

Function	**Role**							
	PM	Design	Dev	T&Q	CM	IM	RM	Deploy
Low-level Sol Design	✓	✓				✓		
Sol Development & UT			✓					
Sol Testing & QA			✓	✓				
Change Management	✓				✓		✓	
Process management	✓				✓		✓	
Interface Design & Integ		✓				✓		
Resource (org) planning	✓						✓	
L3 (Software) support			✓	✓				
Project mgmnt+ govern.	✓							
Production rollout	✓							✓
Vendor/partner mgmnt						✓		
TCQ optimization/reuse	✓	✓	✓		✓			✓

OPERATE

The Digital Age has brought some de-facto alignment between Business and IT at the THINK and BUILD levels, but it is still quite rare to see this extend to the OPERATE level. Considering that the OPERATE level functions mainly in the customers' line of sight, this is indeed awkward. It may be argued with some merit that business cannot concern itself with the nitty-gritty of routine IT operations. All the same, organizations that demonstrate commonality of purpose at the OPERATE level score better on customer experience parameters. For example, business best understands the customers' expectations around the implementation of a solution and an overlap at the OPERATE level would assure that these are faithfully executed by IT. Similarly, on the customer service front, if Business and IT are aligned at the OPERATE level, requests can be prioritized based on customer criticality, rather than rely on an impersonal, automated system which is impervious to customer loyalty. Key functions in the OPERATE band include upselling to existing customers through an enriched end-to-end experience, managing critical infrastructure and optimizing its cost and performance to meet business plans, control of critical assets like servers and customer premise equipment, and very importantly, assuring confidentiality, integrity and availability of business information by building a secure IT environment. All these functions have a clear and present impact on business sustainability and customer loyalty. In other words, a structure which underplays the importance of alignment at the OPERATE level is often responsible for business erosion and customer churn.

Below is a sample list of some OPERATE functions mapped to roles in the structure. I invite you to do a comprehensive exercise here to list all OPERATE functions in your organization and map them to roles.

Table-10C

Function	**Role**							
	L1/ L2Tech Support	Customer Ops	System Admn.	Infra Ops	Field Ops	Analytics & BI Ops	Asset, Policy, GRC	Security & Privacy
Incidence Mgmnt	✓	✓			✓	✓		
Instln & Commning		✓			✓			
Application Support	✓		✓					
Upsell/Cross-sell		✓						
Performance tuning			✓	✓				
Process monitoring			✓		✓			✓
Contact Center Ops		✓						
IT policies							✓	✓
New Tech adoption				✓				✓
Data-center Ops			✓	✓			✓	
Disaster Recovery			✓	✓			✓	
Sys Admn, DBA			✓					
Security + Dataprvcy					✓			✓
Data Management	✓			✓		✓		✓
Business Reports, BI					✓	✓		
Audits & Risk mgmt					✓		✓	✓

Job Specifications Sheet

A job specifications sheet is often considered a rather trivial matter, often ignored. However, it is a very key element of an organization in which alignment between functions is held important. In my view, a job specification sheet should not only be used as a tool for hiring new employees but also be published on a public portal, like the company intranet, visible to the entire organization. It is baffling that people can function together in organizations without any knowledge of what their peers and team members are in the company for. Of course, one generally knows that so and so is a "Business guy," "IT person," "Finance executive" or "HR." But very little, if anything, is known about their job specifications, or charter. If you are working with someone, it is important that you make a small effort to understand their role in the company. It is simple. You don't have a chance of aligning with people if you have no idea of what they do.

This may not appear powerful enough but small things like taking a few minutes to read the job specification of the roles you are hoping to align with goes a long way in institutionalizing BITA in the organization. While it is not pertinent for everyone to understand each nuance of every role, it does help to gain an insight into the purpose, charter, interfaces, etc. of the roles that you are expected to align with. For example, it would be meaningful for a pre-sales executive from business to understand the role of a solution consultant in IT, and vice-versa. I have not yet understood why some companies make it a point to keep job-descriptions 'confidential,' to be visible only to hiring teams. It's a retrograde practice from a BITA perspective.

The purpose of a job specification sheet is to make the role independent of person and bring in continuity. Its utility in the hiring process is of course beyond dispute. Not having a job specification sheet would result in very lop-sided hiring, which is based on the notions of the hiring manager. Two IT Solution Consultants, for example, hired by two different hiring managers in the absence of a common job specification sheet may turn out to be quite diverse and incompatible.

IT Business Analyst [BFSI]

Function	: IT	**Base Location**	: BU Headquarters
Reports To	: Chief Information Officer	**Matrix Reporting**	: SBU Head - BFSI
Level	: AVP	**Desired Profile**	: BTech/MBA with15+ yrs in BFSI
Supervision	: 4-5 associates (in-house and/or partner)	**Interfaces with**	: BU Heads /IT Architects/Delivery/Ops

Purpose of Role: Provide a single window to Business Unit for consultative resolution of strategic and operational issues as an effective Business champion within the IT organization. *Integrate IT with Business.*

Key Skills and Attributes

* Deep understanding of BFSI business imperatives, priorities, trends, regulation and market dynamics
* Ability to translate business requirements into deliverable IT solutions
* Knowledge of IT architecture principles and an ability to correlate them with business roadmap
* Specifically, have a sound technical and business understanding of key business processes
* Preferably should have background in IT consulting and/or BFSI business development
* Knowledge of IT processes, SDLC, operations flow
* Should be able to weigh implications and reconcile the demand/delivery capability to set realistic expectations
* Must be an effective communicator and must have good influencing ability and interpersonal skills
* Should be a team player and strong at conflict management and resolution
* A Positive, Can-Do attitude

Major Responsibility Areas

* Respond to the Business Unit commercial and operational challenges and opportunities to support revenue growth
* Provide thought leading IT insights to the BU and discuss their critical implications /impact
* Promote IT solutions and formulate proposals fitting exactly to the Business needs
* Agree the value and scope of the project with the BU
* Provide metrics on IT-spend and assist with prioritization and rationalization of demand based on RoI etc
* Engage directly with the business teams to prepare work plans, implement recommendations, organize and write business requirements, and participate in new business development.
* Facilitate regular governance and action tracking between IT and BU, and ensure timely and clear communication from IT to Business
* Create and present relevant business-IT metrics and analyze for preventive and corrective action.

If you have done the exercise of enumerating various functions (band wise) and mapping them to roles, as in Tables 10 A,B & C, you would have a high-level idea of each role, which may be used to create (or validate) the job specification sheet. It is strongly advised to do this as the first step to JD development. A job specification sheet is a critical item on the check-list of hiring requirements and any compromise on this aspect is often the lead cause of mis-hiring. Further, as important as reskilling your existing people, is the need to review and reassess the job specifications with changes in business environment.

There may be many ways of creating a job specification sheet, and your organization probably has an established one already. One possible format of a job specification sheet for any given role, like an IT Business Analyst, is reproduced here (This is an example only).

A well-prepared job specification sheet gives a reasonably clear view of what can be expected from a given role. It would, however, be reckless to close the section on job specification sheets without emphasizing that a job specification is only a guideline, and when the need of the hour is to step out for a larger goal, the incumbent is willing and ready to do it. In fact, this attribute is a common component of all job descriptions.

Job-Skills Assessment

BITA is not just a spark that is required to ignite the enterprise into traction, but rather the combustion that keeps the organization in continual motion over smooth as well as rough terrain. In other words, alignment must be *sustained* for the enterprise to create continuous value.

In line with the above, certain methodologies have evolved to assess the individual's developmental needs periodically to reaffirm conformance to BITA requirements and institute developmental actions to ensure that BITA is sustained in the enterprise.

This process is not to be confused with performance management system. It is not required to follow a bell-curve or a ranking system, and its purpose is to *develop*, not appraise. The assessment exercise must be non-evaluative. That is, it should not have a bearing on the person's progression or pay-hike, unlike your company's appraisal system. This will result in a fuller and more transparent assessment, where both the assessor and the assessee are clear that the goal is only developmental.

Well-defined job-descriptions, Business plans, KRAs and value systems are of little use if they fail to set the rhythm for the people in the organization to advance towards their mission. Sustained Business-IT alignment requires that based on the established criteria, clear assessment parameters are defined

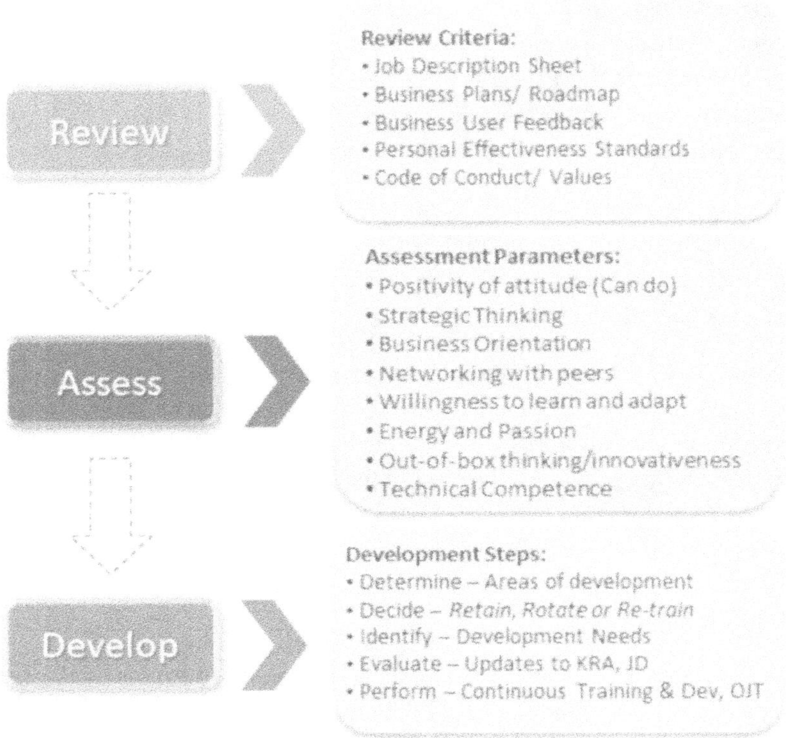
Review
Assess
Develop
Review Criteria:
• Job Description Sheet
• Business Plans/ Roadmap
• Business User Feedback
• Personal Effectiveness Standards
• Code of Conduct/ Values
Assessment Parameters:
• Positivity of attitude (Can do)
• Strategic Thinking
• Business Orientation
• Networking with peers
• Willingness to learn and adapt
• Energy and Passion
• Out-of-box thinking/innovativeness
• Technical Competence
Development Steps:
• Determine – Areas of development
• Decide – Retain, Rotate or Re-train
• Identify – Development Needs
• Evaluate – Updates to KRA, JD
• Perform – Continuous Training & Dev, OJT

for each role, against which developmental needs are continually assessed. In the illustration, I have presented some generic *Assessment Parameters* that are important from a BITA perspective.

Companies may conduct an in-house exercise or use an external consultant to evaluate people on these (or allied) parameters, typically holding interviews and taking feedback from peers, and rating an individual on a 1-5 scale against each parameter. These are very subjective parameters, as can be seen, so the accuracy of results is a factor of the number of people giving independent feedback. As the process is completely non-evaluative and hence transparent, it is best to compare the results with the individual's *own* assessment on the same scale.

Finally, one may be able to create a simple radar graph as shown, which displays the individual's assessment scores (average in case of multiple feedback) against the 'target' fixed for each position/experience-level. Here, we have plotted the chart for John Doe, Solution Consultant. The assessment parameters may also be made specific to roles, drawn directly from the job description.

This display makes it easy to identify the strengths (which is Technical Competence in case of John Doe) and development needs, like Willingness to Learn. If such graphs are created periodically, say once or twice a year, it becomes quite straightforward to assess the individual's progress against defined parameters.

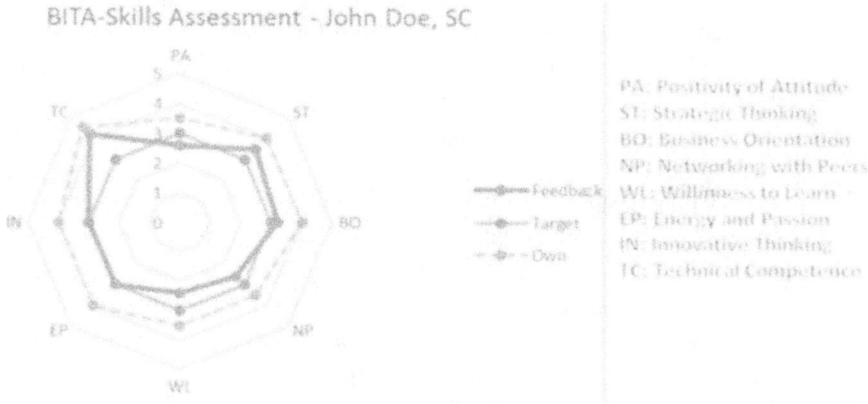

By the way, the parameters, as well as the 'target,' have been picked only for illustration and you may like to decide your own. The 'target' may vary with role and level if you consider this necessary. Having determined the developmental needs, you may ascertain the best course of action, including on-the-job training, mentoring, or refitment of the individual in another role, etc., as the next example illustrates.

Several years ago, I was a function-head at the R&D center in India of a well-known global organization in the telecommunications space. My team consisted of people with the finest minds and skills in the industry, taken from top institutes and the best peer companies. Even though this was before the dawn of the digital era, the nature of the work put a very heavy emphasis not just on picking the right skills but continually developing them to keep up with the complex dynamics and rigors of global R&D. The generation of demand for our services from our parent company in the US, as well as their customers across the globe, depended almost entirely on demonstration of relevant competencies in the workforce. The process of competency review, assessment and development was therefore well-institutionalized in the organization as a best practice that became a subject of case study later by some institutes of learning.

In time, the parent company in the US changed its course from being a *multi-technology* company to focus on a single technology on which it banked its future. This meant that many of its technology units, including the one where I worked, had to be divested, that is, 'sold off' to other companies. My own unit was acquired by an upcoming technology company which saw a great opportunity in this acquisition. The competency levels of the people who had joined their ranks stood out as a clear strategic differentiator, which would be of great value in its mission of achieving global leadership. The challenge, of course, was assuring correct placement of everyone in the expanded structure. In short, achieving *synergy*.

Flowing from its mission, the company set about identifying the right set of competencies, roles, and relationships between functions– particularly Business and IT. They decided to keep the process simple, neutral, transparent and repeatable. New job descriptions conforming to its mission and charter were created, which included the most desirable attributes for each position on a relative scale. They also evolved a comprehensive *assessment process* closely aligned to the one we have discussed above. This assessment played a significant part in the competency development process, as it captured the actual experience and supplemented this by views from an external interviewer, peers, and the employee. *Everyone*, new and old, was required to undergo this process. The outcome of this process was used to ensure the right placements by matching the attributes of each individual with the requirements of every position. Development plans were created along the way to achieve perfect longer-term fitment. It was barely a matter of three months before we had a very consistent team, now over *twice* the size of the original, aligned to the right set of attributes. As the process was designed to be repeatable, it was decided to run this annually to retune the organization to changing needs of individuals and markets.

Competency Assessment Card

Name Jane Smith 65-362 TA

	PA	ST	BO	NP	WL	EP	IN	TC
Experience Profile	3.0	2.5	2.5	4.0	3.5	3.5	2.5	3.0
Ext Interviewer	3.0	3.0	3.5	3.5	4.0	3.0	3.0	3.0
Manager-1	3.5	2.5	2.5	3.5	3.5	0.6	2.5	2.5
Peer-1	3.5	2.5	3.0	4.5	4.0	4.0	3.5	3.5
Self	4.0	3.5	3.5	4.0	4.0	4.0	4.0	4.0
	3.4	2.8	3.0	3.9	3.8	3.0	3.1	3.2

The Business teams were the first to reap the benefits when consistency in meeting time-to-market commitment, quality and innovativeness of the customer solution, and other efficiencies showed up in the results. Unfortunately, I am constrained in naming the company concerned, but being part of the transition, I am very happy to say that this company attained the soundest reputation in its industry segment, with the acquired technology playing a lead role in its journey to the top. This, more than anything else, speaks for the power of a well-planned and efficiently executed organization structure!

Structure as a driver of personal and organizational growth

I was once asked a very good question about structure. The question was: we have been taught HOW to construct a good organization structure, but WHY do we need to invest in building a structure when a collection of people on a common mission can accomplish the goal even *without* a structure? The questioner gave examples of ventures such as farming, building construction, transportation, etc. which do not conform to any structure and yet achieve their missions. In short, as I interpreted it, what are the key drivers for creating a streamlined structure? It is a good question and as I later reflected, an important one as it gives us a basis for building the structure, rather than do it to merely comply with a norm. I would like to conclude this chapter by attempting to answer this question here.

Theoretically, any group of people assigned to perform tasks that accomplish some larger goal make an organization. Take building construction, for example. There is organization here, with people performing distinct functions like brick-laying, welding, plumbing, painting, etc. This organization too, is made of people who are highly *skilled* in their professions. Thus, one cannot say that such an organization differs from a business organization (that works inside those buildings) in the requirement of *skill*. The difference, of course, is in the way a business organization, or an institution is *structured*. So back to the question, why do we need a structure?

A structure enables the *people* of the organization to broaden their view *beyond their immediate assignments* to envision their own as well as the organization's longer-term prospects. Unlike in the case of a building construction project which doesn't have a formal structure but an authority that controls and directs other individuals, a structure provides scope for personal growth and organizational reinforcement. There are five important paybacks that a good structure offers to every individual who is a part of it, as in the following table. Test to see if *your* structure is achieving these outcomes.

Commitment	Passion and enthusiasm to deliver on assigned responsibilities
Development	Opportunities to learn and grow
Alignment	Oneness with the larger organization
Empowerment	Freedom to think and act
Achievement	Motivation to excel

A solid organization with the right structure and people is a great starting point. The job, however, is not finished with getting the right people on board, organizing them in a proper structure and setting their goals and priorities. To become relevant in a booming digital economy, an organization also needs *to let go of some archaic practices which prevent the structure from delivering to its full potential.* In other words, it must create an environment where freedom of thought and action is not restricted by pointless, irrelevant and obstructive rules and policies. Every organization has its quota of these, and I am willing to wager that yours is not an exception.

This is an important aspect and organizations that have overlooked this have witnessed their supposedly stable structures implode upon themselves, leading eventually to their downfall. It is therefore well worth spending a few moments on this often-ignored but vital subject.

Inhibitors, as depicted in the diagram here, are one of the major blocking factors of personal and organizational growth. To identify these, invite feedback from folks, either in team meetings or through online polling, at least once in a year, on unpopular practices in your organization. You may get some mischievous responses that need to be filtered out, but you will also get some relevant inputs worth acting upon. The overarching goal of this exercise, of course, is to provide a productive and conducive environment for people to exploit their full potential, without compromising on the organizational code of conduct. Here are a few general pointers on restrictive practices but I would urge you to create a list that is specific to your own environment before deciding on the practices to be modified or phased out.

1. Keeping people "chained" to a role because the policy requires a minimum term (say one year) to be completed before a re-assignment like a requested transfer can be considered. What purpose is served by this if the person is better suited to the other position and is motivated to move there?

2. Fitting people into a forced Bell-Curve. A bell-curve is derived from the philosophical principle that in a given population X% of people would be super achievers, and the same (or close to) X% would be laggards, and the rest would be roughly average performers. Companies that try to force people into such a distribution invoke insecurities even in the best people. What if most people on one team are super achievers and most people on another team are laggards? The Bell curve will require some laggards to be rewarded and achievers to be punished. While a rough bell-curve is acceptable, insistence on precise fitment, especially in smaller teams (<50) is undesirable and counterproductive.

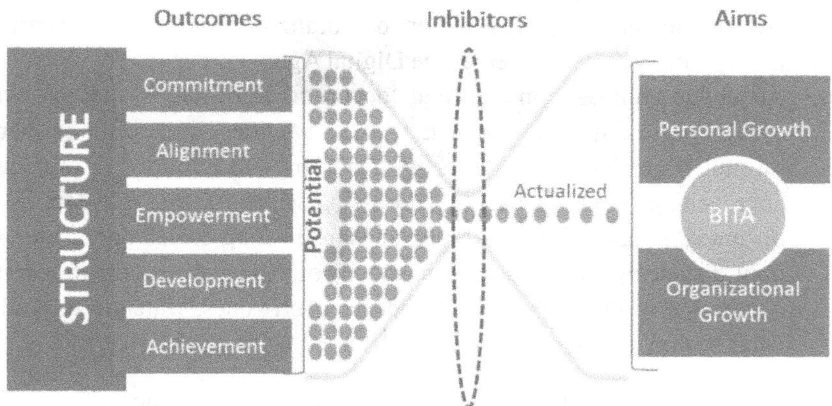

3. Restricting the use of the Internet in the office. Let's get real. We live in the information age. How can blocking people from access to information be productive? If you must, block pornography, drug-use and religious-fundamentalism sites, etc. But why not allow people access to Facebook, personal email, convenience portals like Banking, Ticketing, etc. or even job sites? Times have changed. These things are a part of people's lives, and cutting them off is *not* going to result in higher productivity. Trust me, a workforce that has the *freedom* to stay connected – even if they do not frequently exercise that freedom – is a much happier and more motivated workforce than a restricted one. Try cutting off Wi-Fi (or broadband data) at home for your kids and see what it does to their mood and motivation levels! It's no different in the workplace.
4. A governance system built on command, control and acquiescence. Some companies believe that giving freedom to employees equates to compromising *discipline* which is somehow deemed more important than morale. This could range from strict policies enforcing style and format of communication, requiring approvals for almost everything, and even

curbing the freedom to keep personal memorabilia like photos, etc. on office desk (because it 'distracts'). One of the reasons why companies like Google and Apple are rated as top places to work is that they have not embraced such systems. The only acquiescence you owe as an employee is to the code of ethics.

5. Inflexibility regarding work timings, hours and work-place. This is an 'industrial-age' hangover when card punching machines were installed at factory gates, with wages linked to work-hours. Today, what you achieve is a lot more important than how many hours you worked, or from where you worked (home or office) and organizations that overemphasize fixed hours, strict timings and work desks that are in the manager's line-of-sight are attaining nothing except a more demoralized workforce. Most certainly they are not yet ready to enter the Digital Age.
6. An undue emphasis on a formal 'decorum' in office. In this age where a large part of the workforce is in their twenties, organizations that lay too much emphasis on old-school decorum – like following protocol in approaching senior leadership, addressing senior folks as Mr/ Mrs..., 'sir' or 'madam' instead of their first names, respecting closed doors, etc. – are only distancing themselves from their workforce. Allow full freedom of expression so that people are in their comfort zones, which in turn allows ideas to flow freely.

These are only a few out of dozens of value-subtracting practices. Taking these as a sample, you may like to prepare a fuller list of the practices in your own company that cause frustration and demotivation, while achieving nothing of value. Many of these retrograde rituals are not only injurious to the morale of the people but are also a mill-stone around BITA. How can alignment happen when people are neither inspired nor free to express themselves? If you have such walls, demolish them immediately. They have no role in the modern, business-aligned enterprise structure.

This chapter dwelt on common practices and pitfalls in preparing an organization to meet the challenges of the digital era. As in most of this book, the focus was not on new, path-breaking insights, but on *reinforcing* practices that many successful enterprises have embraced in their pursuit of excellence. Taken in a contextual backdrop, these practices would help to bolster BITA, which indeed is what this book is about.

12 The Process Paradigm

"There are two ways to do something – the right way, and again."

A few years ago, I was in Malaysia as part of the technical delivery team supporting the business on closing a major deal for CRM transformation with one of that country's largest corporate entities. Due to the size of the project and the complexity it entailed, we had formed a consortium of participating companies, led by my company, each bringing its own expertise. There were meeting rounds with various representatives of the customer's team every day, including the Customer Service Delivery organization, the CIO organization, Business Functions and of course, the top management. The schedule required late night huddles to prepare for next day's meetings – ensuring synchronization across decks, feeding in research findings on the customer's environment, compiling responses to anticipated questions, etc.

On the final day, there was a dinner event with all the consortium members and the customer's senior team. During this event, the customer's CIO addressed us to express thanks on behalf of her organization to all the people who had traveled from India, Sri Lanka and Australia and spent ten days working with her teams on scoping out the new project, detailing the design and specifications. She hoped this would lead to the development of a top-notch system, which would be the envy of her competitors. This was all on expected lines of course. What did come as a somewhat surprising, though very pleasant, feedback was her admission of how much she and her team had learned from us on the value of business and technology teams working *together* and delivering so much more than they could have done individually. Then the head of CSD pitched in to say that our approach was like a breath of fresh air because we did not start the meetings by presenting standard PowerPoints on what we were *capable* of offering and then trying to convince the customer how this would (somehow) help him. Instead, he continued, we first spoke of what the customer currently had, the challenges and threats that the current system architecture entailed, and based on this presented a vision of what this company *needed* to achieve its mission. Only after there was a broad level agreement on the system requirements, did we present our *solution.* This showed that much effort had been put into studying the customer's current architecture and its limitations. In short, our approach was focused on where the *customer* wanted to go, rather than on where *we* wished to take him. This resonated very well with the customer and helped achieve the crucial buy-in that is all important in projects of this magnitude, entailing working together for multiple years ahead. Even the CEO mentioned, in his brief address during the toasting ceremony, that he has faced numerous problems in the past due to lack of ownership in projects that involved multiple companies, different functions, etc. But he was singularly impressed with the alignment that was apparent in our approach and expressed the confidence that he would see the same in future too.

Of course, we all felt much pumped up and later had our own little party to celebrate this win! Looking back, I am convinced that in this case, as in many others in today's business world, the most critical factor for the customer was the show of alignment across the constituents, as this gave us that crucial edge over some of our larger competitors who boasted of greater technological depth and price flexibility. In short, the business and technology alignment at work became the key differentiator for us.

The above is a feel-good example that I am sure resonates with some of your own winning experiences – in business or life – but what does it have to do with *process*, you might well ask. Process, as we have all come to understand, is a set of conventions that *prescribe* the way a program must be implemented. Usually, this is a well-documented set with associated policies, forms & templates. But there is no prescription evident in the example. So how is process alignment evidenced here? Let's explore this.

In a typical organization, processes exist at *multiple* levels, each with the purpose of converting an *intention (or a plan) into a manageable result*. Processes at various levels are designed to achieve higher predictability and consistency (or standardization) in the *way* intentions are realized, or "*how*" plans are implemented, to fulfill various obligations– like regulatory compliance, order fulfillment, field operations, project delivery, performance management, etc.

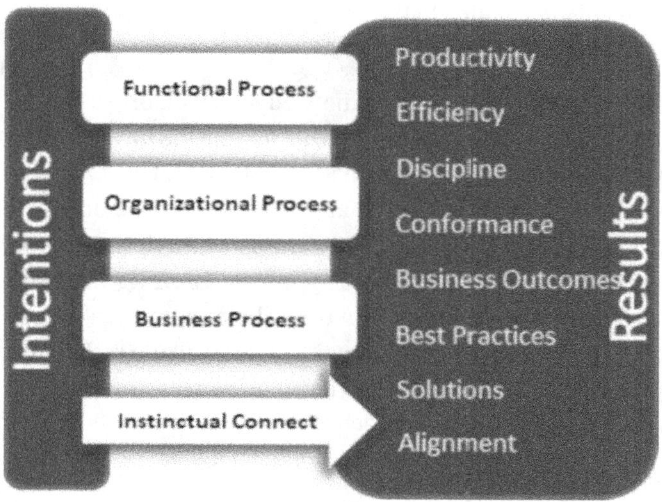

The first level is the *functional* processes. These are processes which are *internal* to the function and do not have a direct bearing on other functions. That is, they are invisible to all but their parent function. For example, the Finance function may have a process for reconciliation of vendor invoices against budget provisions, or the IT function may have a process for periodic data-center equipment maintenance. These processes, while important, operate *within* a function and hence do not have a visible role in the promotion of alignment *across* functions.

The next level is *organizational* processes. These are processes that everyone, irrespective of role, level or function, follows. They do not recognize any functional boundaries. Examples of these are the performance management process, procurement process, travel-expense settlement process, etc. and some IT processes like helpdesk, and allotment of hardware or software resources.

Following this are the *Business* processes – like the billing process, customer complaint logging & response process, supplier relationship management process, etc. – which visibly influence customer (or external stakeholder) experience and hence the business outcome. Business processes have a direct impact on BITA– a customer would, for example, *expect* his bill to be timely and accurate, and ensuring this must be a shared process for Business *and* IT. Business processes are usually well institutionalized through rule-based automated workflows as best practices in customer-experience driven enterprises. But automated business processes, however elegant, may be replicated by others and this may blunt your competitive edge. Therefore, their constant sharpening is essential to stay ahead.

Finally, there is a fourth and less acknowledged level, or perhaps a *connection*, which is *intuitive*, not rule-based. We will call this the *instinctual connect*. This occurs when Business and IT are harmoniously and *instinctively* aligned in such a way that each can relate to and complement the actions of the other in providing imaginative solutions in a complex environment. Written down processes have a significant part to play in *standardizing* the various methods and practices in the organization. But overwhelmingly, creative solutions are a consequence of the *instinctual connection*, which, while respecting the defined and documented processes at each level, leverages the *human* instincts of anticipation, pragmatism, and prudence. The example at the beginning of this chapter is an illustration of the *instinctual connection*.

The instinctual connection – unlike the functional, organizational and business processes – is not a formal and documented system. Think of it this way: you and your friend are on a survival mission, wandering through rocky wilderness, risking wild animals, steep precipices, and falling boulders. Supplies are dwindling fast, and the safety of the base camp is still days away. In this situation, what do you rely on? For one, you are glad that you have each other's support. You shudder to think what would have happened without your friend on this mission. Next, the skills you have and your 'brave-it' attitude play a big part. You also depend on certain laid-down methods that you learned for say, preserving rations and keeping your gear in readiness. But more than anything else, you rely on the inner voice that prompts you to "do what is right." At such a time, all the written down guidelines, or standard operating procedures (SOPs), that you were taught have at best a marginal value in your life.

You guessed it. The above is an allegory for a typical business setting in the intensely competitive Digital Age. Brutal competition, unpredictability, regulatory headwinds and resource limitations are only some of the challenges that continually test your endurance. To survive in this fierce climate, like in your rough adventure in the mountains, you must rely on something more than a set of documented processes.

I know I am treading on rather thin ice here. You are probably not alone in thinking that I am advocating against documented and prescribed procedures in the digital enterprise context. But that's not true. All I am saying is that they are not *enough.* As the gospel tells us, man cannot live by bread alone, meaning that there must be a *higher* spiritual calling in life. That, however, does not diminish the role and importance of bread in man's life. As we shall soon discover, well-defined processes can, and *do*, have a role to play in steering the enterprise to greater success.

Back to the subject of survival in the digital economy. The point being made above was that documented processes and SOPs are not in themselves sufficient to see you through the vicissitudes of modern business. This is where instinctual connections come in. Whether on a survival mission in the wilds or in the whirlwind world of business, these are just what you need to beat the odds. In the tumultuous world of digital business, *BITA is your instinctual connect.*

Process is a vast and very contextual subject and hence not readily amenable to a general treatment. While there may be a loose sort of generalization possible for *organizational* processes, most *business* processes are specific to an industry segment. Our method of breaking down enterprise processes into *functional, organizational* and *business* varieties may be considered somewhat arbitrary by process pundits, but my aim is only to put the spotlight on process *as a tool for Business-IT alignment*, and not on its formulation and engineering. In this chapter, we will focus on process alignment as a competitive edge, while introducing the role and importance of the instinctual connection – those undocumented nuggets of wisdom – into the operational work stream.

Functional Processes

While functional processes are *intrinsic* to a function, it is nevertheless important to appreciate their role in preparing the groundwork for alignment. Without these processes, you may have inefficiencies that could quickly erode your effectiveness and agility. A sales manager may have his own process for obtaining daily sales data from his team which may not impact the working of other organizational units directly. However, if the sales process is not managed effectively, it may lead to delay in required interventions, thereby impacting business results. Similarly, IT may have a process of its own for reconciliation across various databases, which is invisible to business. However, any lapse in this process would impact business heavily. So, the question is not whether functional processes are crucial for enterprise success. They are. The question is if they have a role to play in Business-IT alignment.

The answer to this question depends on whether the enterprise is in the *pre-digital* phase, or is *digital*. In both cases, the role of IT as an enabler of business processes is largely the same. That is, IT must understand crucial processes of the *Business* function and their relationships, not just to automate them, but to optimize and integrate them into the enterprise architecture. If you take the above case of the sales manager, for example, IT must understand where and how sales information is gathered, and define internal processes to capture, process and present data to the sales manager. On the other hand, in the pre-digital phase, there is typically no compulsion for *business* to understand IT functional processes. For example, while business *expects* data sanctity, the *process* followed by IT to achieve synchronization across multiple databases is not a direct concern of business.

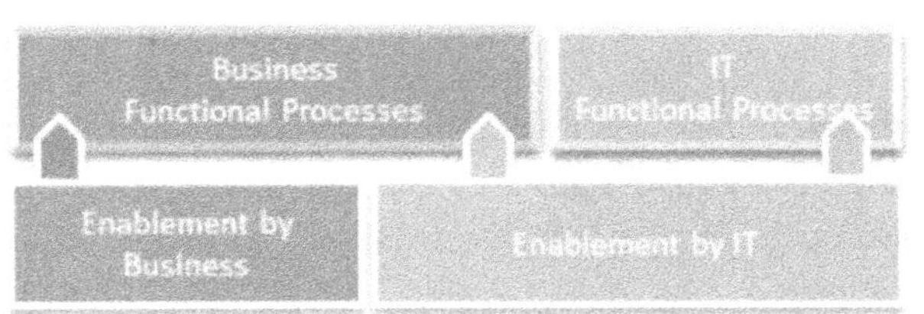

In the *digital* phase, however, where business strongly relies on IT for agile development, enterprise mobility, cloud computing, data analytics and other driving forces, IT functional processes are *integral* to business success, and business must not only understand them but play a key part in their enablement.

Organizational Processes

Organization processes are created to ensure uniformity and discipline across the enterprise. Their primary focus is on organization-wide policy implementation and conformance. Democratization is the essence of organizational processes. For this reason, any deviation is frowned upon even if it seems perfectly logical under the circumstances.

A company I worked for had a policy that every employee up to a certain salary grade must log in to their computer on reaching office and the time of log-in would be recorded as their 'in-time' by the Leave and Attendance process that devoured this information. This application was linked to the salary system, with some backend algorithm to mark x number of accumulated late hours as full-day leave from work. If you were a sales guy who wanted to make an early morning round of his customer before coming to the office, you would be marked late, and only after explanations and approvals from your seniors, could you regularize the entry. Employees often argued that they frequently worked much after office hours, but the system gave no credit for that, while it was quick to deduct hours for late coming, even for very valid reasons. The counter-argument was that reversal of this process could lead to indiscipline and loss of productivity! The company was also worried about 'precedence,' and this drove it to enforce this seemingly flawed process, disregarding its impact on morale and ultimately, attrition. The process defied all logic, yet its proponents could keep it alive years after it exhausted whatever utility it once had.

The biggest problem with the above process was not in the way it was designed or even in the way it was being enforced. The biggest problem here was that it remained *unquestioned* with the passage of time and change in business environment. There is an inherent inertia of 'tradition' and thus many organizational processes suffer from stagnancy, far beyond their useful years.

The important point here is that, like other process classes, organizational processes need to be reviewed and tested for relevance periodically. Many of these are merely ritualistic and serve either no purpose or a detrimental purpose (as the one in above example) and hence must be exterminated as a disease before they can cause irreversible damage. Others, while they could be relevant, may need to be modified to serve the interest of the business better. Bottom-line, do not let organizational processes subordinate common-sense in the name of tradition. Question their relevance often, as the first step to keeping them current and relevant.

Organizational processes no doubt have a role to play in stability and continuance, but purely from a BITA perspective, their function is somewhat delicately placed. If they are not reviewed and recalibrated with changes in the environment, they may, in fact, become detrimental to BITA. On the other hand, organizational processes that are maintained current through regular reviews of their utility and effectiveness, have the potential to form the bedrock for BITA to thrive.

Here are a few examples of how routine organizational processes may impact BITA, positively and negatively.

1. An effective New Employee Joining and Induction process leads not just to newcomers feeling more welcome and comfortable in an alien

environment, but also helps build a base for future collaborative working. The process is not just an HR initiative. It involves all functions, and is an excellent opportunity to bond together, which in turn is great for BITA.

On the other hand, the process could as easily lead to unintended negative consequences. If the content that is used for dissemination to the new joiners is not current and relevant, or is delivered by people who are themselves uninformed and uninterested, or if there is no follow-up action to hand-hold employees in their initial phase, contrary to what was stressed in the orientation, this process could lead to early detachment in employees and a negative impression of the organization which is hard to rebuild.

2. As many of the employee policies and standard operating procedures in a company relate to IT (second only to Human Resources in this aspect), there is an excellent window of opportunity for IT here to align with business through progressive processes. A typical process in companies is the IT Helpdesk, a workflow used for logging, handling, and tracking of all requests made by enterprise functions on IT. It's a great tool for IT to demonstrate its alignment with business through easy access, responsiveness and follow-up.

   Conversely, if the process of logging and handling requests is unfriendly and bureaucratic in the name of implementing 'controls', it ends up in a wide chasm between Business and IT. It is indeed unfortunate if IT, which is the gateway to a company's future in the Digital Age, itself endorses (if not enforces) practices that are out of sync with the times.

   I was at a gathering of ex-colleagues from a company I had worked in. Most of us were not with that company now, but had remained in touch and had decided to have a get-together one Friday evening. One of the prime movers behind this event was conspicuous by his absence, and we were all wondering about this. Finally, we saw him trudging in at around 10.00 pm, when the appointed time was 7.30pm! It turned out that he was held up at the office to give approval on mail to a routine, but urgent, business request from a junior colleague, as he was the head of a key business vertical for his company. He had already given a telephonic approval, but the policy required a written one, and so he had to wait for the mail's arrival in his inbox to could give his approval! I was a bit surprised by this. Couldn't he have done this on his smartphone, while here at the gathering, I asked? He said this was not possible because, despite repeated requests, his IT team had not authorized access to business email on smartphones due to "security reasons." Now, this is decidedly archaic. Amazingly, his employer is an IT services company engaged in next-generation transformation projects for a global clientele! The world, including its clients, has moved on, and yet this company is stuck in the past due to their IT department choosing to transfer its own ineptness to other functions, making people's lives (and business) difficult. Anyone can imagine the state of BITA in such an organization. What an opportunity missed!

3. Staying with IT, one of the organizational processes that are indispensable, is the software license usage and compliance process. Enterprises use third-party software which has terms of use associated with it. Most employees do not go through the fine print of these terms, and thus they are open to involuntary violations, to the huge detriment of the enterprise. An example of this is the downloading by employees of trial versions of software, and 'forgetting' to uninstall them before the expiry of the trial period. Other forms of violation that are subtler can also happen. Such violations expose the enterprise to huge claims by software vendors on the grounds of intellectual property abuse, and remedying them involves substantial payments and loss of credibility. For this reason, IT has strong organization-wide processes for indenting, procuring, installing and use of licensed software. If your organization does not have such processes, I urge you correct this before it is too late. You cannot build BITA on the back of unauthorized software and in the face of I-P lawsuits. If there was one realm which proves that an ounce of prevention is worth a pound of cure, trust me, this is it!

4. Some organizational processes are mandated for reasons of safety of personnel and equipment, though they may not be about BITA per se. There is usually a well-documented and propagated SOP for evacuation in the event of fires, for example. As part of this process, companies conduct periodic fire-drills, and those of us who view these as unnecessary and pointless waste of person-hours obviously have a warped sense of security that endangers not only us but those around us. Laxity on these SOPs threatens life and property and reflects a weak stance on security in general.

I have given the above examples to direct your attention to some common organizational processes in place at most companies. In our definition, an organizational process is one that impacts a very large part of the organization, if not all of it. It may not always be possible to tie back their benefits to BITA directly, but overlooking them could be detrimental in many other ways. It is important to review these periodically and be open to tuning them with the changing environment.

By conducting the following exercise over a wide enough cross-section, you may obtain a fair organization-wide recommendation on the desirable and undesirable organizational processes, which you may like to share with the owners of those processes for required action.

If you have too many processes in the company, take it as a *red flag*. Organizational processes must be kept to the minimum number required. The new generation workforce is not orientated towards too many controls and regulations, which they see as an attack on their liberty. When in doubt on whether to keep or kill an organizational process, the default choice must be to kill. Fewer processes, like lower taxes, result in higher compliance.

Exercise: *List down all the internal processes in your enterprise that you can think of. Classify these under functional and organizational. Against each process, mention "retain", "remove" or "modify" based on your view. For the "modify" category, cite the changes you seek. Get comparative views from your colleagues and peers to check if your views resonate with others.*

Business Processes

Business processes are the collection of methods and procedures designed to serve the *customer* (or a primary external stake-holder: partner, regulator, etc.) of the enterprise. The key thing about these processes is that they must continually be aligned with your customer experience objectives. I have seen a lot of companies start out with an exceptionally well-devised set of processes, only to be overtaken in time by shifting customer expectations and experiences.

In chapter 6, while introducing process (procedural) alignment, I had given a real-life example of a hotel reservation process that failed its customer. Unfortunate as it is, there are many other examples in practically every segment. Rigidity of processes is the chief reason people avoid state-run institutions where bureaucracy runs deep, and changes are difficult to implement. But it is unfair to say that this malaise is confined to government institutions. There are many large private organizations in every sector that have found their comfort zones in archaic processes with scant regard for the experiences their customers go through. I wouldn't make any haste in buying into the stock of such companies.

Just a few days ago, I was at my bank, which incidentally is among the most progressive private banks in the country, to prematurely liquidate a fixed deposit (FD) to meet an urgent requirement. For *opening* this FD, I had been the sole signatory on the required form. Yet I was told that getting the money into my account would need my wife's signature in addition to my own, as ours was a joint account – even though I was the primary (first named) holder. As my wife was out of town, I ended up *failing to get my money transferred to my own account*, due to this absurd process! I had to borrow money from someone to meet the exigency! The gratifying part was that a few days later, the bank manager informed me that they had since changed the process as many had complained. For transfers-in from bank held deposits, primary holder's signature was now sufficient. But the bank lost a lot of goodwill due to its inability (or refusal) to keep its processes tuned to their customers' needs.

Here is another example from a different industry.

It's sad but true that in many management forums, investments in upgrading IT systems are not considered an urgent organizational priority. While no one openly declines the business case for IT, it is often 'deferred' in favor of more pressing needs. IT, to many people (including in management), is like oxygen – it is always there, but rarely noticed, until its absence chokes you. So, the tendency is to 'let things be.' This telecom company I was associated with had a process for extracting data to meet its mandated regulatory obligations from the *secondary* storage system, which was a tape library. As per the process, last 30 days of data was kept on online disk storage (primary), and beyond that, it was kept on tapes (secondary), which were slower, but cheaper. With the disk storage costs plummeting, a case was presented to switch from tape to low-cost *disk* storage, but was 'deferred.' As data volumes grew, so did the tape library, and this company failed three times in a row to meet the regulatory window for providing obligatory information. The result was a huge penalty, which exceeded the cost of changing from a tape library to disk storage. Obviously, at the root here is *process* inertia, not investment capacity.

Both the above examples, though in different contexts, illustrate the need for constant review and adaptation of business processes, instead of waiting for an external trigger.

On the other hand, some new Digital Age business processes like hailing a cab with Uber, or ordering merchandise with Amazon, are not only user-friendly

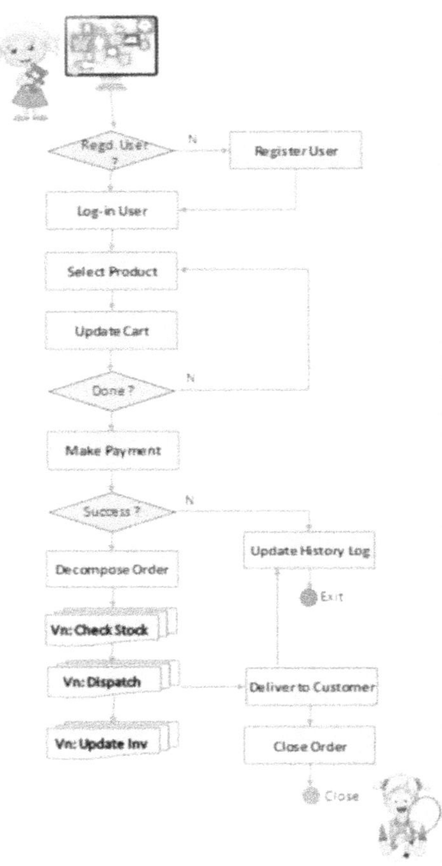

and intuitive but also in lockstep with changes in the market environment and the rising expectations of their customers. This is not by chance. These companies have instituted advanced technologies, like sentiment analytics and data mining, to gauge customer experience parameters and respond to them even before they are expressed. And they have reaped a tidy benefit from this. Today, many digital enterprises attribute their success almost entirely to sleek business processes that keep the customer squarely in the center.

Well-tuned business processes are among the best examples of BITA at work. Think of an enterprise that is into delivery of sports goods from multiple vendors. The company has a convenient website that is supported on different devices as well as browsers. That is, it can be accessed on-the-go by anyone. A visitor to the site is encouraged to select a sport (say tennis) and then the gear that is required – say a tennis racquet. Once you do this, it may prompt you to input your level, like a beginner, hobbyist, pro, etc., and then display an array of matching products to choose from. At this point, you could also specify a make, type or price range. Once you have selected a product, you are guided either to choose more items (like tennis balls) or to a payment gateway. After verifying the payment, the order is confirmed, and an order-ID is issued to you. Then the process of order handling (invisible to you) takes over. For example, if the order consists of multiple items from different vendors, this must be 'decomposed' and sent to each vendor in the chain, with the relevant order and shipment details. At the vendor site, the dispatch and delivery process kicks-in which results in items getting shipped to you from different vendors. When you receive the shipments, an acknowledgment is sent by the deliverer to the front-end company, which then completes the order process and asks you to rate the experience! The flow is illustrated here in a *very simplified* and abridged form, the purpose being only to highlight that *multiple business processes* – each involving both Business and IT working in harmony – are at work to execute a routine customer request. Each box in the diagram is a detailed business process that could span multiple entities.

In this age, the simplicity and elegance of business processes are fundamental to the customer experience. I, for one, can say that I feel privileged to live at a time when I can book my airline ticket using a simple and intuitive process that also enables me to book the seat of my choice, order the meal of my preference and do a check-in, through a convenient application which I can trigger from my mobile phone. And I say this with some authority because I was also around when you had to bus it to the airline's city office, wait in a queue, and then have a paper ticket (like a little chequebook) issued by the agent behind the counter. Options and add-ons? You must be kidding! It was a half-day long process, end to end. Today, having booked the best available ticket, when the time comes I can trigger off another process – hailing a cab to get to the airport. I have already charged up my mobile wallet through yet another business process, which will directly pay for this cab ride without my intervention, as these processes (m-wallet and cab service) are seamlessly linked together for my happiness. On the way to the airport, I suddenly remember I am due on my phone bill payment. No – I don't tell the driver to take a diversion to the phone company's payment center. I just initiate another process from my mobile handset that settles my outstanding bill, while on the move. This is not going to make your eyes wide with disbelief! We are so used to these in this Digital Age that it has become the new normal. In fact, trends like presence, geo-location, and others are already pushing this normal. But at the end of the day, these are simply intuitive and innovative business processes at work, that were fashioned by using IT for creating business value. BITA in motion.

The processes that are now routinely used by customers like you and me are conceptualized by marketers and business people and developed by an IT team. They are then ported to a cloud-based system by another set of IT people, to enable mobility. Somewhere, data on customers' usage and experience is being collected and mined using analytics, the results of which are used by the business teams to tune the front-end process for an enhanced customer experience. Unless they are in perfect harmony with each other, these different operations could soon lead to the enterprise spiraling out of control.

The following illustration depicts the generic pattern of a business process delivery cycle, highlighting the importance of BITA in the conception, construction and rendering of value-creating business services. The *individual* business processes, such as the boxes in the previous illustration, are derived from the process design created together by Business and IT. These may be iteratively developed from scratch or customized using an available framework (COTS), and integrated into the workflow. The processes are designed to capture and analyze information at various stages of the customer lifecycle, which becomes an invaluable input for modeling the revisions in line with changing customer behavior.

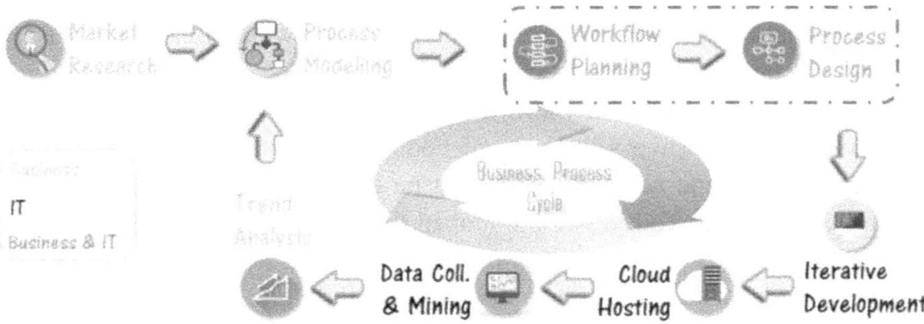

Whether you are a running digital enterprise or an aspiring one, the current environment demands that Business and IT work continuously and harmoniously *as one* in developing and perfecting the customer-driven *business* processes. In this environment, Business and IT share a shared vision which drives them to transgress functional boundaries and have a shared sense of urgency towards accomplishing *organizational*, and not functional, goals.

While this may seem the obvious thing to do, the pursuit of functional goals often overrides larger organizational interests. Business and IT may walk the path together in certain discrete steps of the customer value-creation process, but often do not have an equal stake in the end game. For example, in delivering a critical customer project, Business and IT often define their *goals* as the performance of their functional *roles*. Thus, Business may see its goal as writing the BRS, and IT as development and testing. They are not focused on the common purpose of delivering to the customer on time, cost and quality, but on completing the independent process steps outlined in their functional agendas. This disjoint approach may have had some payback when the goal was automating a set of manual processes over time, but in the context of today's dynamic, customer-driven environment, a much more agile and participative approach is needed.

At this point, let's do a short exercise. List down all the different Business processes running in your organization, i.e., processes that have a bearing on the business outcome or customer experience, in the left column of the following table. Think hard, and try not to miss any critical process. A customer portal, CRM, Bill-payment website, Self-service app, etc. would be some candidates. Having done this, give your considered assessment on a 1-5 scale on the given set of attributes (see definitions following the table). It would be good to do this across several participants from Business and IT.

Business Process	Convenience	Intuitiveness	Flexibility	Simplicity	Diversity	Performance
---						

Convenience: As a *customer*, would you consider that this process contributes to making things convenient for you? [Like ordering items, doorstep delivery, payment options, return policy, refund, etc.]

Intuitiveness: Does the process anticipate needs and/or help the customer make more informed decisions? [Like getting price/fare estimate, travel time, etc. in case of a cab booking]

Flexibility: What is the level of openness to changes in the process? How easy is it to personalize the process for specific markets or segments?

Simplicity: Would your parents, or other people of an older generation, be comfortable using this process without assistance?

Diversity: How accommodative is the process in terms of technological diversity? [Multiple devices & platforms, Cloud, Data Privacy & security, Big data, Analytics, Future trends (like IPv6)]

Performance: How well does the process work under varying load and traffic conditions, on parameters such as speed of response (latency) and stability (downtime)?

When averaged over multiple respondents, this could become a simple yet effective tool for gauging business process effectiveness in meeting the customer benchmark on critical parameters, and for focusing attention on the relative shortcomings. This may then become an additional input for process modeling while considering the next phase of evolution in the iterative process delivery cycle. In fact, you could go a step further with this – create a checklist of 10 or more items against *each* parameter (e.g., ten factors contributing to *Convenience*) and ask people to rate the process on every one of them. The results will greatly supplement your efforts to win your customers' goodwill and stay competitive.

Instinctual Connect – the ICing on the cake

I was at one of those offsite meetings that span a weekend, which one gets used to as part of corporate life. The only difference here was that it happened to be my wife's birthday in that weekend. I did the only possible thing that could rescue me from a sticky aftermath. I placed an online order early in the morning for delivering flowers to her. It required me to select a bouquet online, fill the details, and make the payment. I was surprised to receive a call a few minutes later confirming where I was. They also asked me if it was fine to deliver the flowers to my wife at 9.30am, to which I said yes. I took this to be a routine verification call and thought no more about it.

I reached home the next day. My wife showed me the flowers that she had got from me, which were now placed in a vase in the center of our sitting room. She also showed me the card which had accompanied the flowers. Apart from the usual Happy Birthday, there was a line saying, "wish I could be there in person." Now, this was surprising, because I had given no such instructions. It had not occurred to me. You send flowers by online-order *only* when you are not there! But when I did see it I was glad for this simple message. And I am sure my wife would have been too – and it was probably the reason there was less strain on my arrival than I was anticipating. A happy ending after all!

So, what has this to do with process? Let us go back to the definition of process. It is that series of steps that are taken to convert an intention into a result. This is where we introduce *instinctual connect.* Instinctual connect is a *part* of the steps that must be taken to realize the aim. The difference between a process (business/organizational/functional) and instinctual connect is that in case of process, the defined steps – which are usually documented – are fixed and unchanging. This makes processes very amenable to automation which is why we see a lot of shop floor processes being run by robots in factories. An instinctual connect, on the other hand, while sharing the same goal as a process – viz., converting an intention to a result – is a *variable* human action that is neither documented nor templatized. In other words, it is that *improvisation* which is done to make the process outcome more agreeable.

In my example above, the addition of those simple words was an improvisation, arising from an understanding of the customer's situation. The prescribed process was not bypassed at any point, but an instinctual connect lent *further* fizz to a predictable and comparatively lackluster outcome. Maybe the flower shop had picked this up from long experience, or it was an impromptu act of someone dispatching the order. I am not sure. But who do you think I would go to if in a similar situation again, or if asked to recommend an internet flower delivery service? You guessed it. And why? Because of the instinctual connect. Had it been as per the prescribed process, I may not have complained, but would probably not have remembered the transaction and write about it today.

If the goal of a process is to create a standard product, instinctual connect may not be obligatory. But if your goal is service, you must rely on something that goes beyond templatized processes, which is the instinctual connect. Imagine that the next time you went for a haircut, your hairdresser insisted on *exactly* following a written down process, doing everything with exasperating precision – no room for styling, creativity, etc. I am not sure you will end up with a haircut that would be the envy of your friends. The *improvisation* by the hairdresser makes all the difference!

Quantum physics tells us about the Uncertainty Principle, postulated by Heisenberg. Its core premise is that there is a degree of unpredictability even in the ordered universe, otherwise governed by the precise laws of science. But for this, everything – including our behaviors – would be completely predictable. How dull would that be! It is the same with processes. Without instinctual connect, process outcomes would be dreary and predictable, with almost no room to enthrall its (human) participants. It is the instinctual connect which stimulates a process to achieve more than its potential, and hence this forms a key *tool for differentiation* in a business setting.

Instinctual connect plays a very pivotal role in influencing business outcomes. But this is often ignored, as we are trained to go by the book. Sometimes, we may hide behind the process cover to avoid doing what makes perfect sense but involves some extra steps. At other times, it is the fear of going wrong that pulls us back from doing the right things as opposed to doing things 'right.' Most of us do not recall our experiences with the bureaucracy with much relish primarily due to the boxed processes and the total absence of instinctual connect. Without instinctual connect, a process may, in fact, become a barrier.

An instinctual connect with your customer is obviously a major competitive edge. As we saw in the example at the beginning of this chapter, this instinctual connect with customers stands on a strong foundation of BITA. To enhance your customers' experience at all stages of the lifecycle, an instinctual connect between Business and IT is, therefore, a pre-requisite in this era of digitally driven business. Now, it may be debated whether instinctual connect happens because of BITA, or the other way around. But this is irrelevant. The key point is that for a sustained competitive edge, there must be an instinctual connect between the Business and IT arms of the enterprise.

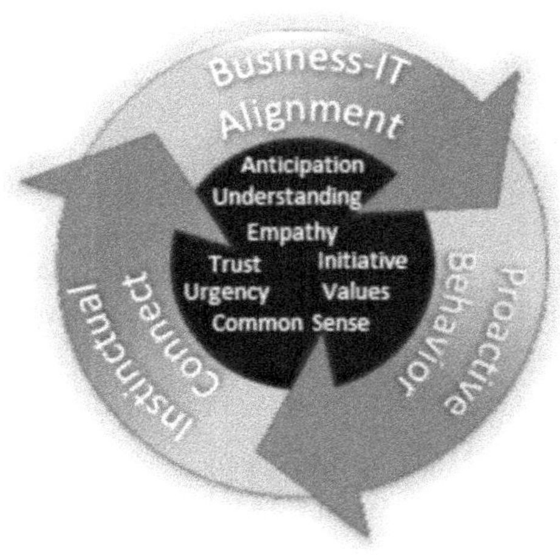

An instinctual connect is situational and intuitive, so it cannot be defined in terms of a rigid set of influencing factors. With time and experience, Business and IT teams learn to be more *proactive* in managing business situations together, resulting in an instinctual connect between them. When there is instinctual connect, Business and IT teams can *anticipate* each other's motives and actions. They can better *understand* the intentions and *predict* the behaviors of each other. There is *trust* between them which enables them to take joint *initiative* (and *risk*) to achieve their common goal. They *empathize* with each other and share the *urgency* to carry a task to completion. Most importantly, they demonstrate the *values* that the enterprise is founded on. The factors that I have *italicized* in this paragraph are core *human* traits, critical for differentiating the enterprise from its peers, that no structured process or automation can produce.

In fact, the process dimension is not the only one to be positively impacted by instinctual connect. It also influences alignment at the intellect and tactics levels, as you can surmise from the above.

You have spent years of effort building and institutionalizing your processes. Some of these have become your lifeline, especially if you are a digital enterprise. Make them work for you. All it takes is a bit of ICing.

Most companies today use an Order Logging System (OLS). This system registers customer orders and provides relevant information to functions involved in the fulfillment process. In a company I worked with, it was common to chat about new orders around the coffee machine informally. In one such case, on hearing about a new order, one of the technical consultants smelt a rat. He went back and pulled up the order in the OLS. His fears were immediately confirmed. A version of one of the software components in the order would not be the best fit in that *specific* customer's environment. It would have worked now but, as per a recent OEM notification, could lead to issues in the *next* upgrade. Now, this was an approved and accepted order, and in general, our process prohibited changes to the order configuration at this stage. What's more, no one would have even noticed a problem. Yet, we went back to the customer and explained the situation, and gave our recommendation for an alternative – a cloud-based solution which would free the customer from such upgrade worries in future. This was much appreciated by the customer. For our company too, it resulted in a multi-year contract as opposed to a single order. The standard OLS process, if followed, would not have provided the same long-term benefits to all the parties concerned. Sometimes, Instinctual Connect only means applying *common sense*.

Exercise: *Reflect on the Instinctual Connect examples in your own company. List down (1) actual cases of instinctual connect that have helped improve the outcome of a business process in your company, and (2) opportunities that exist for future application of instinctual connect, considering the processes you have in place today.*

Tools and Technology

In a modern enterprise environment, there is an abundance of tools and technology to accomplish business objectives. Tools boost performance by enabling higher productivity, faster transactions, accurate and timely availability of information, drilled down analytics and a host of other value-additions. Some of these tools are available commercially for mass consumption, while others are built specifically to serve the needs of an enterprise. Earlier, there were only a few industries that relied heavily on commercial software tools for achieving business results, like CAD/CAM tools for the design and manufacturing

segment. Today, almost every industry relies on software tools for its core operations. Think of banks, airlines, telcos, hotels, utilities, retail or shop-floor. Though diverse in their core focus, these segments are bound together by the adoption of automated tools for their internal (e.g., *ERP*) and external (e.g., *CRM*) operations and use of new technologies like cloud, analytics, and mobility to propel their growth. In a typical scenario, it is these *tools* that fit together as the *building blocks* of the enterprise's business process workflow, glued together by Instinctual Connect.

Using software tools and technology, either as individual productivity boosters or as enterprise process enablers, serves another very important purpose: it *brings Business and IT together* to create a new ecosystem of empowerment and information, better suited to meet the demands of digital markets. However, even in these times, there are numerous adoption challenges associated with new technology, commonly due to ignorance and inertia, or simply tight comfort zones that some people are unwilling to renounce. BITA gets a boost when technology and tools are well-absorbed across the breadth and depth of the organization.

While many new digital enterprises start off well on the tools adoption curve, it is often a challenge to sustain the momentum given the dynamic nature of the business. For enterprises that have *turned* digital, it is an even bigger challenge to drop old practices in favor of technology-driven tools. Everyone is not tech-savvy, nor a fan of technology. It requires a well-focused approach led by top management to sell the value of productivity- and business- enhancing tools, as a cultural shift. Employees must be convinced of the benefits of the tools and their impact on performance – both business and individual. Given the importance of adopting new technology and tools in enhancing your BITA quotient, it is worth spending a few minutes here to look at some simple ways to achieve this.

1. Present a simple user-interface

Whatever the merits of technology in today's business environment, it is not everyone's cup of tea. Even the solution that best fits your business needs is of little value if the entailed user-experience is not great. Too much attention to specifications while ignoring simplicity and intuitiveness in the user-interface is often a major cause of poor adoption. Tools should be 'fun', encouraging users to explore and discover. The more you design your tool for 'dummies', the better will be the rate of adoption. Involve as many users as possible in the interface design. Sacrifice features that add to the complexity, at least in the initial versions. Take a cue from popular applications. Go for tools that can be self-learned, or with minimal training effort. Provide animated demos. Take regular feedback from users. These will help greatly in boosting adoption.

2. Customize your coaching

The usual process of introducing a new technology or tool (like salesforce automation) in the enterprise involves a combination of announcements, demos and training sessions under the assumption that everyone in the organization has a similar grip on technology. In reality, not everyone has the same affiliation for technology, though few people confess to this. Therefore, it is important to individually encourage the adoption through a tailored hand-holding program. This is not as complicated as it may appear because most people *are* tech-savvy and keen to adopt. But you need to consciously on-board the strugglers to excite them into adoption.

3. Enthuse the leaders first

The sway that leaders hold over their teams is far more than any outside expert. This is as true of business as other functions. In the true BITA tradition, the business leaders would be key participants in the earliest stages of technology planning and evolution itself. It is well worth engaging them in the adoption planning and enlisting their support to convey the benefits of the new technology to their teams. If there is any doubt in the minds of the leaders, it is important to remove this before taking the adoption further. The leaders should then be active protagonists of the technology adoption drive, urging their teams through communication as well as by example, like sitting through the initial training programs.

4. Propagate the success stories

Direct evidence of the benefits that the new technology brings is an excellent motivation for adoption. It fires you up to learn and adapt quickly. If a peer or an allied group in the company has been quick to adopt a technology and reap its benefits, make it count. For example, if you have just introduced a multi-factor authentication system using software-token technology to make company laptops more secure against data theft, relate the stories about how folks using this comply far better with the information security policy, have fewer security incidents and can relax more while connecting (remotely) through VPN, etc. Publish weekly or bi-weekly statistics on adoption rate until about 95% is achieved. The last few percent are always more challenging and for these cases a different, more individualized, approach may be required.

5. Recognize the early adopters

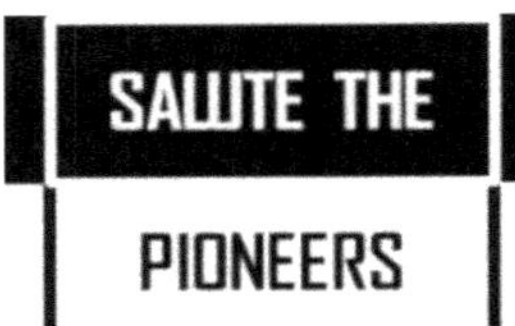

In an ideal world, the prospects of improved business results may be enough to spur 100% of the workforce to adopt new technology. In the real world, however, the promise of recognition (say a Technology-Pioneer Certificate) or a reward is a far more effective spark for adoption. If not for everyone, certainly for a sizeable proportion of users. Institute recognition and reward programs for those adopting the new technology *within a stipulated period.* It works. In fact, the recognition may lead to a higher level of satisfaction which in turn may encourage adopters to induce others among their peers, thus creating a viral effect leading to faster and more widespread adoption.

6. Dis-incentivize the stragglers

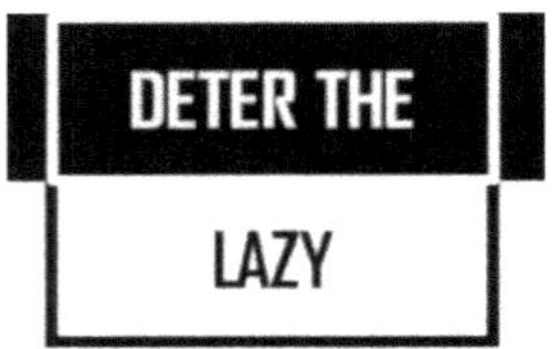

When all else fails, dis-incentives may do the trick. However, this must be resorted to, if at all, when all positive measures have been exhausted. It is a sensitive course that must be broached with caution. First, analyze the root-cause – is there something inherently flawed in the technology? Is there a sub-group that has been slower to adopt than others? Why? In this era, you should not have to threaten people into the adoption of technology ("Do it or else..."). Therefore, such dis-incentives must be soft ones, applied where the only apparent cause is inertia, and intended to promote *enthusiastic adoption* rather than forced compliance. For example, the company may declare that only orders entered using the new tool will be processed for quarterly sales achievement beyond a certain date. I have seen organizations link use of technology to salary payments and performance appraisals, which is totally counter-productive.

7. Build and Nurture Champions

If you are launching an enterprise-wide new process, technology or tool with a potential to transform your business, inspirational leaders and daring pioneers are not enough to get widespread adoption. You need champions, or influencers, from within the teams, who are well-networked, generally respected among their co-workers, and most importantly have a contagious passion for the new technology which they can communicate to their peers in chats around the coffee machine. There are always people who enjoy greater trust among their colleagues. You need to find these evangelists and make them your tools champions – the folks who become spokespersons for the technology, while also being able to sense the pulse and report back to the promoters of the tool on the general mood and perceptions.

As a running, or even aspiring digital enterprise, you must invest not just in creating elegant processes for Business and IT, but in their *fusion.* This is accomplished by linking these processes to a common workflow. The model can be likened to a computer system bus, which is a common link to interconnect different components of a computer system and is used to transfer data between these components. Similarly, the enterprise processes are linked to the *common* workflow, or Information Bus, to achieve harmonization of information (process output) from various parts of the enterprise. Every process on the workflow must test positive to the question: "does this contribute to the accomplishment of the common mission of the enterprise?" If it does not, it's probably just clutter that you should consider getting rid of.

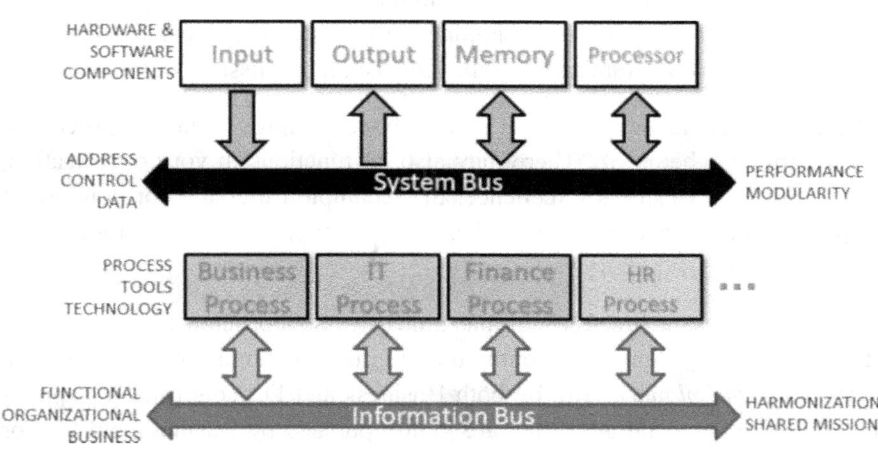

Efforts made to align at the level of functional, organizational and business process, topped by an Instinctual Connect between Business and IT should, one may be inclined to say, be enough for pursuing BITA at the process dimension. One wouldn't be too wide off the mark in making such an assertion. But this is only the *big* picture. There are some other important aspects, often ignored in our fixation with the urgent, which would bear upon making your BITA more comprehensive and enduring. We already looked at the adoption of tools and technology as one such aspect, which if used smartly could strongly bear on your process alignment and eventually on overall BITA. Let us look at some of the other such aspects, purely from the perspective of their impact on BITA.

Continuous improvement

Let's face it. This term has never evoked serious contemplation, nor ever made us pause in our pursuit of larger goals. Doesn't it mean that instead of focusing on what is new, we refine the old? After all, the electric light did not come from the continuous improvement of candles! Well, like any argument, it has two sides. The other side says that unless you continuously improve, you are stuck in the past – and that can never be good in a world which expects you to be in constant traction for survival. A Dreamliner 787 came from the continuous improvement of the Boeing 247 (1933)! BITA belongs in the latter camp. To be fair, continuous improvement is not a *substitute* for out-of-box thinking. If you go back for a second to the illustration of Business Process Delivery Cycle, there is a *continuous* feedback on customer behavior – in *addition* to the input from external market research – which is used to refine the process continually. This is a result of the harmonious interplay between Business and IT, with just one goal – to make things better. Even a momentary break in this cycle signals a failure of BITA and can result in blunting of the competitive edge. If you look at any process-flow diagram and find the feedback loop missing, raise a red-flag.

There are techniques dedicated to continuous improvement of processes, the commonest being 6Σ. There may also be functions in your organization, like Quality or Business Excellence, that champion the case for continuous improvement of processes, and are there for your support. Have you tuned them in?

When we follow a process multiple times, we subconsciously get better at it. However, for alignment, continuous improvement must be pursued in a *systematic and planned* way by both Business and IT. This usually happens by setting incremental goals that are jointly pursued by Business and IT. For example, leveraging big data for continually increasing the level of detail and sophistication in gathering actionable insights on customer behavior. With progressive customer expectations, continuous improvement is your ticket to staying ahead in the game. The key, of course, is never to stop asking the question: "how can we do this better?", with the conviction that there's always a way!

Even right now, there may be several processes in your enterprise that are crying for improvement. Can you single some of these out and start an internal project to tune them to the stakeholders' expectations? I have done this exercise a few times, and trust me, the results are worth the effort.

Change Management

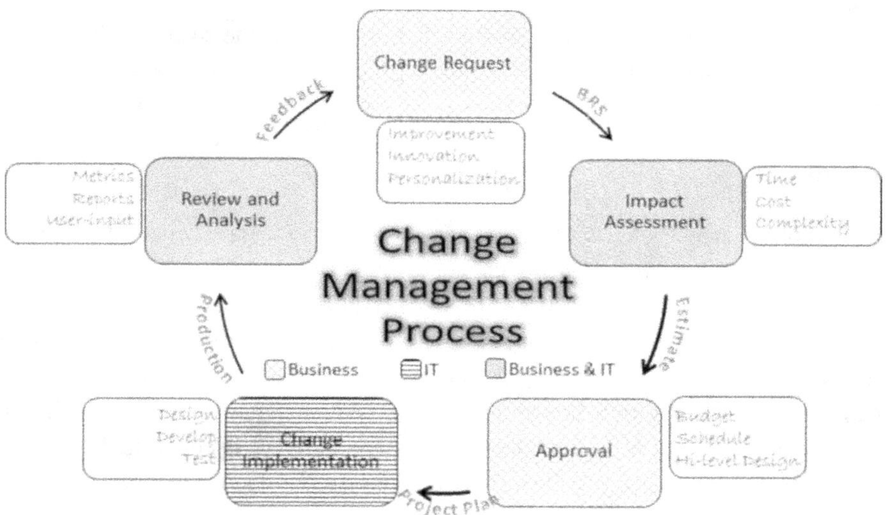

While there can be two sides to the debate on innovation vs. improvement, there can be no argument on the need for managing *change*, which is an inevitability of either track. A key requisite of BITA is the management of change by Business and IT in a shared and disciplined manner, as opposed to an ad hoc approach.

The trigger for change can come from a need for personalization, improvement or innovation. A disciplined approach to managing change requires a constant emphasis on various stages of the cycle as shown here, and tracking the changes made over different versions and releases using advanced tools. If your organization does not have a formal, organization-wide change management process which governs your products, procedures, practices, and policies, it is a warning that you are on a sinking ship.

For applying change management as a lever for BITA and attaining a competitive edge, you may have to go a little bit beyond the standard (as depicted) change management cycle and into the realm of *human connect*. This involves, first and foremost, creating a *sense of urgency* around the change that is shared by Business and IT. Enforced change usually does not accomplish its goals, at least in the longer run. The need for the change must, therefore, be clearly communicated and understood by both Business and IT, as a vision that *motivates* them to its accomplishment. It often helps to appoint *change champions* from Business and IT to rally the forces. Think through the obstacles that are likely to hinder the path of change implementation, and make efforts to remove them *before* they puncture the wheel. There will always be those who resist change, and hindrances only vindicate their stand. Do not let them succeed. In fact, go for some quick wins and try to switch them over with the results. With time, things settle down as the changes mature and are mainstreamed. But by then, it is time for the next change!

Quality

Ever wonder why the term Quality does not mesmerize us anymore? We gloss over the term when we see it appearing in campaigns and ads. Isn't it important now? Well, it sure is, but in this age, quality is *hygiene*. In other words, you are *expected* to maintain certain standards of quality and therefore trumpeting it fails to impress. In a telecom service provider scenario, for example, where customers have easy port-out options, if you cannot guarantee QoS as far as consistency of voice calls and speed of message delivery is concerned, you are out of the market before you know it. And likewise, for other industry segments.

In fact, ensuring quality in your products or services is more important now than ever before. But quality is no longer a tool for *positive differentiation*. While accomplishing your quality goals might not guarantee your place in the market, *not* accomplishing them is certainly the quickest way to exit the market. Today, customers do not *expect* defects in the product or the service, so trying to impress by fixing them quickly will achieve nothing. Quality is a proactive, not a reactive, indicator.

Quality is all-encompassing. It cannot exist in pockets. I was once at a prominent retail store where there were well-marked bays for various categories of merchandise. Shopping carts were in abundance and neatly arranged. The store stocked well-known brands, and if you looked around, there were attendants at hand. Nothing to complain about here. I stocked my cart and moved to the check-out line, paid as per the bill presented, collected my items in the shopping bags provided, and moved out. A few hours later my wife – who checks ALL bills – informed me that there was an over-billing of Rs 197 in the total. I assured her that this was impossible, and most decidedly a mistake with her addition. But anyhow, we went through the addition together, and it turned out she was right! But this was a printed, computer generated bill, and those are never wrong, are they? Well, apparently this one was! It was probably a random, undetected glitch in the billing software and not an intentional and systematic ploy to dupe the customers. In any case, it left a very poor impression of the *quality* at the store in my mind, despite all the other things that were done well. I could not go back, but am sure that if I had, they would have returned the excess with an apology. But even then, my impression of the overall quality would have remained dim.

For quality to be proactively built into the product, Business and IT must work together to embed it into the *design* itself. This is an important corollary of *agile* development. Time-to-market concerns often come in the way of quality assurance and are frequently a cause for some tussle between the Business and the IT delivery folks. In my experience, I have found that it is better to defer a requirement or two to the next cycle (phase) when TTM deadlines loom large than to attempt a short-cut to quality. This, of course, calls for excellent instinctual connect between Business and IT to prevent any loss of revenue or goodwill.

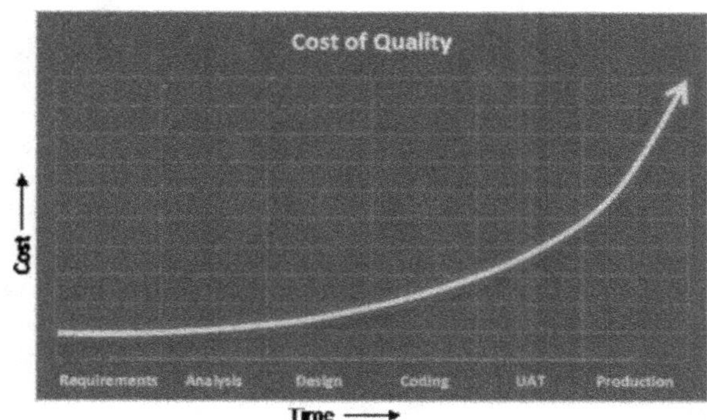

Another matter of concern for both Business and IT is the *cost* of quality. It is imperative that Business and IT understand the implications of delayed discovery of flaws or defects. The earlier a defect is 'caught', the less it costs to fix. A defect that 'escapes' through all the stages of quality assurance (testing) and is first found by the *customer* is the worst kind. Such defects are called, quite predictably, 'escaping defects', and are the costliest to fix both from a monetary and goodwill standpoint. One of the damaging fallouts of the disconnect between Business and IT is the invisibility of the spiraling cost of quality which could manifest in severe margin erosion. BITA is your best bet against such an eventuality.

When you buy your next car, who would you prefer to test drive it? I'm sure you'll like to do this yourself, rather than tell the manufacturer to do it. Yet when it comes to testing new business applications, many organizations let IT, which 'manufactured' the artifact, do the User Acceptance Testing. Unless this final testing is done by a neutral organization – most preferably the Business organization – the product should not be considered fit for commercial launch. If the IT team is a participant in the UAT process in your organization, get this practice stopped immediately.

Quality is hygiene, and it has a major influence on the health of your organization. When it comes to *services*, it is less tangible due to the human component but is as important. Quality of Service relies on Business and IT *sharing* the passion for excellence in spirit and action. In other words, a strong alignment between Business and IT is a *pre-requisite* to product and service quality.

In conclusion, enterprise processes are needed to bring some method to the pandemonium in the business environment. This chapter was not about business process management, but the role of BITA in the enablement of processes. We thus spoke of processes in terms of *functional*, *organizational* and *business* sets, each of which influences BITA in its own way. The *Instinctual Connect* was introduced as an icing on the process pie and an important element in the enhancement of BITA and customer experience. BITA has a high investment in the application of IT-enabled *tools* in the business environment and some simple but effective ways to stimulate adoption assume high importance here.

13 The Intellectual Interlock

"Why fit in when you were born to stand out?"

History has recorded many famous predictions by eminent people, from almost every sphere of human endeavor, which testify to the transcendent nature of the human spirit. Not because these predictions were *accurate* – in fact, they were anything *but* – but because *of their failure to daunt the future generations from breaking the barriers* that they imposed. Here are some specimens from diverse fields.

Computers and communications:

"There is no reason anyone would want a computer in their home.": *Ken Olson*, President, Chairman, and Founder of the Digital Equipment Corporation (1977).

"There is practically no chance that communication space satellites will be used to provide better telephone, telegraph, television, or radio service inside the United States.": *T Craven*, FCC Chief (1961).

"The internet will soon go spectacularly supernova and in 1996 catastrophically collapse.": *Robert Metcalfe*, the inventor of the Ethernet (1995).

Atomic energy:

"A rocket will never be able to leave the Earth's atmosphere.": Headline of an article published in the *New York Times* based on a collective view of the advanced scientific community (1936).

"There is not the slightest indication that nuclear energy will ever be obtainable. It would mean that the atom would have to be shattered at will.": *Albert Einstein*(1932).

"The energy produced by the breaking down of the atom is a very poor kind of thing. Anyone who expects a source of power from the transformation of these atoms is talking moonshine.": *Ernest Rutherford*, known as the father of nuclear physics (1933).

<u>Aviation</u>:

"There will never be a bigger plane built." *Boeing chief engineer*, after the first flight of the Boeing 247 – a twin-engine plane that could hold ten people (1933).

"Heavier-than-air flying machines are impossible": *Lord Kelvin*, British mathematician and physicist.

<u>Entertainment</u>:

"The cinema is a little more than a fad. It's canned drama. What audiences really want is flesh and blood on the stage.": *Charlie Chaplin*, celebrated comic actor, film-maker and composer.

"Television will not be able to hold on to any market it captures after the first six months. People will soon get tired of staring at a plywood box every night.": *Darryl Zanuck*, famous film producer

<u>Military</u>:

"I must confess that my imagination refuses to see any sort of submarine doing anything but suffocating its crew and floundering at sea.": *HG Wells*, British sci-fi writer who still enthralls millions (1901)

"The idea that the cavalry will be replaced by these iron coaches is absurd. It is little short of treasonous.": The *aide-de-camp to Field Marshall Haig*, while witnessing a tank demonstration (1916).

The above examples testify to the fact that the only limitations we have are the ones we place on ourselves. Imagine where we would have been as a society if all 'educated' prophecies about the future had remained unchallenged. Thankfully the passion for questioning set limits prevailed, at least in the more daring amongst us, and our course on the waves of time was re-charted. Think about it. If Einstein had not questioned the famed Newton's law of gravitation, General Relativity – one of the towering achievements of 20th-century physics, and the basis of our present understanding of the

2 GB hard drive from 1996 next
to 64 GB flash storage in 2016

universe – would never have been postulated. Examples like these are everywhere, each hiding countless setbacks, ridicules and frustrations behind that one eureka moment.

The question is what's next? Light-speed travel, Brain-Computer Interface (BCI), Teleportation, Immortality, Interstellar travel, or Colonization of exoplanets? So many possibilities and all considered beyond human scope currently. Indeed, the ramifications are so astounding as to seem utterly unbelievable. Take BCI as an example. It potentially implies that a pair of high-resolution cameras can be interfaced directly with your brain to function as your eyes, and other mechanical devices to function as your limbs. Now, a computer interface, unlike the nervous system, is not limited by proximity and can extend over vast distances. This implies that while you (defined as your brain) are in location X, your 'eyes', 'arms' etc. can extend to locations Y and Z, still controlled by your brain. X, Y, and Z can be on different continents, communicating via satellites in space! In other words, a single human can be all over the globe at the same time. I for one admit to an utter failure to even imagine the implications of this on our civilization.

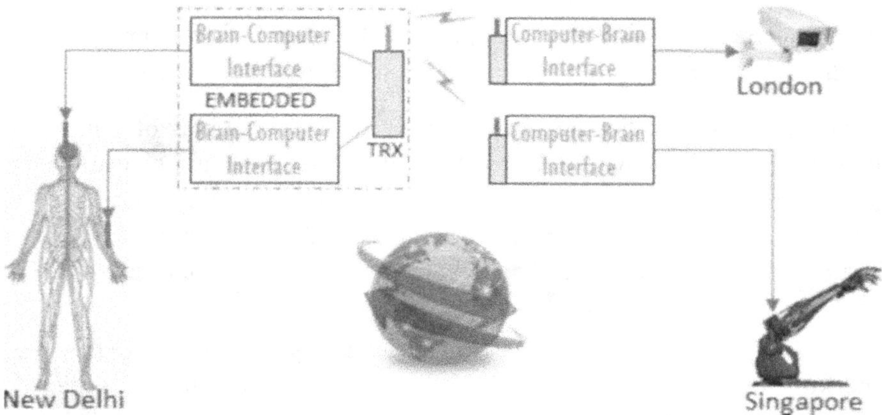

To the charge that I have deviated from the original theme, I plead guilty. In my defense, however, the goal here is to convey the importance of creative thought and *innovation*, the subject of this chapter, in human evolution by stressing that there is no dream too large, no fantasy unimaginable, and no frontiers beyond our reach. Fear of failure, not lack of imagination, is the biggest impediment to innovation.

The terms innovation and creativity are often used interchangeably. Both pertain to ingenuity and are functions of the intellect. It is common to refer to originality in the *artistic* pursuits as *creative*, and in *scientific* and *technological* matters as *innovative*. In the context of a business enterprise, both creativity and innovation are relevant, but there are subtle differences.

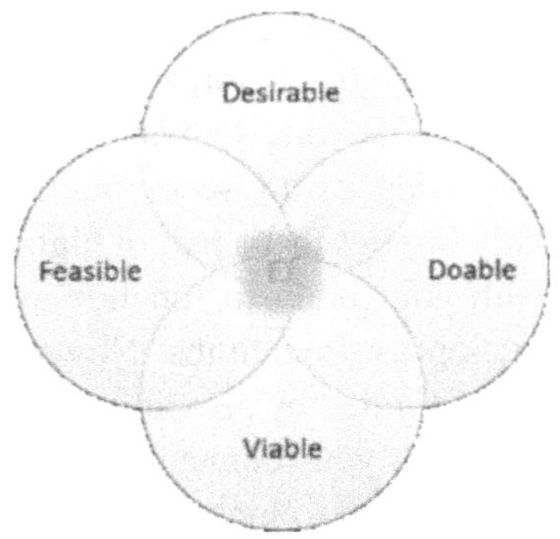

Creativity is about *thinking* new things. Innovation is about *doing* new things. Creativity refers to ideas. Innovation refers to making ideas happen. A creative idea becomes an innovation when it leads to a product, process or practice that is (a) desirable to its users, (b) feasible from a cost and resource standpoint, (c) viable in its market or segment, and (d) doable from a technological perspective. If an idea does not meet all these criteria, it may still be a *creative* one, though not necessarily *innovative*.

Innovation has a lot to do with breaking the confines of established practices and rules, and daring to be different. Hence the term ***out***-of-the-box. I cannot think of even one success story of an enterprise that achieved market leadership by being *similar* to everyone else – employing similar people, doing similar things, producing similar products, but expecting to somehow achieve superior results.

Let's pause here to consider one of many routine examples of innovative thinking in business, with a far-reaching impact on its future course. Doubt and dissent may be a habit of the cynical mindset. But being open to ideas, even from the relatively inexperienced, is the essence of an *innovation-driven culture*, especially in this era when technology is so central to business success.

A mobile telecom company was in an expansion phase to increase the network coverage and capacity in its country of operation. Conventional wisdom dictated that for increased capacity and coverage, you needed to buy a greater quantity of equipment from the network equipment provider (NEP). This was usually an expensive proposition, and given the fiercely competitive nature of the market and wafer-thin margins, any savings here went a good way towards strengthening the bottom-lines. The challenge was to increase capacity and coverage by a factor of X, but cost by a *fraction* of X. Like the very eminent folks in the examples at the start of this chapter, the Chief Technology Officer of this company said, "this is impossible. More capacity requires leasing *more* equipment and hence a proportionally higher cost."

Given the impact of this matter on the business, the teams were asked to deliberate it further and come back with a proposal to the management. The technology and business teams got together to try and find an out-of-the-box solution. One of the participants here was a young business-finance manager (BFM), who raised his hand hesitatingly to ask for permission to make a suggestion. In a nervous tone, he proposed that instead of leasing *equipment* from the NEP, the company should lease *capacity*. But how would that change anything, the more seasoned of the lot queried? He replied that the NEP should be paid for the *traffic carried* by their network, instead of *quantity of equipment* supplied. This, he continued, would force the NEP to *optimize* the equipment required for a given capacity. The whole model changes from being capital expense (equipment) intensive to operating expense (capacity as a service) intensive. It does not require the telecom company to *own* the equipment, just *run* the services, at a much higher utilization rate. It was indeed a breakthrough idea and after some discussion was unanimously adopted. The management loved it, and the model was weaved into the RFP. Of course, the NEPs were a bit uncomfortable initially, but as it still meant good annuity business, joined in enthusiastically later. The model was hugely successful and became the basis of all future contracts between the parties until another breakthrough idea dislodged – or, to be fair, substituted – it from its pedestal, proving that there's always a way to do it better. You just have to find it.

The good thing is that this is not an isolated example. In fact, the *digital enterprise* model, which includes the *aggregation* of goods and services (often of multiple partners) through a simple user interface, is an excellent example of innovation where *established* methods are continually challenged to bring better, faster and cheaper goods and services to millions of consumers across the globe.

The above example also demonstrates the power of *collaboration* in generating innovative solutions. When we are *within* an established system, we become part of it. Inertia chokes innovation. Tom Peters said that change is a door that must be unlocked from *inside*, meaning it must be self-induced. Well, my own experience tells me that it often takes someone from *outside* to unlock the door to new possibilities. Thus, stay receptive. You never know where your next break-through idea is coming from.

Innovation is also sometimes considered synonymous with invention, but there's a difference. Invention is the *seed* that flowers into innovation. In other

words, innovation is the practical consequence of an invention. An invention is often attributable to a single idea or a person behind it, whereas an innovation is its continuous evolution over time by multiple ideas and persons. An invention has a culmination – a single eureka moment. Innovation is an ongoing process.

It's time to pause here for a short exercise.

Can you list at least five things that your company is doing which no one in your industry is doing? It could be products, practices or processes. How many of these are contributing in a positive way to your business results?

Innovation in the Digital Age

We began this book by talking about the power of Intersection. The digital enterprise is the result of an intersection of business with technology. As we have seen in the earlier parts of this book, technology was not always seen as an enabler of business. In fact, some saw it as a threat and even organized protests to block its proliferation. Others intellectualized the subject and discarded the introduction of technology in business as another 'fad', soon to be swept away by the sands of time. It is important to recognize that resistance is a natural human reaction to change. This is perhaps the biggest reason for lack of technological progress in the earlier ages. Today's digital revolution is a consequence of enterprises embracing innovation. If there is one feature that distinguishes the Digital Age from its predecessors – most notably the industrial age and the distribution age – it is the mainstreaming of innovation, or the challenging of established systems, in the formal and informal course of business.

FedEx and UPS started life as document delivery services. Their success was largely owed to their impeccable track record of guaranteed overnight delivery of documents to businesses and individuals in the continental US, making them the undisputed leaders in this in-demand segment. So, when some disruptive digital innovations – like email, low-cost scanners, and PDFs – arrived on the scene, which enabled people to simply email documents to anyone across the globe in a jiffy, did it sound the death knell for these companies? Far from it. Instead of being threatened by these powerful forces, or trying somehow to compete with and beat them, they reinvented themselves and became the leading *supply chain and logistics* companies, emerging as the backbone of e-commerce *by embracing the very technologies that threatened their survival.* From being delivery companies that took advantage of technology, they changed their model to become technology companies that took advantage of delivery. Now, *that's* innovation!

This example is highly pertinent for all of us. It captures the essence of an innovation-driven enterprise environment, which is a precondition for business leadership in the Digital Age. We often relate innovation to imagination and ingenuity only. However, successful innovation requires *all* the following attributes in roughly equal measure, and we see every one of these encompassed in the above story:

What it takes (Innovation requires ….)	**Who it takes** (A person who is ….)
Imagination and ingenuity	Creative
Constantly questioning the conventional	Curious, Contradicting
Adoption of technology	Competent
Unlearning time-honored tradition	Compatible
Embracing Change	Compliant
Taking Risks	Courageous
Overcoming fear of failure	Confident

An enterprise culture is said to be innovation-driven when its people regularly display all the above attributes. Not *only* imagination and creativity (unless you are a well-funded institute of theoretical learning). Now, wouldn't a workforce made up of creative, curious, competent, compatible, compliant, courageous AND confident folks be one to die for? Sure, it would be. But it's rather wishful and brazen to assume that *every* person on your team would possess *all* of these qualities. Which is why widespread and recurrent innovation is rather uncommon. However, the good news is that all these qualities can be found in a *group*. This is the reason that companies with a culture of *collaboration* are

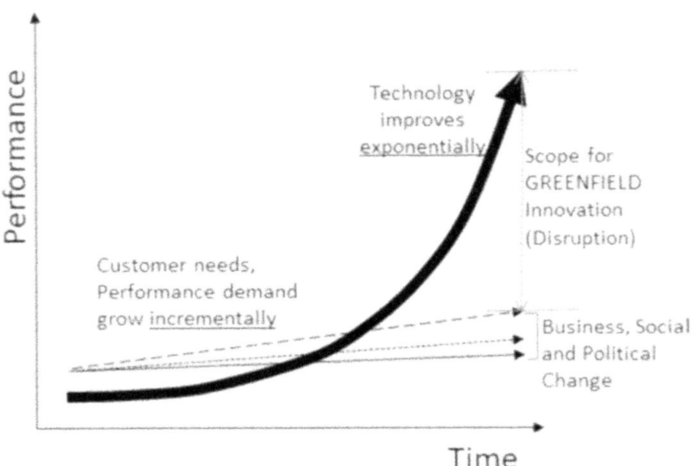

almost always ahead of others in innovation. The other good news is that given the right climate, these qualities can be *nurtured*. For example, a recognition system based on 'dare-to-try' goes a long way in bringing out the streak of creativity and innovation in go-getting individuals.

Innovation has been the subject of in-depth study and many scholarly articles. Our intent here is not to research it but to understand how BITA can be used to leverage it in this Digital Age. To keep our discussion simple and focused, let us tag innovation in two separate buckets. We will term the innovation in the first bucket as **Greenfield**, and the innovation in the second bucket as **Garden-variety**. (These are completely arbitrary labels, don't Google them). All breakthrough innovation – like the Internet, the Maglev (Shanghai), Cloud Technology, Jet-propulsion, 3D Printing, and Driverless cars – is of *Greenfield* type, because it is *disruptive*, suddenly emerging like a towering edifice on a vacant, desolate expanse of green turf. Greenfield innovation happens when the pace of technology dramatically overtakes the pace of social, political and business change. The thing about Greenfield innovation is that you never know when the next one is going to happen. Greenfield innovations don't happen every day, but when they do, they shake things up a bit.

There are countless examples of Greenfield innovation, small and big, that one can easily find on the Internet. It will be inappropriate for me to pick just a few, but I think it may be worthwhile for you to search for developments that pertain to your industry. A lot of great ideas were sparked this way.

Our area of interest here is the more common, but subtler, **Garden-variety** innovation. This is not dependent on the next big thing in science, technology

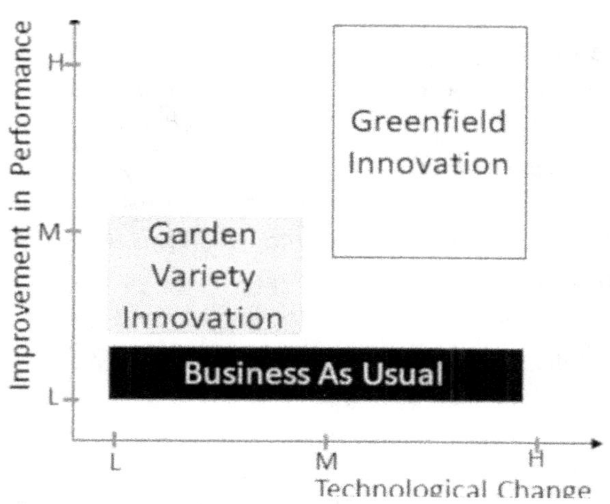

or economics but on the application of thought to everyday matters. The essence of garden-variety innovation is the questioning spirit and out-of-box, or *lateral*, thinking applied to familiar subjects for achieving incremental, but significant improvements. Much of the Garden-variety innovation comes not from scientists and experts, but from ordinary students, employees, business folks, consumers – people like you and me. A great example of a garden-variety innovation is sliced bread! The upside-down ketchup bottle is another! Unless specified otherwise, the term Innovation here will henceforth refer to *Garden variety* innovation.

Innovation can be used to find ways around complex business problems or to gain a competitive edge through differentiation. Here are some familiar examples of BITA-driven innovation in both these contexts:

Competition in the mobile telecom space in India had intensified due to the entry of new operators and ensuing price-wars. Customer retention was becoming a challenge even as tariffs kept dropping. A few companies realized early that this would not be sustainable and turned to innovation instead. At such a time, the companies with a better alignment between their business and technology arms could quickly launch some innovative plans and gain a first mover advantage. These innovations included per second charging (fair usage pricing), dynamic tariff plans based on airtime demand in an area, personalized offers allowing the subscriber to create their own plans, etc. The telcos with innovative offerings had much higher churn-in than their price-slashing peers. In the longer run, these were the operators that have survived, not the price droppers.

A leading domestic airline was losing market share to low-cost competitors on key routes. Its fare structure was competitive, considering the broader

range of in-flight services provided. Hence the loss of market share was quite perplexing to its business executives and shareholders. A focused task group of Business and IT folks got together to crack the problem. It emerged that most travelers used social media actively to invite pre-travel suggestions, as well as shared their post-travel experiences with friends and colleagues. A wealth of information could be mined here. The airline launched a vigorous Voice of Customer (VoC) program using social analytics, web crawlers, etc., to which all key personnel of the airline – from check-in staff to its management – were connected. It was now possible to get concise information *online* on key issues and expectations of the flying public. The airline altered its empowerment matrix to enable its executives to respond better to customer expectations. This helped the airline to adapt their services, fares, schedules, etc. better to customer preferences. It sounds routine now, but the case refers to 2011 when social media as a tool for analysis was not that common.

A telecom company that entered the Indian market relatively late achieved an initial surge in market share and revenues in the rural markets by using innovation to tap into the local, relatively impoverished, population's preference for ready money. As a late entrant, there was little this new company could do by way of differentiation in the predominantly voice dominated rural market in India. It, therefore, decided to swing the mobile-service *retailers* to enhance its value share. These retailers were small-time businessmen, frustrated with the 5-7-day lead time for settlement of their dues from established telcos. This new company spotted the opportunity here and quickly created a system that guaranteed *same day* commission to retailers for new SIMs, recharges, etc. The result was that the retailers started more aggressively pushing for connections from the new company, in anticipation of same day returns. Most of the larger and older competitors could not spot the reason for the sudden proclivity of customers towards this new entrant until it had already garnered a sizeable share.

Probably due to the caution needed in handling money while preventing fraud, the banking sector has been more guarded in taking to innovation, which is equated to risk. In the past couple of decades though, we have seen several breakthroughs in retail banking. For most of us, ATMs,

Internet banking, Mobile banking, etc. are a way of life. These are significant innovations of the disruptive, or Greenfield kind. What about more subtle innovations, of the Garden-variety kind? At least one bank that I am familiar with leveraged the wealth of customer data that banks routinely collect, to create a fully enabled digital services platform using cloud-based data and analytics to deliver personalized services to their HNI customers anywhere and anytime. For example, it could sense if you were on travel and offer local guidance and support, offer tailored investment tips, etc. This BITA-led innovation went a long way in building customer loyalty.

Getting feedback from customers during check out is a common practice with reputed hotels. However, when you see real action on the ground based on these inputs, it is a pleasant surprise. Many times, the solution to customer grievances is not quite straightforward. That's when you need to dial into innovation. A hotel that I once checked into gave an excellent evidence of this. It had received numerous inputs and complaints about long check-in queues at the reception desk and how it caused frustration to even its most loyal customers. The management debated this and came up with a plan. They invited the IT team and worked with them to develop a simple app which was installed on a line of computers in the reception area. Confirmed customers could simply walk up and self-check-in on these terminals, which would spew out a card key, saving not only queue time for guests but also freeing up the hassled front desk personnel to engage in more customer-experience-enhancing tasks. I am sure the thinking was that if airlines can do it, what's stopping hotels? Cross-industry pollination of ideas often works wonders for the business.

I am not from the manufacturing industry, so I am not sure if this is entirely a novel concept, but it sounds like innovation so relating this here. This is about a company that manufactures LED lamps for domestic and industrial use. Due to the savings in power consumption that result from the use of low-wattage LED lamps, these are the highly preferred 'green' alternative to the earlier filament and even the CFL versions. By the way, the LED lamp itself is quite an innovation, but that's not our topic. Many of the reputed companies have struggled to meet demand, resulting in the sprouting of manufacturers in the small-scale sector. By smartly linking raw material supplies – including some items that were being imported – and the projected market demand based on online orders from whole-sellers, this company, a reputed manufacturer, had a firm grip on its production capacity vis-à-vis the required production schedule for the next four weeks. The innovative aspect here was that this firm put up a wall display screen on the shop-floor which tracked the dynamic production target with actual output *in real-time*. Thus, every shop-floor worker knew at a glance the backlog that was required to be cleared and the individual productivity expected. This meant that the supply was never out of sync with demand.

Shopping is going increasingly online. Yet there is a predilection in most of us for the real shopping experience at a proper store, enjoying the touch-and-feel and the ambiance that the outlets offer. How about combining the two for a truly enhanced experience by shoppers? Well, this is precisely what was done by a store chain dealing in the full range of apparel for men and women. This chain used augmented reality (AR) and a quickly downloadable user app for achieving this. A product on shelf-display, say a shirt, had a QR Code associated with it. A customer could use her phone camera to scan this QR code to get a picture of the item and then browse through the entire family of items to choose the color, size, and cut. On display in the mobile would be the detailed picture of the product, its availability status at the store, price and other useful information. The customer could request a trial and if satisfied, add the item in the virtual cart appearing on the phone screen, and move on to other items on the shelves to repeat the experience. After all items were selected, you could make the payment through your mobile – without having to go to a counter – and while exiting the shop, could collect all your items on showing the confirmation code on the mobile, neatly packed and ready for delivery. Thus, you could have a proper storefront experience, without needing a physical shopping cart, or having to stand in a check-out queue. For the store chain too, this resulted in brisker sales, as people have a much higher proclivity for (impulsive) shopping when upfront and close to the goods of their choice. This is another excellent garden-variety innovation that could spawn a new era in retailing.

These are simple examples of the kind that we are familiar with in our work lives. The common theme across them, even while from different industries, is that they are all made possible by a *close alignment between Business and IT*. Many such examples exist, and I am sure you can relate a few from your own workgroup or industry. I have purposely included these, and not some more complex and grandiose ones so that all of us can relate to the power of innovation, and to demonstrate that innovation does not always have to be rooted in an arcane cerebral makeup that few of us are endowed with. The examples also emphasize that the problem that most of us have is not how to get new, innovative thoughts into our mind, but how to get the old ones out.

Much of the innovation in business happens to meet *un*stated customer requirements. This is true of garden-variety innovation as well, as the examples have shown. Being first in the market even with an *incremental* offering may provide a huge competitive edge. Companies with innovation in their veins thus have a major advantage over their larger and better-entrenched peers who value convention over transformation. It was very aptly enunciated by Daniel Muzyka – Dean, Sauder School of Business, University of British Columbia, that "A focus on cost-cutting and efficiency has helped many organizations weather the downturn, but this approach will ultimately render them obsolete. *Only the constant pursuit of innovation can ensure long-term success.*"

Think back. Can you come up with an innovation in your industry – say by your competition – that you found very appealing? Would the same have been encouraged and adopted by your own company? If not, what are the factors that have prevented it? How can they be overcome?

Igniting Innovation with BITA

If innovation were a gift of God given to exceptional people at select times of *His* choosing, it would be perfectly acceptable for you to simply do nothing – except glancing skywards occasionally – until the next inspired idea struck *you.* When/If that happens, you might go out and change the world, but until then, isn't it best to go with the flow? Well, here's the good news – YOU are the chosen one and EVERY moment is the chosen moment! So, the question becomes, what must you do to *unlock* the fountain of innovation within?

To answer this, we need to understand innovation more fully in the context of modern business. Let us step back for a better look. First, unlike an idea, an innovation is not a thought or a brainwave. It is *action* aimed at making ideas happen. A driverless car is an example of this – until it is on the road and making its way through city traffic, it is not a real innovation – though still a good idea. Second, innovation, unlike an idea, is not the product of a single mind but is the result of collective achievement of several minds working in unison, guided by a shared vision. That is, innovation is about making things happen *together*.

INNOVATION
Inherent in Everyone Not Just a select few
Defined by Actions Not Ideas alone
Achieved by Working Together Not Acting in isolation
Happens Continuously Not Exceptionally

Imagine how a car would look and feel if it had a turbocharged engine, but the other accouterments, like gear-box, console, seats, tyres, air-conditioning, etc. were stuck in the dark ages. And third, innovation does not end with one idea or action. It is a *continuous* process which combines a multitude of incremental ideas (and actions) from diverse but related sources in a harmonious way for constant value addition. That is, innovation is *ongoing*. The example we gave earlier for the metamorphosis of Boeing 247 into the modern Dreamliner explains this.

Innovation is thus about alignment at an intellectual level leading to coordinated and continuous *action*. In the digital enterprise context, it is the natural outcome of close alignment between Business and IT, culminating in a shared ownership and pride.

Innovation, while inherent in all of us, needs ignition. This is provided by the right *environment* for it to flourish. The properties we touched upon above are central to building the conditions for innovation to thrive in the enterprise. Inculcating these in your organizational philosophy, attitudes, habits and practices is therefore crucial to creating the environment in which innovation blooms.

For easy reference, these properties are summarized in the accompanying graphic. Though they appear to be rather obvious and uncomplicated, my experience has been that many enterprises lean more towards the properties on the *right*. That is, innovation is the preserve of *just a select few* (whose voice is heard), defined by *ideas alone* (not followed-through), achieved by *acting in isolation* (in a silo structure), and happens *exceptionally* (matter of chance). Think for a moment about how it is in *your* company. Are you leaning more towards the right or the left?

If you glance down the four items on the left in the above illustration, you will observe a common theme, which is *Alignment*. Conversely, the items on the right point to the *opposite* of alignment. This further underlines the power of alignment in harnessing the potential for innovation in the enterprise.

There are techniques available to tap into the innovation potential that is latent in people and organizations. It is probable that you have participated in some great workshops on leveraging innovation – like The Six Thinking Hats, Lateral Thinking et al. If you haven't, it may be useful to get your company to organize one for you soon. Here in this book, our focus is on leveraging BITA for innovation, and we will discuss a few ways to achieve this, revisiting some familiar concepts.

Specific situations may call for different techniques to be employed for distilling the innovation potential of a group, but all these techniques have the above four properties inherent in them, as we shall see. BITA brings in the required diversity of thought and action to leverage this potential fully for enterprise success. In other words, organizations with a strong BITA are much better equipped to tap into the intrinsic potential for innovation by leveraging all its essential properties.

We discussed earlier in this chapter about the inherent personal traits (creativity, curiosity, courage, etc.) that are individually or cumulatively desired in the workforce for stimulating the innovative streak. These traits cut across organizational levels and functions. A business workgroup may not possess every individual trait, but when it teams up with a workgroup from IT, the combined group has much brighter prospects of exhibiting all the required qualities for exploiting the power of innovation. It is commonly seen that groups displaying a lot of ingenuity and serious commitment still fail to deliver truly innovative solutions. Very often, this is because of a missing critical ingredient: ***backbone***. In the absence of this, dissenters get the upper hand and innovation gets choked. In a *collaborative* setting, this – or some other unpalatable outcome – is much less likely. In the discussion that follows on the different means of stimulating innovation, spirited participation of *both* Business and IT is thus at the very core of business value creation.

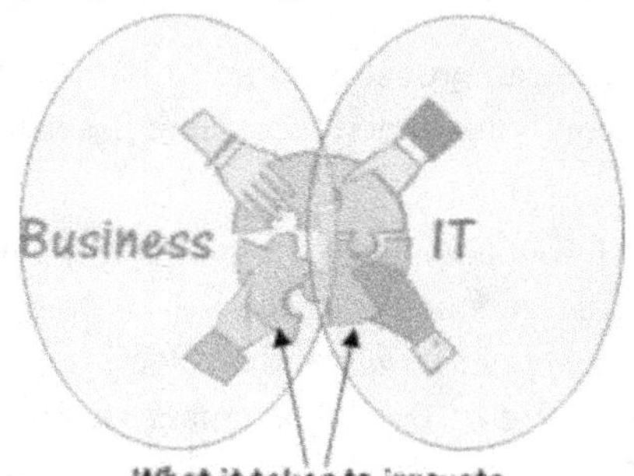

What it takes to innovate

Brainstorming

Perhaps the most common practice in office environments the world over, *brainstorming* is a powerful problem-solving technique. And in the process of problem-solving, it has spawned many a great innovation. The primary focus here is to get many minds focused on a single problem simultaneously, which is conducive to innovation.

As you have heard already, to get the best from brainstorming, you must ensure the following:

1. No domination. Typically, brain-storming sessions with the CEO or other senior folks don't go too well. People are generally uncomfortable about speaking-up and free-flow of ideas does not happen, defeating the very purpose of brainstorming. Avoid this. Brainstorming works best in an uninhibited environment, typically among peers.

2. No evaluation. 'The woods would be very silent if only those birds sang that sang the best.' Same goes for ideas during brainstorming. No idea is too trivial to be ignored. Speak up without fear.

3. Moderation. Moderation is required to ensure that everyone gets a chance to put forth their ideas. The moderator may choose a round-robin method, or any other, but must ensure that every voice is heard and recorded.

4. Follow-up. Nothing frustrates people more than their great ideas going into cold-storage. A brainstorming is not an end but the beginning of an extensive process, whose progress and outcome must be visible to all participants.

You can probably come up with useful and relevant examples of brainstorming from your experience. Here is a sample from mine.

I was engaged as a consulting CIO by an advisory firm ("AF") dealing in mergers and acquisitions, to help leverage AF's in-house IT capabilities for its *client issues*, rather than just keeping its *internal* systems humming. The nature of this engagement was highly confidential, and frankly, I was a bit nervous about how exactly I was to help AF in my interim capacity. It would take me weeks of clandestine research to determine and prioritize the exact issues that required my attention here – and my stint was short and strictly time-bound. Luckily, brainstorming came to my rescue making my task infinitely easier.

On my very first day, I asked for a meeting with all available Business folks and a few senior people from IT. The meeting could only be conducted at 7pm as gathering the busy folks during the day was impossible. I wrote a simple question on the board: "What is preventing the transformation of IT into a business enabler for the company?" Many new and unexpected answers came up. It helped break down the rather broad mission of 'ensuring business success' into more granular statements (like, 'Unclear IT org structure'). We combined similar statements to create a final list of some ten 'real' inhibitors that everyone agreed were hampering the company's chances of success with its existing and potential clients. I then asked the team question number 2: "Which of these must be tackled *right now* in the best interest of AF's *clients*?" There was some debate on this, but we finally reached a list of *four* problems that the team agreed required immediate attention. The meeting closed at this point, with a general sense of contentment.

The next morning, I gathered AF's IT team members and chalked down the four inhibitors as a problem statement. I then posed my third question: "What must we do to overcome these?" After an initial train of the usual suspects, we generated some innovative and out-of-box solutions. The team conceded that they had never got together as a group to think through these problems. But once they got down to it, there was an amazing flow of ideas, backed by a strong and unanimous commitment to deliver. I felt that 70% of my work was done! The plan, when presented to the management team, was quickly accepted and we were assured of their deep and continuous involvement throughout the implementation. All it had taken was a couple of serious brainstorming sessions.

A slight variation of the brainstorming technique is the *brain writing* process, where ideas, instead of being thought aloud, are submitted as written statements, pasted on a board, and collated.

Bucketization

This is a simple technique for organizing the thinking process. It entails breaking down the assignment into smaller and smaller units, or buckets, for generating more numerous and contextual ideas. The following simple example will make it crystal clear and help you apply this in practice.

Everyone who has ever appeared for a job interview is familiar with this most common poser: *Tell us about yourself.* How do you go about this? Well, here is one possible response.

"I am a senior associate with D&X Consulting, which I joined three years ago. I am very fond of traveling, especially to places that are rich in natural

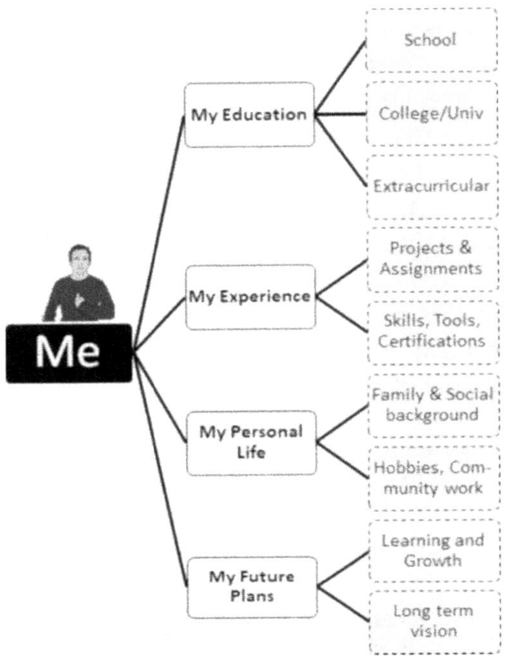

beauty, like mountains and forests. I graduated in computer science near the top of my class three years ago and was among the first to be picked up on campus. I received my last promotion just six months ago, and all my performance ratings have been in the top bracket. I love socializing and am quick to make friends. My company sent me overseas to Europe to work onsite with my client a year ago, and it was an experience of tremendous value, both for my cultural exposure and professional standing. I hail from a small town in India where I did my schooling in vernacular medium but cleared the competition to get into a top university for graduation in computer science. Cricket has been my passion since early childhood, though I couldn't play at a professional level, which is a lasting regret. I am proficient in C++ and have also completed PMI certification successfully. When I was fourteen, I was selected to represent my school in an inter-school debating competition, where I spoke against deforestation. I won that debate. By temperament, I am a curious person who likes to try out new things, as I did in the science lab at my college – sometimes with disastrous results! In the long run, about ten years from now, I would like to become an entrepreneur using my inborn business acumen and acquired professional experience. I am also very tech-savvy, and my friends come up to me for advice on the latest smart devices… (and so on)."

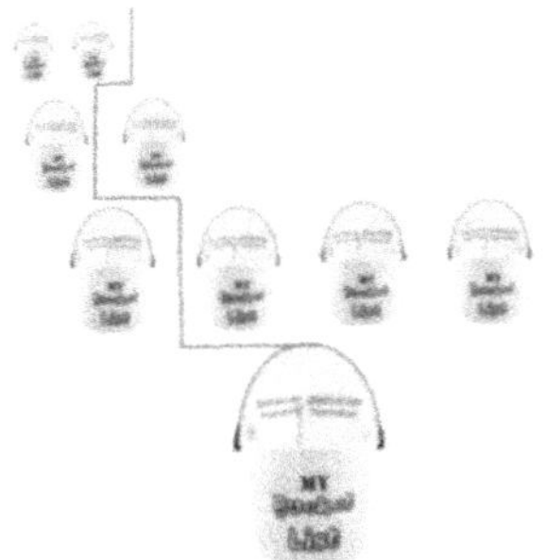

Seems to be a nice enough guy, but there's a problem in the response. To most interviewers, this would blur the view and hence would take away a great deal from his prospects. Can you spot this problem? You guessed it. The response is not *organized,* randomly jumping from one theme to another. Such a response could be prone to gaps and give evidence of a clouded and cluttered mind. A clear thought process would look at breaking up the response into distinct but connected topics, each of which is *individually* thought through before moving on. In the above case, it would be a lot more career-enhancing for the candidate if he were to *organize* his response into topical buckets as shown in the figure here.

I am calling this process 'Bucketizing' because it entails organizing the ideas into successively smaller containers (buckets). There are large buckets (like Education in our example), within which there are smaller buckets (like College). There can be many bucket levels, bringing more granularity to the ideation process. You may decide the order in which you wish to go, but the important thing is that while you are filling a bucket with ideas, you must resist the temptation to jump to a different bucket.

Applying this technique in your business situations is a simple but very effective way of distilling good ideas. It is done best in a group setting with participation from Business and IT folks. Take any business issue, like how to enhance the customers' experience, or how to run the project on cost and schedule, or what should be the specifications of the new product, etc. and apply bucketizing to it. Let us take the last one – deciding the *specifications of the new product*, say, a self-care portal for a mobile service. Instead of doing a brainstorming to generate a wide cross-section of *random* ideas, we'll *bucketize* the process.

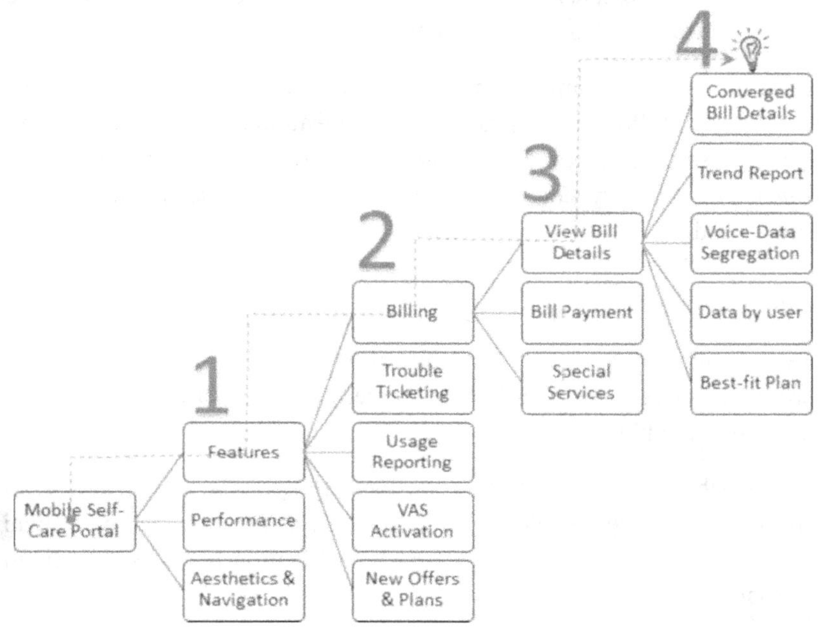

1. Select the largest buckets. In deciding the product specifications, these could be Features, Performance and Aesthetics. [1]

2. Take any of these large buckets, say *Features*. Brainstorm in the combined group on this. You may come up with Billing, Trouble-ticketing, Usage reporting, New Offers and Plans, Value-added Services activation, etc. [2]

3. As the next bucket, brainstorm *one* of the *features*, say Billing. What should this include? You could come up with View Bill details, Pay Bill, Special Billing Services, etc. [3]

4. Now take one of these sub-features, say 'View Bill Details' and brainstorm what must be offered under this head. This could lead to Converged Bill View, Bill Trends, Segregated View of local, Long-distance and Data, User-wise details, Best-fit plan, etc. [4]

5. This process may be continued until you agree within the group that the optimal level for initiating implementation has been reached. There is no limit.

6. The dotted line in the diagram shows the Bucketization path that we took in the example. Repeat the process for other sub-features, moving backward until you have exhausted *all* the buckets up to level 1. The process allows *different* teams to work simultaneously on different buckets.

Contrast this with randomly trying to list down the specifications of a mobile self-care portal, following no structure in the ideation process. *Bucketizing is a great way to set-free those brilliant ideas that you didn't even know were locked in your brain.* At every step, ask this question: "What *other* possibilities exist to break this down?"

Fusion

At the beginning of this book, we spoke of the power of intersection. There is no province where this power is more forcefully apparent than in stimulation of innovative thinking.

Fusion is a byproduct of intersection. Essentially, it is the ability of ideas in one realm to fuse, or blend, with ideas in a *different* realm, spawning innovative concepts. It's a form of cross-fertilization of ideas, germinating new possibilities.

The traditional mercury-based blood-pressure monitoring system had been in use by doctors for decades. Then it occurred to someone, probably an electronics buff, that the vibrations in the arterial wall caused by the inflation and deflation of the cuff around the upper arm could be sensed by a transducer and converted into electrical signals that could produce a digital readout. And thus was born the digital BP monitor, now part of everyone's medical repertoire at home (I am not sure how many homes ever kept those mercury-based contraptions at hand). Had *only* electronics engineers, or *only* doctors, however brilliant in their respective fields, looked at it from their individual points of view, I doubt if such a device would have evolved.

This is an example of fusion between healthcare and electronics, two fields that were once quite apart from each other but are now coming increasingly closer – the digital thermometer and the blood-sugar monitor being other examples of this convergence. The point to note here is that innovation by fusion happens through the mixing of *different* domains to create a new byproduct. Here are some examples:

	Electronics	Music	Health & Fitness	Sports	Automobiles
Electronics		Synthesizer	Digital BP Mon.	Hawk-eye	Digital Dashboard
Music	Keyboard (Piano)		Sony Walkman	Musical Chairs	FM Radio
Health & Fitness	Fitness Band	Aerobics		Squash	Ambulance
Sports	Digital Scoreboard	Floor Gymnastics	Track Bicycle		Formula-1 Car
Automobiles	Electric Car	Car Stereo	Refrigerated-truck	Snowmobile	

These are some randomly selected domains, the purpose being only to explain the role of *fusion* in the conceptualization and creation of innovative products. The matrix has been constructed with the simplest possible items and uses the same set on its horizontal and vertical axes, though this is *not* a precondition of the process. The aim is to *illustrate the concept* using familiar terms rather than to present the most cutting-edge ideas.

As an exercise, create a 10 x 10 matrix of domains that you are familiar with in everyday life (like some of the domains mentioned in the matrix above, and/or new ones like Kitchen, Garden, Entertainment, Communication, Buildings, Education, Transportation – quite literally anything) and at their intersection, jot the familiar product or idea created by the fusion. Next step (more difficult) – any thoughts on what is possible but not yet introduced? You may come up with some completely new ideas and create a revolution – who knows! After all, that's how many product ideas were created.

In the context of business, fusion means mixing ideas and experiences from *different* functions and markets to create innovative products, services, processes, practices or models. Some functions may appear to be far too dissimilar to fuse, but there's always a scope for intersection. The geeks in R&D and the eagles in Legal may seem to have nothing to contribute to each other. But think again. The strong patenting mechanisms that protect (and monetize) hard-earned intellectual property are devised by this union. In the context of BITA, fusion requires BOTH Business and IT to assess new possibilities from different angles for creating market differentiation at their intersection.

Fusion opens immense possibilities for the digital enterprise. Almost all the new age trends around us are results of the *fusion* of digital technologies. And many more opportunities are waiting to be created. Fusion of digital technology trends like Social-Media, Cloud, BDA, Mobility, IOT (all of which are great innovations in themselves) can lead to some striking possibilities.

	Cloud	Big Data	Mobility	Social Media	Internet of Things	Apps
Cloud	IaaS. PaaS.					
Big Data	Analytics-as-a-Service (AaaS). CEM on Cloud	Data Storage, Correlation & Analysis				
Mobility	e-Commerce. Mobile Banking. Personal Cloud.	Navigation, e.g., Google Maps. Mobile BI	Freedom from devices and networks			
Social Media	Video Sharing. Social Cloud Computing.	Sentiment Analytics. Personalization.	BYOD, Message and Media sharing	Audio, Text and Video instant messaging.		
Internet of Things	Smart homes. Smart cities Smart planet.	Predictive Analytics, e.g., Disaster warning	Mobile Device Management. Remote config.	IPv6 based social network of 'things'	Machine-to-Machine Communication	
Apps	SaaS. Interactive Gaming.	Decision Support. Data Mining. BI Apps.	Mobile Apps. Location-based services	Social apps: Facebook, Twitter, Skype	Custom IOT Apps, Embedded apps	Programs running on web servers

The examples given above are quite general, but if smart people from Business and Technology work together on this, there is no limit to the number of unique possibilities at *each* intersection. You can add other domains as well – like Devices, AR and VR, Artificial Intelligence, Machine-Learning, Cyber-security, etc. – to get even more exciting ideas.

Association

This technique builds on the fusion principle. The potential for generating more numerous ideas through fusion, cross-fertilization, and intersections is derived from a simple property of the human brain – viz., it works through *association*. This is a detailed science, but it can be exemplified easily through these simple tests:

1. List down at least 20 hotels that you have stayed in. (If you are not the traveling type, make a list of 20 restaurants that you have been to.)
2. Enumerate 20 different uses of a string (rope).

By the way, the number 20 is purely arbitrary. The idea is to generate the *maximum* possible number of responses in each test. The more, the better.

What did you come up with? More importantly, *how* did you go about it? If you tried to think *vertically* in a *list* form, I am sure you would have found it difficult to reach your maximum potential. On the other hand, if you leveraged the power of *association*, you would have done this in a jiffy. In the first test, the association could be places – think of a *place* you have been to (like Mumbai) and the hotels that you have stayed-in in *that* place. Now think of another visited place (like Helsinki), and the hotels *there* would pop up, don't they? In the second test, the associations could be Games (e.g., skipping, tug-of-war et al.), Home (e.g., clothesline), Adventure (e.g., rock-climbing), Jobs (e.g., packaging, fire-fighting), and many more. Under each association, a myriad of rope-use possibilities exists, some quite innovative. This is far more rewarding than trying to make a *random* list of the uses of rope, as you can easily attest. The power of association makes innovation simple by foraging into the inaccessible regions of your brain. Perfect it through practice, and see the difference!

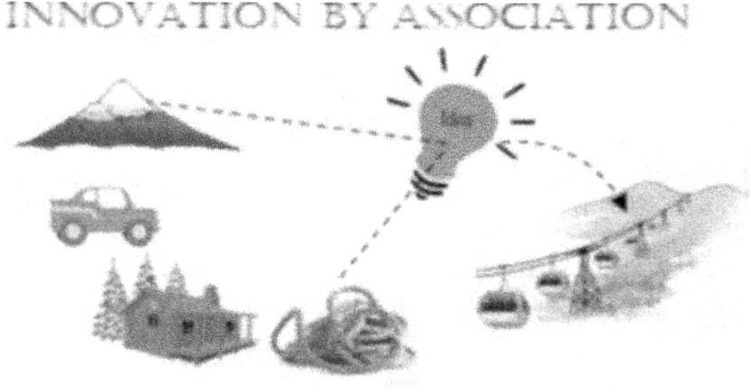

Association can bring out some great ideas in the enterprise environment too and raise the company to new heights of accomplishment. However, for best results, it must be used in a formalized set-up and not in an ad-hoc way. A well guided and moderated association process with the right mix of participants can truly become the cradle of innovation for the company.

Let us take a few of the common situations that enterprises grapple with in the ordinary course of business. By applying the power of association with a dash of BITA, you can turn these into opportunities. But before getting to these situations, I suggest that the following ground rules are strictly followed to get the best ideas unlocked using the association key.

1. Clearly define the problem. Take one problem in one session, as multiple problems blunt the mind's capacity for focus.
2. Agree beforehand that the problem defined in step-1 lends itself to solution by *association* (most problems do, but not all. For example, if you are deciding your PBT target for next FY, association may not be the best choice.)
3. Ensure a good mix of Business and IT people to participate in the exercise.
4. Conduct the session in a focused work-group, or a facilitated workshop, with all the needed accouterments, like flip charts, markers, pads and pencils, quiet ambiance etc.
5. Discourage pre-conceived notions, and encourage every idea – not just the best ones (go back to the section on brainstorming now)

Here are a few examples of situations that could lend themselves to solution by association:

SN	Question requiring innovative answers	Example of Primary Association Key
1	*How can you differentiate your offering in the market?*	Psychological needs
2	*How can you improve the end-to-end experience for HNI customers?*	Moments of truth
3	*How can you reduce customer churn in the state of Maharashtra?*	Districts
4	*How can the alignment between Business and IT be improved in the company?*	Dimensions (Ch-6)
6	*What are the benefits of introducing product X in market Y?*	Demographics
7	*How should our business strategy be different this year?*	Technology trends
8	*What can we do to achieve more enlightened security behavior by employees?*	7-habits (Covey)

For example, in question 1 the drivers of differentiation may be brainstormed against different *human needs and expectations*, stated as well as unstated, as the primary key. You may use the levels in the *Maslow's hierarchy of needs* as association keys to determine human preferences. E.g., under physiological needs (level-1 of Maslow), you may have 'Spend Less' and 'Get More' (for example). Now, what are the features associated with 'Spend less'? Brainstorm this. You may decide Fair Usage Charging, Innovative pricing plans, etc., and under 'Get More', you may decide Personalized features, More Free Calls, and so on. You may successively use these responses as the *next* association keys, before moving to the next Maslow level (Safety). By the time you get to the last level, you will have a bigger and more organized set of differentiators, than a random *list*. Other possible association keys, instead of human needs, here may be market forces, technology trends et al.

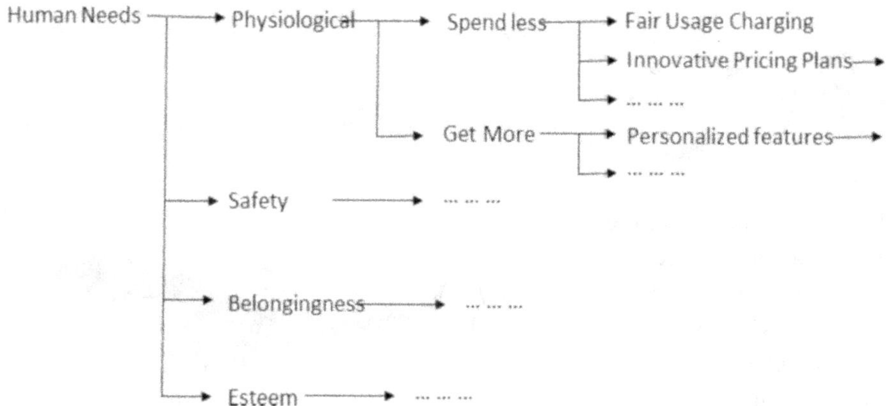

The technique of association does not impose the use of complex or multipart association keys as in the above example. Simple words, symbols, animals/ birds, gestures and pictures can be used just as effectively. Here are some 'cool' examples.

Problem: *Until I get a cup of coffee in the morning, I am unable to function.*
Desire: *To get freshly brewed coffee in bed as soon as the alarm wakes me up each morning*
Solution: *An alarm clock that switches on the electric coffee brewing machine five minutes before sounding off.*
Association: *Coffee machine and Clock*

Problem: *An avid biker, I need safety indicators to alert my movements to motorists in the night, but there is no space on the bike for this.*
Desire: *To give a clear signal of my upcoming actions (like turning, stopping etc.) to motorists*
Solution: *A projector that lights up my movements using my back as a screen, in response to commands from the console on the handlebar.*
Association: *Human body (Back) and display projector*

Problem: *I depend on recipe books for cooking, but often mess it up due to imprecise quantities of ingredients*
Desire: *To put precise quantities of every ingredient and get the advertised flavour*
Solution: *A spoon-like weighing device with a digital read-out of the quantity of ingredient in its bowl.*
Association: *Spoon and digital weighing machine.*

Problem: *I keep misplacing essential items like car keys, wallet and spectacles!*
Desire: *To have these Frequently Misplaced Items (FMIs) announce themselves on my mobile screen*
Solution: *A sensor on the FMIs interacts with a simple app on your phone that displays the precise location of the FMI on a map.*
Association: ***(A)*** *FMI and sensor* ***(B)*** *Mobile phone and Finder-App* ***(C)*** *A and B*

Here's another example. Using the *Eagle* as an Association key, you can target some great *leadership* qualities (You've probably heard this one). The idea is to stimulate the thought process around a topic ("Leadership") using a familiar object, word or form ("Eagle").

Attribute of Eagle	Associated Leadership Quality
Eagles fly high and alone, far above other birds	Don't allow others to pull you down. Stay above negativity and narrow-mindedness.
Eagles have long and accurate vision and can spot their prey from high altitudes	Stay focused on your goals – they are attainable. Look beyond the obstacles.
Eagles do not scavenge. They hunt for new prey	Do not depend on the efforts of others for your success. Be confident, self-reliant and always on the lookout for new opportunities.

Eagles love storms and use the storm-winds to lift themselves higher	Face your challenges head-on, use them to emerge stronger, and having conquered them, raise your sights to higher goals.
Eagles toil hard and faithfully to attain the trust of their mate	to build great partnerships, you need to make investments (physical and emotional) and show commitment.
Eagles prepare the young to fly by making the nest uncomfortable	No growth can be attained without leaving your comfort zone.
Old eagles endure extreme pain and isolation to pluck out their worn feathers and break their beaks and claws so that they can grow new ones	To make yourself ready for new challenges, you must shed old habits, no matter how difficult.

You can try Ant, Gazelle, Lion, Milky way, Everest, Banyan Tree, Tornado, Ocean, and numerous other items to generate ideas similarly around any other topic, feature or aspiration. There is no limit to the possibilities that association opens for stimulating the thought process.

Cross-Pollination

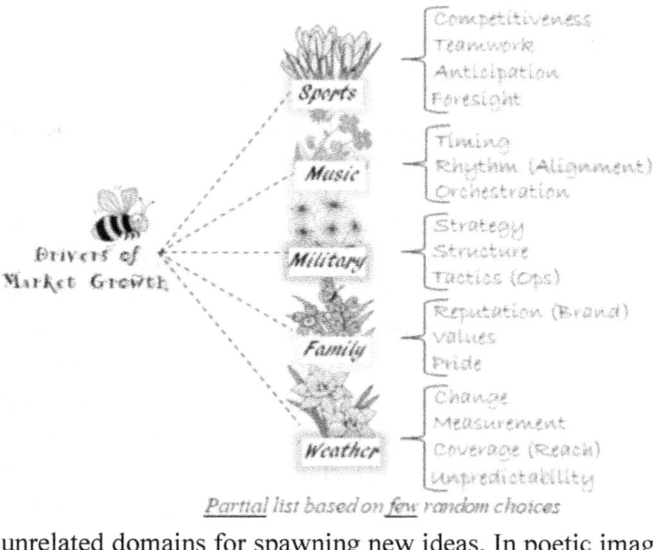

Partial list based on few random choices

A slight variation on the fusion and association techniques, cross-pollination can be used to generate numerous options using the one-to-many principle. Here, you pick a theme, say *Drivers of Market Growth,* and use it to *pollinate* a set of completely unrelated domains for spawning new ideas. In poetic imagery, the *theme* is the *bee,* and the *domains* are *flowers* which are pollinated for extracting the *nectar* in the form of responses (*ideas*). In the illustration, the cross-pollinating 'bee' (Drivers of Market growth) hops across a few *random* 'flowers' (Sports, Music, etc.) to extract a 'nectar' of ideas from each, leading to a broader cumulative set. *Sports* makes us think of competitiveness and teamwork, *Military* of strategy and structure, and so on. You can use this recursively (e.g., *competitiveness* can be the next bee). Cross-pollination is based on the premise that through diversity comes variety.

There are numerous other techniques and tools available for triggering innovation or solving complex problems in ingenious ways. A discussion on every one of these, while instructive, would take us far beyond the intended theme of this book. All the same, let me mention some of the common techniques (other than the ones we discussed above) that I have come across and found useful in generating innovative ideas and solutions. You may like to study some of these in greater detail from other sources.

Cross-boundary group work: Helps cross-functional teams constructively identify solutions to business and organizational problems, by breaking down barriers and fostering openness among participants.

Fishbone: Form of structured brainstorming, performed diagrammatically, to look for root causes.

Flowchart: As diagrammatic representations of inputs, activities, decision points and output for a given plan or process, flowcharts can be an excellent way to find alternate paths to reach the stated outcome.

Force-Field Analysis: Force field analysis is a way to encourage creative thinking by identifying forces that **help** and those that **hinder** the process of getting to the targeted outcome.

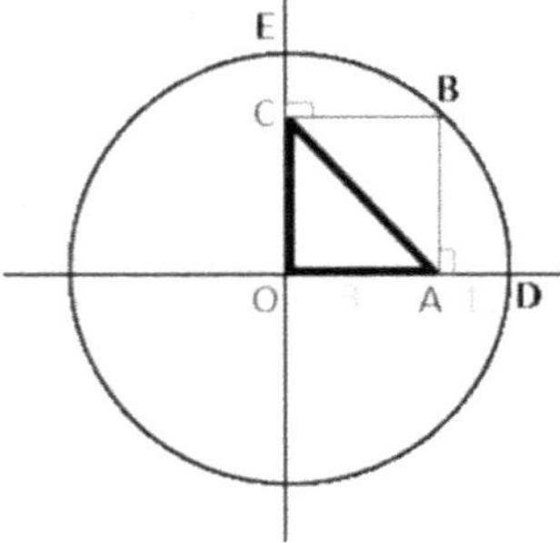

Lateral thinking: Lateral thinking is a creative approach to solving problems and generating ideas using not-so-obvious methods, rules or steps, i.e., the ability to think out-of-the-box. It is one of the most effective tools of creativity. For a detailed treatment of this, I recommend that you read Edward De Bono's book of the same name. Here is a simple example of lateral thinking. In the depicted circle with two perpendicular diameters, only the following are known: O is the center, OA=3, AD=1, BC and BA are perpendiculars on the diameters. Can you determine AC? Think. What did you get? Using the non-lateral (vertical) approach one would somehow apply the Pythagorean rule and come up with $3\sqrt{2}$, while it is nowhere given, or derived, that OC=3! The simple answer, found by *lateral* thinking, is that AC equals OB (*not* drawn) which is nothing but the radius, or 4!

List Reduction: This is a way to logically process the output of a brainstorming session and reduce the number of options to a manageable quantity for further action.

Mind-mapping: This is an individual technique. It enables one to generate and organize solutions around a central topic by capturing ideas along various branches and their off-shoots, like hubs and spokes.

Outcome Thinking: This is a creative process in which different participants visualize the *ideal* outcome of a situation and then share their envisioned outcomes with other group members to reach a concise vision.

Pareto Analysis: Pareto analysis is a great way to separate the 'vital few' from the 'trivial many.' The familiar 80-20 rule is an example of this. It helps the group set priorities by ranking and presenting the data in a bar graph showing the distribution in descending order.

Storyboarding: Storyboarding is a visible process of gathering, evaluating and organizing information. Participants jot down ideas on cards which are put up on a visible board to select the most useful ideas, which are then progressively refined and built upon to reach the most workable set of solutions.

Structure Tree: Structure tree is a systematic way of breaking down the theme into smaller, more manageable topics. They are useful in identifying and selecting problems to work on.

Irrespective of the technique or tool you adopt to galvanize your brain into generating more diverse ideas, always remember De Bono's first law: there is no such thing as the *best* idea. That is, innovation doesn't have a peak, so avenues for scaling higher are always open. Tools only help you find them faster.

Backbone and Empowerment

Based on my experience, people belonging to the *if-you-don't-try-you-can't-fail* school of thought rarely make good innovators. Their emphasis is not on *succeeding* but on *not-failing*. In other words, they are missing the *backbone*, that crucial pre-requisite for innovation, without which great ideas cannot stand on their own. Haven't you ever come across the feeling, when an idea is applauded, that YOU could have done that but weren't sure it would be such a great one? If you want to ride the innovation bandwagon, develop a backbone first: Do not be afraid to voice your ideas.

Related to this, organizations which have successfully leveraged the power of innovation are the ones which have given the *empowerment* to their teams to break free from the clutches and constraints which prevent the free flow of ideas. The *dare-to-try* spirit *must* permeate the organization which is seeking to make a mark in the world as a digital enterprise. Individuals with backbone and enterprises that empower cannot be substituted by any known tools or techniques as levers of human potential.

Applying Innovation

Let us now turn our attention to tapping into BITA for leveraging the power of innovation to transform your company into a digital enterprise, or at the very least, prepare it to surf the waves of the digital ocean. As we have discussed above, there are numerous tools and techniques available for stimulating creative thought, *some* of which we have touched upon. As you head into a territory where being different determines your chances of success and speed determines your survival, the importance of tools, techniques and behaviors that expand *and* catalyze the thinking process certainly cannot be stressed enough. However, the specific tool or process that you employ is a matter of your comfort and the demand of the situation that you are in. I do strongly recommend that before applying the chosen tools or techniques in the real-world, you familiarize yourself with them through workshops and simulated sessions. You'll often find that it is a *combination*, rather than a specific technique, which works best.

Let us apply our simple tools and techniques of innovation to achieve the most important goal which enterprises today are striving for: *digital transformation.*

Digital Transformation

Digital transformation, like beauty, does not lend itself to a single, strait-jacketed definition. It could take many shapes and forms and could mean entirely different things, depending on who beholds it. However, there is one enduring feature that every digital transformation has at its core: a relentless drive for *innovation*. Therefore, the tools of innovation assume the role of tools of *transformation*.

When planning for digital transformation, enterprises (and/or their consultants) first decide upon the key strategic objectives (these KSOs are referred to as

"Transformers" in this discussion), under each of which the potential for value-creation may be unlocked using innovation as the key. These Transformers essentially point the company in the direction it must take to digitally transform itself.

If you have been under some compulsion for a while about taking up digital transformation to *course-correct* your business, you are probably already late in initiating the program. Your ability as an enterprise to envision the future is the real propulsion behind digital transformation, while threat mitigation is just *one* of its many fallouts. Therefore, proactively deciding the Transformers is the critical starting point of your digital transformation journey, and it is best done by asking a simple question: *WHAT must you transform (e.g., Business Model, Customer Experience...) to realize your digital vision?* Even if you do not have a stated digital vision, identifying the real priorities for the future of your business will often result in one.

While the question seems simple enough, answering it may not be a trivial matter, as a mistake here would be an immeasurably costly one. A company aspiring to become a digital enterprise must weigh this question deeply and comprehensively. I recall a recent experience where good practices were indeed followed, but the company was somewhat cavalier in the initial direction setting, eventually succeeding only in arriving at the wrong destination faster. There are both good and bad lessons to be learned from this example. You may like to use it as a case study with suitable alterations to suit your business circumstance. The case refers to a *hosted data-center* provider serving a few corporates, planning a transformation to a full-fledged *public cloud service* (SaaS) provider to a much wider customer base, including SMEs and entrepreneurs. I have taken care to steer clear of any technical aspects, as the intent here is only to demonstrate the use of innovative techniques in a BITA-centric environment.

A hosted data-center provider traditionally renders passive IT resources like servers, storage, etc. along with associated power, cooling, and real-estate, remotely to companies on a tenancy basis. Typical services to corporates include off-premise provision of IT infrastructure elements, SLA-based availability assurance, scale-up/down in real-time based on business exigencies, colocation services, data security, disaster recovery, etc. All these services are provided as a *service* to the corporates, thus providing freedom from capital investments, maintenance worries and most importantly, the unpredictable costs associated with IT operations. The service is popularly known as IaaS (Infrastructure-as-a-Service). From the IaaS provider's perspective, it is a highly capex intensive business entailing huge investments in real estate, power/back-up equipment, HVAC and of course IT infrastructure to serve multiple corporates, all expecting near 100% availability and round-the-clock efficient performance. The IaaS provider also incurs operational costs like equipment maintenance, electricity, fuel (for DG backup plants), and employee expenses covering salaries and overheads for business, technical and other functions. Most IaaS providers maintain state-of-the-art and secure facilities with latest systems and apparatus, including raised vinyl flooring, over-head cable routing with traceability, cold-aisles, biometrics, clean-room environment et al. – all of which entail high costs.

Our company – we will call it XIP (Anonymous Infrastructure Provider) – had a running public data-center, having made substantial investments in its swank facility, IT infra, trained staff, etc. The first two years were a period of growth for the company, with new customer acquisitions being the norm. Over time, XIP started facing challenges, which ranged from unused inventory due to customers opting for public-cloud-based resources, to increased competition and higher overheads. The growth curve started dwindling, and to compound matters, the company's investors were rather unsympathetic." This is a 'high-tech' business and these are 'high-tech' times, so how come the business is not booming as before?", they asked. The company's management decided to take drastic steps *before* reaching the point of no return.

The company called in a top consulting firm for advice. The consulting firm ("XCF") spent a couple of days looking at the company's past performance and present strategy and promptly suggested that the company look at a renewed business model. This, they said, required diverse and innovative ideas and hence proposed an off-site brain-storming session. "Changing the business model" is increasingly considered a panacea for almost all of an organization's business troubles. However, it is easier said than done, and a bit vague by itself. Imagine that you are tasked by your CEO to "change the business model of the company." What, precisely, would you do? Well, our XCF consultant had some ideas. Having got the XIP business people into a room, he wrote a question on the white-board: "What are the top 5 things that must be done to improve the company's top line by 15% in 12 months?" A vigorous brainstorming followed, punctuated by a SWOT analysis, and by the end of the day, the group succeeded in building consensus on five of the many ideas that were generated. It was unanimously adopted that it's a "mission accomplished" if the team could act and deliver on those five ideas.

Six months into the project, it did not really need a detailed formal review to unearth the fact that the company was not going to deliver on its revamped strategy or achieve the much-touted turnaround. If anything, things were going more sharply southwards than before. The signals were clear enough for the XIP management to go back to the consultant – the same, XCF – and re-plan the way forward. This time, though, they decided to use their own internal think-tank, constituted of key Business and IT folks, while the consultant was engaged only to facilitate and guide. After all, who knew the business better? The team concluded that the earlier ideas were indeed good – like enhance virtualization to allocate data-center resources dynamically, create capacity through deduplication, use hi-speed MPLS link to connect the expansion units in different (cheaper) cities, rationalize cost structure for large enterprises, et al. However, all of them simply *built* upon the existing edifice, not *expand* its scope. None of them, in hindsight, appeared a good enough reason to compel new customers to look at XIP.

Indeed, a change of business model had not even entered the equation. It was the *same* business, conducted perhaps more efficiently and with increased vigor and aggressiveness! The root-cause was traced to the initial question ("what are the top 5….?"), which itself postulated that XIP must somehow improve upon the current business only, instead of farming out in new areas. In other words, the focus was squarely on "What are we going to do?" rather than on "Who do we intend to be?" The XIP team brainstormed amongst themselves for the next half a day *only* to get to the right *question* that they must answer to recast their business in a new mold. Finally, the question that was framed, with consensus, was: *"Which aspects of our business must we transform (i.e., refresh, grow or sunset) to take advantage of the new trends and changing customer expectations (instead of being threatened by them)?"* There's no reference in the question to *what* specifically must be done. Just on the identification of the focus areas, or the *key strategic initiatives*. In the earlier question, *the team had to rush into actionable solutions even before the problem had been identified*!

The team then deliberated to generate a range of options in answer to this question. This was done using the Bucketization technique to yield more structured thinking in the group. Some of the ideas were:

Exploitation of new technology trends (Cloud, Mobility, etc.) for business expansion

Alignment between Business and IT (trusted advisory)

Incentives for Innovation (empowerment, encourage risk-taking)

Customer data management (Storage, security & privacy, big data analytics)

Analysis of customer feedback as an innovation driver

Customer Lifecycle management

Future-proofing

Standardization, modularity (for speedy scalability)

….and many others.

These were then prioritized and *grouped* to identify the following three KSOs (the Transformers) which would guide the first phase of the company's transformation to a renewed business model:

Technology

Internal/External collaboration

Customer Experience

Having reached this far, the team used techniques like Association to drill down and come up with innovative ideas individually for *each* Transformer to create version 2.0 of the company. This entailed a collaborative model with ISVs to provide cloud-based application services, and thus expand its customer base to SMEs and entrepreneurs who found it cost-prohibitive to build/buy their own business applications like CRM, ERP, etc. The company has so far shown positive results in its market performance, and I heard recently that its position has moved up a notch in its industry space.

The above example, admittedly a bit elaborate, shows that unless you first address the question of *which* areas need to be transformed to fulfill your vision, the transformation is an exercise in futility.

To re-iterate, deciding on the Transformers is the critical starting point of your digital transformation journey. In the following illustration, I have depicted the opportunities for innovation in a typical digital transformation, showing the transformers on the left. While typical, these are by no means universal. The real Transformers of *your* business must be carefully decided using one of the several techniques for innovation that we discussed in this chapter.

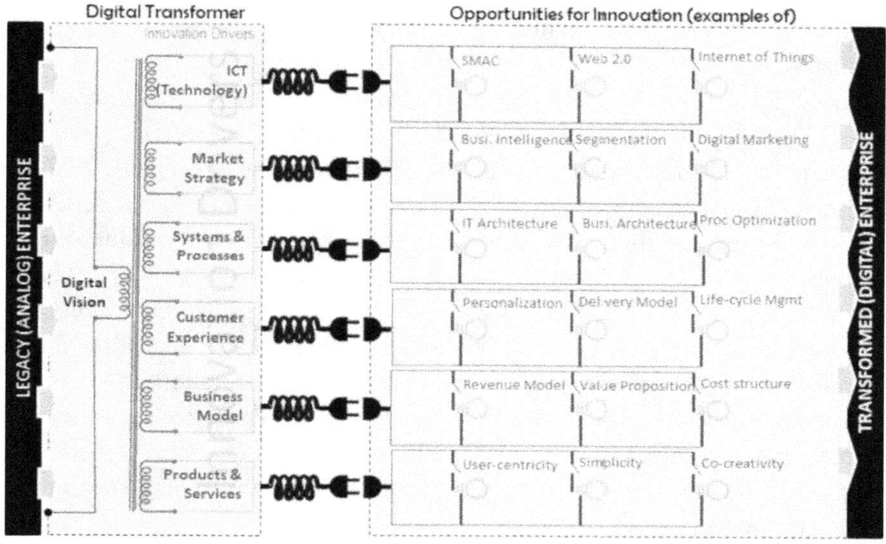

Having decided the Transformers, you may like to "plug" them in independently and in different time-phases depending on how you define your priorities. Or work on several of them simultaneously through separate but aligned teams. For each Transformer, you may like to have a dedicated session (or workshop) to produce as many opportunities as possible, using any of the innovation tools like fusion or cross-pollination. These opportunities, in turn, may be switched "on" as and when the situation dictates. This flexibility (indicated by switches) is important to manage the transformation in a time-bound, priority-driven and non-conflicting manner. The process may be done recursively. For example, the 'Business Model' Transformer throws up "Value Proposition" which may again yield to the cross-pollination technique (say) to generate more specific ideas, and so on.

The illustration here is a *generic* one and is not designed as a master-key to suit every situation. The hope is that it gives the broad guidelines for you to create your own Digital Transformation template.

Digital Transformation, like any business transformation, is a very serious matter for an enterprise. Each Transformer could be a long, arduous and expensive journey requiring intricate planning, strategizing and executing. Choose wisely.

A few quick words on the schematic depiction of the digital transformation framework. The enterprise's vision to transform is converted into individual KSO's (*Transformers* or *Innovation Drivers*) through a collaborative effort involving Business and Technology stakeholders. In other words, all the Transformers derive their power from a common source, which is the organization's *digital vision.* These Transformers can be individually or severally plugged-in into the design of the transformed enterprise, as shown by the plug-and-socket arrangement. This 'plugging-in' may happen in phases, if necessary. Once plugged-in, the Transformers can power up a series of innovations, chosen through a collaborative exercise using various innovation techniques. These opportunities for innovation are shown as lamps which, by the way, are *not* restricted to three per Transformer. Each opportunity for innovation may be 'switched-on', or banked as a rain check, depending on its priority for the business as well as time and cost considerations. This is the reason there are 'switches' shown alongside the lamps. The aim of every digital transformation project is, of course, to light-up as many lamps as possible. Because this is the truest way the enterprise can brighten up its future in the digital economy.

> *Conduct a workshop to identify the Transformers of* ***your*** *Business. (*It will be among the most important exercises you will do as an organization.*) Spot the opportunities for innovation powered-up by each Transformer. Prepare a display showing names of Transformers and corresponding opportunities with* real *bulbs and switches against each opportunity, in your boardroom (your in-house electrician can do this). Get the individual transformation champions and innovators to 'switch-on' a light bulb against an opportunity when the pre-defined threshold for it is crossed. Make it a ceremonial event! Keep increasing the threshold and repeating the process. As a variation, you may use rotary dimmers instead of switches. This keeps innovation happening continuously, and the transparency of the results keeps motivation levels high as well.*

BITA for Innovation

Through this chapter, we have breezed through some techniques, tools and applications that foster innovation in the enterprise, all of which rely on BITA being firmly entrenched in the enterprise core. A shared digital vision, business-

and tech- savvy people, 2-in-a-box approach to customers & markets, are some of the vital building blocks of BITA that are needed to construct the platform for innovation. And this brings us to an important deduction: innovation is the synthesis of *all* the BITA dimensions – culture, strategy, structure, processes, tactics – working in tandem to create a climate in which Business and IT instinctively and continuously Think, Build, and Operate *as one*. Infusion of BITA into the organization's veins is therefore vital to innovation – not just for boosting the metabolism, but for ensuring survival itself.

The typical question that does the rounds at some or the other point in most companies is: Are we ready for the future? Almost without exception, the (honest) answer is No, because there is no 'perfect' state of readiness to meet the demands of an unknown and uncertain future. This realization leads to a fleeting wave of despondency and then to a concerted effort to 'prepare for the future', and that's when innovation becomes the buzz word in the enterprise corridors. All perfectly kosher. But the missing link is the test for *alignment* before you embark on the innovation path. The first question to ask therefore is: Can we achieve convergence across Business, IT, partners and customers to take advantage of the new opportunities and trends? It's always about *alignment*.

In this book, we have discussed methods and approaches to test and improve alignment. If you are looking to take advantage of the inherent potential for innovation in your organization, use these methods – or any other – to build *alignment* before starting out. Innovation is a machine that has at least *two* levers for its operation: Business and Technology.

In the context of the modern enterprise, there is no bigger platform for innovation than its digital transformation. But digital transformation does not happen in a flash. It is composed of Business, IT, as well as enterprise functions and partners continually discovering and developing *incremental* ideas in concert, raising the performance bar higher each time. The companies that accomplished their digital transformation journeys *successfully* did not rely on path-breaking, or greenfield innovation but on exploiting the existing trends like Cloud, Social, Mobility, Big Data, and supplementing them with layers of incremental, garden-variety and home-grown innovation.

Innovation is not a subject that easily lends itself to culmination. Its scope and potential are both limitless. We started this chapter with predictions that could have halted humanity in its tracks, but couldn't. Simply because they failed to dampen the human urge to explore, experiment and embrace new paradigms, and achieve breakthroughs that succeeding generations have not only benefitted from but improved upon. It's a continuous cycle. In closing, let's look at just some of the many innovations that are going to impact our lives and business in the not-so-distant future.

Drones & Flying Cars: These are already out of the test labs. As with most technologies, many of their applications will spawn after their adoption, but some that we *can* envision would be the rapid delivery of packages thus boosting e-commerce manifold, air-surveillance and sight-seeing, air-ambulance and organ transport, and a revolution in transportation enabling access to terrain considered out of reach earlier.

Autonomous Vehicles: Have you bought stock of companies that are developing autonomous (self-driven) vehicles yet? If not, you may have missed a great opportunity. Tesla, Google, Uber are some of the companies that have already broken ground with this revolutionary concept. Autonomous cars are already on the road, and most hurdles to adoption are regulatory, not technical. I am sure the time is not very far ahead when we will wonder how we humans ever trusted ourselves to drive on our own!

Artificial Intelligence: It's been round-the-corner for a long time, and indeed there have been continuous developments in AI, including 'fuzzy logic' embedded in many familiar appliances. AI, with its ability to understand questions posed by humans and search vast memory banks for an accurate and contextual answer, can have unimaginable consequences on the future of business, such as in decision making.

Hyper-Connected world: Connectivity has been at the core of the digital revolution. However, its potential is still largely untapped, with over half of the human population outside its gamut. Add to that the billions of machines that are going to board the communication bandwagon with the proliferation of IoT, and you realize that you have only just scratched the surface yet. Alongside coverage and capacity, the communication speed is also rising exponentially to cater to streaming video and other high-volume data-driven apps.

Cheap Renewable Energy: Solar and Wind energy available abundantly and at low cost (as compared to coal or other fossil fuels) to most of humanity could be among the biggest game changers of the century. Imagine not having to rely on petrol to run your car, or costly hydro-electric or nuclear power for electricity at home and office!

End of Cancer and Disease: Combating deadly diseases has been one of the most absorbing endeavors of scientists throughout history. A world without deadly diseases like cancer and AIDS is perhaps unimaginable to most of us. With some excellent progress in research on combating and effectively eradicating most deadly diseases, cancer included, we might well be opening a new chapter in human evolvement soon.

Stem Cell Research: Discovery of stem cells as the regenerative engine of the body is another breakthrough innovation holding immense potential in the eradication of disease and deformity. Stem cells have already been shown to grow human eyes and enable paralyzed victims the use of limbs again.

Longevity: Recent strides in medical science hold great promise for extension of human life to well beyond 100 years. Not with a frail body, but with the vigor of youth intact! Can you imagine the impact of this on the social as well as workforce demographics, with people ready and able to function easily into their nineties?

Would you bet against any of these happening in your lifetime? I would advise against it. These trends would blend and fuse amongst each other and with several other present and future trends to open possibilities that are beyond our imagination today. The question is not: Can you transform your business to take advantage of these? It is How? And the answer: *Align* first, then *innovate*. You have all the tools. The time to use them is NOW.

14 The Functional Focus

"If you want to go fast, go alone. If you want to go far, go together."

Alignment between Business and IT to take advantage of the opportunities created by the digital era has been our primary focus in this book. I have been an exponent of BITA for many years and have found enthusiastic support for it both in word and spirit in most organizations, especially as the role of technology in business has intensified. But I also came up with a fair share of skepticism based, as deeper probing revealed, on individual biases and pre-conceptions. Let us examine some of the more popular preconceived ideas (PIs) about BITA.

PI # 1: *An excessive focus on alignment could result in diluting the emphasis on functional priorities*. After all, Business and IT are distinct functions with goals and deliverables of their own, which have only a marginal overlap at best. By stressing BITA, one may wonder, are Business and IT trespassing into each other's territory and moving away from their core functional charters? Therefore, is BITA actually *weakening* the organizational pillars that were painstakingly built over the years? This is a concern, often unstated, that takes root in many organizations, even in this day and age. The refrain is that by 'mixing' Business and IT functions too intricately, the organization's core competence could be compromised, rendering it more vulnerable to external threats. As in the game of cricket, the argument goes, specialist batsmen and bowlers both have their place, and if, instead of raising their individual talents, they focus on emulating each other, the game is as good as lost.

This is a point of view that comes from being entrenched too deep and too long in a silo. Simply put, this view is as different from reality as chalk from cheese. BITA is a not a trait that requires Business and IT to *substitute* each other. In which case, it could indeed be argued that BITA could convolute functional charters and competence makeups. The truth is that BITA is not a substitution device, but a force-multiplier. In a BITA centric organization, Business and IT do not just complete each other (as an ensemble). They also *reinforce* each other to higher performance (as a symphony). Therefore, functional charters and core competencies do not need to be redefined for BITA. While an all-rounder or two never hurts, specialist batsmen and bowlers are certainly *both* required. However, they do not *replace* each other but share the mission and *reinforce* the team together. It's the same with Business and IT in the new age business enterprise.

PI # 2: *In the digital enterprise context, Business and IT are merged in a single function, so alignment is a given.* In my experience, I have not come across an organization where Business and IT are indeed merged together and are therefore non-distinct. I am not even sure if that's a desirable state to aspire for. A merger of Business and IT into ONE function implies that they are unidirectional in their strategic outlook, competence make-up and even tactical stance, which is not very conducive to diversity of thought and action. It is the *intersection* of Business and IT that leads to smarter and more innovative ideas, not their parallelism. In the Innovation chapter, we saw how a fusion of *different* domains is necessary for generating out-of-box solutions. Thus, *distinct* but *aligned* Business and IT functions are *required* to broaden the organization's horizons and enable it to take a more holistic approach to market and customer issues. An organization which takes an all-in-one approach in its functional structure would thus be lacking the breadth required to take advantage of the opportunities in the market, that it could have leveraged through distinct but well-aligned Business and IT functions. In conclusion, this PI is unfounded and at the very best, unrealistic. Going back to cricket, a team of *only* all-rounders, expected to outdo the specialists on their turf every time, may be considered by some to be desirable but is unsustainable and unrealistic. You will only end up diminishing your long-term prospects as a team.

PI # 3: *Alignment is an old and overused fad, no longer relevant in this age of innovation.* I was quite surprised to hear this from no less than the CIO of a large corporation. I am sure though that he is not the only one. Where could such a sentiment spring from? I have a few theories. First, catch-phrases are annoying. When we come across over-used jargon, it jars us. Words like "alignment", which are often heard, are equated to jargon and this tends to diminish their role and importance in our minds. The obvious fallacy in the above PI is that if "Alignment" is an overused fad, then so is "Innovation" or – for that matter – "Digital" and "Customer Experience"! Obviously, over-used does *not* mean irrelevant. Second, it is possible that the folks who view alignment as no longer relevant think they have already reached that state of nirvana where nothing further can be done to improve it. Does such a state exist? Even if we hypothesize that it does, the need to *retain* this coveted berth would render alignment anything but irrelevant. Third, I suspect that companies which view alignment in isolation – and not as the root of innovation, customer experience, and other goals – are the ones that see it as a fad. These are companies where alignment carries no strategic importance, and hence may be considered irrelevant.

PI # 4: *IT is that faceless, behind-the-scenes entity, which has almost no scope for aligning with the customer-facing business function.* Or, *IT is too "narrow" and "maintenance-centric" to influence business.*

Anyone who believes that there is some truth in the above statement has clearly not grasped the renewed role of technology in driving business success. But sadly, it's a fact that there are still people who view IT through an extremely narrow lens, and in whose worldview, the above description could be just about right. The other day, a young data analyst with a renowned consulting firm told me how he almost slipped on sending out a customer report due to a glitch in his laptop. "So what did you do?", I asked him. " I just took the laptop to IT to have a look at it", he said. "And what is IT?", I asked. "Oh, it is that window near the reception on the 6th floor where you hand over your laptop so they could figure out the problem and set it right"! This is almost a verbatim conversation. Let me emphasize again: IT is *not* just a maintenance window, but the sum of all activities that leverage technology for the fulfillment of the company's obligations to its stakeholders. Thus, in the above case, the gent who took his laptop to "IT" is himself as much a part of IT as the nameless person behind the window. Throughout this book, our definition of IT has included software and hardware engineering professionals (e.g., architects, developers, integrators), technical consultants, subject-matter experts (e.g., security, compliance), analysts, project managers, *and* the user-support professionals responsible for the upkeep of IT infrastructure. The notion that IT is "faceless" or "narrow" or "maintenance-centric" is reflective of a mindset that is not equipped to tap into the vast potential – and opportunity – that a more inclusive definition of IT opens.

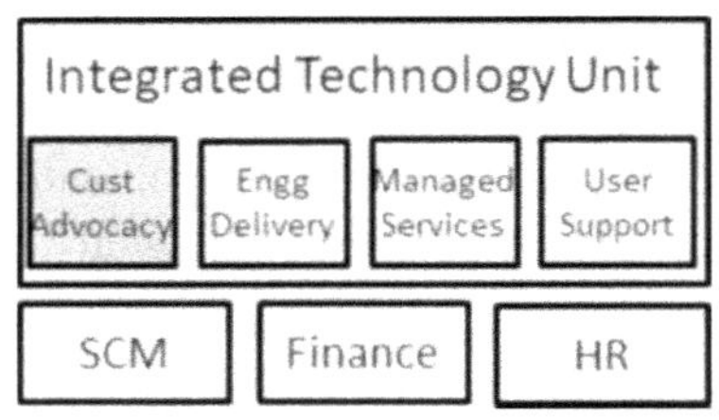

A few years ago, I was associated with a technology company that had made its mark in the US and Western Europe as the leading provider of products and services in its domain. It was now looking at repeating this success-run in the Asian and emerging markets, the new fountainheads of growth, and quite understandably on the cross-hairs of most of its competitors. Our company had to differentiate itself in a new market which was already being courted by the best in the game and had cultural characteristics quite different from anything it had encountered. A core part of its entry strategy was to set up a hub in *India* to serve the needs of the Asia market, and small 'business offices' in most major centers in the Asia Pacific. The core functions that this wheel embodied were *Customer advocacy* (Account management, business consulting), *Engineering Delivery* (Customization, Development, Testing, and Deployment), *Managed Services* (Post-deployment services, Operations & Maintenance Center, Customer SLAs) and *User Support* (IS, Tools and Infra support, availability assurance). A clear distinction of functional charters was paramount to build deep specialization, but the walls between functions were kept porous. Most importantly, all the functions were defined to be a part of one *Integrated Technology Unit*, by which the organization was known. Everyone, irrespective of their functional affiliations, identified themselves as part of the Integrated Technology Unit first and carried the goal of achieving business success in the region, together. Business and Technology functions, by their very design, were seamlessly intertwined to serve the customer through the lifecycle, and hence there were no notions of alignment being a *fad*. Converting a new prospect into a customer was a responsibility of every function. It was a well-understood necessity which was *required* to reinforce the organization. Whether it was entirely due to the strong functional integration evident across the company one cannot say for sure, but the new venture quickly rivaled its counterparts in business traction and credibility. The company soon extended its product-related *research and development* to the center in India, and this too was seamlessly merged into the Integrated Technology Unit. Everyone was part of a well-aligned cohesive group that shared a mission. Contrast this with a set-up where only business folks 'owned' the customer and IT (or Technology) is just a behind-the-scenes support and maintenance facility. An *all-inclusive* technology delivery capability which can leverage the full potential of the organization through a set of integrated functions is certainly not a fad, but a survival kit in the new economy.

The reason for bringing up – and trying to debunk – some of the misconceptions about the function of IT and its alignment with Business is that they could have a serious negative impact on the company's ability to emerge as a strong digital enterprise, which rests on a bedrock of BITA. These misconceptions have their root in a lack of appreciation of the renewed role – and responsibility – of IT in the digital enterprise and its impact on the future of business. *Functional transparency* and *alignment* thus assume decisive implications in determining the fate of the new age enterprise, as we shall discuss.

The function of IT is to *make the business successful.* In fact, the very basis of BITA is that IT must enable business success. One of the primary functions of leadership in the new economy is thus to remove every barrier in the alignment of IT with Business. This calls for a shift from the pure technologist stance that IT leaders tend to define themselves by. In an interview I gave to Economic Times (ET) journal, *ETCIO*, I touched on some general aspects of IT leadership role in the new economy. Excerpts:

Q) Your advice to aspiring CIOs?

My advice to aspiring CIOs would be to expand their horizons beyond technology. It is not easy as that's our comfort zone with most of our lives spent in it. But to cross the same hurdles as I have, it is important to relate to business in particular and people in general. Feel their pain and be a trustworthy partner in their own mission. Technology is just a tool to sculpt your masterpiece, not the masterpiece itself.

Also, do not ever lose sight of your statement of purpose, which is simply this: IT exists to make the business succeed. This is unchangeable. You can define your own path but don't ever lose sight of this goal. Ensure that this is demonstrated in the day to day behavior of the entire IT workforce, which includes your partners. Finally, never expect a quiet moment! Enjoy the roller-coaster. A healthy work-life balance will ensure you have the required charge to keep surging ahead.

Q) The biggest lessons learned in professional career?

I have been fortunate to have experienced the full length of the technology value chain in my professional career with some very renowned Indian and global organizations, from R&D to sales. We tend to define and differentiate, ourselves by our professional expertise in a <u>technical</u> domain. But every technology becomes obsolete or irrelevant, and then so do we. So lesson one is, change is inevitable - embrace it. Many of us at this stage are leaders of people. When you are hiring, counseling or appraising, your actions may have purely business or work-related significance for you. But for the person on the other side of the table, it means his future, his family's aspirations and sometimes his whole life. It is not good to be emotional, but compassion *is certainly required. Not only to be felt but displayed. Hence lesson two is, compassion is human - show it. Lastly, be it in our profession or our life, it is important to have an aim which is unshakeable. It is vital not to be driven by objectives ('what am I going to do?') but by an ultimate goal ('who do I intend to be?'). That's the third and most important lesson I have learned.*

Q) 5 traits of highly effective CIOs?

The CIO role is not just about technology, project execution and cost management but also about people. A CIO must see himself or herself as a business leader, whose sole mission is to make the business successful. First, a highly effective CIO derives the goals and priorities for the IT organization directly from the business goals. He/ she ensures that every person in the team is an empowered stakeholder in the business outcome. Second, he/she does not believe that only seniority and experience bestows wisdom and is keen to learn from everyone, particularly the younger generation. Third, he is passionate about his work. The CIO's role is less about what he does and more about what he inspires. Being passionate about one's goals is the best form of inspiration one can provide. Fourth, he picks and leads an energized team, driven by extraordinary commitment. It always works from the top down. And fifth, he takes a great deal of pride in his work. He knows he plays a very constructive role in shaping the future of the business as well as the larger community. He also knows that there was never a better time to be a CIO, given the influence of information technology in people's lives.

Q) Tips for work-life balance?

Frequent recharge is very crucial but to avail it, you need to ensure undisturbed breaks. Hence a strong second line is important. Equally, an ability to prioritize well and focus on the important, resisting the urge to be pulled into crisis management, will ensure that on a routine basis you are not a late sitter. Use your time during the day well so you can leave the office at a reasonable time. Recognize your capacity and remind yourself that your effectiveness is a direct function of your health, especially as you grow in years. Plan your vacations in advance with your family and intimate your office well ahead. It is preferable to take 2 or 3 shorter breaks in the year than one long one.

Q) Success parameters for CIOs/IT Leaders in any organization?

Being a direct stakeholder in the creation of business value is the surest success parameter for IT leaders. Other critical success factors would include your peer relationships, networking within your industry, and your grasp on technology, which enables you to steer the organization through the surrounding technical maze. The ability to deliver on committed time, cost and quality targets is a very important success measure for IT leaders, as is the demonstrated capacity to recover quickly from catastrophic situations, which are unfortunately a part of an IT leader's backdrop.

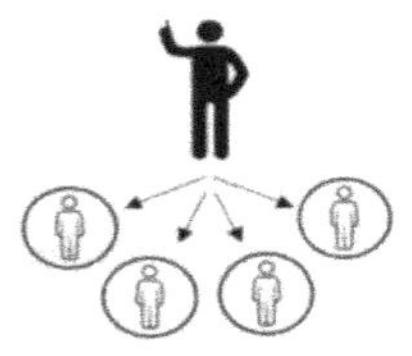

OLD-STYLE LEADERSHI

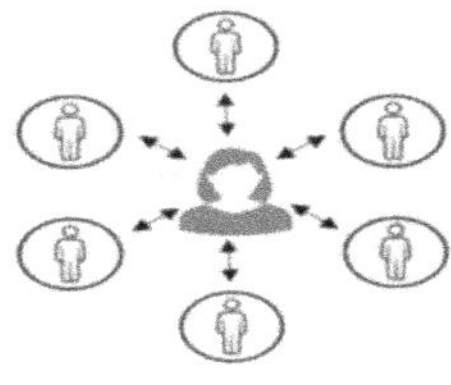

NEW-AGE LEADERSHIP STYLE

Leadership is the capacity that translates an organization's vision into reality. With the advent of the new economy, this idea has not changed. However, the style of leadership has undergone a vast transformation. Most notably, leadership is not about command and control, but inclusiveness. The leader's job is primarily to ensure that all barriers are removed to pave the way for the vision to be realized. In the context of BITA, this means that the Business and IT leaders must focus on creating an enabling environment for their functional priorities to be in sync. It is important to reiterate that Business priorities are *market-driven*, so it is the responsibility of *IT leadership* to assure continuous functional alignment between Business and IT. Business must never change its functional priorities to meet the needs of IT. If that is happening in your organization, it is a *red flag*!

Functional alignment between Business and IT happens when Business can profitably consume what IT produces. Every work product of IT, therefore, must pass the test of contributing to business gainfully. Every decision, policy and action of IT must be able to answer with an emphatic YES to the question: Does this add present or future *value* to the business?

In a nutshell, functional alignment is about defining and maximizing the *Business value of Technology (or IT)*. To bring this into perspective, Business and IT must have convergence on their response to the following questions:

1> What *benefit* must IT produce to be of value to the business?

2> At what *cost* must IT produce this value to the business?

The benefits and costs are not just in economic terms, but are a composite of many factors, determined together by the Business and IT teams, and expressed as an index, or number. In its simplest expression, the Business Value of Technology (or IT), which we shall call **BVIT**, is the combined *benefits* minus the overall *costs*. This, of course, implies that in a BITA driven IT organization, everyone – from the top leadership down – must make it their mission, above all else, to achieve two uncomplicated goals:

- Maximize the benefits of IT to business
- Minimize the cost of IT to business

Obviously then, determination of Business Value of Technology (or IT) concerns itself with finding ways to *measure* the benefits of IT to business, and the cost of IT to business. BVIT could be expressed as simply B – C (where B is the composite benefits and C is the composite cost), or as B/C, or some other agreed expression. I prefer the simple B – C because it can tell you if the value of IT to business is *negative,* and avoids deceptively wide ranges and error values that B/C is prone to. However, it is entirely up to the stakeholders to define the formula through some nifty out-of-the-box thinking. What is important is an agreement between Business and IT, and consistency in the measurement process so that trends can be observed.

BVIT brings out the visible impact of IT, i.e., how it influences the performance and growth of *Business*. Let me reiterate here that IT organizations which are fixated on self-serving internal measurements add next to nil value to business, however pumped up they may feel about their accomplishments.

There are at least a couple of examples in earlier chapters of this book on how internally focused measurements by IT can, at their worst, mislead business due to misinterpretation or false-positive indications, and at their best, have nil or very marginal positive impact on Business. They are indicative of either a clear divergence in priorities or impenetrable silos which prevent any form of functional interlock. In either case, this goes against the grain of BITA. A short example here may help to underline this problem further.

This example refers to a technology company, well reputed in its existing market and growing fast into new markets. The company openly championed BITA and had invested a great deal of management time on instituting its core concepts across the enterprise. BITA here meant alignment between the customer account teams and the technical divisions, viz., product R&D, project delivery, and managed services.

The company had a good track record of supporting its customers. Recognizing this as one of its major competitive strengths, the company decided to trumpet (advertise) the capabilities of its various technology divisions to further strengthen its market position. The reasoning was clear: the technology teams – from product R&D to Managed Services – were responsible for a significant part of the customer lifecycle and thus strongly influenced perceptions in the market. This was a clear differentiator which was underplayed so far, in deference to product led campaigns.

The message was conveyed to the CTO directly to pull relevant information from the various technology arms, in a bid to highlight the company's delivery and technology capabilities to existing as well as prospective customers. The teams got down to work and soon had an impressive compilation. It was of course, clear to the team that customers, or for that matter, their own account teams, would have little patience with internal statistics on the productivity of human and capital resources, and hence the compilation took a different approach. The aspects that went into the presentation included:

- Initiatives taken towards virtualization and the resulting benefits like higher capex utilization
- Measures used internally to optimize development effort in R&D through techniques like ToC (Theory of Constraints), Reuse, etc.
- Set up of Remote Infrastructure Management (RIM) facility to boost efficiency: 80% calls moved to RIM, resulting in 30% reduction in time and cost (effort) to close internal calls.
- Improvements achieved in various performance measures for Service Requests and Call tickets
- Performance statistics of key applications and tools for supporting customer operations
- Architecture diagrams detailing the use of standard components and interfaces.
- Statistics on CMI and Quality at various stages of development lifecycle

The question is: are these metrics indeed useful to the customer? Quite obviously, the presentation is *not* customer-centric. First, an undue emphasis on complex technical terminology (jargon) is a turn-off. Flaunting confusing terms as a means of impressing the customer – in the hope of swaying him – only serves to alienate. Second, the emphasis above is still, perhaps unwittingly, on showcasing the competence and perspective of the *technology* teams, rather than on *real benefits to the customer*! While the customer may indeed be interested in knowing that there is a proper oversight of the technology functions that serve him, what he is paying for is the benefit that accrues to the *customer's organization*. Obviously, the question "What's in it for the customer?" was either glossed over completely or it was assumed that somehow the customer would figure this out from the information provided. This is a very common mistake. If you were a customer, would your decision be materially swayed by the above presentation? I guess not.

Functional alignment is not about doing what is right for IT, but about breaking the shell to do what *matters to the business.* In the above example, all the bulleted actions are 'right', but where they fall short is in being directly relevant to the Business. It would be very hard for a business team member to tie back most of these aspects to direct business benefits. And even harder for the customer.

> ***Exercise****: Can you list five things which the above company should have focused on reporting, that would have genuinely improved the customer's perception and helped the business succeed?*

A good test of functional alignment is to ask the question: *How is the demonstrated action directly helping the customer or business unit in their own mission?* That's all the business is interested in. Every other 'right' action by IT is nothing but an *internal* execution step towards this attainment, and no one is holding their breath to hear about these. In the above example, if you were a business-head, what inference would you draw from the aspects presented, like RIM, Virtualization, SR performance improvements, etc.? These are *interim* steps, not business goals or priorities. The business head's focus would apparently be on aspects like Customer churn and its causes, User acceptance results during pilot run, Order-fulfillment cycle time, Stage-wise Customer experience parameters, root-cause analysis of serious problems, etc. The previous example evidently fails our test, attesting to mismatched functional priorities, or the absence of functional alignment between Business and IT.

As would be evident from the preceding, *functional alignment is about IT understanding the functional priorities of the Business and modulating its goals and priorities to remain in continuous sync with them.* Unlike other dimensions of alignment, functional alignment is *unidirectional*. That is, Business priorities determine IT priorities and not the other way. Service companies with a dominant technology function, like software delivery units, product-led service businesses, etc., often run the risk of following the *reverse* course which could soon lead to their crashing out of the market.

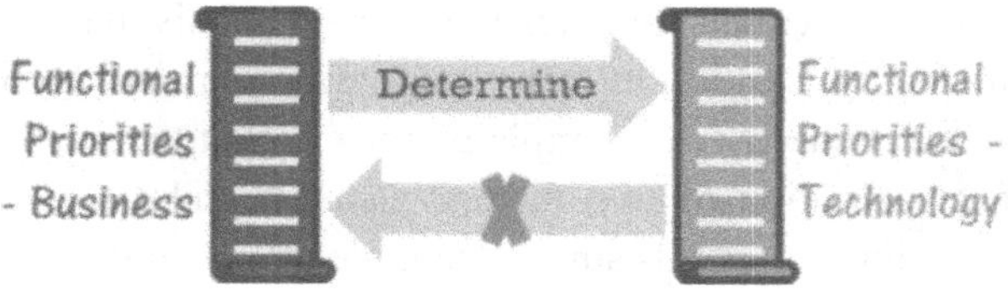

A long time ago, when I was a field support engineer, computer systems were routinely rendered inoperational for reasons outside the customer's control. To mention just a few: a downtime due to technical malfunction extending for days, esp. if the installation happened to be remote; non-availability of required spare-parts to fix the problem; scheduled and unscheduled preventive maintenance; non-availability of trained staff to guide the customer; unattended software bugs awaiting new release, etc. The worst part was this being considered *acceptable*, even though the consequences often impacted the business negatively – like delayed material accounting, invoice generation, management reports (MIS) and so on. Even the business (sales) folks mostly shrugged off the problem, expressing helplessness. Everything was offered on a 'best-effort' basis. Looking back, it is easy to recognize this as the case of IT's functional priorities having the power to decide, and often derail, business plans. I believe that this was one of the chief reasons that IT did not emerge as a real enabler of the business in its earlier avatars. No one trusted IT to be a value creator for the business, as it was perceived as an agency fixated on its internal priorities.

Cutting to the present, we know that such a scenario is inconceivable. The functional objectives of IT are now determined by the level of experience that you aspire to deliver to your *customer*. There are many examples of this encountered routinely, which include planned 'maintenance windows' during off-peak hours, tiered data storage for quick retrieval and recovery of data, hardened security processes (like Firewall, Security Operations Center) to protect customer's information assets, agile and iterative software development, proactive solutions based on CEM probes, and so on. With some IT services, like SaaS, being run on the lines of utility services (like water and electricity) the functional goals of IT can no longer be derived without keeping the functional goals of business in mind. Not in the Digital Age for sure.

> ***Exercise:*** *List at least five functional priorities of the IT, Technology or Service unit of your organization that can be directly traced to the functional priorities of your business unit or customer.*

We will now turn our attention to the determination of BVIT, one of the cornerstones of functional alignment. This has been defined by pundits, including Gartner, in many ways which are no doubt quite erudite and well-researched. My own simple premise is that to determine *value*, one must have a clear notion of two factors: *Benefits* and *Cost*. Without one, the other is meaningless, as this simple example demonstrates.

I remember this incident from a sales training program I attended many years ago. At one point, the facilitator took out a black box neatly tied in ribbon and kept it on the table where everyone could see it. Then he said, "I am willing to give this away for Rs 1000. Any takers?" He didn't say what was in the box. No hands went up. Obviously, people wanted to know what they were getting for their money. He then said, "Okay – here's my last offer. I will give this away for Rs 500. Any takers now?" Still, no one came forward. After some atmospherics, he opened the box, and to everyone's surprise, there was an elegant and expensive wrist-watch inside, costing not less than Rs 2500! He again asked, "Any takers now?" All hands went up! What had changed? It was the same box and content, the same price and the same aspirants. The only difference was that now both the cost as well as the *benefit* were visible and hence people could discover the *value* of the deal – which was quite attractive. The point here is that it is never the cost alone, or the benefit by itself, that determines value, but their *combination.*

BVIT also works on this principle. It is a quantifiable measure derived from an assessment of the benefits *and* cost of Technology (or IT) to the business. Of course, no reduction technique exists that can precisely convert an experience into a number, so a certain amount of subjectivity is inbuilt in the measurement. However, so long as the measurement is done using the same principles over extended periods, it's an excellent compass in the journey to functional alignment.

The Benefits Basket

The first step towards determining BVIT is quantifying the *benefits* of IT (the term IT, as in the rest of this book, includes all the functions involved in technology development, delivery and operations). Depending on the industry, domain or environment that you operate in, the targeted benefits of IT could be different. A network operations team at a telecom service provider has quite a different charter from a project delivery team at a software consulting company. By our definition, however, *both* are part of Technology (or IT) function and have a set of associated benefits for their business/clients. These benefits boost business performance to a much higher level, rendering a clear and continuous competitive edge. To account for the variation across segments, the benefits of IT to Business are grouped under the following four broad categories. The benefits are measured and reported in each of these categories to arrive at the composite *IT Benefits Index.*

- ✓ **Customer Engagement** (Enhancing credibility by fulfilling the obligations to customers/ markets)
- ✓ **Service Excellence** (Creating distinction through superior delivery &operations in all stages of CLC)
- ✓ **Economic Contribution** (Improving profitability through influence on financial performance)
- ✓ **Technology Readiness** (Building capability to take advantage of the digital opportunity)

Almost all the benefits of IT that are relevant to BVIT typically fall under one of the above heads in my experience, though some obliquely. The important point here is to find a consistent methodology for quantifying these benefits. This is usually done by first breaking up each of the four themes into its components as relevant to the industry or environment. While some components lend themselves to direct measurement, others are assessed through collective rating involving feedback from stakeholders.

✓ Customer engagement

The extent to which IT identifies with, assesses, and reports issues that directly impact the *end-user* or *business* is a measure of its customer engagement. For example, the report from IT that shows a month-on-month reduction in insurance claim processing time, or the increase in customer churn along with root-causes, or the end-to-end order-to-delivery time, is an indicator of its customer engagement. Depending on your industry segment, regional links and business direction, the set of customer engagement metrics could be quite diverse. Thus, the metrics which are most relevant to your specific setting must be deliberated and agreed between Business and IT well ahead of production.

Customer engagement is not just about reporting of relevant information. Tools and systems must be pre-built to *capture* the required data at the right time, assimilate it and present it in a comprehensible format to the business. Based on the information presented, IT must be able to institute actions to tune the outcomes to the business aspirations. Tools that extract information on-the-fly from business applications are referred as 'hooks.' These hooks are developed by IT for obtaining business-critical information all the way from the design to delivery of customer or business impacting solutions.

A simple illustration may help absorb this better. Let us take the example of a mobile telecom operating company again, and some features that all of us, as users (customers) of mobile services are familiar with.

Monthly IT Report (illustrative sample)**.** Business Unit: Mobility Retail. Month: April 2018.

SN	Metric	Unit	Target	Actual	Achvmt*
1	Average waiting time at service desk under 30sec	% of calls	98.0%	85.0%	87
2	Prepaid recharges (e2e) completed in under 1 minute	%	99.5%	99.0%	99
3	Customer activation time (CAF to Activation)< 4 Hrs	% of orders	90%	59%	65
4	Voice calls completed without getting dropped	%	99.9%	99.8%	99
5	Average C-SAT rating^ for Service Requests handling	Out of 5	4	4.3	108
6	Post-paid bill accuracy (Zero-error bills out of 1000)	number	1	0.9	111

[Achievement is calculated as the ratio of Actual to Target normalized to a base of 100. ^ The C-SAT rating is the average of customer scores captured at the close of every service request.]*

We could have reported on metrics like product-wise Average Revenue Per User (ARPU), Value and number of monthly recharges, etc., but as these are not directly controllable by IT, they are kept outside the purview of BVIT. The call on what must be included in the value metrics must be a joint one.

As can be noted from the table, unless there are hooks built into the IT systems to extract relevant data, such metrics cannot become a reality (E.g., #4). This is usually not a trivial task as it requires that Business-IT alignment is factored in during the *development* of IT systems. If this is not embedded, you may have to build this using a change request to write internal or external code. Most often, the values are *parameterized* and can be easily changed, rather than being hard-wired. In the case of metric # 1 for example, the horizon may be changed from 30 sec to 25 sec and/or the target from 98% to 99%. Such flexibility ensures that Business and IT stay functionally aligned even as customer and market expectations fluctuate.

The business value on the customer engagement parameters is plotted in the bar graph alongside. The individual score on each parameter may also be displayed as a speedometer dashboard for an intuitive readout. Either way, it is

important to recognize *each* parameter as critical, not just the average. Here, the (non-weighted) average across the six parameters is 95 (simple average of all the six metrics in the earlier table). While the focus is on maximizing the overall value, attention to *individual* metrics cannot be overlooked. For example, you may pull up the average from 95 to 98 by say, further improving the post-paid bill accuracy (#6). But it will do nothing to assuage the feelings of folks who must wait more than 30 secs for their voice to be heard (#1), or the new subscribers whose connections get activated (#3) after their patience wears out! A composite value, which is 95 here is, however, a good indication of the level of alignment on a cumulative scale, and I have found it useful in overall BVIT computations. Both, the forest *and* the trees, are important here. A monthly trend graph on each parameter lends invaluable insight into the direction of movement as an impetus to timely course corrections.

The metrics in the above example pertain to *direct* actions by IT that contribute to business results which have an impact on the company's competitive positioning. IT can also add to business value by facilitating the capture, retrieval and analysis of data that helps the business to more effectively execute on its customer strategy. In the above scenario, this could include Churn Analysis, Customer segmentation and experience parameters at different stages of the customer lifecycle. Virtually, there is no limit to the value that IT can create for the Business by leveraging its most important asset: Information.

Recognizing Business as its most important stakeholder and sponsor, the value measurement by IT in the customer engagement category must respond to the *changes* in the external environment that dynamically redefine business priorities. The ability of IT to stay in lockstep with business is a key indicator of IT's value to the business.

✓ Service excellence

Service excellence is a benchmark that imparts confidence to the Business that the service machinery is well oiled and able to deliver on business commitments, both internal and external. It starts with close engagement between Business and IT to agree on the schedule, cost and quality of the deliverables from IT for meeting the expectations of the market. To accomplish this, the IT skills and processes must stay aligned with the needs of the business.

The two aspects of IT that significantly impact service excellence– and hence business performance – are its Delivery and Operations capabilities. Delivery has a direct bearing on Time (TTM), Cost (development effort, infrastructure and overheads) and Quality (features, performance) of the product or service being sold by the business. IT Operations, on the other hand, have a significant impact on customer retention, requiring IT to not only render excellent service but also capture, process and correlate experience parameters at every stage of the lifecycle towards anticipating needs and fulfilling them before they are expressed. IT Operations also ensure that internal IT systems required for secure and smooth business functioning are seamlessly and transparently available where needed and when needed. Like oxygen.

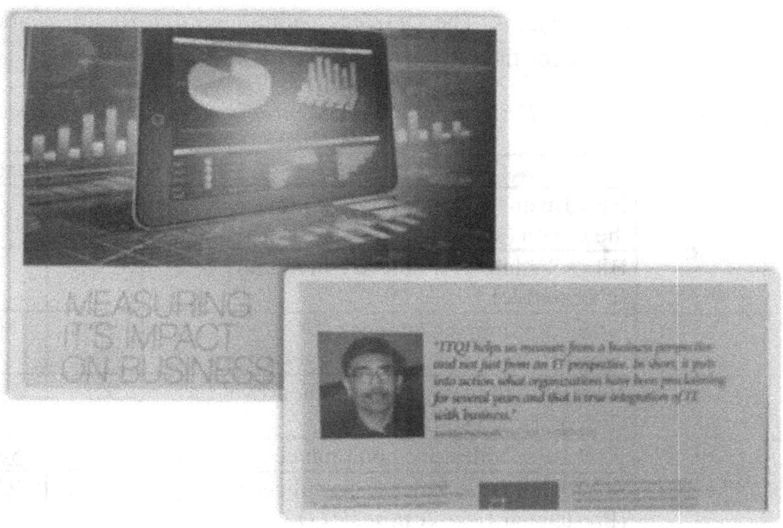

Together, IT Delivery and Operations are the lifelines of business, more so in this Digital Age. Their efficient management requires not just meeting the targeted outcomes, but identifying and monitoring the elements that constitute them. In other words, an ability to *measure* spot performance as well as trends of key delivery and operations parameters is crucial for business value creation. The service excellence metric often referred to as IT Quality Index or Service Quality Index, is a derivative of key IT Delivery and Operations parameters. A few years ago, I had participated in the development of a composite indicator of IT service quality (ITQI) which received wide interest across segments and was included in the Innovation Workgroup's annual yearbook among the top IT innovations. It was a proud and satisfying moment, as it recognized the importance of IT Delivery and Operations metrics in leading the business to success.

Staying with our company, let us consider an example to illustrate how service excellence may be measured and reported as a benefit.

As with most progressive enterprises, this company laid a heavy emphasis on the delivery and sustenance of features, enhancements, and services that impacted its customer and business. As the first step, the company's Business and IT functions deliberated upon the *Delivery-efficiency index (DEI)* that would guide the delivery course from Business Requirements (BR) generation to production roll-out. This was a detailed measurement calling for close engagement of both functions in deciding the key parameters that needed to be quantified and reported to enable the Business to make sensible predictions and rational, data-driven decisions. The Delivery parameters that Business and IT agreed to track monthly for the DEI metric were the following:

Delivery-efficiency index (DEI): Report for the month- April 2018. [Sample]

SN	Attribute	Metric	Target	Actual
B1	**BRs**	New Business Requests (BRs) raised during the month (added)		168
B2		BRs scheduled for delivery in month (cumulative)		193
T1	**TIME**	New BRs: Impact Analysis (IA*) completion on schedule	98%	100%
T2		New BRs: On-time Business approval on Cost & Time estimates	95%	*84%*
T3		New BRs: Milestone compliance (T1*T2)	93%	*84%*
T4		Scheduled BRs: Release compliance (Pre-launch *User Testing[UT]*)	95%	*93*%
T5		Scheduled BRs: UT to *Production* launch compliance	98%	98.5%
T6		Scheduled BRs: Overall schedule compliance (T4*T5)	93%	*91.6%*

C1		Effort adherence (against baseline plan) for scheduled BRs	90%	94%
C2		Effort-saving due to Re-use (actual vs. target) for scheduled BRs	100%	*<u>61%</u>*
C3	**COST**	Cumulative (year-to-date) Effort adherence (against plan)	90%	92%
C4		Cumulative (year-to-date) effort saving due to Re-use (Act. vs Tgt.)	100%	*<u>75%</u>*
C5		BRs in actual use by business/customer post-production	98%	*80%*
Q1	**QUALITY**	Pre-production (UAT) quality (BRs with 0 severe defects in UAT)	90%	90%
Q2		Production quality (BRs with 0 severe or major defects in <1m)	99%	100%

**IA is performed to apprise the business of the impact of the BR on time, cost and functionality*

This is an indicative chart, and the actual metrics to be tracked may vary depending on business need and IT capability. If the terms do not resonate with you, don't sweat. The intent is only to clarify the concept of DEI at a broad level. The composite DEI may be taken as the weighted (if you assign different weights to individual metrics) or simple average of the actual values, which works out to 88%, or 0.88 here.

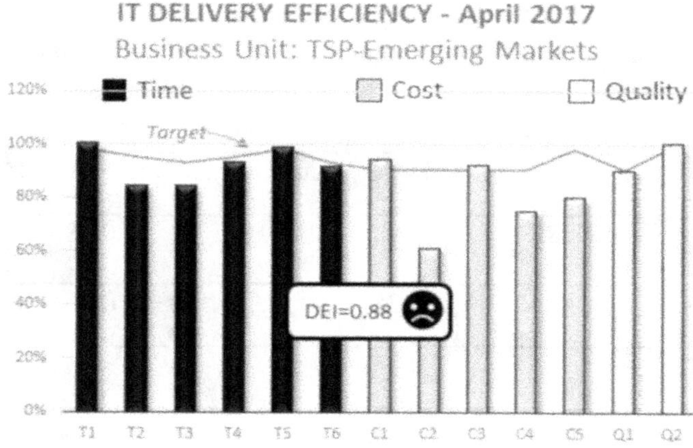

In my experience, I have found it immensely useful to track the delivery parameters along the Time, Cost and Quality dimensions on a month-on-month basis. This requires investment of effort and money to build or buy requisite tools for accurate and unambiguous measurement. It is a worthy investment, with quick RoI through future savings in cost, quality and goodwill. From the chart here, which plots the values from the previous table, it is straightforward to see the attributes that are "under the weather" and need to be pulled up, at least for the month under advisement. Here, for example, the delivery team must focus more sharply on cost savings through re-use (C2), despite adhering to the overall effort plan (C3). This is a common missed opportunity for achieving crucial savings in the delivery effort (measured in person-days) which could be utilized for key projects towards the year-end when the budgets are almost exhausted. The overall DEI of 0.88 is a clear red flag, as the usual 'safe range' is 0.95 and above. A few high scores – like production quality (Q2) or speed of impact analysis (T1) in the example – determined in isolation may lead the team to a state of misplaced euphoria. DEI gives a *holistic* picture and enables timely course correction on the *full range* of attributes that constitute delivery excellence.

Aside from IT Delivery, Service excellence focuses on IT *Operations*. Therefore, the company also identified key *operational* parameters which were simultaneously reported as *Operations-health index (OHI)* in the determination of the comprehensive service quality index. Generally, the parameters that portray characteristics required to *Change (or Transform) the Business* were clubbed under Delivery, and the ones that portray characteristics required to *Run the Business* were clubbed under Operations. This is a definition commonly adopted for IT Delivery and Operations across industries and verticals. In both Delivery and Operations, there are many facets which may be important but are *internal* to IT and the service excellence metrics does not include these. As with Delivery-efficiency index, the first step in the determination of the Operations-health index was to agree on its constituents and the process of their measurement. The company closed in on five operational parameters and their target levels for computing OHI as per pre-agreed method. Here is a sample report with all parameters having equal weight, though this can be varied.

SN	Metric	Target	Curr. Actual	Prev. Actual
1	User Service Requests (USR) Resolution Index	0.98	0.99	0.98
2	Applications-Incidents Index	0.95	0.96	0.96
3	Data-Sanctity Index	0.85	0.71	0.70
4	Business-Continuity Index	0.67	0.67	0.72
5	Information-Security Index	0.90	0.86	0.82

User Service Requests (USR) Resolution Index: This is an index to track the resolution of user tickets. A simple measurement could be <No. of tickets resolved within SLA>/<No. of User tickets received>.

Applications-Incidents Index: This measurement accounts for availability and performance of business-critical applications by tracking the *number* of reported incidents and performance metrics against SLA.

Data-Sanctity Index: This is a tool based measurement that checks for data synchronization across multiple databases as an indicator of the integrity of business-critical data, including customer data.

Business-Continuity Index: This is a composite index derived from the measured performance levels, switch over times and overall reliability of the *recovery* infrastructure (DR).

Information-Security Index: Information Security Index is a measure of confidentiality, integrity and availability of critical data, measured by correlating security logs of reported and prevented incidents.

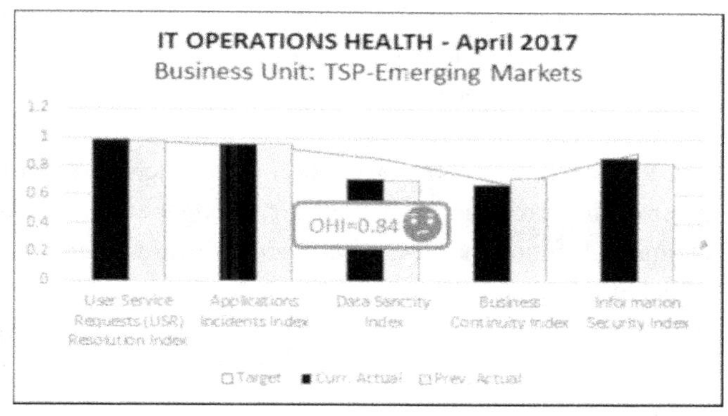

In our example, we have taken the OHI as the simple average of the various parameters, i.e., 0.84. The five factors we have considered to define Operations-health index can generally be applied across industry segments, though the measurement of individual indices and their target levels may vary.

Every industry or enterprise may reach its own verdict on what must be measured (and how) for arriving at the composite OHI. Irrespective of what your list consists of, you will probably require special tools for accurate and objective reporting of the operational parameters.

✓ Economic Contribution

Creation of business value is the primary *purpose* of IT's existence and is not merely a benefit. Everything IT does (or *should* do) contributes to business. The economic contribution of IT to business is usually indirect, but there is also vast (mostly untapped) potential for *direct* economic contribution by IT, which many new-age enterprises have successfully leveraged.

Some years ago, I had the privilege of building and leading the Consulting and Systems Integration (CSI) division for a large European telecom gear maker in the fast-paced Indian telecom market. The division focused on customized 3rd-party solutions and had the dual responsibility of business generation and service delivery, operating as a regional P&L unit. That is, the technical expert who front ended the business proposal as a pre-sales *solutions consultant*, doubled up as the de-facto *solution architect* responsible for planning and design of the customer solution, coordinating across alliance partners, account teams, and of course, the CSI project organization. The entire CSI unit was identified as one of the divisions of the company's *Service* (or *Technology delivery*) organization. The CSI unit contributed handsomely to not just the company's bottom line, but also to the creation of goodwill with highly discerning customers in an intensely competitive market. In this environment, characterized by largely similar companies with similar products and similar people, CSI was a refreshing break as it offered direct engagement between customers and technology function to help build *solutions* that were specific to a customer. This led to improved collaboration, which often resulted in rewarding *upsell* opportunities. The trust and goodwill generated by CSI were also capitalized by other divisions of the company to boost sales. CSI, which was seen by some as a 'gap-filler', quickly metamorphosed into a 'solutioneer.' This is an example, from my own experience, of the potential of Technology (or IT) function to *directly* contribute to the business in enhancing economic value.

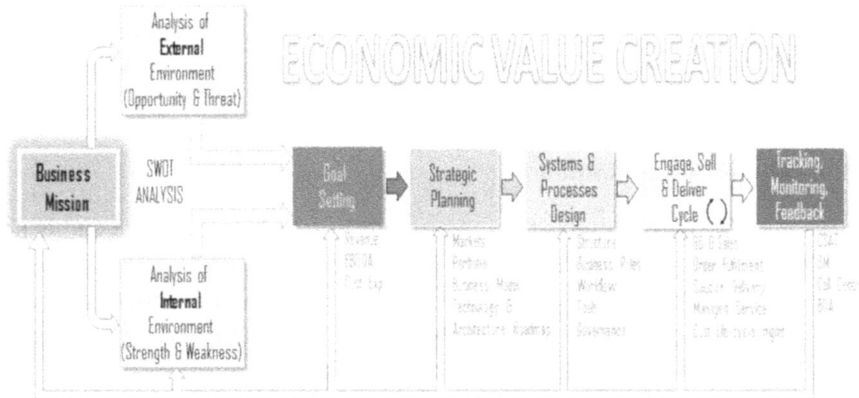

Despite examples like the above, the overwhelming view of IT is still of a support function that can at best *supplement*– indirectly for the most part – the Business efforts towards creating economic value. It is difficult for most to conceive that IT, in fact, *IS* the Business. Or *CAN* be. Even if your organization does not have the replica of a CSI in action, it can surely have one in spirit at least? In other words, if IT can *directly* contribute to the growth of the business by becoming a source of incremental revenue and goodwill, isn't it a distinct benefit? The inhibitors are more often rooted in the cultural and attitudinal stances than in functional abilities or aptitude.

The other instance of economic contribution by IT is where Business and IT are joined at the hip in their approach to economic value creation. Here, IT is not an independent island but an equal stakeholder in the achievement of economic results, like revenue and PAT, carrying the very same economic goals as the Business. It is not a best-effort scenario, where Business merely asks for IT's assistance in responding to an RFP or to explain a technical concept in the proposal to the customer or prospect. Instead, IT and business are partners through *all* the stages of customer and economic value creation process. They swim or sink together. The preceding illustration depicts the keys stages in which Business and IT work as *co-creators of economic value*.

This is a generic model. That is, if Business were to create economic value independently, it would still go through roughly the same stages. In a BITA driven environment, the charge is revved up several notches through *co-creation* of economic value by Business and IT. In such environments, the IT organization is business-led, with a Business Analyst (or equivalent) leading

1. **Sell what people really WANT to buy:** Customers don't buy products or Technology. They buy *experiences* delivered via products or Technology.

2. **ALWAYS Deliver on your promise:** To be successful, you must only promise what you can deliver, and deliver *more* than you've promised.

3. **Do it BETTER than your Competition:** Competition is a good thing. It gets you out of complacency. Remember that somebody can always do it better and that somebody is you.

the charge. Instead of IT coming in for 'support', like assisting with proposals or presentations, the BA here ensures *continuous* engagement of IT at every stage of economic value creation, having shared goals towards the attainment of business results. This requires breaking the shackles and demolishing the silos to put *IT on the front end*, locking step with Business all the way to tap into the vast potential unleashed by the digital economy.

Economic value co-creation is not a matter of chance or happenstance. It requires engagement – in both spirit and action – of Business *and* IT at every stage of the *sales and delivery model*, which evolves from focusing *together* on the three simple, time-tested tenets of business value creation listed alongside. It would indeed be hard for Business or IT to go it *alone* in even one of them, more so in the digital era. If you can measure the contribution of IT to business in each of these three areas in a quantifiable way, it is a giant step for BVIT.

By adopting a collaborative economic value creation model, you may measure contribution by IT in several ways. This could include measuring IT contribution at *every* stage and normalizing the values to a composite index. Or, if you tend to look only at 'the proof of the pudding', you may measure the economic contribution of IT as the achievement of the targeted business *outcomes*, like revenue. Or, you may devise a combination of the above. It's entirely for you to decide how you measure Economic Contribution by IT, but it is important to be consistent.

The IT **Economic-contribution index** (ECI) is a measure of (1) Direct Economic value addition by IT, and (2) Indirect Economic value added by IT through functional integration with Business. Let us take an example here to illustrate a typical way to measure the composite ECI.

First, the Direct economic value addition is the *expected* contribution of IT to business, as measured against a given business target (like sales quota, or profitability target) through direct selling or by capitalizing on upselling opportunities. It can be a simple measurement (say, actual-revenue/target-revenue) or, preferably, a combination of several weighted factors like revenue, profitability, C-SAT, etc. to arrive at a composite value, as shown below.

	Factor	Weight	Target	Actual	Achievement
a	Revenue	40%	USD 1m	USD 800K	0.80
b	Profitability	40%	15%	17.5%	1.17
c	C-SAT Score (scale of 5)	20%	4	3.8	0.95

This gives a weighted average score of (40% x 0.80) + (40% x 1.17) + (20% x 0.95) = **0.98**

Again, this is one of the many possible ways to specify direct business contribution by IT. With a bit of innovation, you can devise better versions.

Next, let us take the *indirect* contribution. As we touched upon earlier, this may require stage-wise measurement of IT contribution based on the economic value creation model. Or one could simply use the *3-point rule* that we just discussed. That is, quantifiably determine the indirect contribution by IT as a response to the following questions:

(1) What is the contribution of IT in creating the experiences (products, services, technology) that customers are willing to pay for?
(2) What is the contribution of IT in delivering the committed value throughout the customer lifecycle?
(3) What is the contribution of IT in bringing the differentiation (Time-to-market, cost and quality of deliverables, etc.) that keeps your organization ahead of competition?

Assessing and quantifying the responses requires breaking each question into constituent topics which are unique to an enterprise environment. An example of a constituent question under 1 could be: How would you rate the speed of operation (Response time in case of Service, Latency in case of Product)? A simple template is used to capture the feedback from business on each constituent question on a scale of 1-5. For simplicity, let us consider each question to have the same weight here. If the average of all responses to questions 1,2 and 3 are 4.1, 3.6 and 3.9 respectively, the indirect contribution score would be 3.87 on a scale 5, which is **0.77**. This may be a good window into IT's indirect contribution, but may not always reflect *actual* business results. Hence this is linked to the business objectives (most often *revenue* achievement) to arrive at the composite index of indirect contribution by IT. If the company's revenue achievement is at 90% of the target, the indirect business contribution index would be 90% x 0.77, or **0.69**.

From the above, we have a direct ECI of 0.98 and an indirect ECI of 0.69. If direct contribution has a weight of 75% and indirect contribution has a weight of 25%, the composite ECI works out to (75% x 0.98) + (25% x 0.69), or **0.91.** In my experience, I have found this measurement to be a highly effective means of ascertaining IT's business contribution, albeit with a margin of error that cancels out over time. You can formulate your own ECI to suit your environment. The above is just one of many possible examples.

✓ **Technology Readiness**

Giving the organization a sharp technological edge is perhaps one of the most significant – and visible – contributions of IT to the enterprise. The degree to which technology is being applied by an enterprise at any given point of time impacts not just its ability to create economic and customer value, but also to attract investment and employment. Yet, it eludes direct measurement. If there is a problem today with technology, it is perhaps that there is too much of it! So, when can you say that you have "right" technology focus, and more pertinently, how do you *measure* the extent of your technology focus as an enterprise? There is detailed research carried out on the measurement of technology, but I daresay that it is somewhat esoteric for everyday use and would probably require a distinct function dedicated to its implementation in the enterprise. But again, with so much riding on technology, you obviously cannot consign it entirely to the realms of subjectivity. Therefore, a simple and practical way to assess the enterprise's technology focus and application for business value creation is the need of the hour.

An effective method of measuring technology adoption is to prepare a basic *template* listing all possible aspirational items under suitable heads. Through periodic surveys and benchmarks, the template can be continually augmented to keep it as current as possible. The extent of adoption in the enterprise against each item is objectively rated on a scale (typically 1-5) using a defined rule-set, and the final index is arrived by averaging out the responses. It is important to assign weights to each item, depending on its criticality to the business. Here is an example of a template along with sample ratings, but it is entirely flexible. You may like to invest time in creating a list that is more pertinent to your environment (ideally through brainstorming), and then keep enriching it with time for greater precision.

Focus Area	Category	Technology	Weight (0-4)	Score (0-5)
External (Business and Customer value)	Digital	Cloud-based business applications and data	3	4
		Hosted Cloud services / offerings for customers	3	1
		Enterprise Mobility (devices, apps)	2	4
		Social Media for tuning into Voice-of-Customer	3	1
		Instant Messaging – business/customer network	1	4
		Big data analytics (real-time analytics)	4	2
		Digital Platform (Architecture building blocks)	4	4
		Data Communication Network (>8 Mbps)	2	4
		Web-based (digital) marketing tools	3	1
		e-commerce platform and gateway	0	0
		Self-care portal for web-based customer service	3	4
	Industry-specific Tech (BANKING)	Java applications (JVMs)	2	4
		Digital Banking Platform	4	4
		Multi-factor cyber-security platform	4	4
		Integration of SM with banking services	3	1
		Biometrics for authentication	3	1
		Digital Wallet	3	2
		Blockchain	1	1
	Generic Business Support Systems	Customer Experience Management (CEM)	4	4
		Customer Lifecycle Management	3	2
		Billing and Payment	4	4
		Business Data Warehouse (DWH)	4	3
		Data extraction and mining	2	3
		Data visualization and presentation	2	4
		Revenue Assurance & Fraud Management	2	4
		Data Confidentiality, Integrity and Availability	4	4

Aligned to WIN

Focus Area	Category	Technology	Weight (0-4)	Score (0-5)
Internal (Productivity and Efficiency)	Digital	Enterprise Mobility - BYOD	2	3
		Internal Mobile apps (or) Mobile Intranet portal	2	3
		Cloud-based access to business apps and data	4	3
		Big Data Analytics	3	2
	Enterprise Productiv-ity	Enterprise Resource Planning (e.g. SAP, Oracle)	2	4
		Relational database management (E.g. Oracle11g)	2	4
		Application Integration (EAI, Web-services, SOA)	2	2
		Functional tech – SCM, HCM, FMS…	2	0
		Information Lifecycle Management	3	1
		Enterprise Software Platform (e.g. Java EE)	3	4
		Architecture standardization (e.g. TOGAF)	4	2
	Enterprise communi-ca-tion	HD Video Conferencing (or) Tele-presence	3	0
		High-speed data communication network	2	4
		Video Conferencing over web channels	2	4
		Secure Instant messaging (e.g., MS Lync)	2	4
		Enterprise-class email solution (e.g. Exchange)	2	5
	Infrastruc-ture	Data storage and management system	2	4
		Application servers on private/public cloud	4	3
		Server/Storage Virtualization	2	4
		Security Firewall	2	4
		Business Continuity (DR)	2	4
		Operations Support Platform (e.g. Openview)	2	1
Future Readiness		Machine Learning	1	0
		Artificial Intelligence	1	0
		3D-Printing	0	0
		IOT / M2M	0	0

Focus Area	Category	Technology	Weight (0-4)	Score (0-5)
Thought Leadership	Learning	Training and development initiatives	4	5
		Tech seminars for business and non-IT	3	3
		Technology-vendor led consultations	3	3
	KM	Knowledge Management Tools	3	2
		Empowered technology council	4	3
	Innovation	Encouragement of dare-to-try spirit	3	2
		Investment in prototypes and Proof-of-Concept	3	1
		Sandbox and incubation labs	3	1

The range of technologies and options is so vast that no list can be even close to comprehensive. Therefore, you must carefully select the tech domains that are important for your business and construct your own template. The good thing is that the list is quite flexible in allowing addition/removal of technologies based on their current relevance, and in changing the weights assigned to individual components, even on a month-by-month basis. *The above categories, technologies, weights, and scores are intended to be only a simple example* that attempts to point us in the general direction of technology measurement at an enterprise level. Here's how.

Let us decide the *weights* first. You may do this in various ways, depending on how important you hold one technology vis-à-vis others. In my own experience, the following classification was found useful in eliminating ambiguity to a good extent.

0	The technology or domain is not (or no longer) relevant to my *industry segment*
1	The technology is relevant to my *industry* segment but not immediately important to my *business*
2	The technology is important for imparting greater *efficiency* to run my business operations
3	The technology is important for creating *differentiation* in the market
4	The technology is critical for ensuring the attainment of strategic goals

In choosing 2, ask yourself this: "Even though this technology does not impart a *unique* edge to my company, could my business run efficiently *without* it?" An "Enterprise-class email solution (e.g., Exchange)" in the above list is an example of such a technology, as are many other technologies deployed for operational and business-as-usual purposes. In the case of 3, the question to ask is: "By adopting this technology would my company's prospects of meeting unstated customer needs, or gaining an edge over its competition, increase?" "Social Media for tuning into Voice-of-Customer" could fall in this category. And by the way, this is a moving target. When something is no longer a clear differentiating edge but an operational need (say due to everyone else adopting it), its weight changes from 3 to 2! In the highest weight category are the technologies without which your *strategic goals* could be compromised. "Customer Experience Management", "Business Support Systems (Like Billing & Payments)" and like technologies would obviously be in this weight category. Similarly, for a banking enterprise, "Multi-factor cybersecurity platform" would be right here. *Despite this classification, you may frequently have to make judgment calls for assigning weights. Stay with them – they usually work. If in doubt, choose the highest weight category.* For example, "cloud-based access to business apps and data" may be relevant from the perspective of 2 as well as 4. Choose *4* here.

The weights which have been assigned above in the example list pertain to an enterprise in the *banking industry-segment*. Depending on the environment the weights may be reassigned because what is strategic to one may be simply an efficiency booster for another, and vice versa.

Similarly, a classification may help in assigning *scores* to each technology element in a less ambiguous manner. Many possibilities exist for assigning scores to each technology, but again, there is no strict formula that would be applicable in every situation – just like for *weights*. You may create your own truth table for score assignment, an *example* of which is given here:

0	Does not exist currently, nor on the roadmap for at least one year.
1	Does not exist currently, but on the roadmap and budget for deployment in next one year
2	Under development or deployment, but not yet tested or moved to production environment
3	Launched and deployed for business operations for < 6 months
4	In active operation for over 6 months, but not upgraded to latest version of the technology
5	In active operation for over 6 months, presently running latest version of the technology

Using this classification, the scores have been populated in our technology list. Having come this far, the derivation of the **Technology-adoption index** (or TAI) is just a simple arithmetic task.

Step-1: Add up all the individual *weights* (w) in the list, to get $\Sigma(w)$. Here, $\Sigma(w) = 155$.

Step-2: Take the product of the weight and score (w * s) in each line (this is not shown in our table)

Step-3: Add up all the individual line-wise products, to get $\Sigma(w * s)$. Here, $\Sigma(w * s) = 439$

Step-4: Calculate the weighted average score, as $\Sigma(w * s) / \Sigma(w)$ which is 439 / 155, or 2.83

Step-5: Compute TAI as (weighted average score) / 5, which in this case is **0.57**

This method generally yields a TAI of 0.70 or less even for enterprises that are well advanced in their tech journeys. A target of around 0.60 is considered quite ambitious here.

While the *industry-specific* technologies are unique to each industry segment, the other technology sets (like digital) are quite universal. It should, therefore, be possible to standardize the list and arrive at a *global benchmark index*. Though this would be a somewhat challenging task, it would have the rich paybacks of creating a universal scale on which enterprises can measure their Technology-adoption index and hence benchmark themselves on an industry, national or global level. That said, the *industry-specific* technologies cannot (and probably should not) get overlooked. If you are a *software company*, for example, you may like to include various development languages (like C, C++, Java), technologies (like Object-Oriented, .Net), tools (like Rational, ASN.1) and methodologies (like Agile) that give you a sharp edge. Or, if you are a *manufacturing firm*, you may like to include shop-floor automation technologies, CAD/CAM and Inventory tracking systems, among others. The TAI may thus be synthesized as a *global index* which encompasses universal technologies, and an *industry index* which covers vertical technologies, as a useful measure of the enterprise's overall technology readiness.

Let us summarize what we finally have on the IT *Benefits* scorecard, from the above computations. Usually, the benefits indices are reported against agreed targets. The component indices are averaged (weighted or linear) to arrive at the composite IT benefits index.

SN	Index	Weight (%)	Target	Actual
1	Customer Engagement (CEI)	20%	0.95	0.95
2	Delivery Efficiency (DEI)	15%	0.95	0.88
3	Operations Health (OHI)	15%	0.95	0.84
4	Economic Contribution (ECI)	25%	0.90	0.91
5	Technology Adoption (TAI)	25%	0.60	0.57
	Composite IT Benefits Index		0.85	**0.82**

The scores above are taken from the earlier computations of individual indices, and the composite IT Benefits Index is arrived at by taking the weighted average of the scores. The weights are assigned arbitrarily here, and these can be tweaked to suit specific situations.

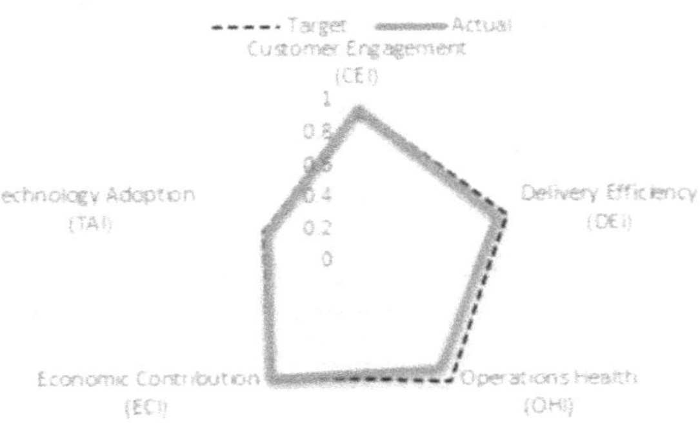

The individual indices and the composite index may be plotted every month in one of many possible ways. Personally, I have found the above representation to be quite useful in sparking the interest of Business and management alike, but you may choose whichever form of representation works best.

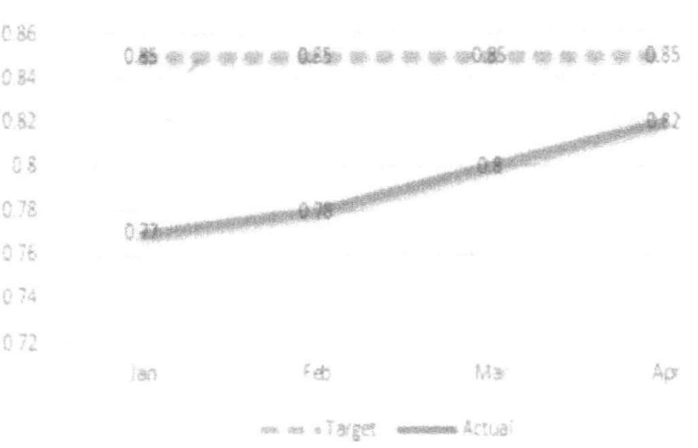

The Cost Factor

As important as it is to have a grip on the *benefits* of IT to business, on their own they fall short of determining the *value* of IT to Business. The *cost* at which these benefits were attained could curtail the overall value. And the cost is not only financial or monetary, but the sum of all the elements which

increase the overhead of doing business. A holistic approach to BVIT requires incorporating both the benefits and *cost* factor in the calculation.

The *Cost of IT to Business* is the sum of all the overheads associated with IT that business incurs to realize the targeted benefits. The most common categories of overhead costs associated with IT are the following. The focus of both Business and IT is, of course, to minimize *each* element of IT Cost to Business.

Examples of Cost Elements

Money	Spent on	Hardware, Software, Personnel, Outsourcing
Effort	Expended for	Access, Response, Speed, Flexibility
Risk	Accepted towards	Security, Compliance, Obsolescence, Regulation
Complexity	Dealt with	Structure, Policy, Process, Technology

On the highway that connects my home to the city, there is a toll plaza. This toll is a huge financial, physical and psychological barrier to the smooth passage of vehicles. Every time I need to drive up to town – which is often – I must cross this toll plaza. The place is a nightmare. The money to be paid per trip, while it adds up to a substantial amount monthly, is the least of the botherations. The delay – or the time cost – is a huge factor, particularly when one is on the way to the airport, railway station, or a doctor's appointment. There is no predictability. Crossing this toll may take anything from 5 to 50 minutes each way as the tail-back often stretches a kilometer! Then there is the chaos. With no proper queuing system, there's breakneck competition among unruly drivers of assorted vehicles – including huge trucks, buses, dumpers, cars, and taxis – to reach the tolling booth. It's the law of the jungle. Lastly, you must contend with rude polling staff who take your money as if they are doing you a favor, in their own time. The toll operator probably sees no incentive in improving things for the very people who keep his cash registers ringing, since he knows they have no choice. It's a matter of perplexity to me as to why the authorities are not taking any steps to dislocate this toll, which lies in an urban area. Be that as it may, it teaches us a few important lessons about the elements of cost. Clearly, the cost is not just monetary. In the above case, I for one would be glad to pay a handsome upfront amount for permanent removal of all obstacles to smooth passage. The toll here includes all the four cost factors outlined above, though in different ways, and then some!

> **Exercise:** *Think of your own IT function. While I am sure that things are not as bad as at the toll plaza in the example, there is always a price, other than the purely monetary one, that Business must pay to IT for reaching its goal. Can you identify these overheads? Not all the imposed toll may be intentional, but Business doesn't see IT the way IT sees IT. It is advisable to take this up as a serious exercise and list down all the intended and unintended 'costs' that Business must 'pay' to get through IT.*
>
> *As the next step, draw out a plan to bring down the IT 'toll' to the minimum possible level. You will see the Business Value of IT spiral steadily upwards just through this simple exercise.*

Staying with the exercise, can you *measure* these costs, or quantify them in a meaningful way? Unfortunately, most of the non-monetary costs of IT are based on experiences or perceptions and thus do not lend themselves to numeric computation. Devising nifty formulae or mathematical models to quantify them may, therefore, be misleading and counter-productive.

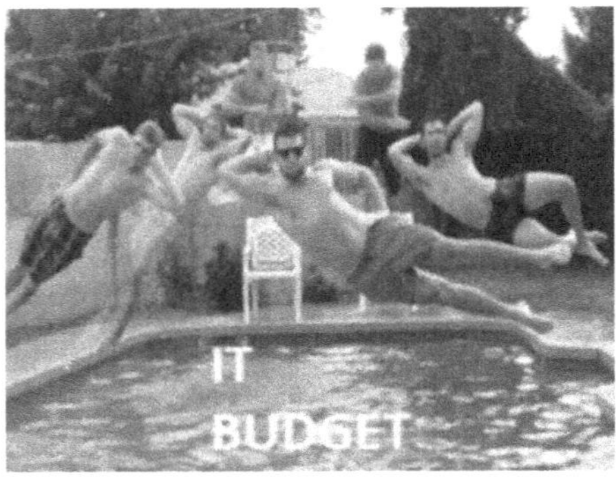

The monetary cost though can be measured, usually against the budgeted amount. Functional alignment requires that the IT budget is not a common pool for everyone to dive in, but a carefully prepared, *business-funded* plan. If you have, say, three business units, each of these units must know – beforehand – what the cost of IT is going to be for them, and they must *agree* to sponsor them. As its sponsors, BUs have a right to decide on how the IT budget is used. The days of unilateral spending by IT are gone. The IT budget for functions like HR, SCM, Finance is generally *distributed across the BUs* in some pre-agreed way (like revenue ratios). Business-aligned IT organizations make it a habit of reporting the IT spends against the budget monthly to respective BUs. Since IT spending directly impacts the bottom-line, the last thing any BU wants is "surprises" on the IT spending front. In all BITA-driven organizations, *IT does not own the IT budget. Business does.* The preparation of IT budget in conformance with business goals and priorities is a detailed science, but we won't go into this here. For now, let us just say that the overall spending against the *business approved* budget is a key measure of the monetary cost of IT to business.

(All amounts in USD Mn)

Business Segment	BU Revenue	% of Ent Revenue	Projects	Infra & Ops	Func Unit	IT Common	IT Budget Estimate
			DIRECT BU Costs		ALLOCATED BU Costs		
BU-A	120	35%	2.0	0.8	0.77	0.95	4.52
BU-B	68	20%	1.5	0.6	0.44	0.54	3.08
BU-C	152	45%	3.0	1.0	0.99	1.21	6.20
Function Units (Combined)	0		1.0	1.2			
IT Common (Opex + Capex)	0		1.2	1.5			
Enterprise	340		8.7	5.1			13.8

*(*Allocation of Function Unit's IT budget is done by distributing the FU budget across BUs in the same proportion as their revenues)*

The above table is an over-simplified view of an IT budget sheet. Broadly, there are two separate cost components from BU's perspective – the *direct* BU-related IT costs, and the IT costs that are *allocated* to BU for shared services. The costs incurred on IT by the common functions like Finance, SCM, HR (e.g., ERP), etc., as well as the common IT costs (like email, security, network, video conferencing, et al.) are usually *charged back* to BUs in some pre-determined ratio. In the above example, we have taken the ratio of revenues, but this could equally be headcount or some other attribute. The *allocated* costs are shown boxed inside the table. For simplicity, we have indicated the allocated costs as a single element, *not* bifurcated into operational costs (opex) which are sunk yearly, and capital costs (capex) which are amortized over several years. The intent is only to give a simple but realistic view of the broad contours of an IT budget.

In this case, the IT budget is 13.8Mn USD for the year, which is the aggregation of the IT budget (direct + allocated) of the three Business Units. This works out to about 4% of the revenue, which for most industry segments is within the ballpark. For tech companies like telecom and software, the ratio of technology budget to revenues could be higher. The *Monetary-Cost index* (MCI) is the difference between actual cost and budgeted cost, divided by the budgeted cost. Since costs *subtract* from the value, the MCI, like all other forms of cost, is ideally a negative quantity. The lower it is, the better. Let us say the measured expenditure on IT at the end of the year is 13.0Mn USD. In this case,

MCI = (Actual cost – budgeted cost) / (budgeted cost), or (13.0 – 13.8) / 13.8. i.e., **– 0.06**

In the case of other (non-monetary) cost factors, there is a much larger element of subjectivity due to which a direct computation is not feasible. The best way to determine the cost associated with these elements, viz Effort, Risk and Complexity, is to jointly develop a template –as we did for Technology Readiness – to obtain perception-based feedback from multiple stakeholders on the various elements of effort, risk and complexity of working with IT, on a scale of 0-5, where 5 represents the *least* effort, risk or complexity. The average of the scores under each 'cost' head across all respondents is computed to get the respective indices, as exemplified in the table below:

Attribute	Index Name	Scale (Max)	Average score	Index value*
Effort*	ECI	5	4.6	0.08
Risk	RCI	5	4.3	0.14
Complexity	XCI	5	4.0	0.20

Effort Elements (5=least effort)	
BA/SPOC Availability	5.0
Escalation matrix	4.6
Speedy Response	4.6
Flexible Policies	4.2

**Index value is computed as (Scale – Score)/ Scale.*

As the Score is always less than or equal to the Scale, the non-monetary cost indices are always positive (that is, they always take *away* from the overall benefits to *reduce* the value), or at best zero, unlike the Monetary-Cost index which *can* be negative, as we saw.

Cost Component	Weight	Index
MCI (Money)	40%	-0.06
FCI (Effort)	20%	+0.08
RCI (Risk)	25%	+0.14
XCI (Complexity)	15%	+0.20
Composite Cost Index (CCI)	**100%**	**+0.057**

The estimation of Business Value of IT (BVIT) is a useful means of assessing the role and contribution of IT to Business in the Digital Age, though the specific method you choose to do so may not be exactly aligned with above sample process. The important thing is that both, the benefits and the cost, must be recognized as constituents of value, rather than benefits alone which unfortunately has been a de facto trend. If you are targeting greater benefits, the cost is usually higher too, as life has taught us in all its walks. Let us take a quick look at the composite cost index in our sample above, and see how it impacts the overall value.

The Composite Cost Index is obviously the sum of the weighted cost indices. It is worth noting that theoretically at least if you can control your monetary costs well within the budget, you may be able to offset the adverse impact of other factors (and vice versa!). Ideally, though, control on each cost factor as an independent contributor should be the aim for an all-round 'feel-good' that goes beyond numeric derivation of value.

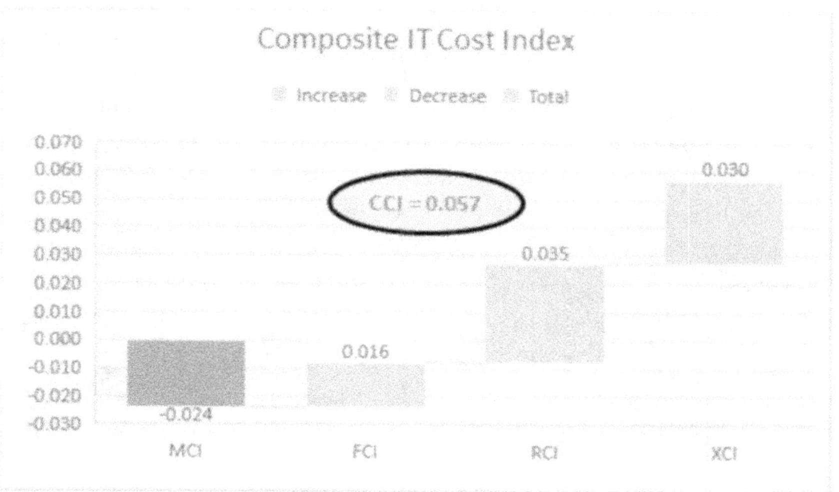

Our overall CCI here is +0.057. This quantity will be taken off the benefits index to arrive at the overall Business Value of IT. As an Index, BVIT is commonly expressed as:

Composite BVIT Index = Composite IT Benefits Index – Composite IT Cost Index

In our sample case, Composite Benefits Index is 0.820, and the Composite Cost Index is 0.057. Therefore,

BVIT Index = 0.820 – 0.057 = **0.763**.

There is no universal BVIT benchmark scale, but in general, a score above 0.65 is considered acceptable, though the more important thing is the *trend* seen over time. If you are moving steadily upwards, it is a better sign than having a relatively higher score that is stagnating, or worse, plunging, over time.

I have often come across the question on the *need* to measure Business Value of IT as a numeric index. After all, if Business is running to plan, and Business and IT are not getting in each other's way, why complicate life by bringing in another parameter to be tracked? Well, for one thing, though the final index as we defined it above is reduced to a numeric value for the sake of comparative assessment, BVIT is more than just a number. It considers many of the *experiential* factors that influence IT contribution to business value creation. It takes both objective and subjective assessment into account to get an idea of IT's overall role in assuring business success while highlighting the individual focus areas - just like a customer feedback survey result, which is a numeric average of opinion-based inputs, but also points to the specific traits that must be focused on for improvement. So with BVIT measurement, except that BVIT is more scientific. BVIT assessment is not only founded on perception-based survey inputs but on direct measurement of business-impacting IT parameters as we saw in our sample. Secondly, if you are in acceptable BVIT range, the chances are good that you will *avoid* some of the fallouts of lack of functional alignment between Business and IT, which are often the root-cause of business failure. The following signals, among others, could point to missing or diminishing value of IT to Business:

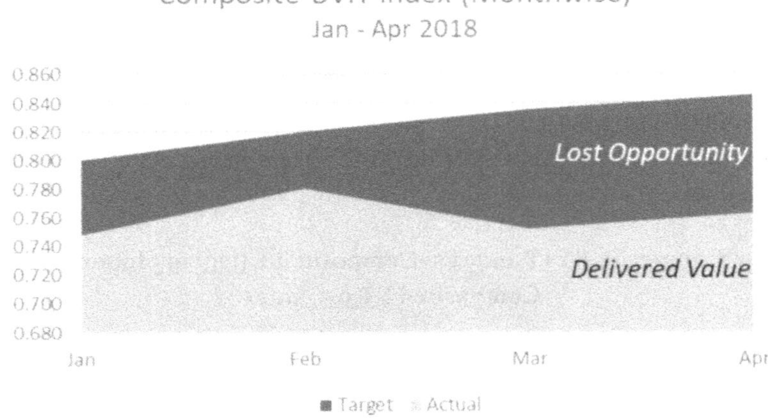

1. Too much money being spent on IT-related items.
2. Lack of visibility into IT costs and outlays (IT costs are an eternal enigma for Business).
3. Unsupportive IT policies, e.g., constraining stance on IT security, software usage, etc.
4. Digital divide within the enterprise (wide gap in technology adoption across functions).
5. Inability to find or reach the right person in IT to get timely solutions to Business problems.
6. Building products/services that no one wants to buy.
7. Launch of new products/services frequently delayed, leading to lost market share.
8. Failure to execute on technology initiatives (e.g., Digital marketing campaign).
9. Insufficient adoption of Social Media and Mobility for Business.
10. Virtually nil instances of IT-led upsells.
11. Archaic processes that have a constraining rather than liberating impact on Business.
12. Missing or inadequate governance structure for Business-IT engagement.

All these (and several more) are direct fallouts of weak or missing functional alignment between Business and IT. The question is, would you rather wait for some of these to show up before you institute systems to track BVIT, or be *proactive* in making BVIT measurement a part of your BITA strategy to *pre-empt* these?

Measuring BVIT is an effective way to gauge the ability of Business and IT to create value together. It is not a rigid process, being amenable to construction according to the specific needs and priorities of an enterprise. You must ask yourself what is important and then weave this into the BVIT measurement. Another good thing about BVIT is that you do not have to wait for a "perfect" setting to initiate it. You can start small, and build gradually to reach higher and higher levels of maturity. It is a continuous process.

There are organizations which have successfully taken the measurement of BVIT from a concept to reality, and as you read this, are in the process of perfecting it to become an accurate barometer of functional alignment. In this chapter, we have used a simple case study to help with constructing and measuring business value of IT in a deterministic, quantifiable and practical way. As many enterprises are still not using a formal method for BVIT assessment, there is an excellent opportunity for you here to get a lead. I hope this chapter can provide the necessary impetus to seize this opportunity.

15 The Tactical Touch

"Strategy without tactics is the slowest route to victory. Tactics without strategy is the noise before defeat".

Let me begin with another old but still relevant story. These were very nascent days of the computer age, somewhere in the mid to late 1980s. Every computer then was a standalone universe unto itself, and the concept of 'networking,' leave alone the Internet, was largely unheard of outside the research and academic world. I was called to attend to a service problem in the minicomputer system at the remote plant of an industrial business house. Getting there (at that time) involved taking an overnight train to the nearest rail station, and from there if you were lucky you got a cab, else, you had to bus it to the vicinity of the plant. The bus dropped you off at a point on the highway which was 6-7 km away from the plant, so the customer had to send a vehicle to pick up its visitors from here. As this was before the mobile/email era, precise coordination was key. I arrived at the plant in the early afternoon, ready to investigate the reported technical problems. As soon as I came in, I was escorted to the office of the plant manager who was apparently not big on small-talk and came straight to the point: did I come ready to deploy the operating system upgrade which was necessary to run his new material-accounting software? I had no idea of this, and more to the point, their hardware was *not supportive* of the new operating system version that was being asked! Turned out that a fortnight ago, our sales manager had visited the plant and when he was apprised of the material-accounting issue, had promptly promised that he would get it fixed by upgrading to the new operating system during the next visit of 'my engineer.' Either the sales guy was blissfully unaware of the limitations of the systems he sold for a living, or he had just parachuted himself out when the going became turbulent. Which I could fleetingly sympathize with because being at the receiving end of the plant-manager's outburst, I can imagine the situation would have been quite nasty for the sales manager.

The issue here is not just that I was caught unawares and subjected to rough treatment. In hindsight, it was perfectly understandable from the customer's point of view. Visits from vendors to this remote place were few and far between, so there were higher expectations from each visit. Plus, he felt let-down by the company's unkept promises. It was bad enough that the sales manager gave false commitments. But not giving even a hint to prepare me for the situation was worse. This when we both worked out of the same office in Delhi, and our seats were just across the aisle from each other! We even had lunch together on many days! This incident led to a serious escalation to the customer's top management, and this being a national account, the top management of our company also got involved. But with all the restoration efforts, the cracks in our credibility were never fully repaired.

To say that such incidents do not occur in today's era of digital business would be economizing with the truth. The style and form are now different, since the channels of communication now permit only a behind-the-scenes interaction with customers for the most part. Whether it is the automated IVR or an executive interaction that set the expectation, your record of *delivering on promises* to your stakeholders defines you much more sharply than your mission statement, technology focus, structure, and processes, or advertisements. The core issue is the *alignment* between Business and IT to uphold the credibility which is built not on promises made, but on *executing* on the promises.

Tactical alignment is about Business and IT locking step for executing not just on the larger company strategy, but on all the explicit and implicit promises to the customer at various moments of truth. In short, it is about *walking the talk.* In today's world of digital business, tactical alignment implies that Business and IT are complementing each other in the execution of the digitization strategy to deliver a superior experience to their customer *throughout the lifecycle*. An environment which promotes open communication to keep Business and IT always in sync is critical to sustaining tactical alignment. The IT systems and infrastructure must be designed to consistently ensure an outstanding customer experience aligned with, or exceeding, the aspirations built through the various touch points. This means that Business is not only aware of IT capabilities and

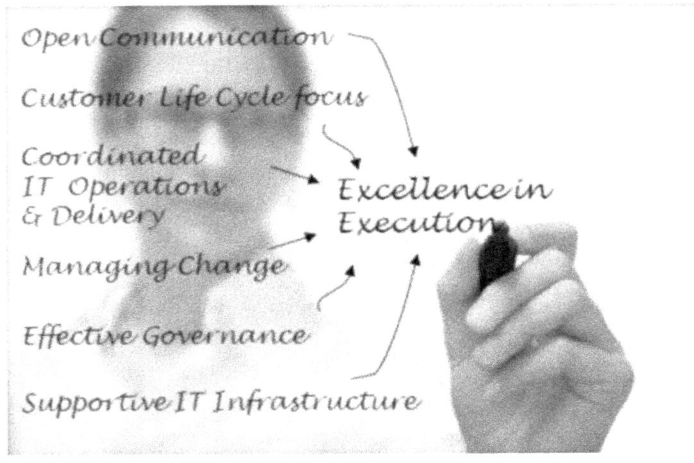

limitations, but is also willing to sponsor changes and enhancements in keeping with the rising customer expectations.

I am not sure if you noticed, but all the characteristics in the illustration above are *qualitative* attributes, not given to precise measurement or the attainment of a *perfect* state. This means that irrespective of where you currently are on the execution curve, you can probably do it better. The following example will hopefully clarify this, by showing that complacency can be catastrophic.

A global technology consulting company that I once partnered with prided itself on its fervent attention to planning and preparation for executing a project. They spent a lot of effort and time in developing an execution plan document that went through multiple layers of review before being approved for roll-out. Not only did this consider the obvious factors like resources and methodologies but also subtler aspects like the adoption of best practices and future-proofing. To all intents and purposes, the model was iron-clad, giving a vivid impression of impeccability. Every conceivable process was boiler-plated and when this company presented its smartly turned out power-point slides attesting to their efficacy, it left no doubt in our mind that we were gaining an infallible partner.

And yet the first project that we co-executed with this company for a prominent client of ours failed. Well, to be fair they were indeed new to the Indian market conditions and probably not quite in the groove with the cultural mores. However, I believe that this was just a convenient excuse. I have worked with many companies on both sides of the divide and am not convinced that one would fail in its very first project in the country for such a reason. If anything, the new company would be inclined to try even *harder* to succeed in a new market. No one just enters a market without a thorough pre-assessment!

Too much rigidity of processes and policies is often at cross-purposes with the goals of tactical alignment. Intuition, anticipation and discernment are some of the unwritten qualities that lead to successful execution. In our case, these were not demonstrated adequately enough by our partner to address the needs of this complex project. Instead of taking a spot decision to accommodate a minor change-request, if you must seek approval from someone far removed from the project, often in another continent, it's an open invitation to failure. The ability to think on your feet and the empowerment to decide and act are as essential to tactical alignment as your time-tested processes and policies.

To cut a long and sordid story short, it was a case of choosing process over perspicacity, and firmness over flexibility, that led to the debacle. When a customer change request was received, it was first resisted, and then reluctantly sent to the headquarters for 'exception approval.' The decorum and form of the governance meets – which I felt were just check-in-the-box affairs anyway – barred such requests to be brought up to the notice of senior folks in our Business and IT teams early enough.

There was no proper local system of handling exceptions and escalations, probably because of the confidence in the efficacy of the regular processes. Hence, an issue could be brought up only in the *next* governance meet a month later! In my 20/20 hindsight, I can assert that the cumulative effect of their processes was a sturdy mill-stone around our necks. If we go back to our illustration of the factors leading to excellence in execution, the apparent weak links, in this case, were (1) **Change Management** process that considered the T0 baseline to be inviolable, and (2) **Governance mechanism** that did not adequately factor exceptions and timely escalations.

"I have not FAILED.
I've just found
10,000 WAYS
that won't work."

I am sure that cases bearing striking similarity to the above have dotted your experience as well. Blind adherence and noble intentions, even when backed by time-tested processes and proven technology, are apparently not sufficient to guarantee successful execution. There is far too much dependence on things happening according to a script, which, as we have all learned – mostly the hard way – is a deceptive notion. Tactical alignment requires us to be inventive and ***make*** things happen. *Together*.

Let's see how we can do this. Firstly, it is important to remember that tactical alignment is the only dimension of BITA that is *visible* to your customers and other stakeholders. That is, *tactical alignment is the showcase of your business.* I would not go to the extent of saying that tactical alignment alone matters to customers, but it certainly is the fastest way to build perceptions about your company. Too many good practices and intentions have fallen by the wayside due to weak or missing tactical alignment. This may be avoided if Business and IT are synchronized in their responses to the set of questions displayed here.

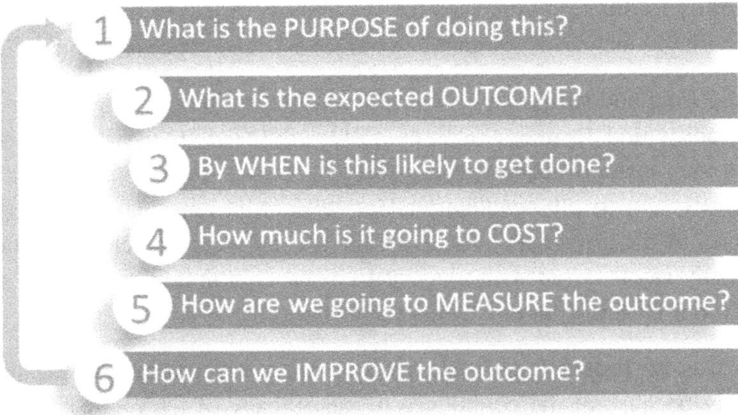

1 What is the PURPOSE of doing this?
2 What is the expected OUTCOME?
3 By WHEN is this likely to get done?
4 How much is it going to COST?
5 How are we going to MEASURE the outcome?
6 How can we IMPROVE the outcome?

These questions broadly apply to most tactical assignments like order fulfillment, service incident resolution, pre- and post- sales consulting, project delivery, etc. I have found this simple questionnaire to be very useful in gauging tactical alignment. The question where I have seen the maximum divergence between Business and IT is ironically not about the cost or schedule (Q 3, 4) but on Q2, i.e., the expected OUTCOME of the assignment. For example, if a customer module (application or server) goes down, Business and IT may agree that the immediate *purpose* (Q1) is to bring the module back into service. But the targeted *outcome* from an IT perspective may be *resolution* of the problem (fix), whereas from a Business perspective it may be the prompt *restoration* of the service (workaround), before resolution. Strong formal and informal communication channels are essential to achieve synchronization. Related to the question of defining the outcome unambiguously, is the need to agree on how to *measure* the outcome (Q5). In the best BITA traditions, Business and IT must achieve harmony on all questions *before* the assignment. But sadly, in a rush to douse our daily fires, we ignore this, bringing our conflicts into the open – right in the customer's view. Here was an opportunity to showcase ourselves in a positive light and instead of seizing it we tragically squandered it, diminishing our prospects. Also, notice that it is a *continuous* loop. After achieving the targeted outcome, Business and IT agree on the way to improve the outcome and the cycle gets repeated.

> **Exercise:** *Take any major project or service that is being rendered by your company to a customer. Ask these 6 questions to relevant folks from Business and IT and compare the answers. Was there agreement on all the answers? If not, which are the key areas of divergence between Business and IT (You may run this for several assignments to confirm the diagnosis)? How can the gaps be minimized?*

If there is an agreement between Business and IT to a fair extent on these six simple questions, chances are that your customers view you in a positive light on your tactical approach to their issues.

Tactical alignment does not occur in only certain pockets of the customer experience lifecycle. It is embedded in every stage of the customer's interaction with the product or service provider. It is important to note here that while your tactical maneuvers are in the customer's line of sight, tactical *alignment* is, in fact, constructed and tempered deep within the nucleus of the enterprise, emanating from its cultural core. From here it spreads to each facet of the organization's persona, in both spirit and action, culminating in an effulgence that reflects in every stage of the customer lifecycle (CLC).

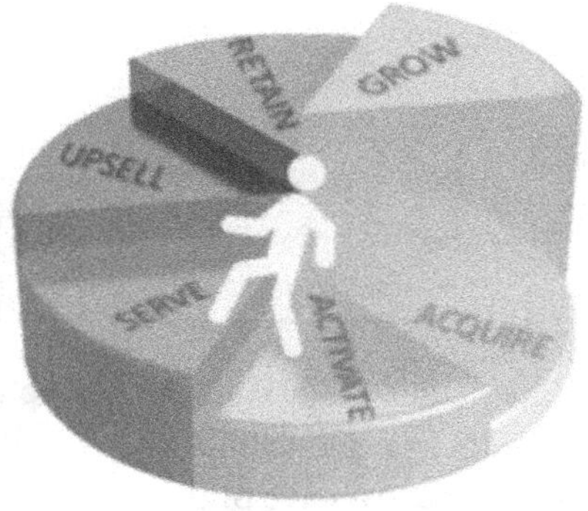

The typical CLC stages are depicted in the figure here. Your actions as a company at *each* of these steps are openly visible to your prospects and customers, and hence have a direct and considerable influence on building perceptions about your company. The only tool at your disposal for avoiding a misstep is tactical alignment between your Business and IT functions, the importance of which is growing in line with your transformation to a digital enterprise. The CLC steps are very steep and slippery, and tactical-alignment is your handrail. Let us look at the salient features of each CLC stage, as it applies in the new age of digital business.

	CLCStage	Actions (examples)	Digital Drivers and Tactical Tools
1	**Acquire**	Lead generation and profiling	Marketing & Promotions, Digital channels
		Customer inquiry (RFP) and response	Needs assessment, Advocacy
		Sales communication and closure	Feasibility analysis, Order-logging
2	**Activate**	Order processing	Automated workflow, orchestration, ERP
		Allotment of services	Tool-based aggregation and provisioning
3	**Serve**	Order Fulfillment	Delivery, Customization and Activation
		Incident tracking and management	Customer Experience Management System
		Service response tracking and analysis	Voice-of-Customer (VoC) and SM analytics
4	**Upsell**	Personalized offerings	Market Segmentation, Targeted campaigns
		Service/Product upgrades	Personalized Offers, Cloud-based models
5	**Retain**	Customer Analytics	Data mining and modeling, Big Data tools
		Loyalty Management	Sentiment Analytics, Loyalty programs
6	**Grow**	New product/service (Co-) development	Incremental, iterative, Agile cadence;
		Customer advocacy, referrals	Trusted Advisory, SM analytics, Collaboration

Exercise: *List the actions under each CLC stage as applicable to your industry. Which stages of CLC are Business and IT teams in your company* ***not*** *perfectly aligned in? In such stages, what are the specific reasons for misalignment? What steps must you take to align on these?*

The essence of tactical alignment lies in the realization – and demonstration – that Business and IT are not bifurcated in their responsibilities towards executing on the expectations of their stakeholders at any stage of the lifecycle. Gone are the days when the business (or "sales") team would deceptively win an order and then expect the IT (Delivery) teams to execute it somehow, while both the Business and IT teams were fully aware of the absurdity of the deal, as this story exemplifies.

A group of adventurers once went on an expedition into a thick forest. While crossing a river, their boat capsized. They all managed to swim to the safety of the river bank, but lost their supplies, including food and gear, except for some basic items like knives, lighters, etc. which were in their pockets. They made rudimentary arrangements to camp until help arrived, which they knew could take days. Their biggest problem, of course, was food, of which there was nothing in sight. From a soggy map that one of the members was carrying, they discovered that this was wild boar territory. They decided to make sharp spears to hunt boar. One of the members announced that he knew a thing or two about boars: they were stupid and docile creatures and would make easy prey. He suggested that half the people team up with him to go boar hunting (as the 'hunters'), while the other half stay back as the 'supporters', to defend the turf and prepare to cook the boar which the hunters were confident of bringing in.

Truth be told, wild boars are extremely dangerous to hunt. They are equipped with thick, razor-sharp tusks and are one of the most intelligent animals on earth. An adult boar weighs-in in excess of 600 lbs. and exhibits extremely aggressive and unpredictable behavior.

A couple of hours after setting off on the hunt, the hunters returned. But not as expected. One of the hunters was on the back of a wild boar desperately wanting to eject himself, while another was being dragged while clinging on to the charging boar's tail, and the others were nervously running along with the party in various defensive postures. They were clearly disoriented and seemed visibly relieved to suddenly find themselves near the supporters, who had a fire burning by now. As soon as they were close enough, the lead hunter – who had rallied the team behind him earlier – announced to the waiting team, now looking rattled and confused, "Here, take this one. It's all yours. We are going back into the forest to bring in the next one." The guy on the back of the boar jumped off and the one being dragged at the tail released the tail, and off the hunting party went, tossing their screaming, roaring and fighting-to-be-free 'victim' to their stunned, unsuspecting, and clueless friends. I don't know the rest of the story, but it probably didn't have a happy ending, at least for the hapless supporters.

Can you spot the relevance of this story to our discussion? The story is unfortunately evocative of the general pattern of working in more companies today than you would imagine. As market competition intensifies, so does the urgency to win business and with it the propensity to overlook the execution angle. In fact, business folks often sermonize about how difficult the market is and therefore the execution teams are *expected* to accept the aberrations that resulted from over-commitment, and 'find a way' to deliver. Many real estate developers, investment brokers and travel agents among others have been known to promise the world to get your order somehow, but when it comes to execution, it is a completely different set of people, who may be well-meaning but are just as flustered as you about how to handle your legitimate requests. The situation is not very different with enterprises in most other sectors. To be fair to the sales folks, it does indeed require exemplary courage to walk away from a lucrative deal only because of the risks associated with execution.

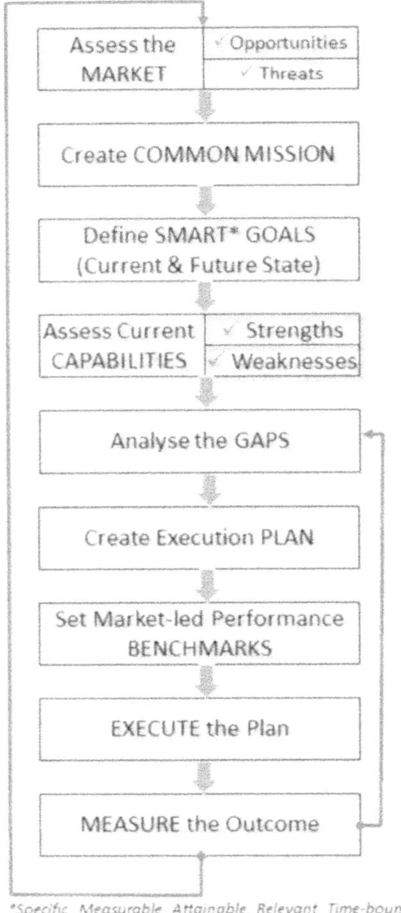

The flip side of the coin is just as sticky. If you accept the order, you are extending an open invitation to early dissonance among the three main participants of the customer lifecycle– Business, IT and customer. It is possible that our story involving the wild boar somehow ended happily for all parties concerned. However, I have never seen a satisfactory end to a narrative that involved a chasm being created between Business and IT early in the customer lifecycle. With time, it only grows.

Obviously, we must find a way out of this quandary. We can neither give up on business nor execution. The only way is to harmonize the two. And this further underlines the role of BITA, particularly on the tactical dimension. Execution is a critical component of tactical alignment, but tactical alignment goes beyond pure execution.

Business and IT must strive for harmony during the *build-up* to execution to assure consistency and predictability in the execution.

The simple flowchart here depicts the various steps *in each CLC stage* that precede or follow the execution stage for sustained tactical interlock. As can be seen, bypassing the preparatory steps and jumping directly to execution could be a recipe for failure. Such an action may result in accidental execution success sporadically, but never in tactical alignment.

At this point, it is essential to reiterate that tactical alignment is about being aware of and executing on commitments to customers (and other stakeholders) on behalf of the *organization*, irrespective of whether they were made by Business or IT. To achieve tactical alignment, it is important to remember that the customer identifies you as the *Company*, not as IT or Business. *That distinction ends at the gate of your office building.*

Combining the above principle with our flow-chart, it is clear that tactical alignment can be assured only when Business and IT are *fully aligned on every step* of the flowchart. The biggest problem in businesses today is not the lack of a process (like the above flow-chart) for executing on their plans. The biggest problem is that the execution happens in silos. That is, the ownership of different steps of the flow-chart is *either* with Business *or* with IT, invisible to each other. This entails frequent hand-offs, and in turn regular conflicts and contradictions. In such a scenario, tactical alignment can never become a reality. This soon shows up in the business performance and the upshot is that companies spend a disproportionate amount of time trying to figure out what went wrong! Now, wouldn't it be far more productive if Business and IT spent the same (or perhaps less) time in aligning on all the process steps *before* the rubber hits the road? Companies that realized this and acted on it achieved a significant lead over those that did not.

Exercise: *Let us go back to the six CLC steps we identified earlier: Acquire-Activate-Serve-Retain- Upsell-Grow. Take each of these steps (one at a time) and apply this to the various steps in our Tactical Flowchart, top to bottom. Can you identify the areas where (1) Process does not exist, (2) Process exists but in isolation (i.e., Business and IT are not sharing the responsibility equally), and (3) Business and IT are well-aligned? Apply due corrective treatment to items in each bucket to tune up your execution fitness.*

As an aside, let us briefly go back to the story of our friends in the jungle. The tactical flow-chart helps us discover the flaws leading to the debacle in a more definite way, opening the path to timely corrective and preventive actions.

×*Assess the Market*: Our team did not do a proper assessment of the market (jungle) before embarking upon the hunting expedition. In the absence of market data, they went ahead based on some completely unfounded assumptions (like boars are docile and easy to hunt) which begged validation.

✓*Create a Common Mission*: The mission, of course, was survival and both teams were alive to this. The story highlights that while it is important to have a common mission, it is not sufficient for achieving success in execution.

×*Define Goals*: There were no clear goals other than *kill the boar* and *cook the boar*. These goals neither provided specific direction nor were aligned to the capability of the team. They could, for example, have increased their strength by hunting *together*, possibly for smaller specimen, making ropes out of vine creepers to trap the boars before spearing, with each member assigned his own responsibilities.

×*Assess Current Capabilities*: The team had no clue about the type of skills and tools needed to hunt wild boar. They proceeded based on speculation and baseless assumptions, which severely dented their ability to acquire the right tools and approach, resulting in complete failure.

×*Analyze the gaps*: Gaps result from the difference between your goals and capabilities. In this case, neither the goals were set, nor the capabilities assessed. Hence gaps obviously could not be analyzed, but it was apparent that they were in abundance.

×*Create Execution Plan*: After splitting into two teams, the hunters just bounded into the unknown jungle with ineffectual spears in no way matched to the requirements of the task. There was no discussion on creating an execution plan, or a back-up in case the plan failed.

×*Execute the Plan*: With nil planning and preparation preceding the execution, the project was doomed to failure. Barring a miracle, the chances of a successful outcome were non-existent.

While the going may still not have been easy, if they had worked according to some system – as in our flowchart – their chances of failure would have been minimized. Or, the process could have redirected the team to a *different* assignment – say hunting smaller animals that must come to the river during the day.

Our process/work-flow here has been over-simplified to cater to a broader sect. It is advisable that you spend some time to create a Tactical Flowchart best suited to *your* environment as a template for sequencing activities and determining pitfalls in execution, for *each* CLC stage.

Tactical basics in the Digital Age

From the jungle, let us now turn our attention to the digital world, a world where digital technology dominates all walks of life, including business. It's a fast expanding world, where the number of entities (applications, things, people) communicating amongst each other is growing exponentially, well beyond the human population. Here, the separation between the cyber and the physical is diminishing rapidly, disrupting existing ways of doing business while spawning new and unforeseen business models. New means, methods, and mechanisms are called into play, not only to make sense of it all but to enable enterprises to deliver a rewarding experience to their customers, as an instrument of survival. The question is, how do Business and IT leverage tactical alignment as a driver of enterprise growth in this altered landscape?

Well, here's the nub: The core principles of tactical alignment stay relevant in this digital world as well! All that has changed is the *tools*. When we look at the many tools at our fingertips today, it becomes difficult to imagine how business was ever conducted without these. But with all their advantages, these digital tools present the challenge of managing wide technological diversity in pursuit of shared tactical goals. *Digital technology platforms*, which enable a host of digital services to be provisioned quickly for delivering personalized experiences, are the bedrock of tactical alignment in today's world. While having 'one-off' digital features like tablet-based sales tracking system for the field force is a positive step, the real value is unlocked only when you can dynamically adapt and apply *different* digital tools in sync with the demands of the business. These demands may change rapidly and unpredictably. An attempt to develop and launch new tools from the ground up in response to every change would render you uncompetitive. A ready digital platform, on the other hand, enables quick creation, reconfiguration and management of digital services and is thus your redeemer in this digital world where speed determines your survival.

A digital platform refers to the apparatus for leveraging various digital technologies and their intersections amongst each other to create new business models, solutions and tools. The *Digital Technology Platform* allows for development and delivery of digital services by leveraging an array of component technologies, isolating the business from downstream complexities of arcane systems. The construction of the business models, applications and workflows, and the integration of the partner eco-system happens at the *Digital Business Platform*, using the convenient building blocks provided by the Digital Technology Platform, as *services*. Together, the Digital Technology Platform and the Digital Business Platform constitute the all-important *Digital Platform*. A digital platform allows enterprises to reap business benefits by speeding up the delivery of new digital services, leveraging Social Media, Enterprise Mobility, Cloud Computing, Big Data Analytics and Internet of Things (IoT).

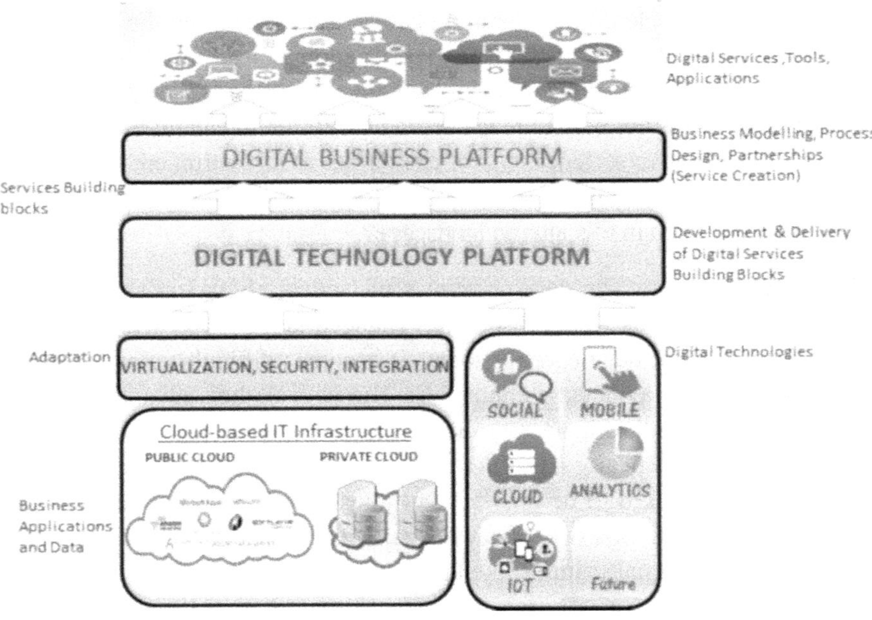

It will be a stretch to say that enterprises that do not have a distinct digital platform are barred from riding the digital wave. However, a functioning digital platform – real or simulated – meets the challenges associated with the launch and operation of digital services, e.g., short TTM, technical complexity, rapid changes and wide diversity (of software, hardware, devices, networks), a lot more efficiently to deliver a unique tactical advantage. The following advantages make a compelling case for its implementation:

(1) It increases the range of solutions by leveraging intersections between multiple technologies
(2) It facilitates standardization of digital architecture
(3) It offers interoperability with other digital platforms
(4) It supports solutions using components from different vendors
(5) It accelerates the digital delivery process

As important as they are, it may be difficult to distill the tactical relevance of these advantages and take them to the Board for seeking approval to the business case for a digital platform. In fact, it might even be seen as an attempt to somehow convince ("sell") by creating confusion. Indeed, it is not very straightforward to tie these advantages back to business benefits. In simple, more business-like terms, the cumulative advantages delivered by a digital platform, emanating from a combination of the above 'technical' advantages, are the following:

1 Creation of new revenue opportunities
2 Reduction in time to market by speeding the product/service development cycle
3 Improvement in customer engagement
4 Penetration of new markets
5 Faster turnaround of customer requests, better customer experience
6 Reduced long-term cost due to single platform for multiple services (e.g., multiple cloud-based offerings)

Surely, these are tactical matters (unlike those in the previous list of advantages) that are best served through close alignment between Business and IT. Before we take this further, it would be good to pause and reflect on their implications on our own organization.

> ***Exercise:*** *Can you identify the discrete digital tools and technologies in use for achieving business outcomes like the six listed above, in your enterprise? Are you currently achieving these outcomes to the maximum potential? Which of the listed outcomes would be better served through the deployment of an integrated digital platform in your organization?*

The above outcomes may not be too different from the targeted business outcomes of the *analog era*. But their achievement in the *Digital Age* is a function of two other critical attributes that were almost non-existent in the analog era: *adoption of digital technologies for business*, and *alignment of*

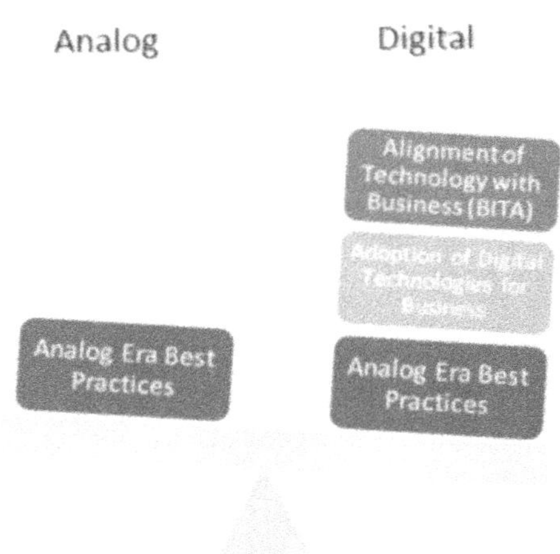

technology with business. Enterprises that show an unrelenting proclivity to embrace these in their tactics as best practices are the undisputed leaders in their domains today.

We have touched on digital technology earlier in this book. The goal here is to assess its *tactical* relevance in new age enterprises. In my experience, enterprises that have adopted the digital platform early have a clear edge in terms of speed and efficacy of operations over their more complacent rivals who await the next big thing (or worse, a catastrophe) to embark on this journey. And with time, the edge gets sharper. Adopting a digital platform in gradual but definite steps in line with the digital maturity of the enterprise is the first and perhaps most important step to tactical alignment in the digital world. I am sure that every enterprise would have its own tale to tell of its crusade to achieve execution excellence in the digital era, like the one below.

This story concerns a well-known company dealing with end-user software products and product-related services. The company has a well-established global presence as well as a sizeable operation in the Indian sub-continent. I was associated with this company as a close partner recently when we executed a systems integration project in a consortium. As one of their executives confided in me, it was a huge challenge to faithfully cater to the demands of the vast Indian market, without compromising on its global policies and practices. While this problem manifested in other geographies as well, it was of unique relevance in India given the sheer size and growth rate of the market. Obviously, it needed a more autonomous mode of working in India, while staying aligned with the larger organization whose brand equity it thrived upon. It was a challenge that affected its business as well as internal operations. To give just a couple of examples of the issues faced by the company, the Indian privacy laws prohibit keeping personal data on servers that were outside the territorial boundaries of India. Thus, the company was constrained in using its global cloud computing infrastructure in the service of the Indian market. Next, India now has good voice and data communication coverage across its length and breadth, but there are pockets of limited data connectivity, erratic electrical supply, etc. Applications designed for the Indian market, therefore, must cater to low and sporadic bandwidth environments, unlike in the more developed world. It represents a big opportunity but is also a tactical challenge.

The global company was quick to recognize that if it passed this opportunity, it would be seized by someone else. It decided to get cracking on this and get a lead over its competition. Some of the issues that the company identified for tackling in the *first phase* of its India Transformation Project were the following:

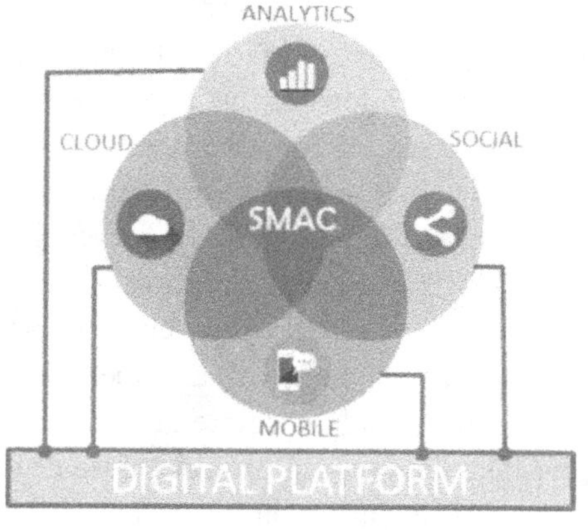

- Establishment of a local data cloud in India that leveraged the applications on its global cloud for the Indian market without transgressing privacy requirements.
- Segmentation of customers to personalize the offering based on customer profile and demographics.
- Making its mobile applications bandwidth independent and resilient.
- Conversion of messaging channels (voice and chat) to vernacular medium.
- Provision of enterprise-app enabled tablets to its field force to access critical market information and customer data on the go.
- Participation in the government's Digital India program by partnering on e-governance initiatives through its cloud and mobility infrastructure.

Given the size and scope of the work, the above can at best be termed a tentative start. But it was something. As you would not have failed to notice, these individual programs necessitated a continuous and robust bond between the company's Business and IT functions and the application of multiple digital technologies serving a single goal. The company developed a dedicated platform to deliver numerous business services using Cloud computing, Big Data Analytics, Social Media and Enterprise Mobility on a common foundation, viz. *digital platform*. Contrast this with the scenario where each service used a separate and disconnected silo for delivery. It would have guaranteed compartmentalization, inconsistency in performance and an inability to get a holistic view of markets and customers. For example, if the company was offering multiple cloud-based services, each service would have required a different cloud infrastructure and offered no way of unified data analytics to get a consolidated picture across services. In the long run, the cost pressures would have crushed business initiatives. Fortunately, the company had the vision of a unifying digital technology platform which it deployed in well-planned phases, and even today, as I write this, it is the undisputed leader in its market. In fact, some even think of it as a monopoly! Which it is not. It is just too far ahead for its rivals to be discernible over the horizon!

The schematic of the Digital Technology and Business platforms shown here is purely at a conceptual level. As with most illustrations in this book, details would take us into a dense and thorny territory, deviating from our chosen path. In any case, there is no standard topology that would apply in every situation, though there is some work in progress to standardize the digital *architectures*. However, it is the nailing down of the *details* that makes execution smooth and predictable. As everyone is not a technologist, the best approach is to use the conceptual framework for seeking consensus and approval, and then give the reins to the technologists to assess gaps and build, integrate and test the required components to achieve your digital mission as a project steered by stakeholders from both technology and business management functions.

A good question to ask at this juncture would be: The Digital Technology Platform is all very good and useful, but what is its relevance to our discussion on the *tactical alignment* between Business and IT? Well, the simple answer is that the adoption of diverse and disconnected digital technologies, working *independently* of each other, may turn out to be counter-productive to tactical alignment.

At a board level meeting of a book publishing company, a decision was taken to deliver a selection of books in the soft-version, that is, downloadable by the user on devices like Kindle. Of course, this is an inevitability that every book publisher is faced with to survive in today's world. Models have evolved to deliver the books through online retailers directly to user-owned devices. The online versions are of course, available at a much lower price than the paperbacks and hardcovers. Yet, since the 'production' costs are very marginal, it is a profitable venture. The big worry, of course, for publishers is piracy, which erodes margins and eventually renders the model unsustainable (Btw, I hope the same doesn't happen with *this* book!). The said publisher created an Online Books Division (OBD) in their company, responsible for promotion and sale of eBooks. They set up a secure cloud linked to online retailers' portals through which customers could browse the catalog, select, order, pay for and acquire the eBooks of their choice.

Now, the book business is heavily dependent on user feedback. Some books become best-sellers while other just languish on bookshelves. Of course, one indication is the briskness of the sales, but even then, publishers and authors depend heavily on qualitative feedback. Another division of the company, let's call it the User Contact Group (UCG), ran applications where any reader could independently upload comments after selecting a book from a list. These apps were mobile-enabled, storing user information and feedback on another public cloud set up by the company. To gauge sentiments from social media and understand reader preferences, the company had shown a great deal of foresight to set up a Data Analytics center. The idea was to base its promotional campaigns on the actual reader feedback in each demographic to boost revenue growth.

It was clear that this company was serious about using technology for business. It made the right moves, and probably spent a good deal of money on technology adoption, including consultants' fee. But there was a problem: Sales did not pick up, and hardly any book from this publisher made it to the top-10 list in any category through the year. Obviously, the company had failed to sense the user pulse and position its products right.

On deep diving into the root-causes, it was discovered that there was no correlation between the feedback received online from critics and readers through the UCG website, and the promotion campaign run by OBD. It appeared that the company was clueless about the sentiments expressed by readers and ended up over-selling the 'wrong' books and under-promoting the ones with excellent feedback! This impacted not only the business but the credibility of the publisher. Further analysis revealed that though the distinct digital initiatives were working well, there was no synergy between them as they were disconnected from each other. Feedback was received through countless channels spread across the country into the UCG site, but there was no way this could be seamlessly passed on to the Data Analytics group, and onward to the Online Books Division, which

had no structured feedback on which to base its promotions. Typically, when you know your aces, you take increased precautions to guard them. When you do not, your guard gets inadvertently lower, resulting in a spike in online piracy, which is what this company witnessed.

I have skipped some details, but the point is that the best digital technologies will fail to come to your aid if they are unable to collaborate with each other for a common purpose. This is where a digital platform comes in as an indispensable tactical tool to enable efficient usage and synergies across various technologies.

As exemplified above and in countless situations across industries, a digital platform is the bedrock of alignment in the Digital Age. It has particular relevance to tactical alignment which is concerned with achieving seamless execution by leveraging multiple technologies and applications of the Digital Age.

You may recall our flow diagram depicting the stages in *strategic* alignment. Let us follow a similar sequence to familiarize ourselves with the different stages of *tactical* alignment, this time taking the help of a hypothetical example to elucidate. Of course, both tactical and strategic alignment begin with the company's *mission and vision statements*. Further, tactics are a function of your strategy. In fact, they are the steps to execute your strategy. Thus, there can be no tactical plan without a strategy in place. Therefore, any depiction of the various stages of tactical alignment must include the strategic goals.

The example here concerns a non-profit start-up agency with the laudable goal of providing medical aid in the world's underserved areas, utilizing the fast-diminishing digital divide, smart devices, applications supporting medical diagnostics and monitoring, and a network of doctors and clinics in the shortest radius around the patient (aggregation). The example is meant only to illustrate the various elements leading up to execution. However, it showcases the appropriate sequence and the questions that Business and IT must answer *together* on the way to achieving tactical excellence in executing various CLC obligations.

Incidentally, this example of ubiquitous medical aid was prompted by the propagation of communication services across the globe. If we can provide unfettered *communication services* to everyone on the planet, why not the far more critical *medical aid services*? There must be a way.

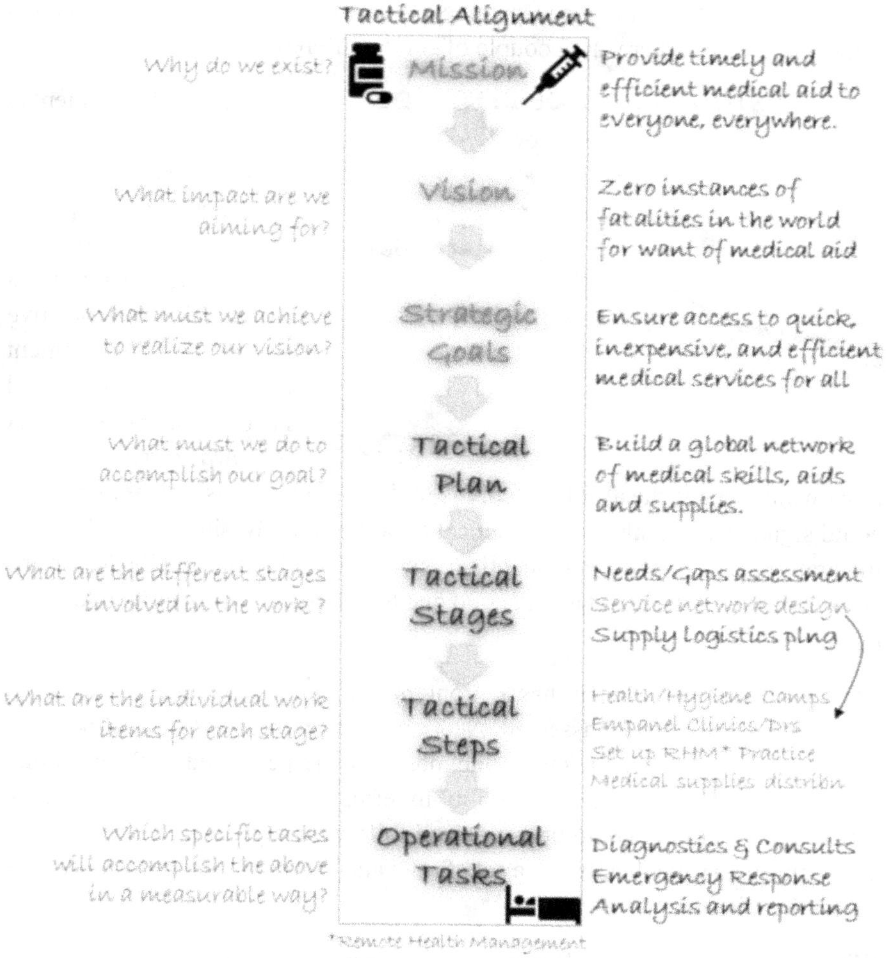

Tactical Alignment

Why do we exist?	Mission	Provide timely and efficient medical aid to everyone, everywhere.
What impact are we aiming for?	Vision	Zero instances of fatalities in the world for want of medical aid
What must we achieve to realize our vision?	Strategic Goals	Ensure access to quick, inexpensive, and efficient medical services for all
What must we do to accomplish our goal?	Tactical Plan	Build a global network of medical skills, aids and supplies.
What are the different stages involved in the work?	Tactical Stages	Needs/Gaps assessment Service network design Supply logistics plng
What are the individual work items for each stage?	Tactical Steps	Health/Hygiene Camps Empanel Clinics/Drs Set up RHM* Practice Medical supplies distribn
Which specific tasks will accomplish the above in a measurable way?	Operational Tasks	Diagnostics & Consults Emergency Response Analysis and reporting

*Remote Health Management

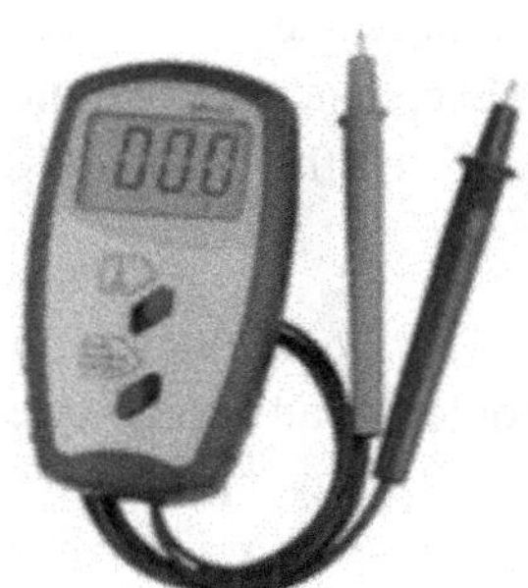

How do you measure tactical alignment? It may neither be possible nor required to reduce tactical alignment to a precise number. In our chapter on functional alignment, we discussed how the value created by Business and IT alignment could be tracked using several indices. These functional indices are also a good measure of the *tactical* alignment between Business and IT. In any case, tracking too many different parameters across various dimensions of BITA could fast become an overhead, outweighing the potential benefits. The attempt, therefore, is to unify measurement to the extent possible.

While we may track the same parameters as functional alignment to gauge tactical alignment, there are a couple of subtle differences.

First, tactical alignment is largely related to *trends*, rather than absolute measures. An upward trend on any of the measurement parameters is indicative of a positive tactical alignment between Business and IT on that parameter. A *downward* trend on the other hand, even if the absolute score is in the top bracket, is a clear alarm that could signal a weakening of the tactical bond between Business and IT. In the illustration, both lines point to identical scores currently (T7), but the lower line is indicative of a stronger tactical bond due to the mostly upward trend to attain this current level.

Secondly, tactical alignment has a strong *qualitative* component which cannot be measured but must be assessed. A lot depends on the spirit of trust between Business and IT, how their actions and intentions are perceived by the customer and other stakeholders, their credibility in terms of meeting commitments, the synchronicity of their communication and follow-through, etc. The best way to assess this is to periodically ask a set of relevant – sometimes tough – questions to test the alignment.

With the enhancement of Business Value being the aim, it is best that the questions to qualitatively assess tactical alignment are organized along the BVIT attributes, viz., Customer Engagement, Service Excellence, Economic Contribution and Technological Readiness, perhaps guided by the concluding discourse below.

Customer Engagement: Customer engagement is the key to long-term competitive advantage, being the primary driver of customer loyalty and hence sustained market leadership through positive references. Many progressive enterprises are discovering the value of engaging customers even prior to the sell-deliver-care cycle, by seeking participation in research, prototypes and pilots. Customer Experience Management systems are ruling the roost in a growing number of enterprises, tracking each interaction through the lifecycle.

Digital technologies like Big Data have effectively helped enterprises to reach the bottom of the pyramid and define systems to measure experience parameters at different stages of the customer's lifecycle, and then correlate them for delivering personalized support. These tactics are aimed at achieving one business outcome: increased customer engagement. Comprehensive tactical alignment requires that the facilitators for these programs are impeccably ingrained into the IT ecosystem.

Measuring and tracking customer engagement, both quantitatively and qualitatively, as a shared responsibility of both Business and IT, is going to be the key determinant of business success in the digital economy.

Companies with their finger on the customer's pulse have always had the edge over those without, and the world of digital business is no exception, even in mass market operations like telecom. If you are unable to relate to your customers' progressive expectations and experiences at every stage of the lifecycle, you clearly do *not* have your finger on the customer's pulse. You would do well to prepare an action plan and an assessment methodology (perhaps in line with the chapter on functional alignment) as your foremost priority. Remember, this is *three-legged* stool – Customer, Business, IT.

Here are a few sample questions for qualitative assessment of tactical alignment on the **Customer Engagement** parameter. The *equivalence* in the response from Business and IT is the determinant of tactical alignment between Business and IT.

1	Which activities are associated with each stage of the CLC [Acquire to Grow] in your enterprise?
2	Of the above, which are the top three contributors to (potential) disengagement of customers?
3	What actions would prevent the customers from disengaging with the enterprise?
4	What are the 3 significant changes in customers' expectations from your enterprise in last 2 years?
5	What are the steps taken by your company to meet these changing expectations?

If both Business and IT give similar answers to these questions or any other set of critical questions around customer engagement, it is an indication of good tactical alignment which could positively influence the business outcome. For example, if there is an agreed method of tracking and improving the experience, as in Q 5, the probability of customer retention is significantly higher.

Delivery Efficiency: Delivery Efficiency has the advantage that it lends itself to more credible quantitative measurement than customer engagement. Its tactical relevance is high, however, as it directly impacts several attributes of business and customer delivery. In general, Delivery Efficiency impacts the following business attributes (the term "product" here connotes both Product and *Service* offerings to customers):

1. Product features and performance (differentiation)
2. Product Quality
3. Time-to-Market
4. Standards conformance and interoperability
5. Scalability and upgradability
6. Extracting maximum value from IT spending

Each of these six attributes is a feature on the tactical landscape. As an example, *product quality* may not immediately strike as a matter of tactics, but it is an indicator of the rigor in user testing by the Business on the artifact developed by IT, and hence is a *tactical* outcome. In other words, if product quality is the reason for customer dissatisfaction, it is clearly a failure of *tactical* alignment. If customer feedback indicates disenchantment with the product quality and the same is not accompanied by a corresponding drop in Delivery-efficiency index, there is obviously a gap between perception and measurement. This further accentuates the need for *qualitative* assessment in ascertaining tactical alignment, even where numeric analysis is relatively straightforward.

The point of the above is that a failure to rise to your stakeholders' expectations could well be rooted in tactical misalignment between Business and IT, more so in the Digital Age. Of course, your culture, strategy, structure, spirit of innovation, etc. all play a part in customer value creation, but *they only set the stage* for the tactical show in which Business *and* IT are the lead performers. Like with any concert, it is not just the individual performance but the on- and off-stage chemistry between the leads that raises the level of enthrallment. That chemistry is called alignment.

Delivery is a back-stage function in many enterprises, left largely to IT. But *not* in digital enterprises. As delivery influences a range of critical business outcomes (see above), alignment between Business and IT is key here. Apart from regular DEI measurements and monitoring DEI trends as determinants of tactical alignment on the Delivery axis, some *critical questions* need to be asked to test for Business and IT being on a common platform qualitatively. These could include the following.

1	How is **change management** handled? What are the various tools/ stages involved?
2	Which stages of the delivery cycle are the biggest bottlenecks to efficient and timely delivery?
3	What are the steps required to eliminate or minimize these bottlenecks?
4	What is in the pipeline for future deliveries to customers/markets (including enhancements)?
5	What is the frequency and charter of *communication* between Business and IT on project delivery?

Again, the important point here is that both Business and IT, having equal stakes in delivery, provide matching responses to the questions such as above. A strong and shared grip on the *change management process*, which is core to delivery efficiency, now goes much farther in building positive experiences than previously imagined. Which stands to reason, given the pace of change in the Digital Age.

Operational Health: Operations are the most visible aspect of tactics. In fact, it is often considered synonymous with tactics. As we have seen, Operations is only one, albeit important, branch of tactics. Before the digital era, operations were primarily seen as an irksome but necessary overhead of the business. The digital era has shifted this from an overhead to an opportunity for gaining competitive advantage. In our context, if Delivery is concerned with *change*, Operations are what keeps the business *running*. A series of internal and external practices make up the Operations universe of the enterprise, as we discussed in the chapter on functional alignment. These practices are aimed at the attainment of some critical business outcomes which include the following.

- Fulfillment of the customer order (commissioning, configuration, etc.)
- Uninterrupted availability of Business and Operations Support Systems
- Efficient Incident Management (service restoration, problem resolution)
- Confidentiality, Integrity and Availability of critical data (security and privacy)
- Disaster Recovery and Business Continuity

Of course, Operations are also concerned with internal productivity initiatives like office communications and user support, but for this discussion, we are leaving these outside the purview of alignment between Business and IT at the tactical level. The Operations-health index (OHI) is a good barometer of operational efficacy (functional alignment) while its *trend* over time is an indicator of tactical alignment. The list of attributes adding up to overall operational health could be much longer than the list above, which is only an indicative sample. It is also dependent on the type of industry the company belongs to. For example, JIT would be a clear measure of Operations Health in a factory or manufacturing environment. The Digital Age is an era of Business-outcome driven IT operations as we discussed earlier in this book with examples from various industries. Therefore, alignment between Business and IT on the Operational axis is one the most critical success factors for Business. Enterprises where Operations are squarely and firmly in the purview of IT often get left behind in the relentless race and *never* reach their aspiration of transforming into digital enterprises. (Notice the emphasis on *never*)

Here too, apart from regular *OHI measurement* as a dipstick for operational health, it is important that Business and IT are aligned with each other in their responses to some qualitative questions, which could include the following (this is a sample list of questions only. It may vary from one environment to another).

1	Which operational parameters are being regularly tracked to monitor your business performance?
2	What are the major operational drawbacks responsible for sub-optimal outcomes?*
3	What is preventing your customer reps (or CC agents) from consistently meeting customer SLAs?
4	What are the top 3-5 actions required to overcome the problems found in Q2 and 3?
5	How does (or can) IT Operations contribute to giving a differentiating edge to your business?

[*E.g. In a firm I was briefly associated with, there was an archaic laptop policy where allotment of laptops was linked to salary grade, not function. So, a GM with an office job had a laptop whereas the sales guy on the road had a to contend with a desktop! And this was NOT in the 80s or 90s, but lately.]

Economic Contribution: The role of tactical alignment in direct economic contribution is best assessed by revisiting our definition of IT. As we have said at several points in this book, IT is not just the faceless, backend entity entrusted with fixing technical problems. IT has a much broader connotation. It encompasses pre-sales technical consultants, business analysts, system architects, project delivery and operations teams, technical specialists, information security officers, and of course, the end-user support organization, among other allied roles. The question is, in this era of technology dominance in business, can a company afford to ignore the combined potential of this invaluable pool to boost the economic performance? Structures and silos are often bigger bottlenecks in leveraging the full potential than skills and enterprising spirit, and the first tactical step is to loosen them. Forget about the 'dangers' of stepping on each other's toes and focus on enhancing economic contribution as your primary purpose. Economic contribution is an outcome that results from Business and IT working *jointly* on the following tactical endeavors:

Generation of opportunities, leads and prospects
Responding to business queries, RFIs
Market/Customer requirements analysis
Creating winning business proposals
Value Demonstrations, e.g., POC/POV
Technical discussions and follow-through
Closure and Contracting
Reference generation and Upselling
Creating an enabling environment – Sales automation (SFDC), Mobility, etc.

When we discussed Economic-contribution index in the context of functional alignment, we touched upon the direct and indirect contribution by IT to Business. As in the case of other tactical attributes, the numeric score here must be supplemented with a qualitative assessment to get a grip on the tactical alignment. However, I would put a higher weight on the numeric score here since this is ultimately about revenue and profitability. Nevertheless, some qualitative analysis would help determine if *both* Business and IT have some skin in the game and thereby if there is potential for upscaling the achievement. Business and IT team members' comparable response to the following *sample* questions will help ascertain this.

1	What are the different stages of the selling cycle in your organization?
2	In what ways *can* IT (in your organization) contribute to business generation?<refer CLC>
3	In what ways *does* IT (in your organization) routinely contribute to business generation?
4	What are the biggest drawbacks to Business-IT cooperation leading to the gap between (2) and (3)?
5	What are the required steps for filling these gaps to generate enhanced revenues in next FY?

These are again sample questions, which may not have universal applicability. But a set of questions for qualitative assessment on this parameter is possible for every environment. A combination of absolute ECI score, ECI trends and qualitative assessment could be your most potent mix for ascertaining the gaps and identifying the right steps towards realizing your full business potential as a digital enterprise.

Technology Readiness: Unlike Economic Contribution where results speak for themselves, the assessment of the tactical angle in *Technology Readiness* takes us into the nebulous territory. How do you gauge the extent of technology readiness, i.e., whether it is *enough*, or if it is *right* for your enterprise? Is a company exhibiting some impressive interactive displays in its front office, or using state-of-the-art electronic whiteboards in its meeting rooms, higher on tech readiness scale than a company which allows its employees to access the company Intranet from their mobile devices? There is no fixed answer. The tactical alignment on the tech readiness front is predicated not on how much or which technology is adopted, but in the spirit of *trusted advisory and thought-leadership that precedes and accompanies the adoption and use of technology for business*.

Tactical alignment here begins with IT continually scanning the market landscape and advising business on the right technologies to navigate that landscape. In far too many companies even today, Business charts the company's technological path independently while IT is only an implementer. That won't work now. IT must lead the technology adoption charge from the front in a modern digital enterprise. The role of IT is chief navigator through the complex technological maze that surrounds the business and often distracts it from its core focus. In other words, IT is the thought-leader on technology, advising and guiding the organization on the efficient adoption and use of technology. From a tactical alignment standpoint, Technology readiness is about Business and IT engaging jointly in the following activities:

Identifying the right technologies for business
Participation in technology solution design (promoting innovative solutions)
Embedding the technology in the enterprise ecosystem (competency and comfort in using the technology)
Promoting use of the technology for business
Calls on setting the sun on old technologies and shining the sun on new ones

Note that deploying and running the solutions and architecture (hardware and software) based on the adopted technologies (say cloud-based in-memory analytics solution) would fall under the purview of *operations*, not technology-readiness. In the chapter on functional alignment we studied an elaborate method of determining the Technology-readiness index, but as we said, a degree of qualitative assessment is required to complete the tactical perspective. Here are some sample questions to test for alignment between Business and IT.

1	Which technologies do you consider most important for your business today?
2	What are the key reasons for failure to adopt all the required technologies in your enterprise?
3	Which technologies are deployed in your enterprise but not fully leveraged for business?
4	Which critical areas of your business could be improved with the adoption of newer technologies?
5	Which technologies do you recommend for phasing out due to lost relevance or newer versions?

Adoption of the right technologies driven by a robust BITA is one of the defining aspects of digital transformation and ultimately your emergence as a successful digital enterprise. The good news is, you already have the potential to achieve this within your enterprise. It only has to be unlocked.

Before we leave the topic, a few words on the roadblocks to tactical alignment. Remember, the essence of tactical alignment is a spirit of camaraderie (*esprit de corps*) that binds the group to a common mission. This tenet sounds simple enough, yet most companies fail to realize their full potential just because they did not consider this an important enough part of their tactical approach. As a result, these companies are stuck in the pre-digital era, when functional independence – not *inter*dependence - was the success mantra.

I do not know the position of management schools on this, but in my own experience, the main inhibitors to tactical alignment between Business and IT are the following. Some are rooted in antiquated practices, and others in rigid mindsets. But with some effort, these can be overcome, yielding positive change.

1	Insufficient formal and informal **communication**
2	IT lacks **knowledge of the business challenges**
3	Business lacks **knowledge of IT capabilities**
4	Business does not have **confidence in IT**
5	IT is a pure **backend function**(at least in the view of Business)
6	Poor **IT leadership**, lacking influencing capabilities

7	Misaligned **strategic priorities**
8	**Tight KRAs** leaving no flexibility with individuals ["not my job"]
9	**Budget inadequacy** leading to failure to acquire/build right tools
10	**Antiquated IT infrastructure,** inhibiting the evolution of **digital platform**
11	Lack of alignment at the level of ***senior*** **Business and IT management**
12	Absence of a shared **sense of urgency** towards business priorities
13	Complex **IT organization structure,** buck-passing
14	Organizational **silos**
15	**Too much hierarchy**: "*Boss* has not directed me to do this, so why should I?"
16	**Lack of initiative** (read lack of **motivation**)
17	**Inertia** (resistance to change. Why me?)
18	**Inadequate partnerships/alliances** (unilateral selection, lack of involvement)

Tactical alignment does not happen in a flash. It evolves. And during the evolution, many of the above (and other) inhibitors will block your path. As you relentlessly move towards your vision in this backdrop, it is natural to miss your step occasionally. I am reminded here of a phrase from the famous HBO series, 'Westworld': *'Evolution forged the entire sentient life on this planet using only one tool – the mistake.'* The message is: You may falter, but that should only make you stronger.

Taken together, the seven dimensions of Business-IT Alignment create the platform on which the successful digital enterprise stands. As we have emphasized in this book, technology plays the lead role in digital transformation, but it is not a substitute for the *other* necessary ingredients in the digital cocktail. Technical superiority undoubtedly lends you an edge, but on its own cannot make you the frontrunner in the race to capitalize on the opportunities opened by the digital economy.

In my experience, enterprises that have enriched their *digital technology adoption* with all the *seven BITA dimensions* are the torchbearers of the digital economy. The combination imparts a winning edge that is hard to beat. Except for the tactical part, much of the BITA iceberg is invisible to us consumers. But the *winning attributes* of successful businesses are not. Check this out for yourself. Think of the many businesses that are trying to make their way through the digital ocean. While many struggle to stay afloat, some clearly stand out –the winds and the waves only making them stronger. What is it that sets them apart?

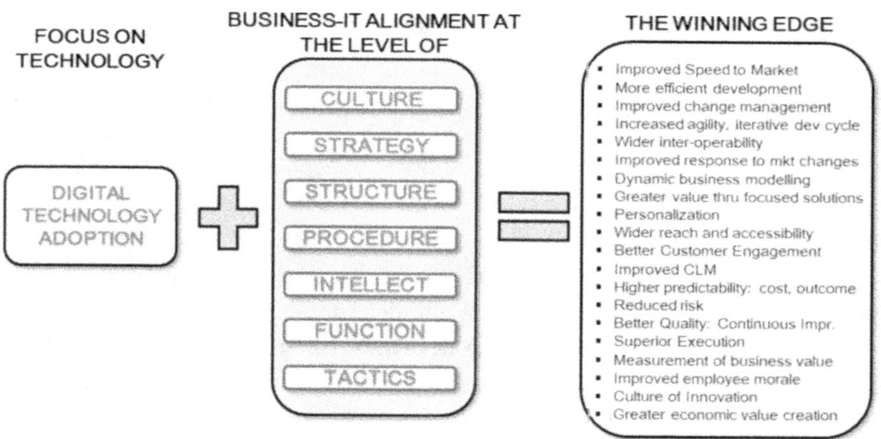

As a keen astronomy enthusiast, I seek answers to common problems in the cosmic intricacy. I am reminded here of the Kardashev scale, which is a measure of an alien civilization's level of technological advancement. There are 4 levels, graded on the *utilization of energy* by the civilization. A civilization that can harness all the energy of its *planet* is called Type-1, one which can harness all the energy of its own *sun* is Type-2, one which can harness the full energy of its own *galaxy* is Type-3 and – hypothetically – a civilization that can harness the energy of the *entire universe* is Type-4. (In case you are wondering, we Earthlings are still years away from even Type-1, reliant as we are on dead plants and animals [fossils] for our energy needs). If we had a similar scale for measuring an enterprise's progress in this Digital Age, I would vote that it is a function of the extent to which the combination of *Digital Technology* and *BITA Dimensions* is harnessed for meeting its business needs.

In the course of this book, we have worked on ways to assess or measure each of the attributes that must be harnessed to attain the winning edge. We measured the dimensional scores using the BITA Calculator earlier, and the *Technical Readiness* was ascertained through the BVIT measurement under Functional dimension. Using these scores, let us develop a simple scale for determining the Type number (out of 8) that your organization falls in. Here is a quick reckoner of our earlier scores for ready reference:

Tech Adoption	Culture	Strategy	Structure	Procedure	Intellect	Function	Tactics
0.57	0.55	0.44	0.56	0.24	0.36	0.21	0.28

In the absence of an industry benchmark score, set a reasonably high but attainable target score for each of the 8 attributes. To start with **0.55** is a good target for all attributes, though you are free to set different targets for each attribute. Now, for each attribute that you have scored *at least* the target, increase your Type by one. In the given sample, you are clearly a Type-3 digital enterprise. You may increase it singly or collectively each year and recheck your Type. Like Type-4 is a hypothetical level on the Kardashev scale, probably Type-8 on our digital maturity scale would similarly be a mite unrealistic. Unless of course, your cut-offs are ridiculously low. While determining your Type, your target on *Technology Adoption* must *always* be achieved. Thus, if your cut-off is 0.55 and you have achieved this for Technology Adoption and two other dimensions, you are Type-3 (as in the example). However, if you have crossed 0.55 on four dimensions, but your Technology Adoption score is less than 0.55, you are still Type-0. By the way, many companies start off their digital journeys as Type-0, so no need for alarm! The aim must be to keep growing.

The digital economy is predicted to gross over USD 1 Trillion by 2022. The proficiencies we have discussed in this book are among its primary drivers. These are going to be decisive in determining who wins and who falls by the wayside. Would you not make some simple investments in the right direction to acquire them *now*, rather than scamper to make course corrections later?

The aim of this book was to emphasize the need for Business and IT to align for taking advantage of the digital opportunity. Individuals and enterprises who have embraced BITA as an instrument of value creation clearly have the winning edge in the digital economy. The understanding of BITA and its infusion in the cultural, strategic, structural, procedural, intellectual, functional and tactical streams of the enterprise is, therefore, a matter of critical importance for a digital enterprise. The good news is that assimilation of BITA does not call for new skills to be acquired or concepts to be learned. It is just application of ideas and practices that we are already familiar with through our experiences and aptitude. The various views, examples, stories, and exercises presented in the book will, I hope, rekindle these to give shape to your aspirations as an individual and your vision as an enterprise.

List Of Acronyms

3-D	Three-Dimensional
AI	Artificial Intelligence
APAC	Asia Pacific
API	Application Programming Interface
App	Application
AR	Augmented Reality
ARPA	Advanced Research Projects Agency
ARPU	Average Revenue Per User
ATM	Automatic Teller Machine
B2B	Business-to-Business
B2C	Business-to-Consumer
BA	Business Analyst
BCI	Brain-Computer-Interface
BFSI	Banking, Financial Services and Insurance
BI	Business Intelligence
BITA	Business-IT Alignment, or Business-Technology Alignment
BPM	Business Process Management
BR	Business Requirement
BRS	Business Requirements Specifications
BSC	Balanced Score Card
BTS	Base Transceiver Station
BVIT	Business Value of IT
BYOD	Bring Your Own Device
CAD/CAM	Computer-aided design/Computer-aided manufacturing
CAF	Customer Acquisition Form
CBI	Composite Benefits Index
CCI	Composite Cost Index

CDO	Chief Digital Officer
CDR	Call Data Record
CEM	Customer Experience Management
CEI	Customer-engagement index
CEO	Chief Executive Officer
CIO	Chief Information Officer
CLC	Customer Lifecycle
CLM	Customer Lifecycle Management
CM	Configuration Manager
CMI	Continuous Measurable Improvement
CMM	Capability Maturity Model
CMO	Chief Marketing Officer
COO	Chief Operating Officer
COTS	Commercial Off-The-Shelf
CPE	Customer Premise Equipment
CPU	Central Processing Unit
Cr	Crore (10,000,000)
CR	Change Request
CRBT	Caller Ring Back Tone
CRM	Customer Relationship Management
C-SAT	Customer Satisfaction
CSI	Consulting and Systems Integration
CSP	Cloud Service Provider
CTO	Chief Technology Officer
DBA	Database Administrator
DEI	Delivery-efficiency index
DMI	Digital-Maturity Index
DR	Disaster Recovery
D-R	Direct Reports
e2e	End-to-end
EA	Enterprise Architecture
EAI	Enterprise Application Integration
EB	Exa Bytes
ECI	Economic-contribution index
EDP	Electronic Data Processing
ENIAC	Electronic Numerical Integrator And Computer

EOY	End of Year
ERP	Enterprise Resource Planning
eTOM	enhanced Telecom Operations Map
F2F	Face-to-face
FA&B (or FAB)	Fulfillment, Assurance & Billing
FCI	EFfort-Cost Index
FCRE	First-Call Resolution Effectiveness
FE, BE	Front End, Back End
FMCG	Fast Moving Consumer Goods
FMS	Facility Management System
GPS	Global Positioning System
GRC	Governance, Risk and Control
GTM	Go-To-Market
HCM	Human Capital Management
HD	High Definition
HNI	High Net-worth Individual
HR	Human Resources
HTML	Hyper-Text Mark-up Language
HTTP	Hyper-Text Transfer Protocol
HVAC	Heating, Ventilation and Air-Conditioning
IA	Impact Analysis
IaaS	Infrastructure-as-a-Service
IC	Integrated Circuit
ICT	Information & Communication Technology
IDE	Integrated Development Environment
IDI	ICT Development Index
IM	Integration Manager
IOT	Internet of Things
IP	Internet Protocol
I-P	Intellectual Property
IS	Information System
IT	Information Technology
ITU	International Telecommunication Union
IVR	Interactive Voice Response
JD	Job description

JIT	Just In Time
JVM	Java Virtual Machine
KM	Knowledge Management
KMO	Knowledge Management Office
KPI	Key Performance Indicator
KRA	Key Result Area
KSO	Key Strategic Objective
LAN	Local Area Network
LED	Light Emitting Diode
LOB	Line of Business
M2M	Machine-To-Machine
MCI	Monetary-Cost index
MDM	Mobile Device Manager
MIS	Management Information Systems
MNP	Mobile Number Portability
MPLS	Multi-Protocol Label Switching
MR	Merged Reality
MRI	Magnetic Resonance Imaging
MS-DOS	Microsoft Disk Operating System
MTBF	Mean Time Between Failures
MTTR	Mean Time To Repair
NEP	Network Equipment Provider
NOTA	None of the above
ODC	Offshore Delivery (or Development) Center
OEM	Original Equipment Manufacturer
OHI	Operations-health index
OJT	On-Job Training
OLS	Order Logging System
OS	Operating System
OTT	Over The Top
P&L	Profit and Loss
PaaS	Platform-as-a-Service
PAT	Profit After Tax
PB	Peta Bytes
PBT	Profit Before Tax
PC	Personal Computer

PI	Preconceived Idea
PMO	Project Management Office
PMP	Project Management Professional
PO	Purchase Order
POC	Proof of Concept
POV	Proof of Value
Q-o-Q	Quarter on Quarter
QoS	Quality of Service
QR Code	Quick Response Code
R&D	Research and Development
R&R	Rewards and Recognition
RCI	Risk-Cost index
RFP	Request For Proposal
RIM	Remote Infrastructure Management
RM	Release Manager
RoI	Return on Investment
SA	Solution Architect
SaaS	Software-as-a-Service
SBU	Strategic Business Unit
SC	Solution Consultant
SCM	Supply Chain Management
SDK	Software Development Kit
SETI	Search for Extra-Terrestrial Intelligence
Sev N	Severity level N
SIM	Subscriber Identity Module
SLA	Service Level Agreement
SM	Social Media
SMAC	Social, Mobility, Analytics, and Cloud
SMART	Specific, Measurable, Achievable, Relevant, and Time-bound
SME	Small and Medium Enterprises
S-M-E	Subject-Matter-Expert
SOA	Service Oriented Architecture
SOP	Standard Operating Procedure
SPOC	Single Point of Contact
SR	Service Request
SRM	Supplier Relationship Management

T&Q	Testing & Quality
TA	Tool Administrator
TAI	Technology-adoption index
TAT	Turn-Around Time
TB	Terra Bytes
TBO	Think, Build, Operate
TCP	Transport Control Protocol
TCQ	Time, Cost, Quality
TOGAF	The Open Group Architecture Forum
TSP	Telecom Service Provider
TTM	Time-To-Market
UAT	User Acceptance Testing
UT	User Testing
VAS	Value-Added Services
VLSI	Very Large-Scale Integration
VoC	Voice of Customer
VR	Virtual Reality
WAN	Wide Area Network
XCI	Complexity-cost index
XHTML	Extended Hyper-Text Mark-up Language
Y2K	Year 2000
Y-o-Y	Year-on-Year

Glossary Of Terms

.NET	Microsoft software-application development platform (Windows-based) supporting language interoperability
Agile development	a set of methods and practices where solutions evolve through collaboration between cross-functional teams
Analog	the opposite of digital. Any technology that doesn't break everything down into binary (digital) code to work is **analog**
Analytics	the discovery, interpretation, and communication of meaningful patterns in data
APIs	a set of instructions and standards that allows two software programs to communicate with each other
Application server	software that allows development, hosting and rendering of web-based applications to users (clients)
Architecture (IT)	the overall design of a computing system's hardware, software, and protocols, and their logical and physical interrelationships
Authentication	the process of identifying an individual, based on a username and password, or biometric techniques
Bandwidth	the amount of data that can be transmitted in a fixed amount of time, or range within a band of frequencies or wavelengths
Big Bang	the event at which the universe came into being and began rapidly expanding from a very high density and temperature state
Big Data	structured or unstructured data that organizations can potentially mine and analyze for business gains, characterized by high volume, velocity and variety
Big Data Analytics	the process of examining **large** amounts of **data** to uncover hidden patterns, correlations and other insights
Big Iron	a term used to refer to a mainframe computer

BITA Calculator	a simple assessment tool for estimating your BITA score. Also referred as BITA tool
Blockchain	a digitized, decentralized, public ledger of all crypto currency (e.g., Bitcoin) transactions
C#	a general-purpose, object-oriented programming language developed by Microsoft within its .NET initiative
C++, Java	general-purpose, object oriented programming languages
Call Data Record	a record that contains data fields which describe a specific instance of a telecommunication transaction
Capex	Capital expense, or funds used by a company to acquire, upgrade, and maintain physical assets
Central Processing System	the brain of a computer, which processes all the instructions given to it. Also referred as CPU
Check-Sheet	a reference 'answer' key used in BITA tool for mapping responses to dimensions
Churn	a measure of the number of individuals or items moving out of a collective group over a specific period
Client	system that rely on servers for processing power
Cloud	a distinct IT environment used for remotely delivering computing services - servers, storage, databases, networking, software
COBOL	common Business Oriented Language. English-like computer programming language used for business data processing
Compatibility	the capacity for two systems to work together without having to be altered to do so
Cookies	small files sent by a website to a user's computer to hold a modest amount of data specific to a user and website
Data center	a facility that centralizes an organization's IT operations and equipment
Data Communication Network	an interconnected system of computing devices capable of exchanging digital data amongst them
Data mining	the process of sorting through large data sets to identify patterns and establish relationships to solve problems
Data probe	devices or programs for retrieving data from the environment for analysis of its type, pattern and trends
Data science	an interdisciplinary field about scientific methods, processes, and systems to extract knowledge or insights from data
Data Visualization	the technique used to convey information by encoding it as visual objects, like patterns and graphs

Data Warehouse	central repository constructed by integrating data from multiple heterogeneous sources
Data-Processing	the collection and manipulation of items of data to produce meaningful information
DB Admin	a role or software responsible for performance, integrity and security of enterprise databases
Digital divide	an inequality relating to access, use or impact of ICT
Digitization	the process of converting information into a digital (computer-readable) format, in which the information is organized into bits
e-Commerce	general term for commercial activity over the internet using B2B, B2B or C2C modes
Encryption	the process of encoding a message or information in such a way that only authorized parties can access it
Engineering	projects delivery unit or organization, e.g., in a software company
Enterprise Mobility	focus on managing mobile devices, wireless networks, and other mobile computing services in a business context
Firewall	network security system to monitor and control incoming and outgoing traffic based on predefined rules
Gateway	a protocol converter used for linking networks or elements which use different protocols
Hadoop	an open-source software framework used for distributed storage and processing of datasets of big data
Host	a computer on a network running server and/or client applications
Instant Messaging	online conversations involving real-time exchange of information over the Internet
Intranet	a private network that is contained within an enterprise
IP-based	a system that uses the set of standards which ensure transmission and routing of data packets over the Internet
IP-centric	technology shift towards packet-based systems suitable for data communication over the Internet
IP-TV	the delivery of television content over Internet Protocol (IP) networks, instead of cable or satellite
IPv6	the most recent version of the Internet Protocol, for identification and location of computers on networks. Replaces Ipv4

Iterative development	breaking down the software development of a large application into smaller chunks and repeated cycles
Java Enterprise Edition (JEE)	a collection of technologies and APIs for the Java platform designed to support "Enterprise" Applications
JavaScript	programming language of the web - a dynamic programming language for providing interactivity to web pages
Kardashev scale	method of measuring a civilization's technological advancement
Line Printer	a machine that prints output from a computer a line at a time rather than character by character
Linux	a community-developed Unix-like open source operating system that is supported on most computer platforms
Machine learning (ML)	the science of getting computers to act by learning instead of being explicitly programmed to do the task
Mainframe	a high-performance computer used for large-scale computing purposes that require greater availability and security
Mediation	the process of collecting usage data from several data sources and delivering it in a specified format for processing
Merged reality (MR)	the merging of real and virtual worlds to create visualizations where physical and digital objects co-exist and interact
Microprocessor	an integrated circuit (IC) which incorporates core functions of a computer's central processing unit (CPU)
Minicomputer	a computer that is intermediate between a microcomputer and a mainframe in size, speed, and capacity
MPLS	a data carrying technique for terrestrial high-speed telecommunications networks
Multi-factor security	security system that requires more than one form of authentication to verify the legitimacy of a transaction
Network	communication fabric for allowing nodes (clients & servers) to share resources
Object-oriented	a programming model based on the attributes of "**objects**" rather than actions, and data rather than logic
Operating System	software that interacts with and manages computer hardware and allows the programs to run
Opex	Operational expense, or ongoing cost of running a product, business, or system.

Platform (architecture)	the foundation of hardware and software on which enterprise applications are built
Plug-and-play	the discovery and use of a hardware component without the need for manual device configuration or user intervention
Portal	a website that brings information from diverse sources, like emails, online forums and search engines, together seamlessly
Real-time	a level of computer (or network) responsiveness that a user senses as instantaneous
Relational database	a common type of database whose data is stored in tables and records, as opposed to a flat file
Reuse	use of pre-developed blocks of software in current development to optimize development effort
Scalability	the capability of a system to handle a growing amount of work, or its potential to be enlarged to accommodate that growth
Score-Sheet	form used in BITA tool for scoring the response from each respondent
Segmentation	the process of dividing a broad consumer market into sub-groups of consumers based on some shared characteristics
Server	a centralized processing system that manages, or serves, files, data and applications
Server Farm	a collection of computer servers to supply server functionality far beyond the capability of a single machine
Shared-service	the provision of a service by one part of the organization to other parts of the organization (like IT or HR services)
Shloka	Sanskrit religious poetry
Silicon	semiconductor material for fabricating Integrated Circuit chips
System Admin	a person who is responsible for the upkeep, configuration, and reliable operation of the computer system
Tape (storage)	data storage medium using spools of magnetic tape which are played on tape drives
Telecom	abbreviation for Telecommunications
Telecosm	a world with an abundance of bandwidth
Time-to-market (TTM)	the length of time it takes from a product being conceived until its being available for sale

Tiered data storage	the assignment of different categories of data to various types of storage media to optimize the cost of storage
Transistor	a semiconductor device used to amplify electronic signals
Unix	a computer Operating System which is capable of handling activities from multiple users at the same time
Virtual machine	an emulation of a computer system, i.e., a computer file, called an image, which behaves like an actual computer
Virtualization	the creation of a software-based, or virtual, representation of something (like a server), rather than a physical one
Voice-over-IP, VoIP	A technology for the delivery of voice and multimedia sessions over Internet Protocol (IP) networks, such as the Internet
Web 2.0	the next version of the world wide web, which emphasizes user-generated content and collaboration
Web browser	a software application for retrieving, presenting and traversing information resources on the World Wide Web
Web services	software that makes itself available over the internet as a service, and uses a standardized messaging system
Web-server	Computers that deliver (serve up) Web pages. Every **Web server** has an IP address and a domain name
World Wide Web	the combination of all resources and users on the Internet that are using the Hypertext Transfer Protocol (HTTP)
Y2K	an anticipated computer glitch related to date change from 1999 to 2000
Y-count	total number of Ys (or 1s) in each column (dimension) of BITA calculator

www.ingramcontent.com/pod-product-compliance
Lightning Source LLC
Chambersburg PA
CBHW061232220326
41599CB00028B/5398

* 9 7 8 9 3 8 7 4 5 6 1 0 5 *